D1527431

"God Ordained This War"

"God Ordained This War"

Sermons on the Sectional
Crisis, 1830–1865

Edited by

David B. Chesebrough

University of South Carolina Press

SCCCC - LIBRARY
4601 Mid Rivers Mall Drive
St. Peters, MO 63376
WITHDRAWN

Copyright © 1991 University of South Carolina

Published in Columbia, South Carolina, by the
University of South Carolina Press

Manufactured in the United States of America

Library of Congress Cataloging-in-Publication Data

"God ordained this war" : sermons on the sectional crisis, 1830–1865 /
   edited by David B. Chesebrough.
      p.   cm.
   Includes bibliographical references and index.
   ISBN 0-87249-753-4 (alk. paper)
   1. Slavery and the church–United States.   2. United States–
History–Civil War, 1861–1865–Religious aspects.   3. Sermons,
American.   4. Secession.   5. Sectionalism (United States)
I. Chesebrough, David B., 1932-   .
E449.G57 1991
252′.00973′09034–dc20   91-6865

For
BRENDA and TIM
With Love

Contents

Acknowledgments

One does not put together a work such as this without realizing his great indebtedness to others. Though space and memory will not allow all of these others to be mentioned, it is imperative that some be.

First of all, I want to express my gratitude to the University of South Carolina Press. Beginning with Warren Slesinger, who has shepherded this project throughout, the personnel of this press have been an outstanding source of helpfulness and support. Their several suggestions have greatly improved the original manuscript I submitted to them.

Two of my colleagues at Illinois State University merit a word of acknowledgment. Dr. L. Moody Simms, Jr., read various portions of the manuscript and aided in its refinement. Dr. Lester Brooks's help in the section on black preaching was significant. My thanks to these two colleagues and friends. They, of course, bear no responsibilities for any weaknesses in the book.

The staff of Milner Library at Illinois State University went out of their way to locate various books and mid-nineteenth-century sermons. Though my many requests must have wearied them, they always appeared to be eager to do whatever they could. In their nationwide searches there were only a few instances when they were unable to locate a particular source.

My thanks also to Sharon Hagan, who typed most of the manuscript. For her typing of the original work and its several revisions I am most grateful.

I would be greatly amiss if I failed to express a very special gratitude to my wife, Terri. Much of the time spent on this volume came out of that which should have been devoted to family. Thank you, Terri, for your understanding, encouragement, and never-failing support.

Finally, I am grateful to those many nineteenth-century preachers for their marvelous sermons. Without their efforts there could be no book such as this. Their passions, talents, rhetorical skills, breadth and depth of knowledge, and involvement in the national concerns of their era made them delightful and fascinating persons to study. Even when I strongly disagreed with a particular viewpoint that a preacher was expressing, I found myself admiring the fervor and the logic that supported such a position. I trust the readers of this book will come to share my appreciation of these clergymen and their homiletic efforts.

D.B.C.

"God Ordained This War"

Introduction

Sydney E. Ahlstrom, the noted authority on America's religious history, has written of the preaching in the nation during the Civil War era: "The pulpits resounded with a vehemence and absence of restraint never equaled in American history."[1] Indeed, to read the sermons of ministers on both sides of the Mason-Dixon Line is to become aware of how greatly the preachers contributed to the war spirit that turned Americans against each other in the mid-nineteenth century.

The contribution of religion, and preaching as a particular and powerful expression of religion, to America's sectional strife in the mid-nineteenth century is a factor of which historians are taking increasing notice. Berringer and his colleagues have noted that "at no time was organized religion in the United States more active politically than in the twenty years prior to the war," and therefore, they assert, that in a real sense "the war was one between the churches of the North and those of the South."[2]

It should be noted that many historians have failed to see religion as playing a vital role in the events which culminated in the Civil War. Kenneth Stampp has edited a volume entitled *The Causes of the Civil War*, a compilation of eighty-two articles which present views of men who lived during the crisis as well as postwar historians. Each article addresses itself to various causes of the war, and not one of them gives religion major attention. Only a very few give religion even minor attention. The same judgment could be made for *Slavery as a Cause of the Civil War*, edited by Edwin C. Rozwenc. James McPherson's book, *Battle Cry of Freedom*, is one of the finest one-volume works that exists on the Civil War. Yet it is disappointing to note how little attention McPherson gives to the role of religion in promoting sectional strife. On the other hand, several historians, and their number is increasing, have taken notice of religion as a primary factor in bringing about the War between the States. As this volume unfolds, the reader will become aware of these sources.[3]

C. C. Goen has claimed that the schisms in the Presbyterian, Methodist, and Baptist denominations at least fifteen years before the war provided a model and inspiration for political division. Thus, he declared, "The denominational schisms, as irreversible steps along the nation's tortuous course to violence, were both portent and catalyst to the imminent national tragedy." Goen elaborated upon the churches' contribution to divisiveness:

> They broke a primary bond of national unity, encouraged the myth of "peaceable secession," established a precedent of sectional independence, reinforced the growing alienation between North and South by cultivating distorted images of "the other side," and exacerbated the moral outrage that each section felt against the other.[4]

Goen believed that the clergy were cognizant of the far-reaching and devastating consequences that their actions would have: "The leaders of the dividing churches were aware of the probable political consequences of what they were doing, and that even so dismal a prospect as the ruin of their cherished political union did not deter them."[5]

William Warren Sweet has written in a similar vein: "There are good arguments to support the claim that the split in the churches was not only the first break between the sections, but the chief cause of the final break."[6] Allen Nevins in his comprehensive account of the Civil War stated that "the divided churches had contributed significantly to the [political] estrangement." [7] Charles Stewart, in his comments about Civil War preaching, has written: "When the United States began to splinter following Abraham Lincoln's election in 1860, perhaps no group had been longer or more deeply involved in the sectional disputes than the clergy."[8]

It seems altogether probable that if the clergy and the churches had not stirred up the fervor and the emotions that they did, the North and South could have found a different way to resolve their differences. However, when each side is convinced that its cause is God's cause, there is little room and not much desire for compromise and amicable solutions. Cultural tunnel vision and ardent nationalism mixed with religious passion is a recipe for intolerance and violence. Recalling the involvement of the clergy and their churches on both sides of the strife, the words of Abraham Lincoln in his second inaugural address become even more meaningful:

> Both read the same Bible and pray to the same God, and each invokes His aid against the other. It may seem strange that any men should

dare to ask a just God's assistance in wringing their bread from the sweat of other men's faces, but let us judge not, that we be not judged. The prayers of both could not be answered. That of neither has been answered fully. The Almighty has His own purposes.

In mid-nineteenth-century America religion in general, and the pulpit in particular, were powerful influences in almost every aspect of national political and social life. The historian Albert Barnes wrote in 1857: "In our country there is no class of men who exert more influence than the ministers of the gospel."⁹ Alexis de Tocqueville, in his observations of mid-nineteenth-century America, claimed there was "no country in the world where the Christian religion retained a greater influence over the souls of men than in America."¹⁰ Beginning in the early 1830s clergymen on both sides of the Mason-Dixon Line began to use this influence to promote and encourage a widening gap between the two great sections of the nation.

Goen has pointed out that it was not merely what the preachers said, but also what they failed to say, that brought on the crisis that ripped apart the national fabric. He concludes his fine book with a scathing chapter that accuses the churches, North and South, of failing to adequately deal with the issue of slavery, and because of this failure bearing a major responsibility in bringing about the Civil War. Several people of that era – James G. Birney, Stephen S. Foster, John Greenleaf Whittier, Harriet Beecher Stowe, Albert Barnes, and others – accused the churches of abrogating their moral responsibility in regard to slavery. The churches chose to place their emphasis upon individual responsibility and "spiritual" matters, and neglected to speak to the great social ills of the day. "An overemphasis on individualism, an inadequate social theory, a world-rejecting ecclesiology – these are clues to the inability of the churches to achieve liberty and justice for the enslaved."¹¹

The fatal flaw in antebellum church leadership was that ecclesiastics were less distressed by the evils of human bondage than concerned with the tasks of institutional maintenance. In the critical decades of the 1830s and 1840s, their efforts were directed more to muting the moral issue of slavery than to confront it forthrightly. . . . By the time they were forced to take a position, it was too late to prevent schism or even to shore up their stand against slavery. Even after the schisms, Northern religious bodies continued to reject abolitionism in order to court supporters in the upper South and border states.¹²

The religion that dominated mid-nineteenth-century America was a religion in the midst of change. At this point in time Americans still sought for strong religious foundations, both individually and nationally. Nevertheless, they wanted religious changes that would correspond to their strong impulses for even more democracy and freedom. The Calvinism of the Puritans, which had emphasized the sovereignty of God and the corresponding depravity and helplessness of man, was becoming less and less palatable to America's religious taste. "The most representative religious thinkers of the period," writes Irving H. Bartlett, "however they might disagree over specific points, found common ground in their attempt to make religious faith palatable to a generation brought up in a democratic faith – a faith that emphasized the rights and dignity of man and the self-improvement of mankind."[13]

These changes are well represented in the Unitarian William Ellery Channing and the evangelist Charles Grandison Finney. Though in many ways these two religious leaders represented opposite ends of the religious spectrum – one a liberal, the other a conservative; one a rationalist, the other holding to a concept of revealed truth; one a Unitarian, the other a Trinitarian – they both demonstrated the changing standards of religious belief and conduct associated with the mid-nineteenth century.

Channing, the father of American Unitarianism, emphasized the rational nature of man and asked people to bring reason to their study of the Bible as they would to any other book. He dismantled the sovereignty of God as taught by Jonathan Edwards and other Calvinists, and spoke of a God who was a morally perfect being, a God whom people follow not because they are compelled to do so but because they are attracted to his virtue. Channing attacked Calvinism as being degrading to man and God. For Channing, there were few limitations that could or should restrict the possibilities of the human mind and life.

Finney, in a democratic style befitting the age, declared that every man was capable of repentance, of turning to Christ, and of receiving salvation. Once receiving salvation, man was capable of moving on to a Christian prefectionism. Thus, both Channing and Finney believed in unlimited human possibilities; both believed that humankind was free before God, capable of accepting and becoming the best, but also free to demonstrate the worst. Both became strong advocates of social reform that would better enable people to achieve their highest potential. Both, with great optimism, believed that America was the land, perhaps the only land, where the highest hopes and possibilities of mankind could be fulfilled.

Something different, however, was happening throughout much of the South. C. Vann Woodward has written that because of the South's preoccupation with justifying slavery, it tended to reject "such popular American ideas as the doctrine of human perfectability, the belief that every evil has a cure, and the notion that every human problem has a solution. . . .In the most optimistic of centuries in the most optimistic part of the world, the South remained basically pessimistic in its social outlook and its moral philosophy."[14] Added to the South's pessimism was a decidedly militant temperament. Tocqueville noted that one of the earliest notions that comes to a Southern man "is that he is born to command, . . . of ruling without resistance. His education tends, then, to give him the character of a haughty and hasty man, irascible, violent, ardent in his desires, impatient of obstacles, but easily discouraged if he cannot succeed upon his first attempt."[15] These basic differences in sectional temperaments and outlooks were reflected in the various religious sentiments and pulpit pronouncements of Northern and Southern preachers.

By the 1830s two major changes had taken place in Southern religion. In the colonial period the Church of England was the established church in the Southern colonies. Because of the Great Awakening and the subsequent Second Great Awakening, Southern religion changed and became basically evangelical in nature, with Baptists and Methodists predominating and the Presbyterians a significant force. The second major change had to do with Southern religion's view of slavery. In the years surrounding the American Revolution many Southern denominations and their people were outspoken in their opposition to slavery. Sometime after that there was a period of silence, a period when it was deemed inappropriate to speak of slavery from the pulpit. By the 1830s, however, most Southern religious leaders began to adopt strong proslavery stances. More will be said on both of these changes as this volume unfolds.

One of the most important characteristics of religion in those years prior to and during the Civil War was the belief that God continually intervened in the affairs of this world. Charles Stewart, who has made an extensive study of the sermons preached in that era, has concluded: "Civil War preaching, northern and southern, was based on the fundamental religious premise generally accepted in

pre-Darwinian America that God controlled the universe and every
thing and action in it."[16]

As one surveys the sermons from the mid-nineteenth century,
this characteristic of perceived divine intervention is observed again
and again. Thus Daniel I. Dreher, an Episcopalian divine from North
Carolina, sermonized in the summer of 1861 that God had ordained
secession: "Nature and nature's God has marked us out for two nations."[17] Daniel Eddy, on the other hand, a Boston minister, declared
in that same summer: "We cannot have two or more republics on this
soil. God and nature have forbidden it."[18]

When the war erupted, there were sermons from both sides em-
phasizing that the conflict had been brought to the nation by God.
Henry H. Tucker, from Georgia, declared in the autum of 1861: "God
is in the war. He brought it upon us."[19] A similar message was delivered by Henry Allen Tupper, also from Georgia, about a year later:
"The Lord, who would deliver us from the snare, led providentially
and imperceptibly into war."[20] Northern preachers echoed the same
theme. Zachery Eddy, from Boston, shortly after the firing on Fort
Sumter, declared: "If the crusaders, seized by a common enthusiasm,
exclaimed, 'IT IS THE WILL OF GOD! IT IS THE WILL OF GOD!'–
much more may we make this our rallying cry and inscribe it on our
banners."[21] Toward the end of the war, on November 24, 1864, Marvin R. Vincent, a Presbyterian cleric from Troy, New York, affirmed
that God had caused the war because of the "great national sin" of
slavery.[22]

In the North preachers saw the hand of God all through the contest. In the early years, when the Union armies were suffering a
series of defeats, the preachers were insistent that God was involved.
John F. Bigelow, a Baptist minister from New York State, in July of
1861 noted that there was little the North could point to in the war
as a sign of God's favor. He urged his listeners to adopt a long-range
perspective, drawing applications from national history, and assured
that God "will make their [Confederates] own wicked rage and demented foolhardiness, if they persevere in the attempts to sunder
the Republic, the means of their chastisement, if not their destruction."[23] In September of 1862 James D. Liggett, Congregationalist
from Kansas, said that the reason the war was not going well for the
Union was because the eradication of slavery was not the first priority of the Northern government.[24] Two months later Alexander H.
Vinton, an Episcopalian from New York City, blamed early Union

defeats upon the North's "profane self-conceit." Vinton claimed that "our disasters may be God's method of delay, to bring us more into felt dependence on Him, and so more in harmony with His plans."[25]

After the battles at Gettysburg and Vicksburg in the summer of 1863, when the tide turned irreversibly in the Union's favor, Northern preachers observed that God was still at work. In the autumn of 1864 Elisha Cleaveland, Congregationalist from New Haven, asserted that God had at last given Union victories in response to Northern prayers, "and how soon and signally have those prayers been answered."[26] About the same time Charles Little from Chesire, Connecticut, declared: "Our hopes? They are unfailing because sustained by the marked interpositions of an Almighty God."[27] Several Northern sermons proclaimed that it was the Emancipation Proclamation that brought God into the war on the side of the Union. W. W. Eells, a Presbyterian cleric from Pittsburgh, on November 26, 1863, declared that after the Proclamation, "He [God] interposed. . . and all thoughtful men should know assuredly that true peace in this land should be built upon the foundation of universal emancipation."[28]

As Northern preachers perceived the hand of God directing both defeats and victories, so did their Southern counterparts. In 1862 Joel W. Tucker, a Presbyterian from Fayetteville, North Carolina, emphasized that every Confederate victory was a sign that Southerners were God's chosen people, and every Confederate defeat was a punishment of sins. Thus, when the battle did not go well for the South, "If the people . . . were to turn with one heart and mind to the Lord . . . He would drive the invaders from our territories. . . . He can turn them as He turns the rivers of water."[29] In June of 1861, J. C. Mitchel from Mobile inquired: "Who can fail to see the hand of God in the whole movement?"[30]

After the Union surrender of Fort Sumter, James H. Elliot, Episcopal rector from Charleston, stated that the Confederate victory was an answer to prayer: "the hand of God seems as plainly in it as in the conquest of the Midianites."[31] After the first victory at Manassas, Stephen Elliot from Savannah proclaimed that the military triumph was "the crowning token of his [God's] love – the most wonderful of all manifestations of his divine presence with us. . . . He has smitten our enemies in their most tender and sensitive point, their invincible power, and has taken from us the funeral shroud of the brave and the young."[32] Because all the worldly and material advantages were with the North, Southern victories could only have been achieved through the intervention of God who rearranged "the boasted arrangements of man."[33]

After the summer of 1863, when Confederate defeats began to mount, the Southern preachers were still convinced that God was directing the conflict. There were divine reasons, they proclaimed, for the sad turn of events, and the most important reason of all was that God was punishing the South for its sins. James Silver has written: "After Vicksburg and Gettysburg there came an avalanche of sermons stressing the sins of the Confederate people."[34] In the fall of 1864 J. L. Burrows said from the pulpit of the First Baptist Church in Augusta, Georgia: "It is universally true, that national judgments have been drawn down by national sins."[35] Many preachers announced that the greatest sin of the South was its abuse of slaves. In 1863 the Rev. Isaac T. Tichenor lamented: "We have failed to discharge our duties to our slaves. I entertain no doubt that slavery is right, morally, socially, politically, religiously right. But there are abuses which ought to be corrected." Tichenor went on to observe: "It is a significant fact that those parts of our country which have suffered the most, in the loss of property, have been the very localities where the abuses have been the greatest."[36]

The Southern preachers pointed to a number of other specific sins of which Confederate citizens were guilty, thus causing God to punish them through military defeats. Those sins included greed, pride, arrogance, the trust in cotton, drunkenness, gambling, cursing, and Sabbath profanations. Burrows complained: "Of what crime in the catalog forbidden by God can we not discover samples every day, and in every section of our land?" He then emphasized what preachers all over the South were saying in the last years of the war. The South's sins were no worse than others, indeed, not as offensive, but because they were God's special people, more was expected of them. Burrows asked: "Do you say we are not worse than other nations? Perhaps not. But we have sinned against clearer knowledge and richer blessings than others and in that proportion our guilt is greater."[37] The implication was unmistakable. Southerners were being punished because they were God's chosen and special people. God expected more from them than he did from others, and they had failed to measure up. The judgment on the South was much like the judgment of God upon the Hebrews in the Old Testament. The sins of other nations may have been greater, but they were not God's people in the way the Hebrews or the Southerners were.

Such a theology had a direct impact upon the war effort and the war's duration. In warfare, the preachers proclaimed, it was not the number of soldiers nor the competency of generals that determined the tide of battle; it was God who brought victory and it was God who administered defeat. Therefore, no matter how bleak a present situation might be, or how disastrous the latest defeat suffered on the battlefield, there was always hope. God could change everything, suddenly and dramatically, if he so desired. So the bloodshed and killing continued in the Civil War long after defeat seemed obvious; for God was the God of history, the God who still worked miracles upon the world's stage, the God who brought forth the impossible, the God who could easily turn heartbreaking defeat into glorious victory. Therefore, when the dark shadows began to fall upon the Confederacy, the clergymen were still there, still inspiring, and still holding out hope. Thus Benjamin Palmer, in December of 1863, before the General Assembly of South Carolina, attempted to rekindle the flickering flame: "The language of true prayer is never the cry of supine imbecility, nor the wail of craven despondency. It is always the language of hope and expectation. . . . I thank God that, in the darkest hour, I have never despaired of the republic."[38] It was the ministers who inspired the South to keep on fighting, to continue the shedding of blood, to perpetuate the carnage, when the cause was obviously lost. Beringer writes:

> Religion played a greater role in the Confederate experience than in that of the Union because the South needed it more, for as military power ebbed away, the will of the people needed more and more reinforcement if the Confederacy was to survive. In a time of defeat, piety could do what military victories did in better times."[39]

It is sometimes debated as to whether preachers and their sermons mold society or mirror it. Beringer, after noting the influence of Southern preachers upon the populace, added a word of caution about that influence: "But one should not presume that the clergy controlled or that they duped the people; if anything, they reflected rather than molded public opinion."[40] The outspoken Unitarian preacher Theodore Parker from Boston, in the years prior to the war, was impatient with his fellow Northern clergymen for their failure to take a bold and forthright stand against slavery. He accused them of being reflectors of current opinion rather than shapers. "Once the clergy were the masters of the people," he affirmed, "and the authors of public opinion to a great degree; now they are chiefly the servants of the people, and follow public opinion, and but seldom aspire to lead it, except in matters of their own craft, such as the technicalities of a sect, or the form of a ritual."[41] It would seem that the vital role preachers and their sermons play in regard to public opinion is that they reinforce beliefs that are currently and popularly held by giving them divine sanction.

For this reason sermons are valuable historical documents, though often overlooked in this regard by many historians. Preachers are a reflection of current thought and practice. Popular preachers, in particular, are popular because they mirror the opinions, hopes, fears, prejudices, likes, and dislikes of a significant number of people. Preachers, like most others, are people of their times, shaped and influenced by the events and ideas of their generation and environment. For instance, one can trace the development of Northern thought and opinions on slavery by observing the evolution of Henry Ward Beecher's sermons on this subject. Paxton Hibben has written that Beecher was "a barometer and record" of what was happening in society. "He was not in advance of his day," wrote Hibben, "but precisely abreast of his day – the drum major's part in more than one sense."[42] A similar observation could be made about many, probably most, preachers. It would be difficult for a clergyman to survive in his vocation if he did not share to a large degree the values and sentiments of his congregation. Sermons, therefore, are documents which reflect current thinking, problems, and issues that occupy the attention and emotions of a large number of people.

This volume contains thirteen sermons from that turbulent time; six from Northern pulpits (Part I), six from Southern pulpits (Part II), and one address by a Northern black preacher (Part III). The first two parts are each subdivided into four chapters. Though the subdivisions or chapters are topically similar for each section of the country, they are not identical because the most significant issues for each side were sometimes different. Thus, chapter 4 for the North is "Assigning of Guilt and Punishment," and the corresponding chapter 8 for the South is "The Lost Cause."

Each chapter begins with a brief synopsis of the issues involved, and many references are made to other preachers and sermons besides those that have been selected for major attention. These introductory pages to each chapter will include some biographical in-

I. NORTHERN SERMONS
  1. Slavery
  2. Sectionalism

  3. War
  4. Assigning Guilt and
     Punishment

II. SOUTHERN SERMONS
  5. Slavery
  6. Sectionalism and
     Secession
  7. War
  8. The Lost Cause

formation on the preacher or preachers whose sermons conclude the chapter. It will be noted that some chapters contain one sermon, while others have two. This represents an arbitrary decision by this editor, who decided that in some chapters one sermon sufficiently presents the issues involved, while in other chapters two sermons are needed for adequate coverage. For example, in the Northern chapter on war (chapter 3), two sermons are included because each sermon represents a different Northern point of view as to why the war was being fought. James D. Liggett said the purpose was slavery, but Horace Bushnell claimed the purpose was for the preservation of the Union. The two sermons represent a major point of contention that raged through the North. In the Southern chapter on war (chapter 7), however, only one sermon is used, and this one sermon by J. W. Tucker adequately represents the dominant Southern point of view.

In selecting the sermons that make up this particular work, three factors were taken into account. First of all, there was the sermon itself. It had to make a specific contribution to an understanding of the category under which it was placed. The sermon had to be well constructed. There are no sermons in this collection that are careless or poor pieces of work. Whether the reader agrees or not with the ideas expressed in these sermons, each one is a carefully considered, well-developed, and powerful piece of prose. The preachers who composed these sermons knew how to use the tools of exposition and rhetoric.

A second factor considered in the selection process was the preacher himself. Not all of the preachers chosen are well known to contemporary minds, but some, perhaps most, of them are. Most who have at least some acquaintance with the history of the American pulpit will recognize such names as Charles G. Finney, Henry Ward Beecher, Horace Bushnell, James Henley Thornwell, Benjamin Morgan Palmer, and Stephen Elliott. All of the men selected were well known in their time and expressed a popular and accepted sectional point of view.

A final factor pertaining to selection was variety. No preacher contributes more than one sermon. Though sermons by Henry Ward Beecher could have been used in each chapter of Part I, and Benjamin Morgan Palmer's sermons in each chapter of Part II, variety dictated that a preacher be used only once. Five denominations are represented in the twelve sermons. Some readers might wish, with justification, for even greater denominational variety. The introductions to each chapter do consider a number of other preachers, along with small portions of their sermons, which greatly increases the denominational diversity. It is this writer's opinion, after reading many sermons from the Civil War era, that the thirteen chosen for this volume are representative of what was taking place in the American pulpit, North and South, during the tumultuous years before and during the Civil War.

Part III, or chapter 9, of this volume is devoted to the subject of black preachers and their sermons in mid-nineteenth-century America. Though black preachers may not have been a part of mainstream America, North or South, they nevertheless did play a part in the sectional strife. Chapter 9 will consider the role and contributions of slave preachers in the South and free black preachers in the North. A discourse from the Rev. Theodore S. Wright, a Northern black preacher, concludes the chapter.

A bibliography that lists over three hundred sermons from the Civil War era brings this work to a close. The sermons are arranged alphabetically by preacher and not chronologically. It is imperative for one who uses this bibliography to observe the date on which a particular sermon was delivered. A few notes are made on each sermon listed, and sometimes direct quotes are used to give the reader a better grasp of the preacher's style and vocabulary.

As one reads these sermons from the mid-nineteenth century, the quality of the discourses, both from the North and South, is impressive. The sermons are extremely well crafted, display excellent vocabularies, and are written by men who were well educated and well versed in several fields of learning. Though many of the sermons are passionate in nature, they nevertheless maintain a sense of rationality and logic.

These sermons have survived because someone took the time and paid the cost of having them put into print. This means that these sermons have their source, for the most part, in the larger and more established urban churches. Out in the small country churches, where the congregations were less sophisticated and the preachers less educated, a different quality of sermon existed. However, most of these sermons were never written out, much less printed, and thus have not survived. Those urban sermons which were printed – several of which have been quoted throughout this work and are listed in the bibliography – and have been passed down to the present era are of high quality. It is the observation of this writer that few contemporary preachers could match the breadth, depth, and fervor of these mid-nineteenth-century sermons, whether from Northern or Southern pulpits.

NOTES

1. Sydney E. Ahlstrom, *A Religious History of the American People* (New Haven: Yale University Press, 1972), 672.
2. Richard E. Beringer et al., *Why the South Lost the Civil War* (Athens: University of Georgia Press, 1986), 84, 86.
3. For a brief but excellent overview of the relationship between religion and politics in those years before the Civil War, see Daniel Walker Howe, "Religion and Politics in the Antebellum North," *Religion and American Politics,* ed. Mark A. Noll (New York: Oxford University Press, 1990), 121–45. In spite of the article's title, it contains insightful information about the South. Howe states that "a proper assessment of antebellum poltical life has to start by admitting the legitimacy and relevance of religious and moral commitments to the politics of the age" (125).
4. C. C. Goen, *Broken Churches, Broken Nation* (Macon: Mercer University Press, 1985), 6, 13.
5. Goen, *Broken Churches,* 67.
6. William Warren Sweet, *The Story of Religion in America* (New York: Harper, 1930), 312.
7. Allen Nevins, *Ordeal of the Union,* 2 vols. (New York: Scribner's, 1947), 2:553.
8. Charles Stewart, "Civil War Preaching," *Preaching in American History,* ed. Dewitte Holland (Nashville: Abingdon Press, 1969), 184.
9. As quoted in Charles Forrester Dunham, *The Attitude of the Northern Clergy Toward the South 1860–1865* (Philadelphia: Porcupine Press, 1974), 5.
10. Alexis de Tocqueville, *Democracy In America* (New York: Knopf, 1966), 303.
11. Goen, *Broken Churches,* 169.
12. Goen, *Broken Churches,* 180.
13. Irving H. Bartlett, *The American Mind in the Mid-Nineteenth Century,* 2nd ed. (Arlington Heights, IL: Harlan Davidson, 1982), 8.
14. C. Vann Woodward, *The Burden of Southern History,* rev. ed. (Baton Rouge: Louisiana State University Press, 1968), 21.
15. Tocqueville, *Democracy in America,* 394.

16. Stewart, "Civil War Preaching," 204.
17. *A Sermon* (Salisbury, NC: Watchman's Office, 1861).
18. *Liberty and Union* (Boston: John M. Hewes, 1861).
19. *God in the War* (Milledgeville: Boughton, Nisbet & Barnes, State Printers, 1861).
20. *A Thanksgiving Discourse* (Macon: Burke, Boykin & Co., 1862).
21. *A Discourse on the War* (Northhampton: Trumbull and Grace, 1861).
22. *The Lord of War and of Righteousness* (Troy: A. W. Scribner, 1864).
23. *The Hand of God in American History* (Burlington, VT: W. H. and C. A. Hoyt, 1861).
24. "Our National Reverses," *Sermons in American History*, ed. Dewitte Holland (Nashville: Abingdon Press, 1971), 247–55.
25. *Man's Rule and Christ's Reign* (New York: John A. Gray, 1862).
26. *The Partiot's Song of Victory* (New Haven: Thomas H. Pease, 1864).
27. *Relation of the Citizen to the Government* (New Haven: William H. Stanley, 1864).
28. *How and Why We Give Thanks* (Pittsburgh: W. S. Haven, 1864).
29. *God Sovereign and Man Free* (Fayetteville: Presbyterian Office, 1862).
30. *Fast Day Sermon* (Mobile: Farrow & Dennett, 1861).
31. *The Bloodless Victory* (Charleston: A. E. Miller, 1861).
32. *God's Presence with Our Army at Manassas* (Savannah: W. Thorne Williams, 1861).
33. David Seth Doggett, *A Nation's Ebenezer* (Richmond: Enquirer Book and Job Press, 1862).
34. James W. Silver, *Confederate Morale and Church Propaganda* (New York: Norton, 1957), 36.
35. *Nationality Insured* (Augusta: Jas. Nathan Ells, Publisher, Baptist Banner Office, 1864).
36. *Fast Day Sermon* (Montgomery: Montgomery Advertiser Book and Job Printing Office, 1863).
37. Burrows, *Nationality Insured.*
38. *A Discourse Before the General Assembly of South Carolina* (Columbia: Charles P. Pelham, State Printers, 1864).
39. Beringer, *Why the South Lost the Civil War,* 101.
40. *Why the South Lost the Civil War,* 97.
41. *Centenary Edition of the Works of Theodore Parker* (Boston: American Unitarian Association, 1907), 11:279.
42. Paxton Hibben, *Henry Ward Beecher: An American Portrait,* (1927; New York: The Press of the Readers Club, 1942), xiv.

Part I

Northern Sermons

SLAVERY

Slavery, far more than any other single factor, was the cause of the Civil War. Sydney Ahlstrom has written: "Had there been no slavery, there would have been no war. Had there been no moral condemnation of slavery, there would have been no war."[1] It was in the "moral condemnation of slavery" that Northern preachers became active participants in the sectional strife. Shortly after the war broke out in 1861, the Northern Methodist preacher Granville Moody exclaimed: "We [the Northern preachers] are charged with having brought about the present crisis. I believe it is true that we did bring it about, and I glory in it, for it is a wreath of glory around our brow."[2]

The antislavery movement, of which the Northern preachers were an important part, became a powerful thrust in the North during the 1830s when abolitionism became a dominant, militant, and uncompromising force in Yankee society. There were earlier voices that condemned slavery. The Quakers had made their protests against the institution since the late seventeenth century. Prominent Quakers who spoke out against slavery prior to the nineteenth century included Francis Daniel Pastorius, Judge Samuel Sewell, John Woolman, and Anthony Benezet. In 1775 some Philadelphia Quakers organized the country's first antislavery society. Several Baptists and Methodists took vigorous stands against slavery in those years surrounding the Revolutionary War. Both of these denominations, however, as the nineteenth century approached, began to accommodate themselves to slavery in order to appease their denominational brothers and sisters in the South.

The American Colonization Society was organized in 1817 for the purpose of raising funds to reimburse slave owners and send their former slaves back to Africa. Churches and ministers played an important role in this organization, which proved to be a failure. The Colonization Society, in various indirect ways, helped to promote slavery. It promulgated the idea of black inferiority and diverted attention away from the institution of slavery itself.

It was the 1830s which brought the antislavery movement to a new intensity and militancy from which there would be no turning back. This new vigor which unrelentingly pressed for the complete abolishment of slavery – abolitionism – was centered in William Lloyd Garrison. On January 1, 1831, Garrison published his first issue of the famous, or infamous, depending upon one's point of view, *Liberator*, in which he stated his uncompromising position. "I will be as harsh as truth," wrote Garrison. "On this subject [slavery] I do not wish to think, or speak, or write, with moderation. . . . I am in earnest – I will not equivocate – I will not excuse – I will not retreat a single inch." Whereas the Colonization Society asked for gradual emancipation through relocation, Garrison and other abolitionists demanded immediate emancipation. By 1843 Garrison was insisting that the North secede from the Union so as to sever itself completely from the diabolical institution of slavery.

Garrison and the abolitionist movement called for the churches and their ministers to participate in this strong and unyielding stance against slavery. On the whole, the Northern clergy responded slowly and with great caution to Garrison's demands. A few, such as Theodore Parker from Boston, supported Garrison and abolitionism without reservation. Parker's admiration for the abolitionists was affirmed as early as his first sermon against slavery in 1841.

> We all know there is at the North a small body of men, called by various names, and treated with various marks of disrespect, who are zealously striving to procure the liberation of slaves, in a peaceful and quiet way. They are willing to make any sacrifices for this end. They start from the maxim that slavery is a sin, and that sin is to be abandoned at once, and for ever. . . . What wonder is it that these men sometimes grow warm in their arguments! What wonder that their heart burns when they think of so many women exposed to contamination and nameless abuse; of so many children reared like beasts, and sold as oxen; of so many men owning no property in their hands, or their feet, their hearts, or their lives.[3]

Many Northern preachers were either openly opposed to abolitionism in those early years of its existence, or thought that it was too radical in its means to achieve desired ends.[4] On October 17, 1833, Joseph Tracy delivered a sermon before the Vermont Colonization Society which was one of the earliest clerical attacks upon the abolitionist movement.[5] In 1834 Simon Clough, a Congregational minister from Fall River, Massachusetts, delivered a sermon denouncing the abolitionists as being antibiblical. He suggested that preachers who espoused abolitionist principles be dismissed by their congregations as false teachers.[6] In 1839 Horace Bushnell from Connecticut, in a sermon that was a response to the abolitionists, warned against hasty antislavery actions and urged that Southern men be given time to correct the abuses of slavery through gradual legislative action.[7] George Junkin, in 1843, before the Synod of Cincinnati (Old School Presbyterian), delivered an eight-hour attack upon abolitionism.[8] One year later Charles S. Porter from Utica urged his listeners to reject insurrectionary efforts (abolitionism) which were tearing America apart, and thus were a greater evil than slavery.[9] Eventually, by the 1860s, various events would occur to swing most of the Northern preachers into the abolitionist camp. Prior to that, however, in the 1830s and 1840s the abolitionists and many Northern churches and preachers were strong in their condemnation of each other even though pastors and members of established churches played major roles in the abolitionist movement. McKivigan has noted that over 56 percent of the officers of the American Anti-Slavery Society (a Garrison-controlled organization) were members of established churches.[10]

The coming of the American Anti-Slavery Society, which was organized in 1833, brought with it new demands for immediate emancipation. By 1840 the Society would have nearly 200,000 members. Some Northern pulpits began their first strong volley, against the "peculiar institution," proclaiming that slavery was not a political issue as the Colonization Society had claimed, but a moral one. Abolitionists and preachers began to speak of a higher law – which superseded all civil laws, including the Constitution of the United States. This higher law declared that because all men were moral beings, none were to be denied their freedom; thus, to participate in such a denial was a grave sin.[11] Northern preachers by the hundreds began to appropriate this appeal to higher law. Nathaniel Hall, a Congregationalist from Dorchester, Massachusetts, in a sermon entitled "The Limits of Civil Disobedience," provided an example of such an appeal. "The principle is," he proclaimed, "that we are bound to obey the requisitions of human law, except where they conflict with the law of God, as made known in our souls and in His Word."[12]

Fairly typical of some Northern preaching at this time were two sermons delivered by the Rev. E. P. Barrows, Jr., in October of 1835 at the First Free Presbyterian Church in New York City. He had recently been called to the pastorate of this church and soon discovered that his new congregation was divided in its views and feelings about slavery. Two sermons were prepared and delivered to this congregation for the purpose of bringing about a unified opposition to slavery. After carefully defining slavery, Barrows presented his arguments as to why slavery was a violation of love, was unjust and evil, and did great moral and mental harm to both slaves and masters. Opposing violence, he asked for a peaceful abolition of slavery. Then he presented a biblical basis for his antislavery position, saying that abolitionism was based upon broad biblical principles rather than specific texts. Barrows was aware that defenders of slavery often appealed to specific biblical texts.[13]

In July of 1834 James Taylor Dickinson from Connecticut delivered a sermon in which he supported the abolitionist position with many references from the Scriptures. Guilt for the sin of slavery, he emphasized, must be shared by the entire nation which had permitted the perpetuation of the institution. Nonslaveholding Christians had a duty to warn slaveholders of God's certain judgment and punishment if slavery persisted. Laws protecting slavery should be nullified by obedience to the higher law of God.[14]

The following year Samuel Crothers, seeking to defuse the biblical argument for slavery, drew a distinction between Hebrew and pagan slavery. Hebrew slavery, he asserted, was a means of paying a debt, and provision was made for eventual emancipation. God's law did not endorse the slavery system of the South (pagan slavery), which doomed a person to perpetual bondage.[15]

During the 1840s the Northern ministers turned up their attacks on slavery, largely because of what they perceived was the expansion of slavery into the territories. The debate over the Wilmot Proviso (1846–47), which would have excluded slavery from any territories acquired by the Mexican War, served to intensify the argument over slavery both politically and religiously. When California applied for statehood at the end of the decade, the balance of fifteen free states and fifteen slave states was threatened. The national temperament was reflected in the pronouncements from the pulpit.

The Boston Unitarian Theodore Parker denounced the Mexican War as a war to extend slavery. On February 4, 1849, he delivered an address at Faneuil Hall where he thundered: "This war is waged for a mean and infamous purpose, for the extension of slavery. . . . We must have more land to whip negroes in." It was a bold gesture to speak against a war that had popular support throughout the nation. Soldiers with bayonets surrounded the meeting at Faneuil Hall. Parker noted this in his discourse: "Here are soldiers with bayonets to overawe the majesty of the people." The preacher was aware that President Polk had said that opposition to the war was treason, and commented: "Your President tells it is treason to talk so! Treason is it? . . . If my country is in the wrong, and I know it, and hold my peace, then I am guilty of treason, moral treason."[16]

Parker led the pace in the clergy's attack on slavery, but there were other Northern preachers, many others, who were not far behind. In 1841 Jonathan Blanchard delivered a lengthy discourse before the Synod of Cincinnati (New School Presbyterian) defending abolitionism from a biblical perspective.[17] Yet in the 1840s several Northern preachers could still be found who vigorously attacked abolitionism and wanted to make some accommodation with slavery. In 1843 Gardner Spring, concerned over increasing sectional differences and tensions, urged a common respect for and loyalty to the United States Constitution. Such a commonality, he hoped, would still bind all Americans together.[18]

In spite of the hopes of ministers such as Spring, by the 1840s differences and tensions had gone beyond retreat, especially in the world of religion. In 1844 the Methodist Episcopal Church divided along sectional lines when the General Conference refused to repudiate its antislavery heritage. One year later the Baptists also divided along sectional lines when the denomination refused to appoint slaveholders as missionaries.

The 1850s have been referred to as "the decade of crisis," those years when sectional tensions in the United States went beyond the point of recovery. The political strains are well known. There was the Compromise of 1850, which contained the hotly disputed Fugitive Slave Law. The year 1854 brought the Kansas–Nebraska Act; 1856, the caning of Charles Sumner on the floor of the United States Senate; 1857, the Dred Scott decision; and 1859, John Brown's raid at Harper's Ferry. These were the events which culminated in the election of Abraham Lincoln to the presidency in 1860, which was shortly followed by secession and war.

The Northern sermons from the 1850s reflect these political

stresses over the question of slavery. Theodore Parker, on March 25, 1850, severely criticized Senator Daniel Webster from Massachusetts for his part in the passage of the Fugitive Slave Law which had been enacted earlier in the month. Speaking of Webster's actions, Parker proclaimed, "I know of no deed in American history, done by a son of New England, to which I can compare this, but the act of Benedict Arnold."[19] On September 22 of the same year Parker expressed his personal determination to disobey that law.

> I will do all in my power to rescue any fugitive slave from the hands of any officer who attempts to return him to bondage. I will resist him as gently as I know how, but work with such strength as I can command; I will ring bells and alarm the town; I will serve as head, as foot, or as hand to any body of serious men, who will go with me, with no weapons in their hands, in this work. I will do it as readily as I would lift a man out of the water, or pluck him from the teeth of a wolf, or snatch him from the hands of a murderer.[20]

In another sermon, delivered on April 10, 1851, Parker urged others to resist the law: "What shall we do? Never obey the law. Keep the law of God." Yet he urged that resistance stop short of violence: "Do not resist with violence. . . . It is not time just yet; it would not succeed. Resist them, by peaceful means."[21] It is of interest to note that Parker's reservations about violence were not moral but utilitarian.

Henry Ward Beecher was also incensed by the Fugitive Slave Law. In an 1859 sermon he declared: "If he [the slave] has escaped and comes to me, I owe him shelter, succor, defense, and God-speed to a final safety. If there were as many laws as there are lines in the Fugitive Slave Law . . . I would disregard every law but God's, and help the fugitive!"[22] Samuel Spear, a Brooklyn minister, asked for lawful measures to correct the "unjust" Fugitive Slave Law. However, he reminded his listeners, man was called to obey God's law first of all, even if that led him to actions for which he must suffer civil consequences.[23]

Not all Northern preachers, however, called for a defiance of the Fugitive Slave Law. John C. Lord asked for patience and obedience to the law until the courts could decide on its legality.[24] In November of 1850 Ichabod Smith Spencer delivered a sermon in which he spoke of Christian responsibility to obey the Fugitive Law.[25] This was a very different stance than the one taken by most preachers in the North.

The Kansas–Nebraska Act (1854), which declared that popular sovereignty in the territories would decide whether new states would be slave or free, greatly aroused the ire of the Northern preachers who perceived the act as one more plot to expand the influence, practice, and boundaries of slavery. The Unitarian minister Thomas Wentworth Higginson called the Kansas–Nebraska Bill a revolution against liberty and the use of law to enforce tyranny.[26] Charles Beecher in a sermon strongly denounced the bill soon after it was enacted into law.[27]

Senator Stephen Douglas from Illinois, who was instrumental in the passage of the Kansas–Nebraska Act, resented the preachers' denunciations of the bill and questioned both their integrity and intelligence.

> It is presented by a denomination of men calling themselves preachers of the Gospel, who have come forward with an atrocious falsehood and an atrocious calumny against the Senate, desecrated the pulpit, and prostituted the sacred desk to the miserable and corrupting influence of party politics. I doubt whether there is a body of men in America who combine so much profound ignorance on the question upon which they attempt to enlighten the Senate as this same body of preachers.[28]

Douglas's charges brought forth a heated response from the clergy. The Rev. Eden B. Foster, a Congregationalist from Lowell, Massachusetts, delivered a sermon in which he defended the right of ministers to discuss slavery from the pulpit, because it was "in accordance with the spirit of the Gospel, and with the lofty purpose to which the pulpit is consecrated." Foster then spoke of widespread clergy opposition to the bill: "When three thousand and fifty [clergymen] from New England alone . . . voice a protest against a political measure, you may be sure the convictions of religious men, and the whole conscience of the country is profoundly moved." The preacher then spoke of the Christian minister's duty to speak on such subjects: "How could you forgive the minister, who is the watchman of the Lord . . . who does not lift up the warning cry if he sees the laws of justice prostrated? . . . Such a measure is the Nebraska Law."[29]

The caning of Charles Sumner by Congressman Preston Brooks from South Carolina heightened the Northern preachers' assault on the South and slavery. Octavius B. Frotheringham, after warning of a spreading slavocracy, charged that the physical attack on Sumner demonstrated how brutal and violent the slave system was.[30] Joseph

Henry Allen from Maine, in a sermon entitled "A Reign of Terror," denounced Brooks's attack on Sumner as a "cowardly assault on a gentleman unarmed and pinioned to his desk." Extending his protest, Allen asserted: "It is important to understand, that Mr. Sumner is the victim of a conspiracy to crush the freedom of congressional debate on that topic [slavery]."[31]

"Bleeding Kansas" that followed the Kansas–Nebraska legislation and the Dred Scott decision of 1857 drew more and more Northern clergy into the antislavery camp. As political and national events intensified, the rhetoric of the Northern preachers heated accordingly. In the midst of these heightened emotions John Brown staged his raid on Harper's Ferry on October 16, 1859, resulting in his capture and execution as a traitor on December 2. The Northern clergy were ambivalent about John Brown. Appreciating his idealism, most preachers questioned his judgment and methods. Henry Ward Beecher personified that ambivalence in a sermon preached after the raid but before Brown's execution. Beecher said that he abhorred the violence, the useless rebellion of Brown. Nevertheless, Beecher could not resist using the incident as an opportunity to shame the South.

> No one can fail to see that this poor, child-bereft old man is the manliest of them all. . . . That wounded old father is the most remarkable figure in the whole drama. The Governor, the officers of the State, and all the attorneys are pygmies compared to him. . . . If they kill the man, it would not be so much for treason as for the disclosure of their cowardice.[32]

The Northern preachers were never unanimous in their opposition to slavery. There remained those who were either neutral toward or advocates of slavery. The most noted Northern clergyman who defended the institution of slavery was the Episcopal prelate of Vermont, Bishop John Henry Hopkins. In 1861 and 1864 he published a work, *View of Slavery*, which startled most of the Northern religious world with its strong defense of slavery. For Hopkins, slavery was a blessing from God.

> In the Providence of God, the negro slavery of the South has been the means of saving millions of those poor creatures from the horrible state in which they must otherwise have lived and died. . . . Slavery in the hands of the Southern masters has been a blessing. . . . The relation of the master to the slave in the Southern states, involves no sin, provided the treatment of the slave be in accordance with the Scriptures.[33]

Henry J. Van Dyke, the noted author and pastor of the First Presbyterian Church in Brooklyn, joined Bishop Hopkins in defending the institution of slavery. On December 9, 1860, Van Dyke delivered a sermon in which he stated that slavery was sanctioned by divine authority, "not as the final destiny of the enslaved, but as an important and necessary process in their transition from heathenism to Christianity." The person who teaches that slavery is a sin, according to Van Dyke, "blasphemes the name of God and His doctrine."[34]

There were other Northern clergy who shared the views of Hopkins and Van Dyke. They were, however, by the 1860s a decided minority in the North. Chester Forrester Dunham has pointed out that three large church bodies in the North — Roman Catholic, Protestant Episcopal, and Lutheran — were virtually silent on the subject of slavery during the 1850s, and that during the Civil War the Lutherans finally took a stand while the other two remained mute.[35]

Two antislavery sermons are included in this chapter. The first example of such rhetoric comes from the noted evangelist Charles G. Finney. The portion included is only an excerpt of the sermon "Doubtful Actions Are Sinful," first delivered in 1835. Finney never devoted an entire sermon to slavery or any other social issue. His sermons always had one of two purposes, and sometimes both: the conversion of sinners and/or the perfection of those who were already Christians. Public issues such as slavery were introduced into Finney's sermons as illustrations or examples of how broad spiritual and moral principles might be applied. G. Frederick Wright, a Finney biographer, has written: "We look in vain in his sermons for any formal discussion on the subject of slavery. His references to it, both in his preaching and in his writing, were frequent and forcible, indeed, but they were casual, and were brought in as illustrations, rather than as his main proposition."[36]

Up through the first quarter of this century historians had largely overlooked the contribution of Finney and his revivals to the antislavery movement. Then in 1933 Gilbert Barnes published his work *The Antislavery Impulse 1830–1844*, in which he found the origin of the antislavery impluse in the religious revivals of Charles G. Finney. In the preface of the book Barnes tells his readers of "a different and incomparably more significant tale of a religious impulse which began in the West of 1830, was translated for a time into antislavery organization, and then broadened into a sectional crusade against the South."[37] William G. McLoughlin has summarized Barnes's discovery of "a different . . . tale."

> [It was] a tale which began with the Great Revival in the "burned-over" region of New York inspired by Charles Grandison Finney (a man as neglected as Weld by historians) and which led through the conversion of Weld and his conversion of other westerners to the formation of a mighty wave of evangelical antislavery sentiment brought about the formation of countless abolition societies and the arousing of a religious crusade against slavery which was more significant and important in the election of Lincoln and the outbreak of the Civil War than the work of Garrison in the East.[38]

Charles C. Cole has written that Finney's "significance in linking evangelism with antislavery cannot be overemphasized."[39] Timothy Smith has also recognized Finney's contribution: "Charles G. Finney probably won as many converts to the cause as William Lloyd Garrison, even though he shunned the role of political agitator for that of a winner of souls."[40] The most notable Finney convert was Theodore Dwight Weld, who became a prominent leader in the abolition movement. After preparing for the ministry at Lane Theological Seminary in Cincinnati, Weld devoted his life to the abolition of slavery. His forceful pamphlet, *American Slavery as It Is* (1839), was one of the most effective abolitionist tracts, and greatly influenced Harriet Beecher Stowe's writing of *Uncle Tom's Cabin* (1852). Weld often criticized his "father in the faith" for failing to take a stronger stand against slavery.

It is sometimes difficult to grasp Finney's antislavery posture because he continually varied his attack on the institution. He took no stand on slavery until twelve years after his conversion. This means that in all his early revival meetings, Finney took no public position on slavery. In 1833, when Finney was persuaded that slavery was a sin, he attacked it vehemently. The New York Anti-Slavery Society was founded at Finney's Chatham Street Chapel in New York City on October 2, 1833. He attended meetings that promoted abolition. On November 3, 1834, Finney and his congregation voted to ban slaveholders and slavetraders from communion in the congregation. He was one of the first to take such an action, believing that such a stance would help to bring about slavery's downfall. Finney's ministry was one of continued vacillation over the slavery issue, at times taking bold stands but then drawing back to more moderate positions that caused some of his abolitionist friends, such as the Tappans and Theodore Weld, to severely criticize him.

After 1839 Finney became more militant in his antislavery comments and actions. This may have been due in part to the fact that Southern Presbyterians, after the schism of 1837, were adamant in pronouncing that they were not going to be enticed by Finney's new theology or abolitionism. In 1839 Finney was elected chairman of the Ohio Anti-Slavery Society meeting in convention. At that convention he introduced nine antislavery resolutions which were "the highlight of the session."[41] In April of 1840 Finney and others, feeling that the Whig and Democratic candidates were not sympathetic to the abolitionist cause, nominated James G. Birney for president under the banner of the Liberty Party.

It is always important to remember that for Finney, everything was secondary to revivalism—even the abolition of slavery. In fact, Finney believed that religious revival would result in the end of slavery. On July 21, 1836, he wrote to Theodore Weld that the whole slavery problem could be solved in two years if only "the publick mind can be engrossed with the subject of salvation and make abolition an appendage just as we made temperance an appendage of revival in Rochester."[42]

Throughout his writings, lectures, and sermons Finney, over and over again, referred to slavery as an "abomination" or "iniquity." He called upon Christians and churches to take a bold stand against the institution, and held the churches primarily responsible for the sin of slavery. "The fact is that slavery is, pre-eminently, the sin of the church. It is the very fact that ministers and professors of religion of different denominations hold slaves, which sanctifies the whole abomination, in the eyes of ungodly men."[43] He was sure that if Christians and churches would take a forthright stand on slavery, the "abomination" would soon disappear. "Let Christians of all denominations meekly but firmly come forth," declared Finney,

and pronounce their verdict, let them clear their communions, and wash their hands of this thing, let them give forth and write on the head and front of this great abomination, SIN! and in three years, a public sentiment would be formed that would carry all before it, and there would not be a shackled slave, nor a bristling, cruel slave-driver in this land.[44]

In 1851 Finney was elected to the presidency of Oberlin College. Though he challenged the students to make revivalism their first priority, Oberlin, under Finney, sent forth many young people who became leaders in the abolitionist movement. John R. McKivigan has written: "Although Finney encouraged his students to concentrate on evangelical rather than antislavery activities, a generation of Oberlin-trained ministers would play a leading role in abolitionist activities among Western Congregationalists."[45] Keith Hardman, a recent Finney biographer, writes: "The school was prevented from veering into several extremes by Finney's moderate position on slavery, and it is no exaggeration to say that his views eventually prevailed among most of the faculty and students of the institution." Nevertheless, Hardman notes that this moderate stance made a great contribution to the antislavery movement: "Finney's attempt to hold a sensible, biblical, moderate stance may have been regarded as a greater contribution to the abolition of slavery than has been generally recognized."[46]

In the sermon at the end of this chapter Finney was concerned with a basic moral principle: "If a man does that of which he doubts the lawfulness, he sins and is condemned for it in the sight of God.... Whether it is lawful itself, is not the question. If he doubts its lawfulness, it is wrong for him." He applied this principle to several concerns: the use of wine at the Communion table, working on the Sabbath, gambling, theater-going, and parties. Not until the sermon was nearly over did he apply his moral principle to the subject of slavery.

The second sermon in this chapter comes from the pen of Theodore Parker, who in the years from 1841 to 1860 was the most outspoken antislavery pulpit voice in the North. He held back nothing and spoke his convictions without regard to the consequences. Parker vigorously attacked what he perceived to be the social and political wrongs of his era: poverty, drunkenness, ignorance, prostitution, political corruption, capital punishment, the privileged who advanced their status at the expense of the underprivileged, the plight of women, and an unjust criminal justice system. It was for slavery, however, that he reserved his severest judgment and harshest words, and devoted his greatest efforts toward its abolishment. About a year before he died, a very sick man, he wrote to his congregation in Boston from Italy, where he was attempting to regain his health: "I have spoken against slavery more than any other concrete wrong, because it is the greatest of all, 'the sum of all villainies.'"[47]

For Parker, at the heart of almost every social evil, and this was especially true of slavery, was the inordinate desire for wealth. In this regard the North participated in the guilt and shame of slavery. He declared that the hated Fugitive Slave Law "was the result of a union of the slave power of the South with the money power of the North: the Philistines and the Hebrews ploughed with the same heifer."[48]

The history of the United States, according to Parker, was a history of freedom versus slavery, with slavery being the winner most of the time. In an address in December of 1848 Parker said that slavery won its first battle in the United States Constitution.

> In 1787, the best and most celebrated statesmen were publicly active on the side of freedom. Some thought slavery a sin, others a mistake, but nearly all in the Convention thought it an error. South Carolina and Georgia were the only States thoroughly devoted to slavery at that time. They threatened to withdraw from the Union if it were not sufficiently respected in the new Constitution. If the other States had said, "You may go, soon as you like, for hitherto you have been only a curse to us, and done little but brag," it would have been better for us all. However, partly for the sake of keeping the peace, and still more for the purpose of making money by certain concessions to the South, the North granted the Southern demands.[49]

In his verbal assaults upon slavery Parker lashed out at some of the most prominent leaders of his day. Senator Daniel Webster and President Polk were two against whom he unleashed his most strident attacks.[50] The Northern clergy were also targets of Parker's rhetoric because of their failure to take a strong enough stand against slavery: "The pulpit is not to be relied on for much aid. If all the ministers of New England were abolitionists, with the same zeal that they are Protestants, Universalists, Methodists, Calvinists, or Unitarians, no doubt the whole State would soon be an antislavery State, and the day of emancipation would be wonderfully hastened. But that we are not to look for."[51]

In reaction to the Fugitive Slave Law, Parker helped to organize the Boston Vigilance Committee, which aided former slaves to escape capture. He hid many blacks in his home until they could find a more secure place. All this was carried out in defiance of the law. On November 7, 1850, he secretly presided over the marriage of two fugitives, William and Ellen Craft, before sending them to England.

In 1855 Parker bore some responsibility (it is still a question as to what degree) for inciting a mob to attempt the rescue of fugitive Anthony Burns from the Boston Courthouse. For this action Parker, Wendell Phillips, and others were arrested and indicted for obstructing the execution of the Fugitive Slave Law. The charges were dismissed on a legal technicality, but it is generally considered that the prosecutors were most reluctant to press charges against someone with the stature and influence of Parker.

Parker did have stature, influence, and popularity, though he was always surrounded by controversy because of his liberal positions both in theology and on public issues. Most of his fellow Unitarians considered him a heretic, and though he was never formally expelled from the Unitarian ministry, from the early 1840s he was actually an independent preacher. In 1845 he and several devoted followers organized a new congregation, the Twenty-eighth Congregational Society, which met at the Melodeon Theater in Boston. In 1852 the congregation moved to the new Music Hall, where three thousand people came almost every Sunday to hear this dynamic New Englander. In 1859 failing health forced Parker to leave his congregation.

As nearly as can be determined, Parker spoke more intelligently, courageously, openly, forthrightly, and with greater impact on the subject of slavery than any other American preacher. Though because of his early death he missed secession and the Civil War by only a few months, he is one who must be considered when the topic of the American pulpit and the Civil War is considered. His well-researched and uncompromising stances paved the way for other clergy and caused these others to appear more moderate and conciliatory in comparison. The fact that many of the Northern clergy spoke against slavery as well and as openly as they did owed much to the example and influence of Theodore Parker, who did so much to sensitize the American conscience.

The sermon of Parker at the end of this chapter was delivered at the Melodeon on Sunday, September 22, 1850. The discourse, entitled "The Function of Conscience," skillfully developed the concept of higher law, or natural and moral law, which was such an important concept in the Northern clergy's antislavery argument. Conscience, according to Parker, is the faculty given to men for discovering and knowing moral law. Very often official and civil obligations, which Parker labeled "Business," come in conflict with obligations to God or natural law, which Parker called "Duty." In every instance a moral man will choose natural law or duty over official law or business. When the laws of state conflict with the laws of conscience, a person of integrity must side with conscience, regardless of civil consequences. "The natural duty to keep the law of God," affirmed Parker, "overrides the obligation to observe any human statute."

Parker applied this principle to the Fugitive Slave Law, which had been enacted by the United States Congress six months prior to the delivery of this sermon. "It is plain to me," said Parker, "that it is the natural duty of citizens to rescue every fugitive slave from the hands of the marshal who essays to return him to bondage; to do it peaceably if they can, forcibly if they must, but by all means to do it."

Parker claimed that something goes wrong with most men when they enter public office; a person's "individual manhood is covered up and extinguished by his official cap." The preacher accused President Polk and other political leaders of this shame for sending troops into Mexico. Parker drew the lesson: "A man does not escape from the jurisdiction of natural law and the dominion of God by enlisting in the army, or by taking the oath of the President; for justice, the law paramount of the universe, extends over armies and nations."

NOTES

1. Sidney E. Ahlstrom, *A Religious History of the American People* (New Haven: Yale University Press, 1972), 649.
2. Quoted in Ahlstrom, *Religious History,* 673.
3. "A Sermon of Slavery," *Centenary Edition of the Works of Theodore Parker* (Boston: American Unitarian Association, 1907), 11:10.
4. For a helpful account in understanding the relationship between abolitionism and the Northern churches, see John R. McKivigan, *The War Against Proslavery Religion: Abolitionism and the Northern Churches, 1830–1865* (Ithaca: Cornell University Press, 1984). Although McKivigan acknowledges the vital role that the Northern churches and their ministers played in the election of Lincoln, and their support of the Union during the war, and even their important part in persuading Lincoln to draw up a statement of emancipation, he tends to downplay their antislavery commitment to a greater extent than do some other writers. Perhaps one reason for this is that McKivigan relies heavily upon abolitionist material for his primary sources. This kind of material would, of course, view the churches as having fallen woefully short in their commitment to the abolition of slavery.
5. *Natural Equality* (Windsor, VT: Chronicle Press, 1833).
6. *A Candid Appeal to the Citizens of the United States* (New York: A. K. Bertron, 1834).

7. *A Discourse on the Slavery Question* (Hartford: Case Library, 1839).
8. *The Integrity of Our National Union* (Cincinnati: R. P Donogh, 1843).
9. *Our Country's Danger and Security* (Utica: R. W. Roberts, 1844).
10. McKivigan, *The War Against Proslavery Religion*, 69.
11. Charles Cole has credited Charles G. Finney, the evangelist, for the development of the higher law doctrine in its application to the abolition of slavery: "Finney's place in the movement [antislavery] has tended to be minimized over the years, not only because the radical abolitionists who wrote histories of the crusades slighted him, but because one of his chief contributions to the cause has been overlooked. Few have ever linked Finney's name with the development of the higher law doctrine. Yet years before Theodore Parker, Seward, or Henry Ward Beecher, Charles G. Finney was preaching that no human legislation could set aside the law of God." *The Social Ideas of the Northern Evangelicals, 1826–1860* (1954; New York: Octagon Books, 1966), 208–09. Timothy Smith gives Finney similar credit: "Finney became the first to elaborate clearly the doctrine that the Christian covenant was supreme in human affairs, a 'higher law' than the Constitution." *Revivalism and Social Reform in Mid-Nineteenth Century America* (Nashville: Abingdon Press, 1957), 156. In his *Lectures on Systematic Theology*, Finney declared: "Nations are bound by the same law as individuals.... No human legislature can nullify the moral law. No human legislature can make it right or lawful to violate any command of God. All human enactments requiring or sanctioning the violation of any command of God, are not only null and void, but they are a blasphemous usurpation and invasion of the perogative of God" (1846; Grand Rapids: Eerdman's, 1964), 227.
12. (Boston: Wm. Crosby and H. P. Nichols, 1854), 17.
13. *The American Slavery Question* (New York: John S. Taylor, 1836).
14. *A Sermon* (Norwich: Anti-Slavery Society, 1834).
15. *The Gospel of the Typical Servitude* (Hamilton, OH: Gradner and Gibbon, 1835).
16. "The Mexican War," *Centenary Edition*, 11:22, 21, 29.
17. *Sermon on Slaveholding* (Cincinnati: n.p., 1842).
18. *The Danger and Hope of the American People* (New York: John F. Trow, 1843).
19. "Reply to Webster," *Centenary Edition*, 11:243.
20. "The Function of Conscience," *Centenary Edition*, 11:304.
21. "The Chief Sins of the People," *Centenary Edition*, 9:44.
22. "The Nation's Duty to Slavery," *Patriotic Addresses* (New York: Fords, Howard & Hulbert, 1891), 212.
23. *The Law-Abiding Conscience, and the Higher Law Conscience; with Remarks on the Fugitive Slave Question* (New York: Lambert and Lane, 1850).
24. *The Higher Law in Its Application to the Fugitive Slave Bill* (Buffalo: George H. Derby, 1851).
25. *Fugitive Slave Law: The Religious Duty of Obedience to Law* (New York: M. W. Dodd, 1850).
26. *Massachusetts in Mourning* (Boston: James Monroe and Company, 1854).
27. *A Sermon on the Nebraska Bill* (New York: Oliver and Brothers, 1854).
28. Quoted in Chester Forrester Dunham, *The Attitude of the Northern Clergy Toward the South 1860–1865* (Philadelphia: Porcupine Press, 1974), 51. Dunham's book is one of the best resources as to the thinking and pronouncements of the Northern clergy on sectional issues just prior to, during, and immediately after the Civil War.

29. "The Rights of the Pulpit," *Two Discourses* (Lowell, MA: J. J. Judkins, 1854), 9–34.
30. *The Last Signs* (New York: John A. Gray, 1856).
31. (Bangor, ME: Samuel S. Smith, 1857).
32. "The Nation's Duty to Slavery," *Patriotic Addresses,* 207.
33. (New York: W. I. Pooley, 1864), 63, 349.
34. "The Character and Influence of Abolitionism," *Fast Day Sermons* (New York: Rudd and Carleton, 1861), 152, 139.
35. Dunham, *Attitude of the Northern Clergy,* 26.
36. G. Frederick Wright, *Charles Grandison Finney* (Boston: Houghton Mifflin, 1891), 140.
37. Gilbert H. Barnes, *The Antislavery Impulse 1830–1844,* introduction by William G. McLoughlin (1933; New York: Harcourt Brace, 1964), xxxiii.
38. *The Antislavery Impulse,* viii.
39. Cole, *Social Ideas of the Northern Evangelicals,* 207.
40. Smith, *Revivalism and Social Reform,* 180.
41. *Social Ideas of the Northern Evangelicals,* 210.
42. Gilbert H. Barnes and Dwight L. Dumond, eds., *Letters of Theodore Dwight Weld, Angelina Grimke Weld, and Sarah Grimke,* 2 vols. (New York: Appleton-Century, 1934), 1:319.
43. Charles Grandison Finney, *Lectures on Revivals of Religion* (1835; Cambridge: Belknap Press, 1960), 301.
44. *Lectures on Revivals,* 302.
45. McKivigan, *The War Against Proslavery Religion,* 49.
46. Keith J. Hardman, *Charles Grandison Finney, 1792–1875, Revivalist and Reformer* (Syracuse: Syracuse University Press, 1987), 365, 364.
47. *Centenary Edition,* 13:377.
48. The Chief Sins of the People," *Centenary Edition,* 9:20.
49. "The Free-Soil Movement," *Centenary Edition,* 11:200.
50. For a stinging verbal attack upon Daniel Webster, see Parker's address "Reply to Webster," *Centenary Edition,* 11:218–47.
51. "The Antislavery Convention," *Centenary Edition,* 11:185.

Doubtful Actions Are Sinful

Charles G. Finney

1837

He that doubteth is damned if he eat, because he eateth not of faith
for whatsoever is not of faith is sin.
—Romans XIV, 23—

Hypocrites often attempt to shelter themselves behind their
doubts to get clear of their duty.

The hypocrite is unwilling to be enlightened, he does not wish
to know the truth, because he does not wish to obey the Lord, and
so he hides behind his doubts, and turns away his eye from the light,
and will not look or examine to see what his duty is, and in this way
he tries to shield himself from responsibility. But God will drag them
out from behind this refuge of lies, by the principle laid down in the
text, that their very doubts condemn them.

Many will not be enlightened on the subject of temperance, and
still persist in drinking or selling rum, because they are not fully convinced it is wrong. And they will not read a tract or a paper, nor attend a temperance meeting, for fear they shall be convinced. Many
are resolved to indulge in the use of wine and strong beer, and they
will not listen to anything calculated to convince them of the wrong.
It shows that they are determined to indulge in sin, and they hope
to hide behind their doubts. What better evidence could they give
that they are hypocrites?

Who, in all these United States, can say, that he has no doubt
of the lawfulness of slavery? Yet the great body of the people will
not hear anything on the subject, and they go into a passion if you
name it, and it is even seriously proposed, both at the north and at
the south, to pass laws forbidding inquiry and discussion on the subject. Now suppose these laws should be passed, for the purpose of
enabling the nation to shelter itself behind its doubts whether slavery is a sin, that ought to be abolished, immediately—will that help

Lectures to Professing Christians (London: Milner and Company, 1837), 24-37.

the matter? Not at all. If they continue to hold their fellow men as property, in slavery, while they doubt its lawfulness, they are condemned before God, and we may be sure their sin will find them out, and God will let them know how He regards it.

It is amazing to see the foolishness of people on this subject; as if by refusing to get clear of their doubts, they could get clear of their sin. Think of the people of the south: Christians, and even ministers, refusing to read a paper on the subject of slavery, and perhaps sending it back with abusive or threatening words. Threatening! for what? For reasoning with them about their duty? It can be demonstrated absolutely, that slavery is unlawful, and ought to be repented of, and given up, like any other sin. But suppose they only doubt the lawfulness of slavery, and do not mean to be enlightened, they are condemned of God. Let them know that they cannot put this thing down, they cannot clear themselves of it. So long as they doubt its lawfulness, they cannot hold men in slavery without sin; and that they do doubt its lawfulness is demonstrated by this opposition to discussion.

We may suppose a case, and perhaps there may be some such in the southern country, where a man doubts the lawfulness of holding slaves, and equally doubts the lawfulness of emancipating them in their present state of ignorance and dependence. In that case he comes under Pres. Edward's rule, and it is his duty not to fly in a passion with those who would call his attention to it, not to send back newspapers and refuse to read, but to inquire on all hands for light, and examine the question honestly in the light of the word of God, till his doubts are cleared up! The least he can do is to set himself with all his power to educate them and train them to take care of themselves as fast and as thoroughly as possible, and to put them in a state where they can be set at liberty.

The Function of Conscience

Theodore Parker

September 22, 1850

Herein do I excercise myself to have always a conscience void of offence toward God and toward men.
—*Acts XXIV, 16*—

There are some things which are true, independent of all human opinions. Such things we call facts. Thus it is true that one and one are equal to two, that the earth moves round the sun, that all men have certain natural unalienable rights, rights which a man can alienate only for himself, and not for another. No man made these things true; no man can make them false. If all the men in Jerusalem and ever so many more, if all the men in the world, were to pass a unanimous vote that one and one were not equal to two, that the earth did not move round the sun, that all men had not natural and unalienable rights, the opinion would not alter the fact, nor make truth false and falsehood true.

So there are likewise some things which are right, independent of all human opinions. Thus it is right to love a man and not to hate him, to do him justice and not injustice, to allow him the natural rights which he has not alienated. No man made these things right; no man can make them wrong. If all the men in Jerusalem and ever so many more, if all the men in the world, were to pass a unanimous vote that it was right to hate man and not love him, right to do him injustice and not justice, right to deprive him of his natural rights not alienated by himself, the opinion would not alter the fact, nor make right wrong and wrong right.

There are certain constant and general facts which occur in the material world, the world of external perception, which represent what are called the laws of matter, in virtue of which things take place so and not otherwise. These laws are the same everywhere and always; they never change. They are not made by men, but only dis-

Centenary Edition of the Works of Theodore Parker (Boston: American Unitarian Association, 1907), 11: 287–315.

covered by men, are inherent in the constitution of matter, and seem designed to secure the welfare of the material world. These natural laws of matter, inherent in its constitution, are never violated, nor can be, for material nature is passive, or at least contains no element or will that is adverse to the will of God, the ultimate Cause of these laws as of matter itself. The observance of these laws is a constant fact of the universe; "the most ancient heavens thereby are fresh and strong." These laws represent the infinity of God in the world of matter, His infinite power, wisdom, justice, love, and holiness.

So there are likewise certain constant and general facts which occur in what may be called the spiritual world, the world of internal consciousness. They represent the laws of spirit – that is, of the human spirit – in virtue of which things are designed to take place so and not otherwise. These laws are the same everywhere and always; they never change. They are not made by men but only discovered by men. They are inherent in the constitution of man, and as you cannot conceive of a particle of matter without extension, impenetrability, figure, and so on, no more can you conceive of man without these laws inhering in him. They seem designed to secure the welfare of the spiritual world. They represent the infinity of God in the world of man, His infinite power, wisdom, justice, love, and holiness. But while matter is stationary, bound by necessity, and man is progressive and partially free, to the extent of a certain tether, so it is plain that there may be a will in the world of man adverse to the will of God, and thus the laws of man's spirit may be violated to a certain extent. The laws of matter depend for their execution only on the infinite will of God, and so cannot be violated. The laws of man depend for their execution also on the finite will of man, and so may be broken.

Let us select a portion of these laws of the human spirit; such as relate to a man's conduct in dealing with his fellowmen, a portion of what are commonly called moral laws, and examine them. They partake of the general characteristics mentioned above; they are universal and unchangeable, are only discovered and not made by man, are inherent in man, designed to secure his welfare, and represent the infinity of God. These laws are absolutely right; to obey them is to be and do absolutely right. So being and doing, a man answers the moral purpose of his existence, and attains moral manhood. If I and all men keep all the laws of man's spirit, I have peace in my own heart, peace with my brother, peace with my God; I have my delight in myself, in my brother, in my God, they theirs and God His in me.

What is absolutely right is commonly called justice. It is the point in morals common to me and all mankind, common to me and God, to mankind and God; the point where all duties unite – to myself, my brethren, and my God; the point where all interests meet and balance – my interests, those of mankind, and the interests of God. When justice is done, all is harmony and peaceful progress in the world of man; but when justice is not done, the reverse follows, discord and confusion; for injustice is not the point where all duties and all interests meet and balance, not the point of morals common to mankind and me, or to us and God.

We may observe and study the constant facts of the material world, thus learn the laws they represent, and so get at a theory of the world which is founded on the facts thereof. Such a theory is true; it represents the thought of God, the infinity of God. Then for every point of theory we have a point of fact. Instead of pursuing this course we may neglect these constant facts, with the laws they represent, and forge a theory which shall not rest on these facts. Such a theory will be false and will represent the imperfection of men, and not the facts of the universe and the infinity of God.

In like manner, we may study the constant facts of the spiritual world, and, in special, of man's moral nature, and thereby obtain a rule to regulate our conduct. If this rule is founded on the constant facts of man's moral nature, then it will be absolutely right, and represent justice, the thought of God, the infinity of God, and for every point of moral theory we shall have a moral fact. Instead of pursuing that course, we may forge a rule for our conduct, and so get a theory which shall not rest on those facts. Such a rule will be wrong, representing only the imperfection of men.

In striving to learn the laws of the universe, the wisest men often go astray, propound theories which do not rest upon facts, and lay down human rules for the conduct of the universe, which do not agree with its nature. But the universe is not responsible for that; material nature takes no notice thereof. The opinion of an astronomer, of the American academy, does not alter a law of the material universe, or a fact therein. The philosophers once thought that the sun went round the earth, and framed laws on that assumption; but that did not make it a fact; the sun did not go out of his way to verify the theory, but kept to the law of God, and swung the earth round him once a year, say the philosophers what they might say, leaving them to learn the fact and thereby correct their theory.

In the same way, before men attain the knowledge of the absolute right, they often make theories which do not rest upon the fact of man's moral nature, and enact human rules for the conduct of men which do not agree with the moral nature of man. These are rules which men make and do not find made. They are not a part of man's moral nature, writ therein, and so obligatory thereon, no more than the false rules for the conduct of matter are writ therein and so obligatory thereon. You and I are no more morally bound to keep such rules of conduct, because King Pharaoh or King People say we shall, than the sun is materially bound to go round the earth every day, because Hipparchus and Ptolemy say it does. The opinion or command of a king, or a people, can no more change a fact and alter a law of man's nature, than the opinion of a philosopher can do this in material nature.

We learn the laws of matter slowly, by observation, experiment, and induction, and only get an outside knowledge thereof, as objects of thought. In the same way we might study the facts of man's moral nature, and arrive at rules of conduct, and get a merely outside acquaintance with the moral law as something wholly external. The law might appear curious, useful, even beautiful, moral gravitation as wonderful as material attraction. But no sense of duty would attach us to it. In addition to the purely intellectual powers, we have a faculty whose special function it is to discover the rules for a man's moral conduct. This is conscience, called also by many names. As the mind has for its object absolute truth, so conscience has for its object absolute justice. Conscience enables us not merely to learn the right by experiment and induction, but intuitively, and in advance of experiment; so, in addition to the experimental way, whereby we learn justice from the facts of human history, we have a transcendental way, and learn it from the facts of human nature, from immediate consciousness.

It is the function of conscience to discover to men the moral law of God. It will not do this with infallible certainty, for, at its best estate, neither conscience nor any other faculty of man is absolutely perfect, so as never to mistake. Absolute perfection belongs only to the faculties of God. But conscience, like each other faculty, is relatively perfect, — is adequate to the purpose God meant it for. It is often immature in the young, who have not had time for the growth and ripening of the faculty, and in the old, who have checked and hindered its development. Here it is feeble from neglect, there from abuse. It may give an imperfect answer to the question, What is absolutely right?

Now, though the conscience of a man lacks the absolute perfection of that of God, in all that relates to my dealing with men, it is still the last standard of appeal. I will hear what my friends have to say, what public opinion has to offer, what the best men can advise me to, then I am to ask my own conscience, and follow its decision; not that of my next friend, the public, or the best of men. I will not say that my conscience will always disclose to me the absolute right, according to the conscience of God, but it will disclose the relatively right, what is my conviction of right to-day, with all the light I can get on the matter; and as all I can know of the absolute right is my conviction thereof, so I must be true to that conviction. Then I am faithful to my own conscience, and faithful to my God. If I do the best thing I can know to-day, and to-morrow find a better one and do that, I am not to be blamed, nor to be called a sinner against God, because not so just to-day as I shall be to-morrow. I am to do God's will soon as I know it, not before, and to take all possible pains to find it out; but am not to blame for acting childish when a child, nor to be ashamed of it when grown up to be a man. Such is the function of conscience.

Having determined what is absolutely right, by the conscience of God, or at least relatively right, according to my conscience to-day, then it becomes my duty to keep it. I owe it to God to obey His law, or what I deem His law; that is my duty. It may be uncomfortable to keep it, unpopular, contrary to my present desires, to my passions, to my immediate interests; it may conflict with my plans in life; that makes no difference. I owe entire allegiance to my God. It is a duty to keep His law, a personal duty, my duty as a man. I owe it to myself, for I am to keep the integrity of my own consciousness; I owe it to my brother, and to my God. Nothing can absolve me from this duty, neither the fact that it is uncomfortable or unpopular, nor that it conflicts with my desires, my passions, my immediate interests, and my plans in life. Such is the place of conscience amongst other faculties of my nature.

I believe all this is perfectly plain, but now see what it leads to. In the complicated relations of human life, various rules for the moral conduct of men have been devised, some of them in the form of statute laws, some in the form of customs and in virtue of these rules, certain artificial demands are made of men, which have no foundation in the moral nature of man; these demands are thought to represent duties. We have the same word to describe what I ought to do as subject to the law of God, and what is demanded of me by custom, or the statute. We call each a duty. Hence comes no small confusion: the conventional and official obligation is thought to rest on the same foundation as the natural and personal duty. As the natural duty is at first sight a little vague, and not written out in the lawbook, or defined by custom, while the conventional obligation is well understood, men think that in case of any collision between the two, the natural duty must give way to the official obligation.

For clearness' sake, the natural and personal obligation to keep the law of God as my conscience declares it, I will call Duty; the conventional and official obligation to comply with some custom, keep some statute, or serve some special interest, I will call Business. Here then are two things – my natural and personal duty, my conventional and official business. Which of the two shall give way to the other, – personal duty or official business? Let it be remembered that I am a man first of all, and all else that I am is but a modification of my manhood, which makes me a clergyman, a fisherman, or a statesman; but the clergy, the fish, and the state, are not to strip me of my manhood. They are valuable in so far as they serve my manhood, not as it serves them. My official business as clergyman, fisherman, or statesman, is always beneath my personal duty as man. In case of any conflict between the two, the natural duty ought to prevail and carry the day before the official business; for the natural duty represents the permanent law of God, the absolute right, justice, the balance-point of all interests; while the official business represents only the transient conventions of men, some partial interest; and besides, the man who owes the personal duty is immortal, while the officer who performs the official business is but for a time. At death, the man is to be tried by the justice of God, for the deeds done, and character attained, for his natural duty, but he does not enter the next life as a clergyman, with his surplice and prayer-book, or a fisherman, with his angles and net, nor yet as a statesman, with his franking privilege, and title of honorable and member of Congress. The officer dies, of a vote or a fever. The man lives for ever. From the relation between a man and his occupation, it is plain, in general, that all conventional and official business is to be overruled by natural personal duty. This is the great circle, drawn by God, and discovered by conscience, which girdles my sphere, including all the smaller circles, and itself included by none of them. The law of God has eminent domain everywhere, over the private passions of Oliver and Charles, the special interests of Carthage and of Rome, over all customs, all official business, all precedents, all human statutes, all treaties between Judas and Pilate, or England and France, over all the conventional affairs of one man or of mankind. My own conscience is to declare that law for me, yours for you, and is before all private passions, or public interests, the decision of majorities, and a world full of precedent. You may resign your office, and escape its obligations, forsake your country, and owe it no allegiance, but you cannot move out of the dominions of God, nor escape where conscience has not eminent domain.

See some examples of a conflict between the personal duty and the official business. A man may be a clergyman, and it may be his official business to expound and defend the creed which is set up for him by his employers, his bishop, his association, or his parish, to defend and hold it good against all comers; it may be, also, in a certain solemn sort, to please the audience, who come to be soothed, caressed, and comforted, – to represent the average of religion in his society, and so to bless popular virtues and ban unpopular vices, but never to shake off or even jostle with one of his fingers the load of sin, beloved and popular, which crushes his hearers down till they are bowed together and can in nowise lift themselves up; unpopular excellence he is to call fanaticism, if not infidelity. But his natural duty as a man, standing in this position, overrides his official business, and commands him to tell men of the false things in their creed, of great truths not in it; commands him to inform his audience with new virtue, to represent all of religion he can attain, to undo the heavy burdens of popular sin, private or national, and let the men oppressed therewith go free. Excellence, popular or odious, he is to commend by its own name, to stimulate men to all nobleness of character and life, whether it please or offend. This is his duty, however uncomfortable, unpopular, against his desires, and conflicting with his immediate interests and plans of life. Which shall he do? His official business, and pimp and pander to the public lust, with base compliance serving the popular idols, which here are money and respectability or shall he serve his God? That is the question. If the man considers himself substantially a man, and accidentally a clergyman, he will perform his natural duty; if he counts the priesthood his substance, and manhood an accident of that, he will do only his official business.

I may be a merchant, and my official business may be to buy, and sell, and get gain; I may see that the traffic in ardent spirits is the readiest way to accomplish this. So it becomes my official business to make rum, sell rum, and by all means to induce men to drink it. But presently I see that the common use of it makes the thriving unthrifty, the rich less wealthy, the poor miserable, the sound sick, and the sane mad; that it brings hundreds to the jail, thousands to the alms-house, and millions to poverty and shame, producing an amount of suffering, wretchedness, and sin, beyond the power of man to picture or conceive. Then my natural duty as man is very clear, very imperative. Shall I sacrifice my manhood to money? – the integrity of my consciousness to my gains by rum-selling? That is the question. And my answer will depend on the fact, whether I am more a man or more a rum-seller. Suppose I compromise the matter, and draw a line somewhere between my natural duty as man, and my official business as rum-seller, and for every three cents that I make by iniquity, give one cent to the American Tract Society, or the Board for Foreign Missions, or the Unitarian Association, or the excellent Society for Propagating the Gospel among the Indians and Others in North America. That does not help the matter; business is not satisfied, though I draw the line never so near to money; nor conscience, unless the line comes up to my duty.

I am a citizen, and the State says, "You must obey all the statutes made by the proper authorities; that is your official business!" Suppose there is a statute adverse to the natural law of God, and the convictions of my own conscience, and I plead that fact in abatement of my obligation to keep the statute, the State says, "Obey it none the less, or we will hang you. Religion is an excellent thing in every matter except politics; there it seems to make men mad." Shall I keep the commandment of men, or the law of my God?

A statute was once enacted by King Pharaoh for the destruction of the Israelites in Egypt; it was made the official business of all citizens to aid in their destruction: "Pharaoh charged all his people saying, Every son that is born ye shall cast into the river, and every daughter ye shall save alive." It was the official business of every Egyptian who found a Hebrew boy to throw him into the Nile, – if he refused, he offended against the peace and dignity of the kingdom of Egypt, and the form of law in such case made and provided. But if he obeyed, he murdered a man. Which should he obey, the Lord Pharaoh, or the Lord God? That was the question. I make no doubt that the priests of Osiris, Orus, Apis, Isis, and the judges, and the justices of the peace and quorum, and the members of Congress of that time, said, "Keep the king's commandment, O ye that worship the crocodile and fear the cat, or ye shall not sleep in a whole skin any longer!" So said everything that loveth and maketh a lie.

King Charles II made a statute some one hundred and ninety years ago, to punish with death the remnant of the nine-and-fifty judges who had brought his father's head to the block, teaching kings that "they also had a joint in their necks." He called on all his subjects to aid in the capture of these judges. It was made their official business as citizens to do so; a reward was offered for the apprehension of some of them "alive or dead," punishment hung over the head of any who should harbor or conceal them. Three of these regicides, who had adjudged a king for his felony, came to New England. Many Americans knew where they were, and thought the condemnation of Charles I was the best thing these judges ever did. With that conviction ought they to have delivered up these fugitives, or afforded them shelter? In time of peril, when officers of the English government were on the lookout for some of these men, a clergyman in the town where one of them was concealed, preached, it is said, on the text "Bewray not him that wandereth," an occasional sermon, and put the duty of a man far before the business of a citizen. When Sir Edmund Andros was at New Haven looking after one of the judges, and attended public worship in the same meeting-house with the fugitive, the congregation sang an awful hymn in his very ears.

Would the men of Connecticut have done right, bewraying him that wandered, and exposing the outcast, to give up the man who had defended the liberties of the world and the rights of mankind against a tyrant, — give him up because a wanton king, and his loose men and loose women, made such a commandment? One of the regicides dwelt in peace eight-and-twenty years in New England, a monument of the virtue of the people.

Of old time the Roman statute commanded the Christians to sacrifice to Jupiter; they deemed it the highest sin to do so, but it was their official business as Roman citizens. Some of them were true to their natural duty as men, and took the same cross Jesus had borne before them; Peter and John had said at their outset to the authorities – "Whether it be right in the sight of God to hearken unto you more than unto God, judge ye." The Emperor once made it the official business of every citizen to deliver up the Christians. But God made it no man's duty. Nay, it was each man's duty to help them. In such cases what shall a man do? You know what we think of men who comply basely, and save their life with the loss of their soul. You know how the Christian world honors the saints and martyrs who laid down their lives for the sake of truth and right; a handful of their dust, which was quieted of its trouble by the heads-man's axe seventeen hundred years ago, and is now gathered from the catacombs of Saint Agnes at Rome – why it is enough to consecrate half of the Catholic churches in New England. As I have stood among their graves, have handled the instruments with which they tasted of bitter death, and crumbled their bones in my hands, – I keep their relics still with reverent awe, – I have thought there was a little difference between their religion, and the pale decency that haunts the churches of our time, and is afraid lest it lose its dividends, or its respectability, or hurt its usefulness, which is in no danger.

Do I speak of martyrs for conscience' sake? Today is St. Maurice's day, consecrated to him and the "Thebaean legion." Maurice appears to have been a military tribune in the Christian legion, levied in the Thebais, a part of Egypt. In the latter part of the third century this legion was at Octodurum, near the little village of Martigni, in Valais, a Swiss Canton, under the command of Maximian, the associate emperor, just then named Herculeus, going to fight the Bagaudae. The legion was ordered to sacrifice to the gods after the heathen fashion. The soldiers refused; every tenth man was hewn down by Maximian's command. They would not submit, and so the whole legion, as the Catholic story tells us, perished there on the 22nd of September, fifteen hundred and fifty-three years ago this day. Perhaps the account is not true; it is probable that the number of martyrs is much exaggerated, for six hundred soldiers would not stand still and be slaughtered without striking a blow. But the fact that the Catholic church sets apart one day in the calendar to honor this alleged heroism, shows the value men put on fidelity to conscience in such cases.

Last winter a bill for the capture of fugitive slaves was introduced into the Senate of the United States of America; the senator who so ably represented the opinions and wishes of the controlling men of this city, proposed to support that bill, "with all its provisions to the fullest extent;" that bill, with various alterations, some for the better, others for the worse, has become a law — it received the vote of the representative from Boston, who was not sent there, I hope, for the purpose of voting for it. That statute allows the slaveholder, or his agent, to come here, and by summary process seize a fugitive slave, and, without the formality of a trial by jury, to carry him back to eternal bondage. The statute makes it the official business of certain magistrates to aid in enslaving a man; it empowers them to call out force enough to overcome any resistance which may be offered, to summon the bystanders to aid in that work. It provides a punishment for any one who shall aid and abet, directly or indirectly, and harbor, or conceal the man who is seeking to maintain his natural and unalienable right to life, liberty, and the pursuit of happiness. He may be fined a thousand dollars, imprisoned six months, and be liable to a civil action for a thousand dollars more!

This statute is not to be laid to the charge of the slaveholders of the South alone; its most effective supporters are Northern men; Boston is more to be blamed for it than Charleston or Savannah, for nearly a thousand persons of this city and neighborhood, most of them men of influence through money if by no other means, addressed a letter of thanks to the distinguished man who had volunteered to support that infamous bill, telling him that he had "convinced the understanding and touched the conscience of the nation." A man falls low when he consents to be a slave, and is spurned for his lack of manhood; to consent to be a catcher of fugitive slaves is to fall lower yet; but to consent to be the defender of a slave-catcher — it is seldom that human nature is base enough for that. But such examples are found in this city! This is now the law of the land. It is the official business of judges, commissioners, and marshals, as magistrates, to execute the statute and deliver a fugitive up to slavery; it is your official business and mine, as citizens, when legally summoned, to aid in capturing the man. Does the command make it any man's duty? The natural duty to keep the law of God over-rides the obligation to observe any human statute, and continually commands us to love a man and not hate him, to do him justice, and not injustice, to allow him his natural rights not alienated by himself; yes, to defend him in them, not only by all means legal, but by all means moral.

Let us look a little at our duty under this statute. If a man falls into the water and is in danger of drowning, it is the natural duty of the bystanders to aid in pulling him out, even at the risk of wetting their garments. We should think a man a coward who could swim, and would not save a drowning girl for fear of spoiling his coat. He would be indictable at common law. If a troop of wolves or tigers were about to seize a man, and devour him, and you and I could help him, it would be our duty to do so, even to peril our own limbs and life for the purpose. If a man undertakes to murder or steal a man, it is the duty of the bystanders to help their brother, who is in peril, against wrong from the two-legged man, as much as against the four-legged beast. But suppose the invader who seizes the man is an officer of the United States, has a commission in his pocket, a warrant for his deed in his hand, and seizes as a slave a man who has done nothing to alienate his natural rights — does that give him any more natural right to enslave a man than he had before? Can any piece of parchment make right wrong, and wrong right?

The fugitive has been a slave before? Does the wrong you committed yesterday, give you a natural right to commit wrong afresh and continually? Because you enslaved this man's father, have you a natural right to enslave his child? The same right you would have to murder a man because you butchered his father first. The right to murder is as much transmissible by inheritance as the right to enslave! It is plain to me that it is the natural duty of citizens to rescue every fugitive slave from the hands of the marshal who essays to return him to bondage; to do it peaceably if they can, forcibly if they must, but by all means to do it. Will you stand by and see your countrymen, your fellow-citizens of Boston, sent off to slavery by some commissioner? Shall I see my own parishioners taken from under my eyes and carried back to bondage, by a man whose constitutional business it is to work wickedness by statute? Shall I never lift an arm to protect him? When I consent to that, you may call me a hireling shepherd, an infidel, a wolf in sheep's clothing, even a defender of slave-catching if you will; and I will confess I was a poor dumb dog, barking always at the moon, but silent as the moon when the murderer came near.

I am not a man who loves violence. I respect the sacredness of human life. But this I say, solemnly, that I will do all in my power to rescue any fugitive slave from the hands of any officer who attempts to return him to bondage. I will resist him as gently as I know how, but with such strength as I can command; I will ring the bells, and alarm the town; I will serve as head, as foot, or as hand to any body of serious and earnest men, who will go with me, with no weapons but their hands, in this work. I will do it as readily as

I would lift a man out of the water, or pluck him from the teeth of a wolf, or snatch him from the hands of a murderer. What is a fine of a thousand dollars, and jailing for six months, to the liberty of a man? My money perish with me, if it stand between me and the eternal law of God! I trust there are manly men enough in this house to secure the freedom of every fugitive slave in Boston, without breaking a limb or rending a garment.

One thing more I think is very plain, that the fugitive has the same natural right to defend himself against the slave-catcher, or his constitutional tool, that he has against a murderer or a wolf. The man who attacks me to reduce me to slavery, in that moment of attack alienates his right to life, and if I were the fugitive, and could escape in no other way, I would kill him with as little compunction as I would drive a mosquito from my face. It is high time this was said. What grasshoppers we are before the statute of men! what Goliaths against the law of God! What capitalist heeds your statute of usury when he can get illegal interest? How many banks are content with six per cent when money is scarce? Did you never hear of a merchant evading the duties of the customhouse? When a man's liberty is concerned, we must keep the law, must we? betray the wanderer, and expose the outcast?

In the same manner the natural duty of a man overrides all the special obligations which a man takes on himself as a magistrate by his official oath. Our theory of office is this: The man is sunk in the magistrate; he is *un homme couvert;* his individual manhood is covered up and extinguished by his official cap; he is no longer a man, but a mere president, general, governor, representative, sheriff, juror, or constable; he is absolved from all allegiance to God's law of the universe when it conflicts with man's law of the land; his official business as a magistrate supersedes his natural duty as a man. In virtue of this theory, President Polk, and his coadjutors in Congress and out of it, with malice aforethought, and intent to rob and to kill, did officially invade Mexico, and therein "slay, kill, and murder" some thousands of men, as well American as Mexicans. This is thought right because he did it officially. But the fact that he and they were magistrates, doing official business, did not make the killing any the less a wrong than if he and they had been private men, with General Lopez and not General Taylor to head or back them. The official killing of a man who has not alienated his right to life, is just as much violation of the law of God, and the natural duty of man, as the un-

official killing of such a person. Because you and I and some other foolish people put a man in a high office and get him to take an oath, does that, all at once, invest him with a natural right to kill anybody he sees fit; to kill an innocent Mexican? All his natural rights he had before, and it would be difficult to ascertain where the people could find the right to authorize him to do a wrong. A man does not escape from the jurisdiction of natural law and the dominion of God by enlisting in the army, or by taking the oath of the President; for justice, the law paramount of the universe, extends over armies and nations.

A little while ago a murderer was hanged in Boston, by the sheriff of Suffolk county, at the command of the Governor and Council of Massachusetts, by the aid of certain persons called grand and petit jurors, all of them acting in their official capacity, and doing the official business they had sworn to do. If it be a wrong thing to hang a man, or to take his life except in self-defense, and while in imminent peril, then it is not any less a wrong because men do it in their official character, in compliance with their oath. I am speaking of absolute wrong, not merely what is wrong relatively to the man's own judgment, for I doubt not that all those officers were entirely conscientious in what they did, and therefore, no blame rests on them. But if a man believes it wrong to take human life deliberately, except in the cases named, then I do not see how, with a good conscience, he can be partaker in the death of any man, notwithstanding his official oath.

Let me suppose a case which may happen here, and before long. A woman flies from South Carolina to Massachusetts to escape from bondage. Mr. Greatheart aids her in her escape, harbors and conceals her, and is brought to trial for it. The punishment is a fine of one thousand dollars and imprisonment for six months. I am drawn to serve as a juror, and pass upon this offense. I may refuse to serve, and be punished for that, leaving men with no scruples to take my place, or I may take the juror's oath to give a verdict according to the law and the testimony. The law is plain, let us suppose, and the testimony conclusive. Greatheart himself confesses that he did the deed alleged, saving one ready to perish. The judge charges, that if the jurors are satisfied of that fact, then they must return that he is guilty. This is a nice matter. Here are two questions. The one, put to me in my official capacity as juror, is this: "Did Greatheart aid the woman?" The other, put to me in my natural character as man, is this: "Will you help punish Greatheart with fine and imprisonment for helping a woman obtain her unalienable rights?" I am to answer both. If I have extinguished my manhood by my juror's oath, then I shall do my official business and find Greatheart guilty, and I shall seem to be a true man; but if I value my manhood, I shall answer after my natural duty to love a man and not hate him, to do him justice, not injustice, to allow him the natural rights he has not alienated, and shall say "Not guilty." Then foolish men, blinded by the dust of courts, may call me forsworn and a liar; but I think human nature will justify the verdict.

In cases of this kind, when justice is on one side and the court on the other, it seems to me a conscientious man must either refuse to serve as a juror, or else return a verdict at variance with the facts and what courts declare to be his official business as juror; but the eyes of some men have been so long blinded by what the court declares is the law, and by its notion of the juror's function, that they will help inflict such a punishment on their brother, and the judge decree the sentence, in a case where the arrest, the verdict, and the sentence are the only wrong in which the prisoner is concerned. It seems to me it is time this matter should be understood, and that it should be known that no official oath can take a man out of the jurisdiction of God's natural law of the universe.

A case may be brought before a commissioner or judge of the United States, to determine whether Daniel is a slave, and therefore to be surrendered up. His official business, sanctioned by his oath, enforced by the law of the land, demands the surrender; his natural duty, sanctioned by his conscience, enforced by absolute justice, forbids the surrender. What shall he do? There is no serving of God and Mammon both. He may abandon his commission and refuse to remain thus halting between two opposites. But if he keeps his office, I see not how he can renounce his nature and send back a fugitive slave, and do as great a wrong as to make a freeman a slave!

Suppose the Constitution had been altered, and Congress had made a law, making it the business of the United States' commissioners to enslave and sell at public outcry all the red-haired men in the nation, and forbid us to aid and abet their escape, to harbor and conceal them, under the same penalties just now mentioned; do you think any commissioner would be justified before God by his oath in kidnapping the red-haired men, or any person in punishing such as harbored or concealed them, such as forcibly took the victims out of the hand of officials who would work mischief by statute? Will the color of a hair make right wrong, and wrong right?

Suppose a man has sworn to keep the Constitution of the United States, and the Constitution is found to be wrong in certain particulars: then his oath is not morally binding, for before his oath, by his very existence, he is morally bound to keep the law of God as fast as he learns it. No oath can absolve him from his natural allegiance to God. Yet I see not how a man can knowingly, and with a good conscience, swear to keep what he deems wrong to keep, and will not keep, and does not intend to keep.

It seems to me very strange that men so misunderstand the rights of conscience and their obligations to obey their country. Not long ago, an eminent man taunted one of his opponents, telling him he had better adhere to the "higher law." The newspapers echoed the sneer, as if there were no law higher than the Constitution. Latterly, the Democratic party, even more completely than the Whig party, seems to have forgotten that there is any law higher than the Constitution, any rights above vested rights.

An eminent theologian of New England, who has hitherto done good and great service in his profession, grinding off the barb of Calvinism, wrote a book in defense of slave-catching, on "Conscience and the Constitution," a book which not only sins against the sense of the righteous in being wicked, but against the worldliness of the world in being weak, – and he puts the official business of keeping "a compact" far before the natural duty of keeping a conscience void of offense, and serving God. But suppose forty thieves assemble on Fire Island, and make a compact to rob every vessel wrecked on their coast, and reduce the survivors to bondage. Suppose I am borne amongst that brotherhood of pirates, am I morally bound to keep that compact, or to perform any function which grows out of it? Nay, I am morally bound to violate the compact, to keep the pirates from their plunder and their prey. Instead of forty thieves on Fire Island, suppose twenty millions of men in the United States make a compact to enslave every sixth man – the dark men – am I morally bound to heed that compact, or to perform any function which grows out of it? Nay, I am morally bound to violate the compact, in every way that is just and wise. The very men who make such a compact are morally discharged from it as soon as they see it is wrong. The forty

Jews who bound themselves by wicked oath to kill Paul before they broke their fast, – were they morally bound to keep their word? Nay, morally bound to break it.

I will tell you a portion of the story of a fugitive slave whom I have known. I will call his name Joseph, though he was in worse than Egyptian bondage. He was "owned" by a notorious gambler, and once ran away, but was retaken. His master proceeded to punish him for that crime, took him to a chamber, locked the door, and lighted a fire; he then beat the slave severely. After that he put the branding-iron in the fire, took a knife, – I am not telling what took place in Algiers, but in Alabama, – and proceeded to cut off the ears of his victim! The owner's wife, alarmed at the shrieks of the sufferer, beat down the door with a sledge hammer, and prevented that catastrophe. Afterwards, two slaves of this gambler, for stealing their master's sheep, were beaten so that they died of the stripes. The "minister" came to the funeral, told the others that those were wicked slaves, who deserved their fate; that they would never "rise" in the general resurrection, and were not fit to be buried! Accordingly their bodies were thrown into a hole and left there. Joseph ran away again; he came to Boston; was sheltered by a man whose charity never fails; he has been in my house, and often has worshipped here with us. Shall I take that man and deliver him up? – do it "with alacrity"? Shall I suffer that gambler to carry his prey from this city? Will you allow it – though all the laws and constitutions of men give the commandment? God do so unto us if we suffer it.

This we need continually to remember: that nothing in the world without is so sacred as the eternal law of God; of the world within nothing is more venerable than our own conscience, the permanent, everlasting oracle of God. The Urim and Thummin were but Jewish or Egyptian toys on the breastplate of the Hebrew priest; the Delphic oracle was only a subtle cheat; but this is the true Shekinah and presence of God in your heart: as this

> "– pronounces lastly on each deed,
> Of so much fame in heaven expect your meed."

If I am consciously and continually false to this, it is of no avail that I seem loyal to all besides; I make the light that is in me darkness, and how great is that darkness! The center of my manhood is gone, and I am rotten at my heart. Men may respect me, honor me, but I am not respectable, I am a base, dishonorable man, and like a tree, broad-branched, and leafed with green, but all its heart gnawed out by secret worms; at some slight touch one day, my rotten trunk will fall with horrid squelch, bringing my leafy honors to dishonored dust, and men will wonder that bark could hide such rottenness and ruin.

But if I am true to this legate of God, holding His court within my soul, then my power to discover the just and right will enlarge continually; the axis of my little life will coincide with the life of the infinite God, His conscience and my own be one. Then my character and my work will lie in the plane of His almighty action; no other will in me, His infinite wisdom, justice, holiness, and love, will flow into me, a ceaseless tide, filling with life divine and new the little creeklets of my humble soul. I shall be one with God, feel His delight in me and mine in Him, and all my mortal life run o'er with life divine and bless mankind. Let men abhor me, yea, scourge and crucify, angels are at hand; yes, the Father is with me!

How we mistake. Men think if they can but get wickedness dignified into a statute, enrolled in the Capitol, signed by the magistrates, and popular with people, that all is secure. Then they rejoice and at their "Thanksgiving dinner," say with the short-lived tyrant in the play, after he had slain the rightful heirs of England's throne, and set his murderous hoof on justice at every step to power,—

> "Now is the winter of our discontent
> Made glorious summer" . . .

and think that sin sits fast and rides secure. But no statute of men is ever fixed on man till it be first the absolute, the right, the law of God. All else lasts but its day, for ever this, for ever still the same. By "previous questions," men may stop debate, vote down minorities with hideous grin, but the still small voice of justice will whisper in the human heart, will be trumpet-tongued in history to teach you that you cannot vote down God.

In your private character, if you would build securely, you must build on the natural law of God, inherent in your nature and in His; if the nation would build securely, it must build so. Out of their caprice, their selfishness, and their sin, may men make statutes, to last for a day, built up with joyous huzzas, and the chiming of a hundred guns, to come down with the curses of the multitude, and smitten by the thunder of God; but to build secure, you must build on the justice of the Almighty. The beatitudes of Jesus will outlast the

WITHDRAWN
SCCCC - LIBRARY
4601 Mid Rivers Mall Drive
St Peters. MO 63376

codes of all the tyrants of the Old World and the New. So I have seen gamblers hurry and huddle up their booths at a country muster, on the unsmoothed surface of a stubble-field, foundation good enough for such a structure, not a post plumb, to endure a single day of riot, drunkenness, and sin; but to build a pyramid which shall outlast empires, men lay bare the bosom of the primeval rock, and out of primeval rock they build thereon their well-joined work, outlasting Syria, Greece, Carthage, Rome, venerable to time, and underneath its steadfast foot the earthquakes pass all harmlessly away.

All things conspire to overturn a wrong. Every advance of man is hostile to it. Reason is hostile; religion is its deadly foe; the new-born generation will assail it, and it must fall. Of old it was written, "Though hand join in hand, the wicked shall not prosper," and the world's wide walls from the remotest bounds of peopled space, laugh out their loud and long "Amen!" Let Iniquity be never so old and respectable, get all the most eminent votes, have the newspapers on her side, guns fired at her success, it all avails nothing; for this is God's world, not a devil's, and His eternal word has gone forth that right alone shall last for ever and for ever.

O young man, now in the period of the passions, reverence your conscience. Defer that to no appetite, to no passion, to no foolish compliance with other men's ways, to no ungodly custom, even if become a law. Ask always "Is it right for me?" Be brave and self-denying for conscience' sake. Fear not to differ from men; keeping your modesty, keep your integrity also. Let not even your discretion consume your valor. Fear not to be scrupulously upright and pure; be afraid neither of men's hate, nor even of their laugh and haughty scorn, but shudder at the thought of tampering with your sense of right, even in the smallest matters. The flesh will come up with deceitful counsels—the spirit teaching the commandments of God; give both their due. Be not the senses' slave, but the soul's freeman.

O brother man, who once wert young, in the period of ambition, or beyond it, if such a time there be, can you trust the selfishness, the caprice, the passions, and the sin of men, before your own conscience, renounce the law of God for the customs of men? When your volcanic mountain has been capped with snow, Interest, subtler than all the passions of the flesh, comes up to give her insidious counsel. "On our side," says she, "is the applause of men; feasting is with us; the wise and prudent are here also, yea, the ancient and honorable, men much older than thy father; and with gray hairs mottling thy once auburn head, wilt thou forsake official business, its solid praise and certain gain, for the phantom of natural duty, renounce allegiance to warm human lies for the cold truth of God remote and far!" Say, "Get thee behind me," to such counsellors; "I will not stain my age by listening to your subterranean talk."

O brother man, or old or young, how will you dare come up before your God and say: "O Lord, I heard, I heard Thy voice in my soul, at times still and small, at times a trumpet talking with me of the right, the eternal right, but I preferred the low counsels of the flesh; the commands of interest I kept; I feared the rich man's decorous rage; I trembled at the public roar, and I scorned alike my native duty and Thy natural law. Lo, here is the talent Thou gavest me, my sense of right. I have used each other sense, this only have I hid; it is eaten up with rust, but thus I bring it back to Thee. Take what is Thine!" Who would dare thus to sin against infinite justice? Who would wish to sin against it when it is also infinite love, and the law of right is but the highway on which the almightiness of the Father comes out to meet His prodigal, a great way off; penitent and returning home, or unrepentant still, refusing to be comforted, and famishing on chaff and husks, while there is bread of heavenly life enough and yet to spare, comes out to meet us, to take us home, and to bless us for ever and for ever?

SECTIONALISM

As the Northern preachers stirred an antislavery sentiment in the North, they became a vital factor in promoting a sectionalism whereby the North saw itself as superior to the South; superior morally, intellectually, and culturally. Theodore Parker drew the distinction as sharply as any preacher in the North. In an 1848 sermon, which smacked of strong provincialism, he proclaimed:

Who fought the Revolution? Why the North, furnishing the money and the men, Massachusetts alone sending fourteen thousand soldiers more than all the present slave states. Who pays the national taxes? The North, for the slaves pay but a trifle. Who owns the greater part of the property, the mills, the shops, the ships? The North. Who writes the books — the histories, poems, philosophies, works of science, even the sermons and commentaries on the Bible? Still the North. Who sends their children to school and colleges? The North. Who builds the churches, who founds the Bible societies, missionary societies, the thousand-and-one institutions for making men better and better off? Why the North. In a word, who is it in seventy years has made the nation great, rich, and famous for her ideas and their success all over the world? The answer is still the North, the North.

Well, says the calculator, but who has the offices of the nation? The South. Who has filled the presidential chair forty-eight years out of sixty? Nobody but slaveholders. Who has held the chief posts of honor? The South. Who occupy the chief offices in the army and navy? The South. Who increases the cost of the post-office and pays so little of its expense? The South. Who is most blustering and disposed to quarrel? The South. Who made the Mexican War? The South. Who sets at naught the Constitution? The South. Who would bring the greatest peril in the case of war with a strong enemy? Why the South, the South. But what is the South most noted for abroad? For her three million slaves; and the North for her wealth, freedom, education, religion![1]

In an 1851 sermon Parker echoed a similar theme. Because the South had disregarded higher law, its society had paid a price: "Ask the Southern States of America to show us their rapid increase in riches, in civilization; to show us their schools and their scholars, their literature, their science, and their art."[2] Nevertheless, Parker lamented that the South was much more committed to its way of life than the North was to its. "Southern slavery is an institution which is in earnest. Northern Freedom is an institution that is not in earnest."[3]

In 1854 Horace Bushnell delivered a sermon whose theme was that the South was culturally inferior to the North. Though the South was proficient in dining, hunting, harangue, and political skill, the North had iron which the South lacked. The North was superior in learning, culture, art, and letters. Of the South, Bushnell proclaimed, "The scholarship, the philosophic and esthetic culture, the originative art . . . are barbarized of necessity by the element of slavery and make a very sorry figure in the world of letters."[4] George M. Frederickson has pointed out that the reason Bushnell opposed the Fugitive Slave Law and supported conflict over the sovereignty issue was not humanitarian or antislavery concerns. "It was New England chauvinism," wrote Frederickson, "which led him to advocate forcible resistance to the Fugitive Slave Act and armed conflict in the territories. . . . His sense of a Southern threat to the institutions and traditions of the North led him to side, for all practical purposes, with the Parkers and Higginsons."[5]

Henry Ward Beecher, of whom more will be written at the end of this chapter, said that one of the fundamental differences between the two sections of the ntion was that the North was national in character, whereas the South was sectional. On April 14, 1861, one day after Fort Sumter had surrendered to Confederate forces, Beecher addressed this issue:

> There has been a spirit of patriotism in the North; but never, within my memory, in the South. I never heard a man from the South speak of himself as an American. Men from the South speak of themselves as Southerners. . . . And in the South the feeling has been sectional, local. The people have been proud, not that they belong to the nation, but that they were born where the sun burns. They are hot, narrow and boastful. . . . They have been devoid of that large spirit which takes in the race, and the nation, and its institutions, and its history.[6]

Later in the same year Beecher complained that "the South had been overrun with pestilent heresies of States rights."[7]

Throughout the war Northern preachers continued their verbal assaults upon the South as an inferior culture. In the summer of 1862 Dr. Edward Everett Hale, Unitarian minister and author of *The Man Without a Country*, proclaimed: "The end of the present war must be the civilization of the Southern states. It will not really end until that civilization is secured. . . . We are to introduce into the South and Southwest, new men, new life, and a higher civilization."[8]

In May of 1864 the Rev. Nathaniel Hall presented a report, by means of a sermon, on his recent three-week trip through Kentucky and Tennessee: "It seems indeed to the Northern stranger that he has fallen back generations from the civilization he has left. . . . You seem to yourself to have come among a different nation, upon a different age; among those who have been slumbering, while the rest of the world has moved on."[9]

Soon after the assassination of President Lincoln, the Rev. Daniel C. Eddy of the Baldwin Place Congregational Church in Boston spoke of the fundamental differences he perceived between the South and the North:

> Argue as we may, our Southern people are a different race. Slavery has given them a different idea of religion. . . . Slavery has barbarized them, and made them a people with whom we have little in common. We had an idea of Southern civilization when Judge Hoar was driven out of Charleston, . . . when Sumner was bleeding in the Federal Senate, . . . when ornaments were made for Southern ladies of the bones of the brave soldiers killed at Bull Run, . . . in the atrocities perpetuated upon our poor soldiers. . . . And now we have another exhibition of it in the base, wanton, assassination of the President.[10]

In the antebellum years some Northern clergy looked upon the South as such a distasteful part of the Union that they advocated the Garrisonian position whereby the North should separate itself from the South. In 1851 Charles G. Finney, coming to the realization that revivalism was not going to bring an end to slavery, suggested "the dismemberment of our hypocritical union."[11] Finney detested the thought of living in a nation where slavery existed. It was better to separate from such an evil. He exclaimed: "To adopt the maxin, 'Our Union even with perpetual slavery,' is an abomination so exercrable as not to be named by a just mind without indignation."[12]

In two sermons delivered in 1854 Eden B. Foster, a Congregationalist minister from Lowell, Massachusetts, proposed the secession of the North from the Union as a last resort to check the spread
of slavery. Inherent in the slavery system, said Foster, were such
evils as cruelty, ignorance, immorality, and sin.[13] On April 4, 1861,
less than two weeks before the cannons from Charleston began to
bombard Fort Sumter, Zachery Eddy urged the North to free itself
from the burden of Union with the South so that the North might
more fully "develop all those forces of a high, Christian civilization."[14]
Later in the month, on April 28, after the surrender of Fort Sumter,
Eddy changed his mind and advocated war to save the Union.[15]

A few Northern preachers seemed quite willing to allow the South
to break with the Union. As late as 1860 Henry Ward Beecher was
ready to let the South secede in peace. He held to the traditional fear
that the nation was expanding too rapidly for the maintaining of
peace and order.[16] When the cannons boomed against Fort Sumter,
Beecher changed his mind and took the position that no section had
the right to secede. For Americans, Beecher exclaimed, the right of
revolution had ceased to exist: "If we will legalize and establish the
right of any discontented community to rebel and to set up intestine
governments within the government of the United States," then we
would have no government at all. That would be "the right of
disintegration."[17]

When it was asked in England why the North did not allow the
South to secede, Beecher, in a speech at Exeter Hall in London, on
October 20, 1863, had a reply.

> It is said, "Why not let the South go? Since they won't be at peace with
> you, why do you not let them separate from you?" Because they would
> be still less peaceable when separated. Oh, if the Southerners only
> would go! They are determined to stay – that is the trouble. We would
> furnish free passage to all of them if they would go. But we say, the
> land is ours. Let them, and leave the nation its land, and they will have
> our unanimous consent.[18]

Most Northern preachers came to view secession with great foreboding. On January 4, 1861, George P. Fisher delivered a sermon in
the chapel of Yale College which attacked the compact theory of
government. "Society," affirmed Fisher, "is not a compact to be dissolved at the caprice of the parties which are bound to it."[19] In the
same year George L. Prentiss, a professor at Union Seminary in New

York, delivered a sermon in which he sought to demolish the Jeffersonian argument which would vindicate rebellion and secession and spoke of the historical and religious necessity of one nation.[20] On Independence Day of 1861 William T. Dwight, in a sermon preached at City Hall in Portland, Maine, warned that if secession were allowed to succeed, the United States would lapse into the colonial orbit of England or France.[21] Chester F. Dunham has summarized the gradually changing positions of many Northern ministers from peaceful dissolution to coerced union:

> Slowly but surely the idea of secession and peace was transferred into secession and coercion. . . . Secession seemed to be a threat at the very foundation of society. . . . The Clergy put forth a mighty effort for peace. When that failed, then many and possibly most of them rallied loyally for a supreme war effort. There was a minority who dissented — through Quaker pacifist ideals, sympathy with the South, or resistance to the Administration.[22]

The greatest contribution of religion to the sundering of the nation may well have been the denominational schisms of the Presbyterian, Methodist, and Baptist denominations in 1837, 1844, and 1845 respectively. The three denominations represented 94 percent of the churches in the South: the Methodists had 45 percent; the Baptists, 37 percent; and the Presbyterians, 12 percent. Though these denominational schisms will be considered in greater detail in chapter 6, it needs to be noted here that these religious divisions served as a model, motivator, and predictor of the political division that would follow some years later. Henry Clay recognized the serious implications of the splintered denominations when, in 1852, he commented: "I tell you this sundering of religious ties which have hitherto bound our people together, I consider the greatest source of danger to our country. If our religious men cannot live together in peace, what can be expected of us politicians, very few of whom profess to be governed by the great principles of love?"[23]

The sermon included in this volume to demonstrate Northern preaching on sectionalism is by Henry Ward Beecher, the most popular preacher in mid-nineteenth-century America. William G. McLoughlin has put Beecher's popularity in perspective:

> For at least three decades Beecher was the high priest of American religion. His pulpit was the nation's spiritual center. . . . Millions read him, millions heard him, millions believed in him. Beecher was the first American clergyman to attain a national audience which acknowledged him as its spokesman; the first to make it part of his regular practice to speak out on every significant political and social issue; the first to make a point of being seen with Presidents, to campaign for Presidents – in short, our first, self-appointed national chaplain.

McLoughlin went on to credit Beecher with formulating and promulgating the concept of American "civil religion."[24]

Sinclair Lewis once referred to Henry Ward Beecher as "a combination of St. Augustine, Barnum, and John Barrymore."[25] Lionel Crocker, who has devoted many years to the study of Beecher's rhetoric, emphasized that "Beecher will be remembered as one of the greatest preachers produced in America, if not in the world." Crocker continued: "His influence upon the content and composition of sermons in the United States, if not in the world, must be reckoned with by any historian of the Protestant Church. The influence of his pulpit upon so many important men and movements of the nineteenth century has caused for Beecher a place in history."[26]

Beecher's first church was in Lawrenceburg, Indiana (1837–49). His second charge was the Second Presbyterian Church of Indianapolis (1839–47), where he is credited with converting his congregation from a strong proslavery group to a strong antislavery group. In 1847 he became the pastor of the newly organized Plymouth Church (Congregational) in Brooklyn, where he would minister for the next forty years until his death. In 1849 the church burned down and a new one was built. It was constructed according to Beecher's design. He did away with the traditional pulpit in favor of a platform that extended into the congregation. He told the architect: "I want the audience to surround me, so that they will come up on every side, and behind me, so that I shall be in the center of the crowd, and have the people surge all about me."[27] The seating capacity of the church was 2,100, but folding chairs were fitted to the ends of the pews, people sat on the pulpit stairs, and many stood so that the capacity could be stretched to 3,200. For forty years Beecher preached to crowds of about 3,000 every Sunday, both in the morning and evening.

Because Beecher believed that the important element of Christianity was how life was lived in the here and now, he worked and preached for a reformation in society. He was involved in the temperance movement, championed women's suffrage, and was a strong proponent of good government. Another area of reform to which Beecher dedicated his life and his talents was the antislavery movement. More than anything else, Beecher's name has been associated with emancipation. At the Plymouth Church he would receive fugitive slaves. Impersonating a Southern slave auctioneer, he would call for bids on the fugitives. Moving his audience to tears on behalf of the fugitive (almost always a light-skinned, young female), he would take the money bid and purchase the fugitive's freedom.

When Kansas became embroiled in a bitter and bloody strife over the slave question, Beecher organized shipments of guns to the Free-Soil settlers in Kansas. Beecher claimed the guns were for defensive purposes. Because the boxes which contained the weapons were labeled "books," the shipments became known as "Beecher's Bibles."

He was a strong advocate of the new Republican party, believing it to be the party of justice. In 1856 Beecher vigorously campaigned for John C. Fremont for president, and in 1860 for Abraham Lincoln. After Lincoln was elected and took office, Beecher openly and strongly criticized him for being too slow on the emancipation issue. Nevertheless, a mutual friendship remained intact, and there is good evidence that Beecher had some influence on the thinking of the president.

Above all, Beecher's antislavery sentiments were most clearly demonstrated through his sermons and addresses. In the fall of 1863 he traveled to England, where his powerful and persuasvie oratory helped to turn English thinking in favor of the North.

The sermon which concludes this chapter, "Against a Compromise of Principle," was delivered on November 29, 1860. The sermon's date is important to an understanding of its meaning. Earlier in the month Lincoln had been elected to the presidency. Beecher had campaigned openly and vigorously for Lincoln. After the election agitated excitement ran high in the South and threats of secession were rampant. Beecher welcomed the excitement: "Excitements among a thinking people tend to clearer convictions. . . . Do not be afraid because the community teems with excitement. Silence and death are dreadful."

Throughout the sermon Beecher declared what he perceived to be the differences between the North and South, differences which made the North a superior culture. "The Southern States, then, have organized society around a rotten core, – slavery: the North has organized society about a vital heart, – liberty. . . . The distinctive idea of the Free States is Christian civilization, and the peculiar institutions of civilization. The distinctive idea of the South is barbaric institutions. In the North mind, and in the South force, rules."

Beecher was willing to allow the existence of slavery within the borders of the Southern states, but on two matters he would not compromise; obedience to the Fugitive Slave Law and the extension of slavery into the territories.

> We do not ask to molest the South in the enjoyment of her own institutions. But we will not be made constables to slavery, to run and catch, to serve writs, and return prisoners. . . .
>
> Keep your institutions within your own bounds: we will not hinder you. . . . But if you ask us to augment the area of slavery; to co-operate with you in cursing new territory; if you ask us to make the air of the North favorable for a slave's breath, we will not do it!

Beecher, in this sermon, did not want secession, but neither did he fear it: "If secession and separation should come, – which God forbid! – which can best bear it, freedom or slavery?" Even at this late date, Beecher says nothing about the forcible prevention of secession.

NOTES

1. *Centenary Edition of the Works of Theodore Parker* (Boston: American Unitarian Association, 1907), 11:205–06.
2. *Centenary Edition*, 9:87.
3. *Centenary Edition*, 9:197.
4. *The Northern Iron* (Hartford: Hunt & Son, 1854).
5. George M. Frederickson, *The Inner Civil War: Northern Intellectuals and the Crisis of the Union* (New York: Harper, 1965), 46. Thomas Wentworth Higginson was a Unitarian minister greatly influenced by Parker. After hearing a Parker address Higginson led an antislavery mob on an assault of the Boston Courthouse in 1854 for the purpose of freeing a fugitive slave. In 1856 Higginson went to Kansas and took up arms to fight for the free-state forces. He and Parker helped to subsidize John Brown's raid. Though they may not have known exactly what Brown was up to, they had few misgivings about the bloody results. When the war broke out, Higginson became an officer in the Union army.
6. *Patriotic Addresses* (New York: Fords, Howard, & Hulbert, 1891), 276–77.
7. *Patriotic Addresses*, 334.
8. Quoted in Chester Forrester Dunham, *The Attitude of the Northern Clergy Toward the South 1860–1865* (Philadelphia: Porcupine Press, 1974), 86.
9. *The Moral Significance of the Contrasts Between Slavery and Freedom* (Boston: Walker, Wise, 1864).
10. *The Martyr President* (Boston: Graves & Young, 1865).

11. William G. McLoughlin, *Modern Revivalism: Charles Grandison Finney to Billy Graham* (New York: Ronald Press, 1959), 112n.
12. Charles G. Finney, *Lectures on Systematic Theology* (1846–47; Grand Rapids: Eerdman's, 1964, 227.
13. *Two Discourses* (Lowell, MA: J. J. Judkins, 1854).
14. *Secession: Shall It Be Peace or War?* (Northampton, MA: Trumbull and Gere, 1861).
15. *A Discourse on the War* (Northampton, MA: Trumbull & Gere, 1861).
16. William G. McLoughlin, *The Meaning of Henry Ward Beecher* (New York: Knopf, 1970), 208–09.
17. *Freedom and War* (Boston: Ticknor & Fields, 1863), 96–97.
18. *Patriotic Addresses*, 559.
19. *Thoughts Proper to the Present Crisis* (New Haven: Tuttle, Morehouse and Taylor, 1861).
20. *The Free Christian State and the Present Struggle* (New York: W. H. Bidwell, 1861).
21. *The Nationality of a People Its Vital Element* (Portland, ME: N. A. Foster, 1861).
22. Dunham, *Attitude of the Northern Clergy*, 79–80.
23. Quoted in C. C. Goen, *Broken Churches, Broken Nation* (Macon: Mercer University Press, 1985), 106.
24. McLoughlin, *The Meaning of Henry Ward Beecher*, 252, 254, 253. Robert D. Linder has defined civil religion as "a way of thinking which makes sacred a political arrangement on governmental system and provides a religious image of a political society for many, if not most, of its members. . . . It is a religious way of thinking about politics, which provides a society with ultimate meaning." Linder writes of the development of civil religion in America: "Over the years the American civil faith has grown conceptually from evangelical Protestantism-in-general, to Christianity-in-general, to the Judeo-Christian tradition, to theism-in-general." Writing of contemporary American civil religion, Linder states: "Modern American civil religion, therefore, is an alliance between religion and politics which transcends separation of church and state and permeates every level of national life. As such, it rests on a politicized ideological base: (1) there is a God; (2) his will can be known and fulfilled through democratic procedures; (3) America has been God's primary agent in modern history; and (4) the nation is the chief source of identity for Americans in both a political and religious sense. According to this world view, Americans are God's chosen people, a New Israel which made the exodus to the Promised Land across the sea and became a 'city on a hill,' a light to the nations proclaiming the message of democracy as the socio-messianic doctrine that will lead the human race to freedom, prosperity and happiness." "Civil Religion," *Dictionary of Christianity in America*, ed. Daniel Reid (Downers Grove, IL: InterVarsity Press, 1990), 281–83. For what may be the classic article on civil religion, see Robert N. Bellah, "Civil Religion in America," *Daedalus* 96 (Winter 1967): 1–21.
25. Sinclair Lewis, foreword, Paxton Hibben, *Henry Ward Beecher: An America Portrait* (1942; New York: Beekman, 1974), vii. Hibben's book may be the most critical of all the many Beecher biographies.
26. William Norwood Brigance, ed., *A History and Criticism of American Public Address*, 2 vols. (New York: Russell & Russell, 1960), 1:272, 292.
27. Quoted in Robert T. Oliver, *History of Public Speaking in America* (Boston: Allyn and Bacon, 1965), 376.

Against a Compromise of Principle

Henry Ward Beecher

Thanksgiving Day, November 29, 1860

And there was delivered unto him the book of the prophet Esaias. And when he had opened the book, he found the place where it was written, The Spirit of the Lord is upon me, because he has anointed me to preach the Gospel to the poor; he hath sent me to heal the broken-hearted, to preach deliverance to the captives, and recovering of sight to the blind, to set at liberty them that are bruised, to preach the acceptable year of the Lord."
—Luke IV, 17–19 —

These words are remarkable, to-day, for their meaning and for their historical position. The first sermon which Christ made, upon entering his public ministry, was this one at Nazareth, where he had been brought up. That he chose these words in entering upon his mission – these words, of all the Law, of all the Psalms, and of all the Prophets – gives them peculiar significancy. And, when we consider their contents, they become yet more memorable, since they were the character and index of his mission, – the text not only of his sermon, but of his life. Christ came to save the world, – not laws, not governments, not institutions, not dynasties, but the *people*. The fulfilment of his mission is to be looked for in the condition of nationalities and the character of peoples. Though peace breathe balm over all the world, and every law is obeyed, and every government rides among the people, as a man-of-war dressed for holiday, upon a tranquil sea, there is no reason for rejoicing if the people are ignorant and their capacities are undeveloped; if they are mean and sordid, and their morals, like a Chinese foot, are cramped too small to walk upon. But though there be wars and rumors of war, revolutions and tumults, the world is prosperous if by these convulsions the race is freed from oppression, thoroughly aroused, and incited to bolder enterprise and to nobler moral character.

Freedom and War (Boston: Ticknor & Fields, 1863), 28–56.

We are, then, to study the advance of Christ's kingdom in the whole aspect of the world. The Church is of the people. God's Church includes the whole human race. Our separate churches are but doors to the grand spiritual interior. The good men who love God and man with overruling affection, of all nations, and of every tongue, are the true Church.

To-day we are assembled to give thanks for national mercies. I need not remind you of the year that is closing. Who knew, when January set her cold, calm face toward the future, that she was the herald of such a summer? When was there ever a year so fertile? so propitious to all industry? It has been a procession of rejoicing months, flower-wreathed and fruit-laden, – a very holiday year!

The soil awoke with new ardor; everything that lived by the soil felt the inspiration. Every root, and every blade, and every stem, and every bough has this year tasked itself for prodigal bounty. Except a narrow strip, this continent has been so blessed with husbandry as to make this year memorable even among years hitherto most eminent. The meadow, the tilled fields, the grazing pastures, the garden, the vineyard, the orchard, the very fence-row berry-bushes and wild wall-vines, have been clothed with unexampled bounty and beauty. Nature seems to have lacked messengers to convey her intents of kindness, and the summer, like a road surprised with quadruple freights, has not been able to find conveyance for all its treasures. The seas have felt the divine ardor. The fisherman never reaped such harvests from the moist furrows of the ocean as this year. These husbandmen of the sea, who reap where they have not sowed and grow rich upon harvests which they have not tilled, have this year put in the crooked hook for their sickle with admiring gladness for the strange and unwonted abundance of the deep.

All the sons of God rejoice, and all good men rejoice. It needs but one element to complete the satisfaction. If we could be sure that this is God's mercy, meant for good, and tending thereto, we should have a full cup to-day. That satisfaction is not denied us. The Mayor of New York, in a public proclamation, in view of this prodigal year, that has heaped the poor man's house with abundance, is pleased to say that there is no occasion apparent to him for thanksgiving. We can ask no more. When bad men grieve at the state of public affairs, good men should rejoice. When infamous men keep fast, righteous men should have thanksgiving. God reigns and the Devil trembles. Amen. Let us rejoice!

But it is not now to these topics that I shall confine my remarks. I propose to glance at other reasons for thanksgiving.

1. The advantage and increasing influence of nations which, in the main, tend to conserve human liberty, and the decadence and dwindling of those nations that have flourished by exaction and tyranny, is a matter of gratulation. It should make good men glad when wicked men and wicked nations grow weak.

2. The emergence of the connom people to that degree of political power that makes it necessary now for the whole of Western Europe to ask their permission for the establishment of any throne or monarchy is cheering and auspicious. Crowns were once made of gold beaten out on the people's backs. Now the strongest crowns are made of paper, – the paper votes of the common people. Therein we rejoice, and will rejoice.

3. The resurrection of Italy is another memorable event of the year. I see as many tokens of a Divine presence in Italy as of old there were in the emancipation and conduct of the Israelites from Egypt. That such a conjunction of events should have taken place; that such a monarch as Victor Emanuel, who almost reconciles republicans to kings, should have sat waiting; that such a consummate statesman, of noblest patriotism, as Cavour, should have been prepared and waiting; that such a hero, simple, true, pure, disinterested, self-sacrificing, skilful, and lion-like, as Garibaldi, should have come at the hour, are marks of the planning of God. Men never devise such combinations. It would have been significant had either of these men come singly. That all should have come together, – a solider to bat down the old despotism, a statesman to organize the new liberty, a just and patriot king to preside over the people's government, and a people, divided for centuries, but now at last united, – this reveals the mind and will of God. Let us rejoice!

4. The growing moderation of the Russian monarchy, the quiet improvement of the people, the emancipation of the serfs, ought to engage the attention and receive the sympathy of every Christian people. There is a great work begun in Russia. This gigantic nation, the antithesis of America politically and geographically, is, like her, almost half a globe of herself. The end we cannot now even suspect. Prophets are dead. God no longer tells beforehand what he is going to do. But, by the clearing that has been made for the foundations, by the materials that are gathering, and by the workmen that are

employed, we judge that no mean structure is about to rise to the glory of God. There is an immense History now in birth. Let us hope that the unmeasured future will be for Humanity, Justice, and Piety!

5. In the rest of the world there are signs, but more remote, of good. Heathen nations are growing weaker, Christian nations are growing stronger. The nations of Heathenism are imbecile. The nations of Christianity are of vigorous stock, and have a future. Already Christian nations rule the world. Who may war, how long, for what, with whom, depends upon the will of Christian peoples. There is a Christian police around this globe!

6. Our own land has not been behind. In this march of nations our country has kept step. We know it by the victory of ideas, by the recognition of principles instead of mere policies, by the ascendency of justice, and by the witnessing and ratifying rage of all who love oppression and oppressors.

To-day should not be profaned by partisan congratulations; but we should be ungrateful to God, who has guided us through peril and darkness, and at length brought us forth into illustrious victory, if we did not to-day remember, with profound gratitude and devout thanksgiving, the resurrection of the spirit of liberty from the graves of our fathers!

The tree of life, whose leaves were for the healing of the nations, has been evilly dealt with. Its boughs have been lopped, and its roots starved till its fruit is knurly. Upon its top has been set scions of bitter fruits, that grew and sucked out all the sap from the better branches. Upon its trunk the wild boar of the forest had whetted his tusks.

But now again it blooms. Its roots have found the river, and shall not want again for moisture; the grafts of poisonous fruits have been broken off or have been blown out; mighty spearmen have hunted the wild swine back to his thickets, and the hedge shall be broken down no more round about it. The air is fragrant in its opening buds, the young fruit is setting. God has returned and looked upon it, and behold, summer is in all its branches!

To some it may seem that the light in this picture is too high, and that the background is not dark enough. I do not wish you to think that the background is not dark; for it is. There is excitement. There is brewing mischief. The clouds lie lurid along the Southern horizon. The Caribbean Sea, that breeds tornadoes and whirlwinds, has heaped up treasures of storms portentous, that seem about to break. Let them break! God has appointed their bounds. Not till the sea drives back the shore, and the Atlantic submerges the Continent, will this tumult of an angry people move the firm decrees of God. He who came to open prison doors, to deliver captives, to loose those that are bound, – he it is that is among us. We are surrounded by airy hosts greater than those which the prophet of old saw filling the mountains. God is with us. The very rage of wickedness shows his presence.

While we tremble, then, let us rejoice; not triumph, nor boast, nor make invidious comparisons, nor throw fuel of passions into the flames already too hot. But, with a sober, temperate, and beneficent joy, let us give thanks to God, that he has begun to recall this nation from a course that would have wrought utter destruction; and that now, though waves are beating, and the tempest is upon the ship, she has changed her course, and heads right away from the breakers and the sand!

But be sure that, in these times, there can be no safe navigation except that which clings to great universal principles. Selfish interests, if they are our pilots, will betray us. Vain glory will destroy us. Pride will wreck us. Above all, the fear of doing right will be fatal. But justice and liberty are pilots that do not lose their craft. They steer by a divine compass. They know the hand that holds the winds and the storms. It is always safe to be right; and our business is not so much to seek peace as to seek the causes of peace. Expedients are for an hour, but principles are for the ages. Just because the rains descend and winds blow, we cannot afford to build on shifting sands. Nothing can be permanent and nothing safe in this exigency that does not sink deeper than politics or money. We must touch the rock, or we shall never have firm foundations.

I. Our prosperity had its beginning and continuance in Natural Laws. God's will in nature and in human society is the source of human strength and human wisdom. No matter how many are with you, if your councils are in the face of divine principles. Peace, regardless of equity, is a treacherous sleep, whose waking is death. It is not half so necessary to have a settlement as it is to have a *right* settlement. In the end, right political economy will work out prosperous national economy; and if for want of faith in the safety of rectitude you abandon sound and proved principles, or let them go by default, all your good intentions will not save you from national misrule and national wasting and destruction. The mariner who should take refuge in the Maelstrom, thinking it a safe harbor, would learn quickly that good intentions are good follies when men run against natural law. And for men to think that this nation has been prospered on account of the skill, the wisdom, or the arrangements or combinations of men, is the worst of infidelities. While papers and parties are in full outcry, and nostrums are advertised, and scared politicians are at their wits' ends, (without having gone far, either,) and men of weak minds are beside themselves, and imbeciles stand doubting in the streets, know ye that the way of peace is simple, accessible, and easy! Be still. Stand firm. Have courage to wait. Money is insane. Fear is death. Faith in Justice, and in Rectitude, and Trust in God, will work out safety. The worst is over. Our Northern apathy to freedom and our greed of commerce are a thousand times more dangerous than Southern rage and threat. Moral bankruptcy will ruin us all. No other bankruptcies will harm us!

Let us have firm courage, kindness of temper, willingness to make concessions in things of mere policy, but no concession of principles, no yielding of moral convictions, no paltering with our consciences. Thirty pieces of silver bought Christ and hung Judas. If you sell your convictions to Fear, you give yourself to a vagabond. If you sell your conscience to interest, you traffic with a fiend. The fear of doing right is the grand treason in times of danger. When you consent to give up your convictions of justice, humanity, and liberty, for the sake of tranquility, you are like men who buy a treacherous truce of tyrants by giving up their weapons of war. Cowards are the food of despots.

When a storm is on the deep, and the ship labors, men throw over the deck-load; they cast forth the heavy freights, and ride easier as their merchandise grows less. But in our time men propose to throw overboard the compass, the charts, the chronometer, the sextant, but to keep the freight!

For the sake of a principle our fathers dared to defy the proudest nation on the globe. They suffered. They conquered. We are never tired of praising them. But when we are called to stand firm for principle, we tremble, we whine, we evade duty, and shuffle up a compromise, by which we may sell our conscience, and save our pocket.

It is rank infidelity, and, at such a time as this, stupendous infatuation, to suppose that the greatness of this nation ever sprung from the wisdom of expediency, instead of the power of settled principles. Your harbor did not make you rich; you made the harbor rich.

Your ships did not create your commerce; your commerce created your ships; and you created your commerce. Your stores did not make traffic. Your factories did not create enterprise. Your firms, your committees, your treaties, and your legislation did not create national prosperity. Our past greatness sprung from our obedience to God's natural and moral law. We had men trained to courage, to virtue, to wisdom. And manhood, – *manhood*, – MANHOOD, – exercised in the fear of God, has made this nation. Men are God's vicegerents; and if they will govern as he governs, then they shall be creators, too, in this world. The reason we have prospered in days past is not that we have known how to duck and dodge and trim; it is not that we have known all the minute ways of microscopic statesmanship: it is because we have known just enough to see the way in which natural law and God's kindgom were going, and to follow them. It is a simple thing; it is no secret; and accursed be he that counsels the people to seek peace and prosperity by abandoning the causes of it, and that leads them into destruction by leading them into the arms of a tinselled folly!

II. Let no man be foolishly fearful of Excitement. Our age marks the growth of the world by this: that excitement is now wholesome. When men low down in the scale begin to be stirred, the most active part is excited, which is passion. But when men have outgrown barbarism, and live in moral and intellectual elements, then excitement rouses up the higher nature. Among a savage people, excitement works downward and rages; among a Christian and civilized people, it works upward and toward peace. Excitements among a thinking people tend to clearer convictions, to surer intuitions, to more heroic purposes, and loftier enthusiasms. Do not be afraid because the community teems with excitement. Silence and death are dreadful. The rush of life, the vigor of earnest men, the conflict of realities, invigorates, cleanses, and establishes truth. Our only fear should be lest we refuse God's work. He has appointed this people, and our day, for one of those world-battles on which ages turn. Ours is a pivotal period. The strife is between a dead past and a living future; between a wasting evil and a nourishing good; between *Barbarism* and *Civilization*.

The condition of the common people always measures the position of any nation on the scale of civilization. The condition of Work always measures the character of the common people. It is not where the head is, but where the feet are, that determines a nation's position. By ascertaining where the working people are in the North and in the South, you can determine the respective positions of these two sections of our country. I need not tell you what is the relative position of these two extremes and opposites on any scale of Christian civilization.

The Southern States and the Northern alike found poisonous seed sown in colonial days. The North chose to weed it out. The South determined to cultivate it, and see what it would bear. The harvest-time has now come. We are reaping what we sowed. They sowed the wind, and they are about to reap the whirlwind. Let us keep in view the causes of things. Our prosperity is the fruit of the seed that we sowed, and their fears, their alarms, their excitements, their fevers, their tumults, and their rages are the fruit of the seed that they sowed. Ours is wholesome; theirs is poisonous. All, now, that we demand is, *that each side shall reap its own harvest.*

It is this that convulses the South. They wish to reap fruits of liberty from the seed of slavery. They wish to have an institution which sets at naught the laws of God, and yet be as refined and prosperous and happy as we are, who obey these laws; and since they cannot, they demand that we shall make up to them what they lack. The real gist of the controversy, as between the greatest number of Southern States and the North, is simply this. The South claims that the United States government is bound to make slavery as good as liberty for all purposes of national life. That is the root of their philosophy. They are to carry on a wasting system, a system that corrupts social life in its very elements, to pursue a course of inevitable impoverishment, and yet, at every decade of years, the government is, by some new bounty and privilege, to make up to them all the waste of this gigantic mistake! And our national government has been made a bribed judge, sitting on the seat of authority in this land, to declare bankruptcy as good as honesty; to declare wickedness as good as virtue; and to declare that there shall be struck, from period to period, a rule that will bring all men to one common municipal and communal prosperity, no matter what may be the causes that are working out special evils in them.

The Southern States, then, have organized society around a rotten core, – slavery: the North has organized society about a vital heart, – liberty. At length both stand mature. They stand in proper contrast. God holds them up to ages and to nations, that men may see the difference. Now that there is a conflict, I ask which is to yield? Causes having been true to effects, an effects true to causes, these gradually unfolding commercial and political and moral results having been developed in the two great opposing extremes of this country, the time has come in which they are so brought into contact that the principle of the one or the principle of the other must yield. Liberty must discrown her fair head; she must lay her opal crown and her diamond septre upon the altar of Oppression; or else Oppression must shrink, and veil its head, and depart. Which shall it be? Two queens are not to rule in this land, one black and the other white; one from below and the other from above. Two influences are not to sit in culminated power at the seat of influence in this nation, one dragging and pulling toward the infernal, and the other drawing and exciting toward the supernal. No nation could stand the strain to which it would be subjected under such a state of things.

There is a Divine impulsion in this. Those who resist and those who strive are carried along by a stream mightier than mere human volition. Whether men have acted well or ill, is not now the question; but simply this: *On which side will you be found?* This controversy will go on. No matter what you do, God will carry out his own providences with you or without you, by you or against you. You cannot hide or run away, or shift the question, or stop the trial. Complaints are useless, and recriminations foolish and wicked.

The distinctive idea of the Free States is Christian civilization, and the peculiar institutions of civilization. The distinctive idea of the South is barbaric institutions. In the North mind, and in the South force, rules. In the North every shape and form of society in some way represents liberty. In the South every institution and element of society is tinged and pervaded with slavery. The South accepts the whole idea of slavery, boldly and consistently. The North will never have peace till she with equal boldness accepts liberty.

While liberty and slavery are kept apart, and only run upon parallels, there may be peace. But there is no way in which they can be combined; there is no unity made up of these deadly antagonisms. And all devices, and cunning arrangements, and deceitful agreements, are false and foolish.

The truth that men cannot hush, and that God will not have covered up, is the irreconcilable difference between liberty and slavery! Which will you advocate and defend?

There are three courses before us: –

1. To go over to the South.

2. To compromise principles.

3. To maintain principles upon just and constitutional grounds, and abide the issue.

1. Shall we, then, obliterate from our statute-books every law for liberty? Shall we rub down and efface every clear and distinctive feature of liberty? Shall we assume that one is just as good as the other, – slavery and freedom? Are we, for the sake of peace, to go over to the South, yield our convictions, and our moral influences, and our whole soul and body of teaching and conviction?

This course is not to be thought of for a moment, whatever it may be theoretically considered. As a matter of fact, you know, and I know, and everybody knows, that there will be no change in the convictions of the North. We have reaped too bountifully from the seed we have sown to change. Our method of moral and political tillage will be the same as heretofore.

2. Shall we then compromise? We are told that Satan appears under two forms: that when he has a good fair field, he is out like a lion, roaring and seeking whom he may devour; but that when he can do nothing more in that way, he is a serpent, and sneaks in the grass. And so, it is slavery open, bold, roaring, aggressive, or it is slavery sneaking in the grass, and calling itself compromise. It is the same devil under either name.

If by compromise is only meant forbearance, kindness, well-wishing, conciliation, fidelity to agreements, a concession in things, not principles; why, then we believe in compromise, – only that is not compromise, interpreted by the facts of our past history! We honestly wish no harm to the South or its people: we honestly wish them all benefit. We wish no harm to their commerce; none to their manufacturers; none to their husbandry; none to their schools and colleges; none to their churches and families; none to their citizens, who are bone of our bone and blood of our blood, and who are in many eminent respects united to us in a common historic glory. We are far from wishing them diminution or feebleness; so far from it, we most heartily and sincerely, and with much more earnestness than they reciprocate, with them riddance of their trouble. We neither envy nor covet their territory. We are not jealous of their honors. We would that they were doubled, and double purified. All that belongs to the South; all that with liberalest construction was put in the original bond, shall be hers. Her own institutions were made inviolate in all her States. The basis of representation in the South was made broader than in the North, and property, as well as citizens, sends represen- tatives to Washington. We will not complain. The common revenue and the common force of the nation protect them against intestine revolt. Let it be so. The Constitution gives them liberty to retake their fugitive slaves wherever they can find them. Very well. Let them. But when the *Congress* goes beyond the Constitution, and demands, on penalty, that citizens of free States shall help, and render back the flying slave, we give a blunt and unequivocal refusal. We are determined to break any law that commands us to enslave or re- enslave a man, and we are willing to take the penalty. But that was not in the original bond. That is a parasitic egg, laid in the Constitu- tion by corrupt legislation or by construction.

We do not ask to molest the South in the enjoyment of her own institutions. But we will not be made constables to slavery, to run and catch, to serve writs and return prisoners. No political hand shall rob her. We will defend her coast; we will guard her inland border from all vexations from without; and in good fath, in earnest friend- ship, in fealty to the Constitution and in fellowship with the States, we will, and with growing earnestness to the end, fulfil every just duty, every honorable agreement, and every generous act, within the limits of truth and honor; all that, and no more, – *no more*, though the heavens fall, – no more, if States unclasp their hands, – *no more*, if they raise up violence against us, – NO MORE!

We have gone to the end. There is no need of compromise in this matter, then. It is a plain, simple matter. It is never mystified except when bad men have bad ends to accomplish, and bring up a mist over it.

Let us look things right in the face, then, and speak some plain truths. We are approaching times when men will not hear what they will listen to now; so let us drop the seed beforehand.

1. The secret intentions of those men who are the chief foment- ers of troubles in the South cannot in anywise be met by compro- mise. They dread as much as we hate it. What do those men that are really at the bottom of this conspiracy mean? Nothing more or less than this: Southern empire for slavery, and the reopening of the slave-trade as a means by which it shall be fed. Free commerce and enslaved work is their motto. They will not yet say it aloud. But that is the whispered secret of men in Carolina, and men outside of Car- olina. Their secret purpose is to sweep westward like night, and in- volve in the cloud of their darkness all Central America, and then

make Africa empty into Central America, thus changing the moral geography of the globe. And do you suppose any compromise will settle that design, or turn it aside, when they have made you go down on your knees, and they stand laughing while you cry with fear because you have been cozened and juggled into a blind helping of their monstrous wickedness?

They mean slavery. They man an Empire of Slavery. They don't any longer talk of the *evil* of slavery. It is a virtue, a religion! It is justice and divine economy! Slaves are missionaries. Slave-ships bring heathen to plantation-Christianity. They imagine unobstructed greatness when servile hands shall whiten the plains from the Atlantic to the Pacific with cotton. Carolina despises compromise. She means no such thing as liberty. She does not believe in the word. It is rubbed out. It is gone from her constitution and from her Bible. Its spirit is departed from her legislature and her church.

And do you think, poor simple peeping sparrow, that you can build your poor moss and hair nest of compromise on the face of the perpendicular cliff, that towers a thousand feet high, with the blackness of storms sweeping round its top, and the thunder of a turbulent ocean breaking upon its base, – and God, more terrible than either, high above them, meaning Justice and Retribution!

2. But in so far as those States are concerned that are contiguous to Carolina, and do not mean these things, even for them compromise can never reach, nor even any longer mollify, the causes of complaint; for I hold that the causes are inherent in them, not in us. And they are endless. If you cure one, another will spring up in its place. You cannot compromise with them except by giving up your own belief, your own principles, and your own honor. Moral apostasy is the only basis on which you can build a compromise that will satisfy the South!

No compromise will do good that does not go back to the nature of things, and change moral qualities. To be of any use, compromise must make the slaves contented, slavery economical, Slave States as prosperous as Free States. Compromise must shut the mouth of free speech, or it will send the shafts of truth vibrating into the midst of slavery. Compromise must cure the intolerance of the plantation, the essential tyranny of slave-owners. It must make evil as prosperous as good, enforced drudgery as fruiftul as free labor.

What compromise can there be between sickness and health? Between violence and peace? Between speech for liberty and speech for despotism? There may be peace between opposites, but no harmony, no compromise. If the South is fixed in her servile institutions, the North must be equally firm in her principles of liberty.

You cannot prevent, in the present state of this land, the departure of the children of opposition. You might as well attempt to prevent the tides of the Atlantic ocean. You might as well attempt to prevent vegetation in the tropics. Till the heavens be no more, and their orbs cease to draw, men will aspire, and will follow aspiration. There is too much light in the North, and even in the darkness of the plantation, to keep men in slavery. When one man gains his freedom, twenty men will know it, and to gain theirs will do what he did. Every hour there will be men who will take their life in their hands and risk all for liberty. It is of no use to tell the South that it shall not be so. It is of no use to whisper to them, and say, "Your trouble shall cease; we will fix this matter to your satisfaction." God never made brick or trowel by which to patch up that door of escape. By night and by day slaves will flee away and escape.

Compromise is a most pernicious sham. To send compromises to the South would be like sending painted bombs into the camp of an enemy, which, though harmless in appearance, would blow up and destroy them. Suppose you tell the people there that when their fugitives come North they shall be surrendered? Will you not please to catch them first? You know you cannot. There are five hundred men that run through the Northern States where there is one that stops or is turned back. They know it, you know it, we all know it! The radical nature of the feelings of the North is such that they will hurry on the black man and trip his hunter. If the managers of parties, the heads of conservative committees, say to the South, "Be patient with us a little longer, do not punish us yet, let down the rod and the frown, spare us for a short season, and we will see that our slaves are returned to you," do you suppose there will be a fulfilment of the promise? You know there will not. I know there will not. I would die myself, cheerfully and easily before a man should be taken out of my hands when I had the power to give him liberty, and the house was after him for his blood. I would stand as an altar of expiation between slavery and liberty, knowing that through my example a million men would live. A heroic deed, in which one yields up his life for others, is his Calvary. It was the lifting up of Christ on that hill-top that made it the loftiest mountain on the globe. Let a man do a right thing with such earnestness that he counts his life of little value, and his example becomes omnipotent. Therefore it is said that the blood of the saints is the seed of the Church. There is no such seed planted in this world as good blood.

I see that my words are being reported; and as free speech may get into Charleston, some men there may see what I say; and let me say this to my Southern brethren: We mean to observe the Constitution, and keep every compact into which we have entered. There are men that would deceive you. They are your enemies and ours alike. They would tell lies to you, but we will not stand up and indorse them. I tell you that as long as there are these Free States; as long as there are hills in which men can hide, and valleys through which they can travel; as long as there is a loaf in the cabin, and water in the cruse; as long as there is blood in the veins, and humanity in the heart, – so long the fugitive will not want for sympathy and help to escape!

I say, again, that we are bound, as men of truth and conscience, to look this matter in the face, and ask, "Is there any benefit to be expected from compromises?" My friends, we are not reasoning about a matter of which we have had no experience. From the beginning we have been living on compromises. Now there is history, and we can make scientific inductions from facts, and know the results of certain courses. Do you suppose that if, knowing what you know now, you had sat in the original convention to frame the Constitution, you would have made compromises? Persons say, "Are you wiser than your fathers?" Yes! A man that is not wiser than his father, ought not to have had such a father, if his father was wise! Our fathers, when they laid the foundations of that structure, did the best that the wisdom of that time would enable them to do; and they were wise men, – much wiser, doubtless, for their time, than we are for ours. But, nevertheless, we may know now; better than they did then, what their wisest course would have been. When Carolina refused to come into the Confederacy except on the ground of certain favors to slavery, then was the time to have said to her, "Stay out."

Do you suppose that when Carolina infamously said, "I will not come in unless you will give me leave to traffic in slaves from 1790 til 1808," – do you suppose that then it was wise for our fathers to give her what she demanded? I do not blame them; they acted up to the best light they had; but if we, knowing the facts that we know now, had done what they did, we should have been infamous.

When, later, the compromise of 1850 was set on foot, there were not wanting, as there are not wanting now, men who lifted up their voices in favor of compromise; and I think that very few who saw the effects of compromise at that time believe it to be a cure. They promised finality. They took renewed courage, and with a strong arm of injustice destroyed a compromise still anterior to theirs, – namely, the Missouri Compromise, – itself a wickedness only paralleled by that which destroyed it. It ought not to have been made; but after it was made, it should have been removed only for purposes of liberty, and not for purposes of oppression. We sold our birthright for a mess of pottage, and the pottage was then stolen!

We have had, then, a long experience of the virtues and merits of compromise; and what has been the result, except growing demands, growing impudence, growing wickedness, and increasing dissatisfaction, until at last excitements that used to come once in twenty years began to come at every ten, and now once in four years, and you cannot elect a President strictly according to constitutional methods, without having this nation imperilled, banks shaken, stores overturned, panic created, and citizens terrified. You have come to that state in which the whole nation is turmoiled, and agitated, and driven hither and thither, on account of the evil effects of compromise.

It is asked, "What shall we do?" We should speak the truth about our feelings, and about our intentions. The North should have nothing to do with half-way measures or half-way men. A whole man is good if he is imperfect; but a half-way man has no place in heaven, he has no place in hell, and he is not wanted on earth! We do not want half-way measures, nor half-way men. We want true men, who will say to the South: "The North loves liberty, and will have it. We will not aggress on you. Keep your institutions within your own bounds: we will not hinder you. We will not take advantage to destroy, or one whit to abate, your fair political prerogatives. You have already gained advantages of us. These we will allow you to hold. You shall have the Constitution intact, and its full benefit. The full might and power of public sentiment in the North shall guarantee to you everything that history and the Constitution give you. But if you ask us to augment the area of slavery; to co-operate with you in cursing new territory; if you ask us to make the air of the North favorable for a slave's breath, we will not do it! We love liberty as much as you love slavery, and we shall stand by our rights with all the vigor with which we mean to stand by justice toward you."

In short, the North cannot love slavery or cease to love liberty;

she cannot conceal her sentiments or restrain the immoral power; she cannot prevent the irritating contrast between Free States and Slave States; she cannot prevent the growing intelligence of slaves, nor their love of liberty, nor their disposition to seek it, nor the sympathy that every generous soul must feel, nor the humane and irresistible wish that they may succeed in obtaining freedom; we cannot sympathize with the hounds that hunt them, nor with the miscreants employed to witness against them, nor with the disgraced Federal officers that are bribed with double fees to convict them: the North cannot either permit her own citizens – colored men, Christians, honest and industrious, and many of them voters a thousand times better fitted for the franchise than the ignorant hordes of imported white men that have cheated their way against law and morals to the exercise of the voter – to be subject to seizure as slaves under the odious and ruthless provisions of an insulting Fugitive Slave Law, without providing for them State protection; we will not assist in inflicting upon free territory an evil which we abhor, and which we believe to be the greatest blight that can curse a people; we will not accept the new-fangled and modern doctrine that slavery is national and universal instead of the doctrine of our fathers of the Revolution and of the Federal Constitution, who regarded slavery as local, existing not in the right of a national law, but only by force of special law: certainly we will not apostatize from the faith of our fathers only for the sake of committing disgraceful crimes against liberty!

Let not the South listen to any man who pretends that the North will look kindly or compromisingly upon slavery. In every other respect we may be depended upon for all sympathy, aid, and comfort. In this thing we shall give the strictest and most literal obedience to those constitutional requirements which we hate while we obey and beyond bare and meagre duty we will not go a step.

Now, can any man believe that peace can come by *compromise*? It is a delusive hope. It is a desperate shift of cowardice. It will begin in deceit and end in anger. Compromises are only procrastinations of an inevitable settlement with the added burden of accumulated interest. Our political managers only renew the note with compound interest, and roll the debt over, and over, until the interest exceeds the principal. It is time for a settlement. We may as well have it now as ever. We shall never be better prepared. It will never be so easy as now. It would have been easier ten years ago, and yet easier ten years before that. Like an ulcer, this evil eats deeper every day. Unless soon cauterized or excised, it will touch the vitals, and then the patient dies!

The supreme fear of Northern cities is pecuniary. But even for money's sake, there should be a settlement that will stay settled. Compromises bury troubles, but cannot keep down their ghosts. They rise, and walk, and haunt, and gibber. We must bury our evils without resurrection. Let come what will, – secession, disunion, revolted States, and a ragamuffin empire of bankrupt States, confederated in the name of liberty for oppression, or whatever other monstrosity malignant fortune may have in store, – nothing can be worse than this endless recurring threat and fear, – this arrogant dragooning of the South, – this mercantile cringing in the North. Every interest cries out for Rest. It scarcely matters how low we begin. We have a recuperative enterprise, a fertile industry, a wealth of resources, which will soon replace any waste. Let the gates of a permanent settlement be set up in bleak and barren granite, and we will speedily cover them with the evergreen ivy of our industry. But perpetual uncertainty is destructive of all business. That is not a settlement that only hides, that adjourns, that trumps up a compromise against the known feelings of both parties, and which must inevitably fall to pieces as soon as the hands that make it are taken off. Shall every quadrennial election take place in the full fury of Southern threats? Is the plantation-whip to control our ballot-boxes? Shall Northern sentiment express itself by constitutional means, at the peril of punishment? Must panic follow elections and bankruptcy follow every expression of liberty? And what are the precious advantages which the North reaps, which make it worth her while to undergo such ignominy and such penalty?

Every advantage that can be reckoned belongs to the North. Ours is the population. Ours is free labor. Ours is a common people not ashamed of toil, and able to make Work a badge of honor. Ours is popular intelligence, competitive industry, ingenuity and enterprise. We put the whole realm and wealth of Freedom and Civilization against Slavery and Barbarism, and ask what have we to fear? If secession and separation must come, – which God forbid! – which can best bear it, freedom or slavery?

The North must accept its own principles and take the consequences. Manliness demands this, – Honor demands it. But if we will not heed worthier motives, then Interest demands it. If even this is not strong enough for commercial pusillanimity, then Necessity, inevitable and irresistible, will drive and scourge us to it!

When night is on the deep, when the headlands are obscured by the darkness, and when storm is in the air, that man who undertakes to steer by looking over the side of the ship, over the bow, or over the stern, or by looking at the clouds or his own fears, is a fool. There is a silent needle in the binnacle, which points like the finger of God, telling the mariner which way to steer, and enabling him to outride the storm, and reach the harbor in safety. And what the compass is to navigation, that is moral principle in political affairs. Whatever the issue may be, we have but one thing to do, and that is to look where the compass of God points, and steer that way. You need not fear shipwreck when God is the pilot.

The latter-day glory is already dawning. God is calling to the nations. The long-oppressed are arousing. The despotic thrones are growing feeble. It is an age of liberty. The trumpet is sounding in all the world, and one nation after another is moving to the joyful sound, and God is mustering the great army of liberty under his banners! In this day, shall America be found laggard? While despotisms are putting off the garments of oppression, shall she pluck them up and put them on? While France and Italy, Germany and Russia, are advancing toward the dawn, shall we recede toward midnight?

From this grand procession of nations, with faces lightened by liberty, shall we be missing? While they advance toward a brighter day, shall we, with faces lurid with oppression, slide downward toward the pit which gapes for injustice and crime?

Let every good man arouse and speak the truth for liberty. Let us have an invincible courage for liberty. Let us have moderation in passions, zeal in moral sentiments, a spirit of conciliation and concession in mere material interests, but unmovable firmness for principles; and—foremost of all political principles—for Liberty!

chapter 3

WAR

Prior to the Confederate bombardment of Fort Sumter in April of 1861, the Northern clergy were divided as to whether war could be justified as a means of holding the Union together. The shelling, however, tended to draw the great majority of Northern preachers together in support of the war. Henry Ward Beecher is an example of the transition. As late as 1860 he had been willing to allow the Southern states to secede in peace. On April 14, 1861, the day after the surrender of Fort Sumter, Beecher delivered a sermon which demonstrated he had changed his mind. In a dramatic piece of rhetoric Beecher urged his audience to prepare for battle and not to shrink from a fight because the cost would be great. He was convinced that the Union's cause was a holy cause. God was with the Union, and, if they pressed their cause with vigor and courage, they would surely triumph. Though war was wicked and wretched, Beecher asserted, "I hold that it is ten thousand times better to have war than to have slavery." The sermon was filled with emotive words, phrases, and sentences.

> I love our country. . . . I hold that to be corrupted silently by giving up manhood, by degenerating, by becoming craven . . . is infintely worse than war. . . . We want no craven cowards; we want men. . . . They have fired upon the American flag. . . . Let every man that lives and owns himself an American, take the side of true American principles; – liberty for one, and liberty for all; liberty now, and liberty forever.[1]

Edmund B. Wilson, a Unitarian minister from Salem, Massachusetts, proclaimed in a sermon on April 20 that the shelling of Fort Sumter brought about a unified determination in the North to prevent secession. "One week before all was uncertainty," he affirmed; "there was apathy, doubt, gloom. . . . [Because of Fort Sumter] we are one people."[2]

Several Northern preachers testified of their conversion from sympathy to hostility toward the South. In the fall of 1861 Gardiner Spring, pastor of the Brick Presbyterian Church in New York City, said:

> When the first indications of this conflict made their appearance, all my prepossessions, as is well known, were with the Southern states. . . . But when I hear so few kind words . . . when crafty politicians . . . blind and enslave the minds of people . . . when I learn that secession was preconcerted and determined in years gone by . . . when I see these things my convictions are strong that we have reached the limit beyond which forbearance may not be extended.[3]

Henry A. Boardman, of the Tenth Presbyterian Church in Philadelphia, also in the autumn of 1861, expressed a theme very similar to Spring's. Having previously expressed a desire for conciliation with the South, Boardman now felt betrayed by the Confederacy. He could no longer sympathize with those by whom "this rebellion was concocted many years ago. . . . The one cherished object of these men was to destroy the Union."[4]

Most of the Northern clergy supported the war effort. Dunham has summarized: "By and large, the Northern Clergy in most cases officially, and in almost all other instances unofficially, loyally supported the Federal Government . . . and directly or indirectly opposed the cause of Southern Independence."[5] The support, however, was not unanimous. Some of the Northern clergy were "disloyal," a term used to describe a variety of positions: pacifism, the abhorrence of war as a means of settling disputes; copperheadism, the lending of comfort or aid to the enemy; neutrality, the refusal to take a position on the war; and passive resistance, the refusal to observe various patriotic amenities. Whatever hindered the war process was "disloyalty." There are no figures as to the number or percentage of Northern ministers who were labeled "disloyal." It is known that life was made very difficult for some of them.

In the very early stages of the war the predominant theme expressed over and over by Northern preachers was that the Union must be preserved. In January of 1861, after the secession process had begun and the clouds of war were gathering on the horizon, Henry W. Bellows, in a sermon at All Souls Church in New York City, declared: "We are not going to war, I trust, to force fifteen states to live under a Government they hate. But we will go to war to save order and civilization, with any faction, conspiracy, rabble, or political party that strives, in illegal and treasonable ways, to break up the Government."[6] On April 21, 1861, the Sunday following the surrender of Fort Sumter, A. L. Stone, in a sermon at the Park Street Church in Boston, stated the cause and purpose of the war as he saw it: "It is not an anti-slavery war we wage," he stated; "not a sectional war; not a war of conquest and subjugation; it is simply and solely a war for the maintenance of the Government and the Constitution."[7] The following week, at the North Broad Street Presbyterian Church in Philadelphia, E. E. Adams proclaimed that the preservation of government was the cause of God, and thus rebellion could not be justified.[8]

When the war did not go well for the Union in its early phases, the preachers found a different purpose to emphasize – emancipation. Several preachers, in fact, proclaimed that the reason for Northern losses was that, for many Northerners, preservation of the Union was a higher priority than emancipation. On November 21, 1861, the Rev. Henry Kimball delivered a sermon in the First Congregational Church of Sandwich, Massachusetts, where he announced that Union defeats were due to the federal government's failure to take a stand against slavery. The ship of state had come upon a storm that would not abate until "Jonah" (slavery) was thrown overboard. Kimball proclaimed: "It is preposterous for us to suppose that we can keep up long before a civilized world, and nourish the very cause of all our disasters. The venom of slavery is in the fang of treason; let us extract the poison, and the teeth of rebellion will be drawn."[9]

Henry Ward Beecher, on November 26, 1861 – the first Thanksgiving of the Civil War – reminded his listeners: "We are fighting, not merely for our liberty, but for those ideas that are the seeds and strength of liberty throughout the earth." Beecher noted the lack of unity in the North over the slavery issue.[10] On October 5, 1862, William A. Gaylord, at the Congregational Church in Fitchburg, New Hampshire, declared: "It is this spirit of despotism [slavery] that we are called to combat."[11] By this point in the war the dominant theme of preachers was no longer the salvation of God-ordained government, though that issue was still very important, but the emancipation of the slaves.

Beecher and several other Northern preachers began to exert pressure on Lincoln to issue a proclamation of emancipation. When Lincoln issued a preliminary Emancipation Proclamation in September of 1862, many Northern preachers exclaimed that the Union had, at last, found the key which would open the doors of victory. Israel E. Dwinell, on October 19, 1862, at the South Side Church of Salem, Massachusetts, delivered a sermon recognizing the importance of the Proclamation for the North. "The cause of the war is clearly slavery," he said; "and we tried for a long time . . . to fight the war, and save sin; and God would not suffer it. . . . Now we are openly and directly on the side of God; and now we may hope to have His favor."[12] The following month Frederick G. Clark, at the West Twenty-third Street Presbyterian Church in New York City, declared that the issuance of the Emancipation Proclamation meant that God was now clearly on the Union side.[13]

Though the saving of the Union and the emancipation of the slaves were the primary themes of sermons during the war, there were other subjects that were often expressed. War was justified, even glorified, by the Northern preachers. In an 1861 sermon William H. Goodrich from Cleveland affirmed that goodness and progress can triumph only when contested on the battlefield:

> You will mark it as a fact of general history, that in the establishment of great rights, and the overthrow of great wrongs, there has always come a point where the issue must be fought out in battle. Rooted wrong and ancient despotism never yield that last point, till they are confronted with force greater than their own. Selfish power, even when deserted by its old advocates, and disowned by the surrounding world, will always make one last stand, and will yield only when conquered and abased.[14]

Several preachers spoke of the virtues that can accompany war. In September of 1861 S. P. Leeds delivered a sermon at the Congregational Church at Dartmouth College where he decried the softness, laxity, and unwarranted leniency that had permeated the country. Leeds rejoiced, however, that war would bring forth better characteristics. Soft-headed people would be pushed into the background, "while men of deeds come to the front."[15] S. D. Phelps, on April 18, 1862, at the First Baptist Church of New Haven spoke of the positive traits that soldiering would bring to young men who enlisted for war. Camp life would instill a "hardier and stronger [people], both in physical endurance and in moral vigor." Americans had degenerated and become effeminate through luxury and ease, according to Leeds. The returning soldiers would provide the nation with "moral and Christian heroes ... stalwart influences ... a purer and more stable Republicanism."[16]

In an 1862 sermon Samuel T. Spear, at the South Presbyterian Church of Brooklyn, proclaimed that the war would result in the United States being recognized as a great military power, a "first class nation, whose ability to defend its rights will protect it against injury."[17] On Thanksgiving Day of 1863 Ray Palmer of Albany, New York, was grateful that the Civil War had given the United States a real history. "People from other lands," Palmer said, "will come to visit and survey our battlefields, at Fort Donelson and Shiloh, Vicksburg and Port Hudson, Murfreesboro, Antietam and Gettysburg, as we have gone to examine those of Thermopylae and Marathon, of Cannae and Pharsalia, of Bannockburn, Angincourt and Waterloo. So we shall take our place and influence among historic and classic lands."[18]

Though many Northern preachers pushed and attempted to pressure Lincoln into issuing a statement on emancipation, often criticizing him for not acting swiftly on that subject, they were generally supportive of the president throughout the war. Henry Ward Beecher was one of those who had publicly chastened Lincoln for his failure to act rapidly on emancipation, yet on most everything else Beecher was a staunch supporter of the nation's leader. On September 28, 1862, six days after Lincoln had announced the Emancipation Proclamation, Beecher delivered a sermon denouncing slavery and strongly defending Lincoln's use of the war powers that were coming under question from several quarters in the North.[19] In 1861 J. B. Bittinger of Cleveland was an early supporter of Lincoln's use of war powers which suspended certain civil rights. To those who protested such actions, Bittinger replied that "so-called freedom of speech and press" were a mask for "foulness of vituperation" or "unblushing mendacity."[20] In the same year Cyrus D. Foss, in a sermon to Brooklyn Methodists, proclaimed strong support for limiting freedom of expression. "We talk of the freedom of the press as something sacred," Foss exclaimed. "We have exalted it into a demi-god which is profanation to touch or speak against. . . . Free speech and a free press are essential to the stability of republican institutions; but let neither insolently claim to be in such sense free as to be beyond any check."[21]

When Lincoln ran for reelection in 1864 against George McClellan, most Northern preachers who brought politics into the pulpit were

strong supporters of Lincoln. On October 9, 1864, O. T. Lanphear of
New Haven urged the reelection of Lincoln as the surest way to realize peace. He denounced a vote for McClellan, the supposed "peace
candidate." "The man who casts his vote in the election now pending," Lanphear said, "in favor of a peace not won by the conquests
of our armies, does the rebel cause more service, if possible, than he
could by joining the rebel army."[22]

A few Northern preachers, in their attempt to portray the war
as a battle between good and evil, filled their sermons with accounts
of Southern atrocities, atrocities based upon rumors and for which
there was little evidence. Such preaching was not typical, but it did
happen. The following lines are from a sermon by Edwin B. Foster
at the First Congregational Church in Springfield, Massachusetts,
in 1862.

> They [Southerners] dig up the decaying remains [of Northern dead]
> and tear the scalps from the heads of the departed, as vultures tear
> the flesh, that they may make drinking cups of the skulls. With strange
> powers of invention, almost their own ingenuity of mechanism, they
> manufacture the bones of our dead into rings and castanets and whistles,
> then hawking them abroad, as an article of merchandise, they coolly
> pocket the thirty pieces of silver.[23]

The Northern preachers also tried to bolster support for the war
by warning what would happen if the Southern "rebellion" should be
successful. A. L. Stone from Boston declared if the rebellion should
succeed, all legitimate authority would break down in America, forcing Americans "back from friendships and brotherhoods and all alliances, to the instincts of the forest brute." He urged his listeners
to "strike for Law and Union, for country and God's great ordinance
of Government."[24] Henry Post, at the Presbyterian Church in Warrenburgh, New York, warned of the consequences if the South should
be successful in its secession efforts. "We should sink to the level of
the European nations," he declared; "the hope of the world would
turn into a nation too feeble, too inherently jealous, to preserve its
high station. . . . The star of the western hemisphere would set amid
lurid clouds, no more to rise."[25]

James H. Moorhead tells his readers that most of the Northern
clergy – most specifically the Baptists, Congregationalists, Methodists, and Presbyterians – viewed the Civil War in apocalyptic and
millennialistic terms. The United States as the New Israel was going

through the Apocalypse on its way to the millennium, the Kingdom of God on earth. The kingdom could come only through suffering and the clash of arms. "God was violently overturning the old, corrupt order and was bringing the disparate forces of history to a climatic resolution in one place and time. It has been granted to Americans to fight the definitive battle that would ensure the future happiness of the nation and the world."[26]

The apocalyptic and/or millennialistic themes recurred again and again in Northern sermons. These themes were emphasized even before the war began. On January 4, 1861, Herman Humphrey stated that in spite of crisis, the United States would not be deterred from its great divine mission. "Would He [God] have brought us hither and given us so much work in prospect for bringing in the millennium," he asked, "if He had intended to pluck us up, just as we are entered upon the work?"[27] Later in the same year, after the war was in progress, Nathaniel West, Jr., at the Second Presbyterian Church in Brooklyn, affirmed that when the war was over, God would commission the United States to be "a national Israel and servant of the Lord, fit for the Master's use."[28] Later in the year William B. Sprague emphasized that a Northern victory would bring in "a flood of millennial glory."[29]

On Thanksgiving Day of 1863 Henry Clay Fish, pastor of the First Baptist Church in Newark predicted a Union victory and described his vision of the new America:

> I see it. I see it. The war successfully ended; the bondman everywhere a freeman; the degraded white man everywhere educated and ennobled; the diverse elements in the national composition fused and welded inseparably together; local jealousies and animosities at an end; treason and traitors expelled from the country; the heresy of state sovereignty and secession killed; . . . a school house and church in every district; the people taking the highest type of civilization – intelligent, God-fearing, liberty-loving, self-governed, and bound together in one tender and beautiful brotherhood.[30]

The following year at Thanksgiving time Sherman Canfield spoke of the importance of going through the fire on the way to the millennium. "On its way towards the millennium," Canfield exclaimed, "the Kingdom of Christ occasions strifes and conflicts by causing a portion of a world lying in wickedness to differ from the rest. The very goodness, frankness, and courage which it produces in its subjects, renders them odious to evil doers."[31] When the war was over, James T. Robinson, pastor of the First Baptist Church in North Adams, Massachusetts, announced: "The great Republic, tried by fire ... but terrible and glorious, ascends through smoke and flame to unending sway and splendor."[32]

On April 14, 1865, Henry Ward Beecher gave the address at the raising of the Union flag over Fort Sumter. He had been invited to do so by President Lincoln, who would be assassinated the very night of Beecher's address. In that address Beecher summed up what he felt the Civil War had accomplished.

> First, that these United States shall be one and indivisible. Second, that States are not absolute sovereigns, and have no right to dismember the republic. Third, that universal liberty is indispensable to republican government, and that slavery shall be utterly and forever abolished. . . . These are the best fruits of the war. They are worth all they have cost. NO MORE DISUNION! NO MORE SECESSIONS! NO MORE SLAVERY![33]

The first sermon that ends this chapter is by the Rev. James D. Liggett, who began his career in law and journalism. In 1858 he began a study of theology and was ordained in the Congregational Church the following year. He held pastorates in Leavenworth and Hiawatha, Kansas. In 1877 he left the pastoral ministry and founded the Detroit Home and Day School in Detroit, Michigan.

The sermon "Our National Reverses" was preached on September 7, 1862, in the First Congregational Church of Leavenworth. At the time this sermon was delivered the war was not going well for the Union, and Liggett asked why. He was sure that the South was in the wrong and that God did not support their cause. Why then the Union defeats upon the field of battle? The reason, he answered, was because the Union had ignored God's priorities. The North was fighting to preserve the Union first, and then, perhaps, to eradicate slavery. God's priorities were precisely the other way around. Liggett castigated Lincoln for his emphasis on saving the Union and his neglect of the slavery issue. "Our President has said, and all his policy has been, to preserve the national life and slavery too, if he can." Not until the North made the abolition of slavery its first goal would God grant victory in war. "When the nation is fit for final victory He will grant it; and it will be signal and complete."

The second sermon is by the eminent New England Congregationalist Horace Bushnell, clergyman and theologian, who looked at the war from a very different perspective than Liggett. For Bushnell the primary purpose of the war was preservation of God-ordained government.

Bushnell was one of the most innovative theologians in American history. Many of his innovations were not congenial to some of the rigid orthodoxy of his day, and certain ministers in Connecticut sought, unsuccessfully, to bring him before an ecclesiastical tribunal for heresy. Some of those innovations caused quite a stir in the mid-nineteenth century, but over time became widely accepted in many quarters of American Christianity. Bushnell emphasized that truth, especially religious truth, could best be apprehended by intuition rather than by logic or reasoning. He held that spiritual matters could not really be expressed through words. Words might be suggestive of religious truth, but never definitive. Bushnell tended to downplay the necessity of a religious conversion and said that a child should grow up as a Christian, never knowing himself to be otherwise. This emphasis caused many churches to place a greater emphasis upon the training and nurture of the young. He redefined the doctrine of the Trinity, reinterpreted the meaning of the cross, and blurred the line that traditionalists had drawn between the sacred and secular.

On the national issues of his time, Bushnell vigorously opposed the Fugitive Slave Law, but he was never an abolitionist. Prior to the war he sought for ways of reconciliation. After the war began, he supported the Union, not because of the slavery issue, but because he believed that government was a God-ordained institution against which there was no right of revolution or secession. Bushnell had great faith in Lincoln, and his support for the President never wavered even in the most uncertain days of the war. When the war ended, Bushnell shared in the millennialistic dream, looking forward to a better and more noble America.

The sermon "Popular Government by Divine Right" was delivered on Thanksgiving Day of 1864 in the South Church of Hartford, Connecticut. Bushnell's discourse is a lengthy, sophisticated, political science treatise whereby he established the authority of government in a doctrine which resembled the divine right of kings. "The magistrate," asserted Bushnell, "is a sovereign over the people, not they over him, having a divine right to bind their conscience by his rule." The states rights position, once advocated by John C. Calhoun and continually advocated by most in the Confederacy, was, according to Bushnell, a heresy – a denial of a sovereignty established by God.[34] "Our whole civil order," proclaimed Bushnell, "is the ordinance of God." The war, therefore, was an instrument of God to preserve what the Almighty had ordained. "Every drum-beat is a hymn, the cannon thunder God, the electric silence, darting victory along the wires, is the inaudible greeting of God's favoring word and purpose." Though the abolition of slavery was an important rationale for the war, it was secondary to preserving the institutional order God had established. This was a very different stance than the one advocated by James Liggett.

NOTES

1. "The Battle Set in Array," *Freedom and War* (Boston: Ticknor & Fields, 1863), 84–110.
2. *Reasons for Thanksgiving* (Salem, MA: Observer, 1862).
3. *State Thanksgiving during the Rebellion* (New York: Harper & Bros., 1862).
4. *Thanksgiving in War* (Philadelphia: C. Sherman and Son, 1861).
5. Chester Forrester Dunham, *The Attitude of the Northern Clergy Toward the South 1860–1865* (Philadelphia: Porcupine Press, 1974), 143.
6. "The Crisis of Our National Disease," *Fast Day Sermons* (New York: Rudd & Carleton, 1861), 293–310.
7. *The War and the Patriot's Duty* (Boston: Henry Hoyt, 1861).
8. *Government and Rebellion* (Philadelphia: Henry B. Ashmead, 1861).
9. *The Ship of State Bound for Tarshish* (Boston: Geo. C. Rand and Avery, 1861).
10. "Modes and Duties of Emancipation," *Patriotic Addresses* (New York: Fords, Howard, & Hulbert, 1891), 322–41.
11. *The Soldier God's Minister* (Fitchburg, NH: Rollstone Printing Office, 1862).
12. *Hope For Our Country* (Salem: Charles W. Swasey, 1862).
13. *Gold in the Fire: Our National Position* (New York: John H Duychinck, 1862).
14. *A Sermon on the Christian Necessity of War* (Cleveland: Fairbanks, Benedict and Co., 1861).
15. *Thy Kingdom Come: Thy Will Be Done* (Windsor, VT: Bishop and Tracy, 1861).
16. *National Symptoms* (New Haven: Thomas H. Pease, 1862).
17. *The Nation's Blessing in Trial* (Brooklyn: Wm. W. Rose, 1862).
18. *The Opening Future: or, The Results of the Present War* (Albany: J. Munsell, 1863).
19. "National Injustice and Penalty," *Freedom and War*, 311–40. In this sermon Beecher also claimed that Southern women, more than Southern men, bore a special blame for slavery. "Southern men have been tame and cool," Beecher said, "in comparison with the fury of southern women."
20. *A Sermon Preached Before the Presbyterian Churches of Cleveland* (Cleveland: E. Cowles and Co., 1861).
21. *Songs in the Night* (New York: N. Tibbals and Co., 1861).
22. *Peace by Power* (New Haven: J. H. Benham, 1864).

23. *The Constitution Our Ark in the Storm* (Springfield: Samuel Bowles, 1862).
24. *The Divineness of Human Government* (Boston: Henry Hoyt, 1861).
25. *A Sermon* (Albany, NY: Weed, Parsons and Co., 1861).
26. James H. Moorhead, *American Apocalypse: Yankee Protestants and the Civil War 1860–1869* (New Haven: Yale University Press, 1978), 43.
27. *Our Nation* (Pittsfield, MA: Henry Chickering, 1861).
28. *Establishment in National Righteousness* (New York: John F. Trow, 1861).
29. *Glorifying God in the Fires*, (Albany, NY: C. Van Benthuysen, 1861).
30. *The Valley of Achor a Door of Hope; or, The Grand Issues of the War* (New York: Sheldon and Co., 1863).
31. *The American Crisis* (Syracuse: Journal Book and Job Office, 1865).
32. *National Anniversary Address* (North Adams: W. H. Phillips, 1865).
33. "Address at the Raising of the Union Flag over Fort Sumter," *Patriotic Addresses* 676–97.
34. After John C. Calhoun made the transition from ardent nationalist to ardent states righter, he proposed a number of ideas to limit the power and authority of the federal government. In 1828 he initiated the doctrine of nullification, a process for states to follow when they disagreed with a federal law. At such times states should call for a state constitutional convention to decide if the offending law was constitutional. If the convention declared the law unconstitutional, then a recommendation was made to the state legislature to declare that law null and void in that state, and the state would interpose itself between the federal law and the citizens of the state. The nullification process was attempted in a tariff dispute with Andrew Jackson, over various issues prior to the Civil War, and in the 1950s and 1960s as a means of fighting federal civil rights laws. Later in his career Calhoun would advocate government by a "concurrent majority" as a means of protecting local interests against encroachments by the federal government. In such a doctrine the government would be composed of various interest groups throughout the nation. A negative vote of one interest group could veto a piece of federal legislation. This was Calhoun's alternative to straight majority voting, which at that time was working against the South. It was against these various expressions of states rights that Bushnell was arguing. For a more involved discussion on Calhoun's theories of states rights, see Robert M. Calhoon, *Evangelicals and Conservatives in the Early South, 1740–1861* (Columbia: University of South Carolina Press, 1988), 175–85; John C. Calhoun, *A Disquisition on Government and Selections from the Discourse*, ed. C. Gordon Post (Indianapolis: Bobbs Merrill, 1953); and Lacy K. Ford, "Republican Ideology in a Slave Society: The Political Economy of John C. Calhoun," *The Journal of Southern History* 54 (Aug. 1988): 405–24. The works by Calhoon and Ford offer several helpful bibliographical suggestions.

Our National Reverses

James D. Liggett

September 7, 1862

> And the Children of Israel inquired of the Lord, saying, Shall I again go out to battle against the children of Benjamin my brother, or shall I cease? And the Lord said, go up; for to-morrow I will deliver them into thine hand.
>
> *—Judges, XX, 27–28—*

The facts connected with this passage of Scripture are such as to present a question in relation to God's dealings with his people of great interest and practical importance.

A few wicked and worthless men of Gibeah, of the tribe of Benjamin, committed a most horrible outrage upon a Levite and his wife, who had taken lodgings for a night in their town. No reason for the act is given in the narrative, and none can be supposed by us except their own devilish desire to commit wickedness. It was unprovoked and devilish. As the news of it spread through all the tribes of Israel, the greatest indignation was excited in all hearts; and the people came together en masse to decide what to do. With one voice they said, the perpetrators of so great a crime must be speedily and terribly punished; and they demanded of the Benjamites that the criminals be delivered up for punishment. But, instead of complying with this reasonable and righteous demand, the whole tribe of Benjamin took offense at the action of the other tribes and prepared to resist them by force of arms.

Under these circumstances no choice of action was left to the other tribes but to enforce justice and assert the authority of the nation by the sword. Hence they went out against Benjamin with four hundred thousand trained men of war, many of whom had seen actual service in the battlefield, thus arraying at once the whole military power of the nation against one little tribe. Their purpose seems to have been to make sure and thorough work. There were no delays or

From DeWitte Holland, ed., *Sermons in American History* (Nashville: Abingdon Press, 1971).

want of earnestness in the prosecution of the war. The cause was doubtless just; the nation was united in its support; the symbols of national authority were with them; and the result shows that God himself was on their side, and against Benjamin. Yet the Israelites were unexpectedly and disgracefully beaten in the first battle; and also in the second.

There were four hundred thousand men of valor, representing the national authority, with justice and the divine approval, on the one side; and only twenty-six thousand rebels and wrong-doers on the other; yet the wrong-doers triumphed in two successive pitched battles, slaying in the two engagements fourteen thousand more than their own entire army.

Now, on the theory that God has something to do in these conflicts of men, and that all his attributes are always pledged to the side of justice and right; how shall we explain this remarkable piece of history? Certainly not by the more than semi-infidel saying attributed to Napoleon, that "God favors the strongest battalions."

Surely some superhuman influence was in the conflict, otherwise the result in the first battles would have been different. Taking merely human power and valor into the account, it is incredible that twenty-six thousand men could defeat and rout an army of four hundred thousand men of equal valor in a fair and open conflict. Shall we say then that God was, even temporarily, on the side of wicked men and wrong-doers, and gave them the victory? Certainly not. But we must say that his power was exerted as to result ultimately in the greatest good to Israel, whom he did really favor; and the greatest evil to Benjamin, whom it was his will and purpose to punish with a most signal punishment. The facts will make this interpretation clear.

(a) Israel did not consult God, their king and leader, as was his duty to do before making that war; but a mass meeting of the people was called, and a Congress of the chief men of the tribes deliberated and determined for themselves the question of duty.

(b) They were evidently actuated by a wrong spirit; that of revenge rather than an humble and conscientious desire to vindicate the cause of justice in the fear of God.

(c) In the heat and haste of passion, they evidently sought to glorify themselves rather than God.

(d) They evidently trusted in their own superiority of strength for an easy victory, and forgot their dependence on the God of battles. God required of them when they went to war at all, not only and solely that it should be in a just cause, but that they should first submit the decision of that matter to him; and then prosecute it with motives and feelings consistent with a holy cause, and in a confident dependence upon himself for success. In this way he undertook to train them to follow him as their leader, and to educate them for his own peculiar people, ready to acknowledge and glorify him at all times and in all things.

But you will observe that the only question which they at the outset submitted to him for decision was one of minor importance, which doubtless arose from ambitious rivalry. It was "who shall lead us?" Who shall have the most responsible position and reap the most glory from the war? Who shall be the Commander-in-Chief of the united armies? The Lord nevertheless decided this question for them. He said "Judah shall go up first," and of course the chief man of Judah became the chief man of all. Nor can we doubt that he was the right man in the right place, because God chose him. But with all that, they were not prepared for victory. The conditions upon which God could grant them success were not complied with.

After their first defeat they were greatly mortified and grieved, even wept out their tears of bitterness before God; but evidently had not really discovered the true cause of their failure and disaster.

They encouraged themselves, instead of seeking direction from God, and set themselves in battle array the second time, and then after having done so, sought God's advice whether to fight or not. Having first decided the question of duty for themselves, the act of submitting it to God was doubtless a formal, rather than a sincere submission to his will. Their purpose was already fixed, and no answer contrary thereto would have been heeded. But God's answer was again given. He said "go up." He approved the war. His will was that they should prosecute it still further and to the bitter end; yet he determined in his wisdom to make it the means of correcting Israel, as well as of punishing Benjamin, and the former object had to be first accomplished.

Israel had one Bull Run disaster, and had passionately resolved to avenge it, and wipe out the disgrace at all hazards; and their feelings of pride and unholy ambition, alike dishonoring to God and degrading to themselves made another such disaster necessary. Again they are defeated and massacred in heaps on the same bloody and fatal field. This second defeat brought them to a proper sense of their own weakness and error. While in their vain glory and zeal, they undertook the correction of other transgressors, they found themselves corrected. This time they go to God with fastings, tears and confessions. This time their tears are not those produced solely by regrets for their losses and disgrace; but there are also tears of penitence for their own sins in forgetting and departing from the Living God; and they for the first time humbly and honestly submit the question to him: "Shall we go out and fight against Benjamin, our brother, again, or shall we cease?" This time, there was a sincere willingness either to fight or not, as God's will should indicate; a willingness to obey him, even though it involved their own disgrace by a base submission to the victorious arms of an inferior foe. The answer of God, as before, is "go up," and with it the promise also "tomorrow I will deliver them into your hands."

The state of mind to which they had been brought, and the lesson of dependence which they had learned, were such as to make victory a blessing, and not a curse to them, as it would have been under their former state of feelings.

This, then, makes this seemingly dark chapter of the Divine Providence luminous and instructive. God is always consistent with himself, and works for righteous ends. If his hand is for a time against even his own people, it is not in anger, not without a just reason, and for a glorious purpose. If he uses his enemies to scourge his own people, and to correct them, it is in mercy, and it does not follow that his favor is even temporarily with his enemies, and against his own people, but the contrary.

This history and its lessons of instruction are old, but today they seem to us new and profitable.

Almost the very same history is being acted over again in our country. Thus far the parallel is almost, if not entirely perfect; and if as a nation we shall only heed the lessons which the past and the present teach us, it will be perfect to the end. If by our past reverses we shall be made willing to be corrected as Israel was, then shall we yet be victorious over all our enemies. Let us trace the parallel briefly.

Certain wicked men, of the Southern tribes of our Confederacy, inaugurated rebellion by the commission of the greatest crimes known to the laws of God or man, and have continued to prosecute it in the same spirit of wickedness. The effect of their acts of rebellion was to arouse the loyal people of the whole land to a pitch of excitement and indignation very much like that excited in the tribes of Israel, when they heard the news of the crime of the men of Gibeah. The hearts of the people, as in that case, were also knit together as the heart of one man. The unanimous decision was that the rebellion must be subdued.

The laws of God and man, the welfare of the whole nation, and the interests of the human race at large, and of future generations seemed plainly to every right-hearted and right-minded man, to require that these criminals must be punished. In this the whole nation, the slaveholders and those who sincerely sympathized with them excepted, was heartily agreed. And for this object it was determined that the whole power of the nation should be at once employed. The first campaign was inaugurated, and after some successes, ended with a great defeat. The people wept sorely and were greatly disheartened, but they encouraged themselves, and again set themselves in battle array against the enemy. The second campaign was inaugurated on a scale much larger than the first. We felt that no power could withstand our new armies as disciplined, equipped and commanded; and with impatient confidence, we sent them forth to wipe away the disgrace of former defeats. Again after various successes and doubtful victories, this campaign also has ended in failure; and our national existence, involving the cause of liberty and justice, is in greater peril than ever. The men of Belial, and the tribes that sustain them in their great wickedness are again triumphant and defiant.

A loyal people are again in mourning for the thousands of good and valiant men who have fallen in disastrous conflicts. Why is it? O God of Justice! why is it?

There is an adequate reason for these terrible calamities and disappointments. But God does not in fact look with favor upon such schemes of conspiracy against liberty and humanity as the authors of the rebellion are endeavoring to carry out. That cannot be. God forbid that any man should think so for a single moment! All the attributes of his nature are clearly against that system of human bondage which they are avowedly fighting to establish; which they have boastingly laid down as the corner stone of the frail superstructure of the aristocratic and military government which they hope to erect upon it.

We cannot come to the conclusion that our enemies are in the right and that God is with them; and if they are in the wrong God cannot be the friend of their cause.

Where then is the trouble? If the question is put, "Shall we go out again and fight against the rebels?" the principles of justice and right, and the law of self-preservation, as plainly answer in the affirmative and as authoritatively as if an audible voice from Heaven uttered the words of permission, "Go up." Look at this question in whatever light we may, — religiously, politically, socially, and with reference to the welfare of other nations as well as our own, and the answer is the same. No choice of action is or ever has been left to us but to fight, or treasonably betray the high trusts which the past has committed to us; and which the generations of all the future plead with us to sacredly guard for them. But notwithstanding all this, the promise does not seem to come as yet — "tomorrow I will deliver them into your hands." As to what seems to be duty, all agree, and there can be no mistake; but as to what is to be the result, and when it shall be attained, all are equally in darkness and doubt. Such perils and uncertainties surround us, that we can only walk by faith. And if, indeed, our reverses have brought us, or shall soon bring us, to this point, there is good hope for us yet. If as a people we shall thus walk, God will then speedily lead us to victory, but by the path of righteousness.

Such questions, as who shall lead our armies, may well be laid aside if God shall be pleased to lead them. Well may we lay aside our confidence in merely human leadership, since all our most competent military commanders, separately and unitedly, have been unequal to the task of achieving victory either by genius, science, numbers or personal prowess. Our armies have always fought bravely and well; and the tens of thousands of our noblest ones have fallen as heroes only fall. We could not, in reason, ask them to do more. Yet, in the main, we are defeated. The stubborn hosts, after the fortunes of hundreds of important and bloody battles, face each other on substantially the first battle-fields of the war. It is time then to lay aside the question of leadership, since thus far there has been neither success, nor glory for any. If other conditions of success were complied with, we have men enough competent in skill and courage for any responsibilities that may be imposed upon them.

But rather let us define our objects and settle our policy, and see to it that they are such as we can confidently ask God to maintain for us. What, then, are we fighting for? Is it for what we often meaninglessly call "our glorious Union"? Is it for a Union representing the principles of justice and liberty to all, or merely a Union in name and form, without regard to what it represents? If it is for the Union as it recently was, corrupted and perverted by the very men who have destroyed it, to subserve in all possible ways the base ends of the slavery power and interest, then that is one of the things that can never be again. The antagonisms of the old Union – Liberty and Slavery – destroyed it; and the same antagonisms, if attempted to be preserved, will forever keep its fragments asunder. Is it for the old Union, under which free men of the North were made, like blind Samson, to grind in the mills of the political Philistines of the South? Then, God in his mercy has saved us by our defeats from such a fate. Is it that we may again be made like poor, eyeless Samson, an object of sport and derision for these same Philistines of the South? Then, God give us strength to shake down the old fabric ourselves, and let us, like men, perish in the ruins. But that question is already settled by the past. Let the dead bury their dead. The question is now, whatever it may have been twelve months ago, no such thing as "the restoration of the Union as it was." Let that most stupid and transparent of all fallacies, which has already cost so much blood and treasure, be abandoned. Let us break away from the fallacies and prejudices of the past which, like withes, have bound us in helplessness; and in manly strength grapple with the living issue of the agonizing Present. That issue is Liberty or Slavery. The rebels have resolved to destroy the nation that they may establish Slavery. Shall we hesitate to destroy Slavery that we may preserve the nation? Because it has come to this, that the nation must perish or that which strikes at the nation's life must perish. Our President has said, and all his policy has been, to preserve the national life and slavery too, if he can. He has tried it, and the experiment has certainly been tried long enough. The nation faints under the terrible and protracted torture. God thunders in his ears from the rivers and valleys of the West and mountain fastnesses and plains of the East, which the blood of our slain has made red in vain – "You cannot." The honest judgment of all loyal men decrees to him in terms that are imperial – "You cannot," and, what is more, "You shall not." All the sacrifices which a noble people have made and are pledged still to make, protest against a longer continuance of the ruinous experiment. Why, then, is what seems to be the will of the whole nation thus balked by the stubborn will of one man? In the midst of all the popular outcry for Liberty and the destruction of Slavery, I think I hear God saying to us – "Are you as a people, after all, ready to do justice? The rebels are fighting for Slavery; are you fighting for Liberty in the true sense, and from principle? Is it from a sense of justice to the slave, or a feeling of revenge and hatred towards the master that you ask Slavery to be destroyed? Is this nation fit in heart to do this great work of God?" If not, then must he, by still greater reverses and afflictions, prepare our hearts and make us fit to receive upon our brows the wreath of victory which his own holy hands shall place there. Our God is a jealous God and looks on the heart. Let us endeavor, through outward signs, to look a little further into this nation's heart. What means the heathenish and God-defying sentiment uttered by a distinguished orator and applauded by a great crowd, "I hate the Negro, but am willing, for my own safety, to let him shoot a rebel, reserving the privilege of scorning and persecuting him afterwards?" What means the recently enacted black code of the great patriotic and Liberty professing State of Illinois? Do the sons of the would-be-glorious State die by the thousands for the liberty of the black man, as of the white man, and then by a vote almost unanimous, deny him a resting place for the sole of his weary foot on their own boasted free soil? What means all the howl of objection against allowing black men, who were good enough to fight the battles of our country under Washington and Jackson to bear arms and help to fight the same battles under Lincoln? What means the most extraordinary spectacle of the President of our great nation, inviting to his own council chamber a large number of as intelligent and respectable colored men as he could find, to insult and degrade them by telling them, "Your presence in this country is offensive, injurious and intolerable to the white race, and I am authorized, by the representatives of the nation in Congress assembled, to say to you that your expenses shall be paid, if you will be gone from our sight and the land of your unfortunate birth forever"? What mean these and very many other things, to which I cannot now allude, but that there is yet in the heart of the nation a deep-seated and unjustifiable hatred of the enslaved race of this country? – a spirit which is at once the root and the fruit of Slavery. "Whosoever hateth his brother, is a murderer." And shall we not, from this divine rule of judgment, also say that whoever hateth an oppressed race of men in our midst is an oppressor? This hatred is the very essence and soul of the system of Slavery. It has kept, and it today keeps it in existence. Judged by this just rule, we are a nation of slaveholders still. Is this nation then prepared in heart to take off the shackles from four millions of black men and do justice by them? If God will punish the slaveholder for his sin, as we believe He will, is it not just in him first to correct the spirit of the slaveholder in the hearts of those whom he intends to make the instruments of that punishment? Will he honor this generation with the championship of freedom, while it is imbued with the principles and feelings of despotism? I believe he will indeed thus honor this generation, but not until he has made it fit to bear the honor; not until he has purged the nation's heart of the poison of Slavery.

These facts and principles, thus merely hinted, are sufficient, as it seems to me, to explain to us God's dealings with us; how he is against us, and yet not against us, as he was against Israel and yet all the time for him. If our pro-slaveryism is not the particular and only cause of his chastisements – if I am wholly mistaken in this, then there is some other cause; and still the general principle upon which I have explained His dark providence is undoubtedly true. Let him that has a better solution or a more faithful admonition to give, not for a moment hold his peace, but cry aloud, spare not, and show this people their transgression.

In the vast changes wrought already in the hearts of the people by the defeats we have suffered and not by the victories we have won, we can plainly see that God and not man is working a mighty and rapid revolution for us. It may seem to us to move slowly, too slowly while the life of the nation is wasting away in torrents of blood, but the engine of God's power propels it; and it must and will move on, through all the friction and weight of man's opposition – "through on time." This is our faith; and let it be the ground of our hope. In the meantime let us be patient and not despair, but work on, seeking to work in the line of God's direction. The Lord says "Go up." Other defeats and greater may yet be necessary; how many and how great He only knows, yet He says, "Go up again," and again. When the nation is fit for final victory He will grant it; and it will be signal and complete. What the near future has in store for us no man can tell; yet having faith in God and the certainty of human progress under God, though your eyes and mine may not behold it, I believe that the future of this nation shall be more glorious than the past; and that no drop of precious blood will have baptised the yet virgin soil of our beloved land in vain. Unborn generations will yet praise God for the defeats of our armies, as well as the victories which He shall hereafter grant unto them. These are not the bitter words of treason, but the joyful words of loyal faith and hope. But for this interpretation of what is otherwise dark and inscrutable, I should despair of the present and the future of my country. If God be indeed against us, then are we undone. Let our constant and submissive prayer be—"Thy will be done, O God, and fit us to do it."

Popular Government by Divine Right

Horace Bushnell

Thanksgiving Day, November 24, 1864

> And their nobles shall be of themselves, and their governor shall proceed from the midst of them and I will cause him to draw near, and he shall approach unto me: for who is this that engaged his heart to approach unto me? saith the Lord.
> —*Jeremiah XXX, 21*—

Taken, as by the sound, these words appear to be a kind of American Scripture; and still more, when the notably English word "nobles" is substituted, as it should be in correct translation, by the singular word *chief* or *leader*. Then the declaration is that God will now be united to their chief or governor, so that while he is one of the people, — exalted, or called from among themselves, — he shall consciously and even visibly rule by a divine sanction. In the restoration at hand, it shall not, in other words, be as it was before, when the kings and captains of the land were so often idolaters, or infidels, but the discipline the people have had in their bitter captivity shall have brought them and their rulers in, at last, to God, and given to their government a crowning authority under religious ideas and sentiments. "And their chief shall be of themselves, and their governor shall proceed from the midst of them; and I will cause him to draw near, and he shall approach unto me; for who is this that engaged his heart to approach unto me? saith the Lord";—who, that is, but me, by my own

Building Eras in Religion (New York: Charles Scribner's Sons, 1910), 286–318.

strong Providence in their captivity, and the restoration now of their lately broken country and government?

Just as we ourselves, in this dreadful war-struggle by which we are trying to vindicate and establish our shattered unity, have our public feeling itself so visibly tempered by religion, and have it even as a pleasure, in our proclamations, dispatches, and speeches, to submit ourselves, in homage and trust, to the sacred name and Providential rule of God. Just as now, for the first time, we issue a religious coin, with the motto: *"In God we trust."* Just as many too of our countrymen, dissatisfied with the irreligious or, at least unreligious accident, by which our Constitution omits even the mention of God, began a year ago, and this day are again assembled in Philadelphia, to advocate the memorializing of Congress for an amendment, among others, to the Constitution, that shall make some fit acknowledgment of God and of the fact that human government stands in true authority only when it rules in the emphasis of religious sentiments and sanctions.

What, I propose, accordingly, on the present occasion, is to follow the train of suggestion started by the words of the prophet, showing especially this; that popular governments, or such as draw out their magistracies by election from among the people themselves, are not likely to be completed at the first, but have commonly to be completed historically afterward, and get their moral crowning of authority by a process of divine discipline more or less extended. How this process works, in our own case, it will be my endeavor to show. And I hope to make it appear, to the satisfaction of you all, that we are now come to the final establishment of our government in those religious sentiments and ideas, which are at once the deepest bases and highest summits of a genuine state authority. This, I think, we shall discover and even thankfully accept, as being the true meaning of the present awful chapter of our history. No people of the world were ever sheltered under institutions so genial and benign as ours. They have yielded us blessings of freedom and security hitherto, which no nation of mankind has ever enjoyed in the same degree. But our sense of allegiance, or civic obligation under these institutions, we have always felt and now more than ever perceive, has hitherto been thin and flashy; as if they were, after all, inventions only of man and not the ordinance of God. What more stunning evidence could we have than the fact of this horrid rebellion, – a whole third of the nation renouncing their allegiance, even as by right, without so much as an apparent thought of crime! In this view let us welcome God's process of training and see if we can trace it.

Before proceeding, however, with the more direct matter of our inquiry, let us first glance a moment at the philosophic foundations of government, that we may clear a way for the exposition of fact that is to follow.

The more deeply we consider this matter of civil government, the more nearly impossible it will be, on mere grounds of philosophy, to construct a government without some reference to a Supreme Being.

Thus, if we say that the law is to be grounded in right, right is a moral idea, at whose summit stands God, as the everlasting vindicator of right. If we imagine that mere enforcements will create obligation, apart from any moral consideration whatever, we have only to observe that when statutes are enforced by fines, no good citizen is satisfied because, having broken the statute, he has paid the fine. Enforcements create fear but never obligation. True obligation towers above all enforcements. No touch of it is ever felt, till the subject hears the state, unseen yet somehow divine, commanding through the laws enacted.

If we imagine that the human will of magistrates may somehow create law and wield authority, what do we find, in every real government, but that the magistrates themselves are as truly bound by the laws as the private subjects are; and the insensible, corporate, everywhere electric presence of the state will have magistrates and people all alike submitted to it, as the instrumentalities and objects of its sway?

How plain is it, too, that civil obligation takes hold of the conscience, whenever it is truly fastened upon the subject of government! And what is the conscience, but that summit of our nature where it touches God?

Nor is it any objection that the subjects of many real governments are idolaters and have no rational conception of God. Enough that their conscientious obligations under law will reach higher than their understanding, accepting with implicit and potential homage the Being whom, as yet, they do not think or know.

Regarding the state then as having a legitimate and proper right of government only when it is a factor, so to speak, in the Divine government itself, it becomes a very considerable question, when it may be so considered. I cannot undertake, of course, to settle all the

difficult points of casuistry that may here be raised. I am not required to show whether the governments in Poland, France, and
Mexico are the ordinance of God, nor whether the governments of
Charles I. and Louis XVI. have ceased to be. It must be enough that
government, in the ordinary condition of mankind, is universal, just
as gravity is universal in matter. And as gravity is just as real and
practically the same to them that do not know it, as to them that
do, so is God's ordinance of government the same to them who only
have it by impression, as to them who have it by knowledge or opinion. The real fact is that we have a nature configured inwardly to the
civil state, and are, in fact, civil-society creatures. We do not even
conceive the possibility of living without government. We fly to it,
even the world over, as the necessary shelter of our life. It may be
this or that, it may be in the chieftain of a clan or tribe, it may be
a wild, ungenial, or even a bloody and barbaric absolutism; be it
what it may, the civil-society nature invests it with a gloomy and
blind sovereignty, and bows to it as to some higher kind of being,
closer to God or the gods. And so the world is parceled off, in all
ages, into governments in the most incongruous and grotesque as
well as the most august shapes, yet all alike, with only here and there
an exception, received with unquestioning homage, and bearing rule
in acknowledged right and authority.

Futhermore, as civil government is one of the greatest interests
of mankind, there is either no such thing as Providence, or else it
must also be one of the principal cares of Providence. And it will
almost always be felt that the government in power is in such a sense
historic, that it could not well be different from what it is. In that
view it will be accepted as a kind of Providential creation. And this
is very specially true of our own. It was not necessary for God to
give it authority by saying from the sky: "This is from me." Enough
that if we do not hear the voice, we feel the hand. First, there is given
us a beginning here, in provinces, or colonies, hereafter to be called
states. We are set crystallizing, as such, in the bosom of the common
law of England, receiving, in that manner, all the great principles of
right and liberty that are the heritage of Englishmen. Next, we are
cut off from all distinctions of blood, which might give us a possible
king and nobility. And so, when we came to institute a frame of government we were literally cornered into just the government we have.
We must be states and also the United States. We had, in fact, the
name upon us before we spoke it, and the Constitution in us before

we saw it on paper. The Philadelphia Convention did scarcely more, in fact, than draw out the constitution already framed by Almighty God in the historic cast of our nation itself. We do not all say this or see it; many of us do not see distinctly any thing, but that certain men asserted certain magic formulas, which are conceived to have done everything for us. Still we have the feeling, all of us, that we have just the government that belongs to us; which is, in fact, the same thing as a feeling that it is the creature of God's Providence. Moral and religious ideas come slow and arrive late, but what we have had implicitly as a feeling is now, I trust, to be felt more distinctly, and even formally thought and acknowledged.

Leaving now these generalities behind us, we go on to sketch the process by which our American government is to be thus consummated and to become a full-toned, proper government, under moral and religious ideas. I call it a process; and as every such process advances by crises, not by an imperceptible growth, there appear to have been three such crises that must needs be passed. Let us note them in their order; first, the two that are already passed, and then the third, which we are passing now.

First, we have the stage of self-assertion or declared Independence, in which our new state of order began. It was no single champion that got us in his power and fought us into separation, to be the prize of his own chieftainship. That would have inaugurated a monarchy or absolute government, not a free and popular government. We undertook as a people, just opposite to this, to champion our own right and assume a new civil condition for ourselves. And this we should naturally do, by reverting to principles conceived to be most fixed and absolute. To separate was to rebel, and rebellion could stand by no mere argument of liking, or convenience, or interest, or passion. We began thus to conceive that we had certain inborn natural rights, and very soon also to maintain them by a stiff and sturdy assertion; sometimes, it would seem, by a considerable over-assertion.

In some cases, our leaders had been considerably affected by the political theories of Rousseau and other French infidel writers, who began at the point of what they called nature and natural right in men, contriving how civil society might arise, and could only arise lawfully, by their consent, or compact, or vote, and the surrender of their individual rights, to make up the public stock of powers and prerogatives in the state. In other cases and parts, we had been shaped historically by our popular training in the church, and the little democracies of our towns and colonial legislatures, and so had become ready, as the others, to make a large assertion of our inborn, sacred rights and liberties. As a natural result, the two schools flowed together, coalescing in the same declarations of right, and the same impeachments of wrong, followed by the assertion of a common independence.

In this manner, without any very nice consideration of our meaning, or precisely defined criticism of our principles, we bolted on the world in our famous July declaration. The pressure of the time was too close to allow any very deliberate measurement of ideas. Appealing thus to "the laws of nature and of nature's God," we declare it "to be self-evident that all men are created equal," – a very much easier thing to say, than to show wherein they are equal, or that simply created men, born into no social and civil distinctions, have any where existed, since the time of the creation, – also, that "they are endowed, by their Creator, with inalienable rights," to secure which "governments are instituted, deriving their just powers from the consent of the governed." And so we have New England and Virginia, Puritan church order and the doctrine of the French Encyclopedia, fused happily together in the language of Mr. Jefferson, and the "Creator" and his friends are duly honored by admission to a considerable place in a really atheistic bill or doctrine. Our new political order which is older, in fact, than this document, is yet chronologically born of it, – though not, in any sense, of the matter of this preamble. This is not the sober fact of our history, but only the paradise of the July orators.

Far be it from me to satirize this very dear chapter of our nationality. The doing was grand, but the doctrine of the doing was eminently crude, as Mr. Jefferson very well knew how to be. In a certain possible sense it was true, but in the sense in which it is commonly understood it can only operate and has always operated destructively; working as a kind of latent poison against all government from the first day until now, as we shall by and by see.

The true merit of this document, for merit enough it has, lies in the bill of facts and grievances stated afterwards, not in the matter of the preamble. Probably some of these facts are a good deal exaggerated, but we may take them all together, and sum them up in a single inclusive impeachment, which is true beyond debate and amply sufficient; viz., that the British mother country was holding us only

as provinces to be farmed for her own uses, and not with any thought
of benefit to us; keeping us for trade and taxation, and place, and
office, giving us no voice in the parliament, and permitting us, in
fact, NO FUTURE. Exactly this too, was what every American felt;
this was the real grievance that stung our people, and that sting was
God's inspiration in their bosoms. And now, what living man, having
simply reason for his attribute, will imagine that God's high Providence could have meant this vast, almost continental region of the
new world to be, for all time, the mere convenience and farmhold
subserviency of a little patch of island three thousand miles away!
We talk about the right of revolution and puzzle ourselves much in
that kind of question. There is certainly no such right in government
itself, or under government; which is the really new doctrine asserted
in what is called the right of secession. If there is any right of revolution at all it is a right against government that is really no government; and it cannot stumble any one to admit that such a right exists. Be that as it may, we undertook no proper revolution of the
mother country, but leaving all her laws and magistracies still standing as before, we simply assert the right to be, and have a future
ourselves. The real fact was that we had the momentum, in our feeling, of too vast a future, and slung away the British king and parliament just because they undertook to be the centre of gravity for us,
even as an asteroid might for the sun. Weight of being, – here is the
real argument, – weight of being began to be felt here, and the laws
of proportion, consciously or unconsciously working in us, threw us
into separation, as it were by the laws of arithmetic, or what is not
far different, by the sentence of God. We revolted transcendentally,
for reasons deeper than we conceived; such as we could only feel. The
case was peculiar. There had been many revolutions; never before,
that I know, a separation by specific gravity.

Had we been able to conceive the matter in this way, at the time,
it would have saved us the necessity of, alas! how many pernicious nostrums, accepted from that time onward as maxims even of political
philosophy. There was no need of adverting to some original, barely
created, ante-civil equality, as the paradise of all true right and reason;
contriving, with Rousseau, how we gave up, by consent, these primal
honors of equality, and surrendered this and that natural right, to
make up a pool of endowment large enough for the outfit of a government. We never had, as individual men, any one such right to surrender, – no right to legislate, make arrest, imprison other men, try

them, enforce contracts, investigate titles, punish frauds and wrong doings. Governments have such rights because we have them not, and we have them not on the ground that governments have them for us. And governments are as old as we. We are not born sole men or monads, afterwards if we can to come into society and manufacture government from below. We are born into civil society as we are into the atmosphere; we were already born into British civil society and became legitimate subjects of it; this too, with as little right of consent as whether we should be born at all. The only question was whether, having been grown as a seed in the capsule of that stem, we had a right to get ripe and let go connection, so to become a stem by ourselves. No greater fiction is conceivable, than that we fell back in our act of separation from the mother country upon an original equality, to give up a part of the same by compact, and so become a state. It is very true that we are all equally human, equally entitled, in the right of our inborn conscience and eternity, to the best possible chances of intelligence and character. But if we undertake to assert that we are all, by nature, equally entitled to a government by consent, and to count one in the public suffrage of such government, it may be very well for us, Americans, that it is so; better, in fact, than any thing else; but I know not where there is any such universal principle. A born magistracy, however unequal, be it kingly, or noble, is good without consent, if only it rule well. What can be more preposterous for us, or a conceit more fatal to our moral sobriety, than to assume that there is no legitimate government in the world and never has been, to the present hour, but our own, in the principle forsooth that all governments "derive their just powers from the consent of the governed?" No such consent, whether express or implied, was ever a fact. It never has been, even with us. Our own original consitutions were made, in general, by the votes of property-holders. Minors and women, that is a full two-thirds of our people, are excluded still from any such consent, and, what is more, forbidden even the right of dissent. We male citizens too, of the living generation, have never, in fact, had the opportunity of consent to the United States' government; and how little any such consent may signify, we plainly see, in the fact that the laws are, at this very moment, fighting down with sword and gunpowder, whole sections of country that have been protesting many years against its sovereignty. They are going to be governed, we still say, but where is their consent? Alas, had no such half-principle, or no-principle of consent been asserted, how different might our condition be!

Furthermore, it is a remarkable fact that, after this rather high sounding appeal to supposed foundation principles of government, in many cases we did not organize any new government whatever, but went on generally with the old state governments, just as they were, only declaring them to be "Independent States." We did not even declare ourselves to be a nation. Neither did we, in fact, organize a nation. The Articles of Confederation were only a machine contrived to make the states work together; a harness and not a Constitution. There was a Congress and the Congress had a President, or presiding officer, but there was no President of the republic; no supreme court, no criminal code, and no right of criminal proceeding; no right of taxation or impost, save by the states; no law, in fact, which directly touched the person of any citizen; nothing but a right to get men and means for the common purposes, by requisitions on the states, where the congress voted only by states, — each state, great and small alike, having a single and, of course, equal vote. And even then the vote had no compelling sanction; it was simply an appeal to the good faith of the states. What, in this view, had become of the ultimate principles announced, with so great philosophic pretension, in the preamble of the declaration!

It was something, doubtless, that the states were independent states, but we had, as yet, no common government; for the confederation was only a league, and not, in any sense, a government. But the governments, that is, the states, went on bravely together, and fought the battle finally through, held together firmly by the outside pressure of the war. Then came the day of trial. As soon as the outside pressure was gone, the loose-jointed machinery of the league began, at once, to fall apart. The states laid impost duties in their own right; they often gave no heed to the requisitions of the congress, killing them as it were by simple silence; the public credit gave way; the paper money lost value; the common devotion grew slack, collapsing in blank apathy and hopeless discouragement. Whoever looks over the sad picture given by Mr. Hamilton, in the *Federalist*, will see that a complete lapse, under atrophy and final extinction, was close at hand.

This brings me to the second stage or crisis in the process of our advance towards a complete government, viz., which we passed in the organization of our National Constitution. Here the effect is, though it is not commonly so stated, to drop the mere machine, or harness of common working for the states, and create or institute a proper government for them. Before, the states were sovereign, and were not subjects at all, in the sense of being under government. There is now to be a power created that can move, without moving solely through states; the new government is to have a new order of subjects, viz., the people themselves; holding them in terms of direct allegiance to itself. "The great and radical vice," says Mr. Hamilton, "in the construction of the [then] existing Confederation, is in the principle of legislation for *states* or governments, in their corporate, or collective capacities, as contra-distinguished from individuals." (*Federalist*, No. XV.) And, again, "We must incorporate into our plan those ingredients that may be considered as forming the characteristic difference between a league and a government, and must extend the authority of the Union to the *persons* of the citizens, the only proper objects of government." (*Federalist*, No. XV.)

Hence the Constitution; wherein we get a President or National Chief Magistrate, a right of impost general, of taxation, of military levy, of Courts of Admiralty and a criminal jurisdiction, a Supreme Court with a right of appeal from the state courts, arraignments for treason, every thing that belongs to the highest functions of a supreme government.

Now there begins to be a ring of authority and decisive obligation in the civil order of the Republic. The people feel the contact now of its laws, and rejoice in the sense of a new born nationality. I need not sketch the picture; sufficient to say, that no people of the earth were ever before as free, and secure, and prosperous, and happy. Our progress, accordingly, even astonished ourselves. A national feeling, too, was growing up, silently and imperceptibly to ourselves, and the state feeling was subsiding into a more nearly domestic or household sentiment. Both kinds of allegiance are dear to us, but the higher allegiance raises a higher devotion; even as the flag which represents it everywhere, in every sea and clime and field of common battle, becomes a symbol more significant and sacred than the flags of the states. The states, too, have consented knowingly to have it so. They had rights of government as individuals never had, and it is matter of indubitable and sober history that they did surrender certain very eminent rights, to endow the prerogatives of the general government. And to make it a sacrifice more free, and give the act a greater solemnity, the People of the States, in place of the State Legislatures, themselves voted the surrender. And so it results that the states are governments in virtue of their reserved rights, and the State general or nation is a government in virtue of its contributed rights. Both are sovereign in their sphere; both govern as final authorities. Only it results, of course, that the General Government is a higher and more eminent sovereignty, according to the more eminent powers of peace, and war, and final appeal, that are given it.

Still there is a weak spot here, and it was growing weaker for a long time, till finally, four years ago the bond was broken asunder. This weak spot and final break of order began at what is called "the State Rights doctrine" of Mr. Calhoun. He takes ground here exactly opposite to Mr. Hamilton and the *Federalist*, maintaining still "that there is no immediate communication between the individual citizens of a state and the general government. The relation between them is through the state." (Letter to Gov. Hamilton.) This being true, the governmental function proper, viz., that of authority to bind the private wills and consciences of personal subjects, falls to the ground, and nothing, after all, is really gained by the Constitution. Still we have no government as before, but only a league.

The claim of Mr. Calhoun is perfectly unhistorical and against even the letter of the Constitution beside. Has the man who wants a patent for his new invention or a copyright for his book, no immediate relation to the general government? Has the smuggler, the counterfeiter of national bills and coins, the perpetrator of treason, the suitor of one state claiming dues of the citizens of another, – have none of these, and ten thousand others, expressly provided for in the Constitution, no relation to the general government except through the state?

It is very true that the preamble of the Constitution reads: "We, the people of the United States ordain and establish," and it is also true that they voted the Constitution by states. All the more proper was it that the legislatures had never been appointed to surrender, but only to administer, the State Rights. These rights, in fact, could only be conclusively and absolutely surrendered, just as in fact they were, by the people's vote. It is also true, as Mr. Calhoun so pertinaciously insists, that the surrendering party will naturally expect to be judges themselves of what they have surrendered. And so too, will the party receiving the surrender. And then whose judgment will be strongest in effect, and uppermost in prerogative, that of a little, turbulent, uneasy state faction, or that of a great nation having all its mighty concerns of benefit and blessing embarked in the general unity? It is very true that the great nation thus constituted may usurp to itself powers never granted, just as the small state may factiously deny or claim powers that have been granted. And if it be hard upon the small state when it is oppressed in this manner by the nation, it might also be hard upon a much vaster scale, if the general order of the nation were compelled to submit itself to the bramble judgment of a factious little state and consent after all to be a nation only by sufferance. It must be enough for the states that exactly this kind of risk was submitted to by them, in their vote of surrender, and that no such eminent sovereignty could be created without a consent to the risk. The judgment of the stronger and superior party must prevail. Otherwise, if every state has a right to decide peremptorily on what she has surrendered, she has in fact surrendered nothing. In that simple right asserted, goes down the whole mighty fabric so carefully built, and the sublime fathers and founders have their fool's errand revealed by the discovery that the mere whim or conceit of a faction has even the right to shiver all their work in pieces!

But the root of Mr. Calhoun's famous state rights speculation was not, after all, in the Constitution, as he persistently claimed; it was deeper than he even knew himself; viz., in the fact that he had received, with such implicit trust, the spurious brood of false maxims that began early to be hatched by our new theories of liberty, and took them into his very life with such unquestioning facility, that, without being at all aware of it, he had not even the conception of government left. My words are carefully measured when I say this. I have made exploration of his writings, with this very point in view, and I do not anywhere find that he has the conception of a real government, or of anything higher than a league. Indeed he testifies, in fact, himself that he has not. Thus he writes: (Letter to Gov. Hamilton) "according to our theory, governments are in their nature trusts, and those appointed to administer them, [that is, the magistrates,] trustees, or agents, to execute trust powers. The sovereignty resides elsewhere, in the people, not in the government." What kind, now, of government is that which has no sovereignty in itself, and is under a sovereignty residing elsewhere? And then what kind of government there is in a mere trusteeship, where, as he continually insists, the trust may at any time be revoked by the principal, as in common law, will be seen at a glance. And if any of us should imagine that he is speaking thus only of the general government, let it be observed, that he says, "governments" in the plural; showing that he has no conception of a government even in the states which is more than a trust, terminable at will, and having no real sovereignty!

Now in this wretched figure of statesmanship, you perceive that he only takes up what he conceives to be the accepted doctrine of the country, yielding himself to it with unquestioning trust; for he says, not "according to my theory," but "according to *our* theory." And he had a good right to that kind of reference. What have our orators and public men been saying and repeating for these many years, but what Mr. Jefferson began to say at the first, – that "government has no right but in the consent of the governed;" that "all the powers of magistracy are delegated powers;" that "the people are sovereign;" that "self-government is the inherent right of states;" that "the people are the spring of all authority;" that "the will of the people is the highest law;" – going on thus, without limit, in the ring of as many thousand changes, as our one miserably ambiguous and mischievously untrue maxim will permit! Even such a writer as Mr. Hamilton, wanting above all things a government, was so far taken, unwittingly, by this kind of chaff, as to say: "The fabric of American empire ought to rest on the solid basis of the consent of the people. The streams of national power ought to flow immediately from that pure, original, fountain of all legitimate authority." (*Federalist*, No. XXII.) So generally prevalent, in short, and so unquestioningly received is this kind of maxim, that I run a considerable risk of parting company with this audience, if I do not explain what I mean by dissent from it.

I dissent from it then, because it affirms the possibility of making a real government over man by man; a government, that is, without ascending into the region of moral and religious ideas, or going at all above the mere wills of voters. As if any forty thousand, or forty million wills, taken as mere wills, could have any, the least right to command, or set obligation upon my will. According to our scheme of order under the Constitution, these forty millions of wills may, by their suffrage, choose the magistrates, and that, for us Americans, may be the best scheme possible, the ordinance even of God; but it does not follow that the binding authority of such magistrates is carried over into them by distillation, or transfer, out of the wills of the

people. They only designate, by vote, the men who are to be magistrates, just as they are designated by birth in other countries; and
their oath before God and God's ordinance in the Constitution make
them more than simply designated men; viz., magistrates, with authority to bind.

Such is the general account to be made of our popular elective
function as related to government, or to magisterial right and authority. And all the thousand axioms we repeat, as our political confession, are in this way easily reduced to the small residuum of truth
that belongs to them.

Thus, if we say with Mr. Calhoun, that "government is a trust,"
it is very true that the voters signify a trust in the men when they
vote for them; and so does the woman signify a trust in the man,
when she becomes his wife, but it does not follow that her act of
trust makes him an agent and herself his principal, with a right
to recall his trusteeship when she pleases. She passes over no hus-
bandship by her trust; and as little does the voter pass over a magistracy; neither one nor the other has any such functional right to
pass. To reason with Mr. Calhoun that wherever there is a trust,
that is, a confidence exercised, there is of course a legal trusteeship,
is only to play with words without distinguishing their meaning.
Even God himself would, in this manner, be only our trustee and we
his principals.

So of "the sovereignty of the people," of which we hear so often.
In our scheme of order, the people are certainly arbiters in the matter of election or designation. And so, if the magistrates were designated by lot, a lottery wheel or wheel of fortune might be; but shall
we all begin therefore to say that the sovereignty is in the wheel,
assuming it too for a universal axiom that wheels are inherently
sovereign in states? If we only mean by the sovereignty of the people,
that, in our particular scheme, nobody gets into place save by the
popular vote, that is very well; a grand distinction of our system,
and a sheet anchor of security for our liberties. Still the magistrate
is sovereign over the people, not they over him, having even a divine
right to bind their conscience by his rule.

In the same way, we are to interpret all we have to say of "self-
government," or "the right of self-government." "By nature," says Mr.
Calhoun, following after Mr. Jefferson, "every individual has a right
to govern himself," deducing then all true right in government from
the right of self-government in the individual. He does not see that

the word he plays upon changes meaning, that, by self-government in a person, we mean simply self-keeping, or self-restraining, and suppose no such thing as command or authority at all, unless it be in God, whose all-governing law we are simply restraining ourselves to keep. Our particular people do, indeed, choose their magistrates, and then, not governing the magistrates, the magistrates govern them. Just so near they come to self-government as – not to touch it.

We deceive ourselves again by a like imposture of language, when we say: "that magistrates have only delegated power." Doubtless they are in by election, but there is no passing over of powers in the vote. Not one of the supposed powers was ever in the persons of the voters, or by any possibility could be. They are all from the Constitution, the sanction of God's Head Magistracy going with it.

You perceive, in this manner, how we have been taking down all magistracy from the first by trying to get up authority from below, that is, out of man himself. Our very axioms go for the destruction of magistracy; ignoring always the fact so grandly and even philosophically put by an apostle, when he says: "there is no power but of God." There was never a finer way of government for a people than God has given us, and the special grounds of personal security we have in our equal suffrage, and the choosing of our own magistrates, are the admirable distinctions we may fitly value and cherish. Still the whole shaping of the fabric is Providential. God, God is in it, everywhere. He is Founder before the founders, training both them and us, and building in the Constitution before it is produced without. Our whole civil order is the ordinance of God saturated all through with flavors of historic religion, sanctioned every way by the sanction, and sanctified by the in-dwelling concourse of God. This it is that crowns the summit of our magistracies, and is going to give us finally the most sacredly binding, most indissoluble government in the world.

But as yet we have not come to this. For a long time we have been trying, as it were, to shake off Providence and law together, and we have so far succeeded that even the conception of government was beginning to be a lost conception. Perhaps these nostrums of atheistic philosphy must needs reveal what is in them before they can be duly corrected. The conceit must be taken out of us, enough to stop us in asserting, for axioms, doctrines that impugn the right of all governments in the world beside; recoiling by a most fit retribution, that takes away even the idea of government as for ourselves.

Be this as it may, we have, at last, come to the point where only blood, much blood, long years of bleeding can resanctify what we have so loosely held and so badly desecrated. To what else could we be descending, for these generations past, when winnowing out, as we have been doing, all the sacred properties and principles of the great fabric God had constructed, and reducing it to a mere budget of "sovereignties," "consents," "trusts," "delegations of power," contrived "balances," and other as feeble pretences of philosophy. And yet we have not got on with our desecrations as fast, and come to the crisis of disruption as soon, as might have been expected. Mr. Calhoun wrote secession, but did not live to see it. Strange to say, it did not come half soon enough to meet the flash expectation of Mr. Jefferson himself. With a lightness quite unworthy of a great statesman, he says: "The late rebellion in Massachusetts, 'the Shay rebellion,' has given more alarm than I think it should have done. Calculate that one rebellion in thirteen states in the course of eleven years, is but one for each state in a centry and a half. No country should be so long without a revolution." (Vol. II, p. 331.) And taking his French principles of government no one ever would be; it would have a revolution every year.

Be that as it may, the fearful time has finally come. By the unwisdoms put upon it in the name of philosophy, and the state-right speculation that much admired philosophy has nourished, our noble fabric has been fatally weakened, and is now for the present only a possibility, or government in abeyance. And so the great third crisis of which I am to speak is upon us.

Let us see then, how we are now going to complete and establish the state of government. To get these false axioms qualified, or expelled, so as to let in the rule of government, and make it solid in the people's heart for ages to come, saving all that is genuine, all that is free, is a truly difficult matter; but it will now be done. Let it be our thanksgiving to-day, that we can distinguish the manner and be certified of the result.

In the first place, what are we doing but exactly this,—fighting out the most pestilent heresy of the nation, that which, under the plausible name of "state rights," has taken away every semblance of right in the government; that which revokes every function of law without so much as a pretext of grievance? We are saying continually that slavery is the cause of the rebellion, and it is true; but slavery could never have drawn out a pin of the public order, if every pin had not been first loosened by the false maxims repeated, every bond of unity and dignity shivered by the pretentious usurpations of the state rights arguments and cabals. What now are we doing? Marching down these arguments, pounding them down with artillery, never to stop marching, or stop pounding, till they are trampled so low and ground so fine that no search can find them. Our issue is made up, we are going to have a government, – no more by sufferance, but a government.

We are going also to vindicate the supremacy of the law, just where it broke down. We chose a President not liked in certain quarters. Without one pretended injury from him, whole states rebelled. Now we have chosen him again, and the issue is made up, not upon some other, but upon him. They shall come back thus and submit themselves to him at the very point of their outbreak, and the sacred right of election shall be vindicated. So that as he stole into Washington to assume his office, the leaders of rebellion may steal out of the land, if they can, to bemoan as exiles the ignominy of their treason, and die with the stamp of God's visible frown upon their awful crime.

In the terrible contest waged, the government meantime is girding itself up in decision, and wrestling like a giant with every sort of foe; with conspiracies, treacheries, factions secret, agitations public, midnight arsons, foemen in the bush, armies in the field. The grapple of law is upon us, and we see that government, after all, is somewhat of a reality even with us. We thought we could do as we pleased, and were all sovereigns. We saw velvet gloves on all magistracy. Poor Mr. Buchanan did not know any thing he could do to coerce a state! We wake up now in the discovery that our goverment has, after all, some thunder in it. That thunder too, is going to roll its reverberations down through all our future history, and what we now feel is going to be felt, a hundred fold more deeply, as long ages hence, that we have the strongest, firmest government in the world.

Again, it is a vast and mighty schooling of authority that we have in our armies. Nothing goes by consent, or trust, or individual sovereignty here. The power is not delegated here and liable to be recalled. Authority here lifts every foot by the drum-beat; defies all weather, and water, and mud, and swamp; forbids even hunger and sleep; and squaring the massed legions, hurls them in the face of gunpowder and over the flaming edges of defence. This it was, this military drill, so exact and sharp and systematic, that made the Romans, always at war, the great law nation of the earth. This is the kind of lesson we are taking by the million now, and the result will be a great moral intoning of our allegiance, such as we could never have had from any other discipline. Why, that single flag of ours means even more to us now than the Constitution of the United States did four years ago. And the man who should set himself to get one stripe or star out of it would fare as Mr. Calhoun did not, in that life-long public advocacy by which he dismembered the Union itself.

Slavery again, we are dealing death blows upon that. I say not how it shall go, but go it must; nay, it is already broken to the fall, if we touch it by no civil action whatever. No human power under heaven can put it on its feet again and make it stand. What too, are we all beginning to say, but to add our hearty Amen to its final departure? There was never a funeral where the mourners were so many and so happy. We breathe more freely, as soon as we begin to think that human slavery is gone. We are clear thus of that miserable hypocrisy to our own first principles, that has so long shamed our feeling and made our very government seem hollow. We touch bottom now in moral ideas, and do not skim the surface any longer in lying platitudes that we do not ourselves respect. The demoralizations are all stopped, and we feel it in us to be true for liberty and right, true for the law, and the good, great government our God has given us.

Meantime, what are we doing so constantly, and in so many ways, to invoke the sanctions of God and religion? We are not wanting, any of us, to get our affairs away from God as we used to be. We associate God and religion with all that we are fighting for, and we are not satisfied with any mere human atheistic way of speaking as to means, or measures, or battles, or victories, or great deeds to win them. Our cause, we love to think, is especially God's, and so we are connecting all most sacred impressions with our government itself, weaving in a woof of holy feeling among all the fibres of our constitutional policy and government. We think much of the righteous men who have gone before us, and of their prayers descending upon us, and the sacred charges they have committed to us. There is an immense praying too by day and by night in all parts of the country; wives, mothers, children, fathers, brothers, praying for the dear ones they have sent to the field, for the commanders, for the cause; soldiers fighting and praying together, and many of them learning even in the field to pray and catch heroic fire from God. Oh! it is religion, it is God! Every drum-beat is a hymn, the cannon thunder God, the electric silence, darting victory along the wires, is the inaudible greeting of God's favoring word and purpose.

And, lest we should forget the religious mood of the time, what forbids that, if we go into the revision of the Constitution advocated by many, we take just pains to record our thanksgiving in it, by inserting in the preamble some fit recognition of God? Not that we are to think it a matter of consequence to compliment God by inserting there his name; not that we are to think of inscribing there some evangelic article of doctrine; it must be enough, – and so much ought to be done as a matter of philosophic conviction, – to cut off all our noxious theories of government by man, and make it the recorded sentiment of the nation that all true authority in law is of a moral nature, and stands in allegiance to God.

How certainly, again, last of all, do we consecrate or hallow any thing that we make sacrifices for! And what people of the world ever made such sacrifices of labor, and money, and life, as we have made for the integrity of our institutions? How many of our choicest, noblest youth, have yielded up their lives in the field? How many commanders, who were taking their place with the world's great heroes, have fallen to be mourned by a sorrowing country? Blood, blood, rivers of blood, have bathed our hundred battle-fields and sprinkled the horns of our altars! Without this shedding of blood, how could the violated order be sanctified? And to see the maimed bodies, and the disfigured, once noble forms, and go into the desolate homes, and listen to the plaint of the mourning children, – Oh! it is a sacrifice how great that we are making! This is the price we are willing to pay for our country and its laws.

And what shall be the result? One only result can there be. Nothing can be so evident as that we are now in a way to have our free institutions crowned and consummated. A great problem it was to connect authority with so great freedom. The free maxims we began with and took with no qualification were continually demoralizing our conceptions. The government had but a feeble connection with moral ideas. Now it is to be the ordinance of God, and nothing is to have a finer sound of truth for the ages to come, I trust, than that famous opening of the 13th chapter of the epistle to the Romans: "Let every soul be subject unto the higher powers; for there is no power but of God." And when we have come to this, there is no government on earth that compares for strength with ours. Nay it has about as nearly proved itself already in that figure as it could be desired to do. We did not know how strong it was before. Nobody had any conception of the immense strain it could bear. How bright is the future now of such a government and nation! Hallowed by so many battle-fields, and these by the tribute of so many histories, and sung by so many songs of the great poets of the future, how dear, and sacred, and glorious will it be! And God be thanked it was our privilege to live in this great day of crisis, this always-to-be-called heroic age of the republic!

Let no one imagine that here we shall have reached the goal of our progress. Now that government has ceased to be itself a demoralizer, as it has hitherto been, we may look even for a new-begun growth in the moral and religious habit of the nation. What many have been fearing, with so great and even rational dread, a final collapse in public vice and anarchy, will be a destroying angel passed by. There will, instead, be a great and sublime progress in character begun. There will be less and less need of government, because the moral right of what we have is felt. And as what we do as right is always free, we shall grow more free as the centuries pass, till perhaps, even government itself may lapse in the freedom of a righteousness consummated in God.

Assigning Guilt and Punishment

As the war wound down and it became certain that the Union would be preserved, Northern preachers struggled with and were divided over the question as to how the defeated South should be treated. Some emphasized stern justice, condemnation, and punishment; others spoke more of reconciliation, forgiveness, and leniency. The Rev. S. F. Bliss, on April 9, 1865, preaching at the Universalist Church at Barre, Vermont, asked for understanding toward the South. "We have no right," he declared, "to mingle with our gladness [at the close of the war] any emotions of exultation over our vanquished foe; any glorying in their shame. We ought to remember that we have been accomplices in the crime that has brought this ruin upon them."[1]

Following the assassination of President Lincoln, however, voices of conciliation and leniency markedly decreased in the North, and most pulpits thundered that stern justice must be administered upon the South. The Rev. Leonard Swain of the Central Congregational Church in Providence, Rhode Island, spoke of this change in attitude in a sermon delivered on the Sunday following Lincoln's death:

> We had overpowered our enemy, and now we were to use magnanimity and mercy, and waving all further retribution, we were to leave him to be punished by his own reflections, while we on our part, hastened to welcome back to the family circle. . . . All this is brought to an end at once and forever by the dreadful event which hangs all the sanctuaries of God in mourning to-day.[2]

Thus, after the assassination many Northern sermons were filled with anger toward the South, demanding swift and severe retribution. George Dana Boardman, in a sermon at the First Baptist Church of Philadelphia, called for a swift punishment upon all Southern leaders: "Unquestionably, if ever the halter was a fit instrument for ridding the earth of monsters, it is the case of these murderers, fiendish traitors, who inaugurated and guided this colossal and gory treason."[3] On April 16, 1865, the Rev. J. B. Wentworth delivered a similar message at St. Mark's Methodist Episcopal Church in Buffalo.

> These traitors are guilty of the highest crime known to human law. . . . To pardon their crimes would be a treason to civil justice. . . . It is necessary that these great villains should be executed according to the law, in order to impress upon the public's consciousness the idea that Justice is the basis of the state.[4]

One of the most vitriolic of all attacks leveled upon the South by a Northern preacher was delivered by Alonzo Quint at the North Congregational Church in New Bedford, on April 16, 1865. "Carry your perjuries to other shores," exclaimed Quint; "England is a good place for you. This land is sick of your presence. You are a stench in the nostrils of honest men. Go, Virginian descendants of transported convicts. Go, you who have lived by oppression and robbery. Never return. Your heritage is gone. Return, and the rope awaits your first step upon our shores."[5]

Several of the Northern preachers made a careful distinction between Southern leaders and the masses. George Dana Boardman wanted to banish all Southern leaders from the borders of the nation, but to "speak words of forgiveness and good to the multitudes they have duped."[6] Leonard Swain echoed a similar theme. "Let the leaders of the rebellion," he declared, "or a suitable number of them, be tried, sentenced, and executed for treason. . . . Then justice, having had its place, and the majesty of the law having been honored, mercy may have its exercise, and the people of the rebellious states be forgiven."[7] At the East Congregational Church of Ware, Massachusetts, A.E. P. Perkins demanded that certain Southern political leaders never hold office again. "The idea," fumed Perkins,

> that such men as Breckenridge, Yulee, Benjamin, Hunter, Mason, Toombs, Slidell, and others like them, infamous for perjury and treason, should ever, by any possibility, appear in the halls of Congress, or upon the judicial bench, or should represent us in foreign courts, as they may do if they are restored to their full civil standing, is too great an outrage to every sentiment of decency and patriotism, even for a moment to be entertained.[8]

Two Southern leaders who seem to have come in for special attention by Northern preachers were Jefferson Davis and Robert E. Lee. Dunham has summarized the postwar attitudes of the Northern clerics toward Jefferson Davis.

> The Northern Clergy, who discussed Davis in their sermons, editorials and articles christened him the arch criminal, to be slaughtered as a guilty scape-goat for the sins of his people for which he was responsible. Hemp was a fitting adornment for this public example. There was also a minor amendment to the penalty of hanging; banishment or exile.[9]

The verbal attacks on Robert E. Lee were not as universal as those on Jefferson Davis, but the attacks that were leveled were severe in nature. Justin R. Fulton, pastor of Tremont Temple (Baptist) in Boston, made a reply to those in the North who praised the fighting ability of Lee. "We cannot bear to hear," he exclaimed, "such men as Robert E. Lee, Judge Campbell, and others praised. The blood of our starved brothers, in different rebel prisons, cries out against them. . . . It is no honor to rebel, and to have bravely fought. Fighting in support of a crime is murder."[10] Gilbert Haven, a Methodist minister from Boston, accused Lee of complicity in Lincoln's assassination. Booth "was but the dagger's point," said Haven; "Lee [was] its polished handle. . . . The yet unharmed general attempted to assassinate a nation. . . . He, too, is a murderer."[11] Dunham has written of the accusations Northern preachers made toward the noted Southern general: "Lee was thus responsible for military slaughter, for the starvation of Northern prisoners, for dishonesty in violating his oath to support the United States, for being a traitor and a rebel, and fighting in a criminal and murderous cause."[12] Thus, most Northern clergymen who orated on Lee demanded swift, sure, and stern punishment for the Southern commander.

Some Northern preachers were particularly harsh in their judgments of their Southern counterparts. Southern clergymen were denounced as false prophets, the chief advocates of slavery, the most ardent supporters of secession and war, and the primary architects of hatred and slander. The Rev. Lyman Abbott, who would succeed Henry Ward Beecher as the minister of Plymouth Church in Brooklyn, spoke of the apostate Southern clergy.

But as for me, I would rather trust the Southern soldier, and as readily receive the Southern politician, as reinstate the Southern clergy. . . . We cannot trust the Gospel of liberty and humanity to Dr. Hoge in Virginia, or Dr. Palmer in New Orleans. We might better intrust the civil government with Vance in North Carolina.[13]

In September of 1865 the *Christian Secretary* (Baptist) of Hartford, Connecticut, accused Southern ministers of still holding to their proslavery and secessionist dreams.

The assertion that the clergy of the South adhere more obstinately to the lost cause of rebellion than the politicans is doubtless true. They went into it on principle . . . that it was their duty, in order to save the divine institution of slavery, and they have not yet given up the argument, although divine Providence has abandoned the institution. . . . We make the record with no malice toward the parties concerned, but we do earnestly wish that they might see the error of their position, and abandon it. That they will see it if they live long enough, we have no doubt.[14]

The Northern clerics wanted it known that their demands for retributive justice stemmed only from high and noble motives, and not the desire for revenge. On April 16, 1865, Charles S. Robinson, at the First Presbyterian Church of Brooklyn, remarked that judgment toward the South must not be administered from motives of revenge, but retribution.[15] Richard Eddy, a Universalist from Philadelphia, asserted: "Justice shall have its course with those who instigated and led this Rebellion. I speak not of revenge . . . but the justice which comes from judicial trial, the execution of the penalty which the law has provided for treason."[16] E. S. Johnston, minister of the Second English Evangelical Lutheran Church of Harrisburg, Pennsylvania, declared that it was God who wanted vengeance to be executed upon the South and mortals must not hinder it. "Vengeance," Johnston said, "belongs to God. To us as a Government he has entrusted the execution of his punishments on the guilty. It is neither wise nor safe for us to arrest the vengeance which does not belong to us, but to God."[17]

The ministers offered several suggestions for the reconstruction of the South. In addition to the punishment of Confederate leaders, the preachers suggested a variety of remedies for what they perceived as the South's ills. Some advocated a virtual military dictatorship over the South. A reordering of Southern political arrangements was imperative. Many, perhaps most, Northern clergy advocated black suffrage. Others called for a religious reconstruction of the South of which Northern preachers would be the chief architects. Blacks and poor whites were looked upon as fields ripe for a missionary harvest. Henry B. Smith called for a peace plan that involved the elimination of the Southern "caste" system and the introduction of Northern churches and institutions of philanthropy into the South. "Especially," Smith emphasized, "must we use all means to raise up the class of freedmen to the dignity and responsibilities of their new positions, as men and as citizens."[18]

The concern for the freedmen was echoed in many 1865 Northern sermons. In April, Henry Martyn Dexter, who would later become a noted church historian, delivered a sermon in which he spoke of the necessity of dividing rebel lands among the former slaves. Yet, he cautioned, the government must not interfere with questions of social equality. "If we can trust the grass to grow," said Dexter, "and the trees to blossom and bear fruit . . . we can trust the great mass of emancipated negroes to become thrifty farmers and mechanics, and valuable members of the great industrial body, by natural promptings of opportunity and self-interest, in the propitious air of freedom."[19] In June, Henry L. Edwards, at the Congregational Church of South Abingdon, Massachusetts, called for black rights. "And let us give," said Edwards, "the long degraded negro his due. Give him the Bible, and the ballot, as well as the bullet. If he has used the one as well as we, he will the other. . . . Qualify the freedman to read, and write, and vote, as soon as possible, and let him make the most of himself that he can."[20]

Though many Northern preachers had expressed great interest in emancipation of blacks, there was less concern about social equality. Henry Ward Beecher may have been typical in this regard. In a sermon delivered on October 29, 1865, at the Plymouth Church, after speaking about the necessity of the abolition of slavery, Beecher declared that abolition, however, did not translate into social equality. "Declaring the colored man's right to citizenship in this country," said Beecher, "does not make him your equal socially. . . . I have never seen the time when I desired black people and white people to intermarry." Saying that he doubted there would be universal suffrage in the South, Beecher affirmed that he advocated property and educational tests as qualifications for voting – the very qualifications that would endure for the next one hundred years in the South. Beecher exclaimed: "I do not at once expect to see universal suffrage in the South; but if the Southern people will not agree to universal suffrage, let it be understood that there shall be a property and educational qualification."[21]

In this same sermon Beecher demonstrated that he was in the minority of Northern ministers by asking for leniency and charity toward and reconciliation with the South.

> Now that war has ceased from our midst, nothing can better crown its victories than a generous and trustful spirit on the part of the citizens of this nation toward those who have been in error. And if I have not in past days been delinquent in the duty of defending liberty against the assaults of men . . . so now I am glad, on the other hand, to be early and equally persistent in advocating lenity, charity, sympathy, and, as far as I may in consistence with duty, forgetfulness.

Dunham has written that "the conciliatory attitude of Dr. Beecher represented only a minority of Northern Clergy. The vast majority shared the opposite views."[22]

Washington Gladden, "father of the social gospel," was another who consistently asked for compassion in the treatment of the South. On the Sunday following Lee's surrender to Grant, Gladden implored:

> I must firmly believe that by a hearty and considerate kindness to the southern people we can restore the old relations of amity; nay, that we can establish new relations of friendship which shall be far closer and more enduring than the old ones were. . . . There is room for the exercise of a true chivalry, – opportunity to show our southern friends that we know how tender a feeling is wounded pride, and how to treat it with the gentleness and respect that are the only medicine adequate to its cure."[23]

Gladden recalled that his appeal for a conciliatory approach toward the South fell mostly upon deaf ears: "Of the few hundred who listened, a score may have been convinced; but a voice like this affected the raging of the populace about as much as the chirping of the swallows on the telegraph pole affects the motion of the Twentieth Century Limited." Beecher and Gladden were not expressing the dominant and popular Northern attitude. Gladden seemed well aware of this.

Over time, however, the majority of Northern preachers began to adopt a position closer to Beecher's on reconstruction and the role of blacks in the South. In 1866 Beecher declared that he was generally satisfied with the progress of reconstruction and once again emphasized that it would take time for the freedmen to become the social equals of whites.

> Civilization is a growth. None can escape that forty years in the wilderness who travel from the Egypt of ignorance to the promised land of civilization. The freedmen must take their march. I have full faith in the results. If they have the stamina to undergo hardships which every uncivilized people has undergone in its upward progress they will, in due time, take their place among us.[24]

Beecher failed to say what their "place" was, or how long "in due time" was supposed to be. It has been noted that Beecher didn't believe that citizenship made the freed slave the social equal of whites. Such racial views help to explain why Beecher could support President Johnson's veto of the Freedman's Bureau, and why he did not press for full black suffrage without restrictions. The black man was on his own and he must prove himself. "For I tell you," intoned Beecher, "all the laws in the world cannot bolster a man up so as to place him any higher than his own moral worth and natural forces put him."[25]

In taking such a position, Beecher stood with an increasing number of the Northern clergy. McKivigan has written of the soft support for blacks among Northern ministers. After saying that the primary motive for most Northern clergy in taking a stand against slavery was expediency rather than true antislavery commitment, McKivigan concluded: "Because of these fragile origins, the churches' commitment to the welfare of blacks proved no better than that of other northern institutions to weather the storms of Reconstruction."[26]

An example of a clergyman who was once an ardent antislavery proponent, but after the war lost interest in the black cause, was the Unitarian Thomas Wentworth Higginson. Greatly influenced by Theodore Parker, he led an assault on the Boston Courthouse to free a fugitive slave in 1854. In 1856 he went to Kansas, took up arms, and fought for the free-state forces. He helped to subsidize John Brown and became an officer in the Union army after the war began. Yet soon after the war, George M. Frederickson asserts, Higginson became disinterested in the freedmen's cause, and showed "surprisingly little interest in the problems of Reconstruction after 1868."

> He made no significant contribution to the discussion of events in the South until 1878, when he made a tour of South Carolina to inquire

into the condition of the freedmen under "conservative" rule. Higginson found all going well enough for the Negro, despite the fact that he was now at the mercy of the Southern whites. His final answer to the great problems to which he had devoted many years as an abolitionist and commander of Negro troops was "local self-government" for the Southern states, trusting to the benevolence of Southern gentlemen . . . or, in the event that matters got out of hand, to the ability of the Negro to emigrate from areas where his life was intolerable.[27]

Frederickson concluded that Higginson was typical of many Northern intellectuals who "ignored the whole problem and turned to other things."

The sermon that concludes this chapter was delivered by the Rev. Robert Lowry, a Baptist minister, on Easter Sunday of 1865 — two days after the assassination of Lincoln. Understandably somber in tone, the sermon expressed the people's love and admiration for Lincoln: "How much we loved him. . . . He was God's gift for the crisis. . . . He was the appointed instrument of God." An interesting side note in the sermon is the need Lowry felt to apologize for Lincoln attending a theater. "It cannot be said that the President went to the theatre because he loved to be there." The sermon expressed great expectations for the new President, Andrew Johnson. This was a common sentiment that would shortly turn to bitterness as the clergy began to perceive that Johnson was far too lenient in his plans for the South. Toward the end of the sermon Lowry, apparently with great agitation, proclaimed that the assassination had united the North in demanding a harsh justice upon the South. "We have lost all sentiment of *clemency*. . . . There is one deep, loud cry for *justice!*"

NOTES

1. Quoted in Chester Forrester Dunham, *The Attitude of the Northern Clergy Toward the South 1860–1865* (Philadelphia: Porcupine Press, 1974), 168.
2. *A Nation's Sorrow* (Providence: n.p., 1865).
3. *Addresses* (Philadelphia: Sherman & Co., 1865), 18–19.
4. *A Discourse on the Death of Abraham Lincoln* (Buffalo: Matthews and Warren, 1865).
5. *Southern Chivalry and What the Nation Ought to Do with It* (New Bedford, MA: Mercury Job Press, 1865).
6. *Addresses*, 20.
7. *A Nation's Sorrow*.

8. *Thanksgiving Sermon* (Boston: T. R. Marvin and Sons, 1865).

9. Dunham, *Attitude of the Northern Clergy*, 180.

10. *Radicalism* (Boston: J. E. Tilton, 1865).

11. *A Memorial Discourse on the Character and Career of Abraham Lincoln* (Boston: James Magee, 1865).

12. Dunham, *Attitude of the Northern Clergy*, 183.

13. *Attitude of the Northern Clergy*, 195. Palmer will be referred to several times in Part II of this book. Moses Drury Hoge was installed as the first pastor of the Second Presbyterian Church of Richmond in 1845, a position he held until his death in 1899. Under his leadership the church became one of the most influential in the Presbyterian denomination. During the Civil War he served as a volunteer chaplain while carrying on his own church work. In 1862 he ran the blockade from Charleston, and went to England to obtain Bibles and other religious books for the Confederate army. He was an ardent defender of and spokesman for the Confederacy.

14. *Attitude of the Northern Clergy*, 195.

15. *The Martyred President* (New York: J. F. Trowbridge, 1865).

16. *Three Sermons* (Philadelphia: H. G. Leisenring, 1865).

17. *Abraham Lincoln* (Harrisburg: Theo. F. Shaffer, 1865).

18. *Our Martyr President* (New York: Tibbals & Whiting, 1865), 329.

19. *What Ought to Be Done with the Freedmen and with the Rebels?* (Boston: Nichols and Noyes, 1865).

20. *Discourse Commemorative of Our Illustrious Martyr* (Boston: Wright and Potter, 1865).

21. "Conditions of a Restored Union," *Patriotic Addresses* (New York: Fords, Howard & Hulbert, 1891), 713–35.

22. *Attitude of the Northern Clergy*, 182–83.

23. *Recollections* (Boston: Houghton Mifflin, 1909), 147–53.

24. *Patriotic Addresses*, 741.

25. *Patriotic Addresses*, 731.

26. John R. McKivigan, *The War Against Proslavery Religion: Abolitionism and the Northern Churches, 1830–1865* (Ithaca: Cornell University Press, 1984), 200.

27. George M. Frederickson, *The Inner Civil War: Northern Intellectuals and the Crisis of the Union* (New York: Harper, 1965), 195.

Sermon

Robert Lowry

April 16, 1865

And the victory that day was turned into mourning, unto all the people.
— 2d. Samuel XIX, 2 —

You do not expect a sermon to-day. I have no sermon to give you. The air is laden with sorrow, and our hearts are plunged together in one common grief. The mind refuses to think of anything but the great public calamity. Our dear, good President is dead! We are all mourners today. It is not for me to comfort you; we can only weep together in our overwhelming family bereavement.

We have looked forward to this day as the Resurrection Sunday of our Lord. We had adjusted our minds to the contemplation of the event, which broke the seals of the dark world, and opened up life and immortality to the sons of men. But the smile has fled from our faces to-day. We weep as at a burial, though we stand by the empty grave of our Savior. There is no jubilant music from the organ to-day. There is no glad song of victory on our tongues to-day. No bright flowers of gladness decorate our church to-day but, instead, we sob forth our funereal dirges. We cover our faces and drop our bitterest tears. We hang these walls with the deep drapery of woe. We droop our beautiful flag over the pulpit, the gaze on its craped folds till our eyes cannot see it for the tears that blind them. Why does the sun shine to-day? It seems to mock us with its brightness. We could have wished that the heavens had been hung in black, and the clouds had wept their sympathy. We have no heart for sunshine. We are prostrate in our profoundest grief.

We did not know how much we loved him. We have talked of his geniality, his tender-heartedness, his patient endurance, his broad common sense; but we thought of these qualities with the quiet appreciation which attends familiarity. We only learn his great worth when he is taken from us. We feel now how good a man he was, how great, how noble.

Matthew Simpson et al., *Our Martyr President, Abraham Lincoln: Voices from the Pulpit of New York and Brooklyn* (New York: Tibbals & Whiting, 1865), 303–315.

Four years ago the people called him to preside over a country drifting toward a whirlpool. It was a time when the largest experience, the clearest statesmanship, and the most intelligent tact were scarcely adequate to meet the appalling demands of the crisis. He went to Washington, taking with him neither policy, nor statecraft, nor the learning of the schools; but he carried there a lofty patriotism, a sterling honesty, and a full American manhood. The work before him was not one of courtly genuflexion in the reception room. The time for fresh thoughts and manly vigor had come. He was God's gift for the crisis. We did not all think so then. The surge of popular excitement sometimes swept far beyond the cool stand-point of the President. When rebellion seemed to be strengthening itself in every point, and even asserting superior prowess on the battle-field, there were not wanting those who clamored for this policy and that, and poured the vials of their hasty anger on the head of the patient President. But no menace of friend or foe could drive him into a policy, when the essential elements of a policy that would endure had not yet germinated. He stood amid the conflict of passion and opinion, as one who felt that the issues of the problem were with him. And with this temper he has filled the years of his administration. He had learnt that "he that ruleth his spirit is better than he that taketh a city." How well he has performed his task, a mourning nation is now ready to acknowledge.

There was not a nerve in his body that did not thrill with love for the Union. He lived only for the Union. If a commander was appointed or deposed, it was that the Union might the better be defended. If a change was made in the cabinet, it was in subserviency to the interests of the Union. If the just demands of the government on foreign powers were held in abeyance, the integrity of the Union was the all-controlling motive. In the early stages of the rebellion he announced that, with slavery or without slavery, the Union must be saved. To this sole end he gave his wearisome days and sleepless nights. For this consummation he issued his proclamations, or withheld his signature from the laws of Congress. While it was possible to preserve the unity of the nation without invading the institutions of the States, he forbore to interfere with domestic laws. When it was evident that the salvation of the Union demanded the extirpation of human bondage, he did not hesitate to write the immortal paper that gave freedom to four millions of enslaved humanity.

If the people were slow to give him all their confidence, they learnt at last to look to him as their worthily-trusted chief. It is seen now that he was the appointed instrument of God, more than even the choice of the people. When this conviction fastened itself on the popular mind, it was not difficult to determine that, in the midst of an unsettled struggle, we should have no change of rulers. There were those who deemed him yet to be below the level of the crisis. But the popular will swept them away like chaff. We said that the man who had conducted us through four years of fearful war, and made himself the target for traitorous hatred, should carry us through to its completion. We elected him for a second term. Not even an opponent possessed of extraordinary personal accomplishments could divert the instinct of the popular heart. All classes accepted the decision of the ballot. We gave ourselves up to no vehement rejoicings, but we cherished a calm satisfaction in the result. We felt that the country was more safe in the hands of its now tried leader, than it could be under any new administration. We looked hopefully for the end.

Nor did we wait long. The expression of the popular will gave nerve to the government, the army, and the people. Faction was silenced, and loyalty became more clearly defined. Rebel sympathizers slunk out of sight, and military combinations closed more effectively on the focal points of the insurrection. With crushing weight fell the final blows. City after city was taken; fort after fort captured; army after army beaten; till the whole loyal land shouted for victory, and gave thanks to God that our beloved country was saved. How gaily our flags leaped up to the mast-head! How joyfully our guns thundered out the rejoicings of the people! How sympathetically our hearts fluttered with the restored banner of Sumter! The heavens were growing brighter every hour. Charleston, the cradle of the rebellion, was a desolate ruin. Richmond, that became its coffin, was a captured city. The insurgent government were fleeing before our arms. The rebel chief had become a fugitive from the justice that pursued him. The bastard rag that flaunted its insolent folds in the sight of Washington, hid itself from the face of the national banner. The rebel hosts that had defended the strongholds of treason for four years, were conquered and shattered. From the subdued capital of the Slave Confederacy, the President sent dispatches to the federal city. O, how glad we have been over the victory! What blessing God has been pouring upon us, till we could scarcely find room to contain it!

And now, behold these emblems of woe! Look at these strong

men weeping! The nation that two days ago surged with joy, now heaves with unutterable grief. The flags creep sadly down to half-mast. There is crape on our banner to-day, and crape on our hearts. We are over-whelmed in our great affliction. We are unable to think calmly, or speak without quivering lips. We are in a paralysis of sorrow. It has come to us in a moment. It has smitten us when we were most jubilant. "The victory this day is turning into mourning, unto all the people." Would that it were only a *rebel son* that had been slain. But the head of the nation has been snatched from us. The friend of the people has fallen. We have lost our father. The kind, the good, the loved ABRAHAM LINCOLN lies dead at the capital. Alas! how can we bear a grief like this!

Shall I speak to you of the honored dead? His glorious deeds are known to us all. He needs no eulogy from the pulpit. His sublime life is cherished in the hearts of his countrymen. His death of martyrdom will cover his name with *immortelles*. Shall I tell you that he was *patriotic*? You know that every heartbeat was devotion to the country. He lived for his country. He died for his country. Who else could have done her so much good in the terrible ordeal of civil war? Whose death could have brought her to such bitter tears, as his?

Shall I tell you of his *humanity*? The columns of the press beam with the records of his tenderness and sympathy. How pathetic was that exhibition of his loving heart at City Point. Six thousand sick and wounded soldiers lay in the hospitals. The President was on his way from Richmond to Washington. The pressure of public business could not deprive him of an interview with these brave defenders of the republic. He moved down the long lines of prostrate men – visiting each cot – taking the sick soldier by the hand – laying his fingers on the pale brow – speaking a kind word to this one and that – till he had shed sunshine in every invalid's heart. In the midst of this philanthropic work, an agent of the Christian Commission approached him with a request that he would give them the pleasure of entertaining him in their tent. "No," replied the warm-hearted President, "I have only so many hours to stay at City Point, and all that time must be devoted to the soldiers." Dearer to him were the answering smiles of those wounded soldiers, than all the honors which official dignitaries could bestow upon him. How feelingly will those brave men now cherish the memory of that visit, with its tender hand-pressure; and words of affectionate sympathy!

Shall I tell you of his *religious character?* This, from its very nature, has engaged our attention less than his patriotism and his humanity. And yet, how deeply are we concerned in it this morning. We long, as Christians, to follow him beyond the river into whose waters he so suddenly entered. For him there was no death-bed pre-paration. The blessing of a sick chamber, granted to many a soul for reflection and faith, was not vouchsafed to him. Can we look with a cheerful gaze through the death mist that closed so suddenly around him?

I venture to express my conviction that Abraham Lincoln was one of the Lord's people. It is impossible to penetrate the inner life of a man in his position, as we can that of a private and familiar citizen. But there are at our command a few important elements, strengthening a conviction that he had "passed from death unto life." Our lamented President is known to have been a *man of prayer*. It may not be that when, in 1861, he uttered his last request in Spring-field, "pray for me," he grasped the full blessing for which he asked. But never did Christians pray for a ruler more sincerely and more importantly, than for our over-burdened President during the last four years. And if the White House has not heretofore been regarded as holding intercourse with the court of heaven, it is certain that for months past its walls have looked on the bent form of the Chief Magistrate invoking the grace of Almighty God.

A clergyman in New York, having business with the President, sought an interview early in the morning. Being detained in the waiting-room longer than seemed to be indispensable at that time of day, he inquired the reason of the President's non-appearance. He was answered, that this hour was employed by the President in the reading of the Scriptures and prayer, and no interruption would be permitted until these sacred exercises had closed.

When little Willie Lincoln passed from earth, the mind of the bereaved father was deeply affected by thoughts of death. But the vortex of public duties held him from pursuing the serious thoughts to which his mind had been directed. But when he stood on the battle-field of Gettysburg, and beheld the graves of the brave men who had gone down to death for the principles of which he was the exponent, such a sense of the presence of God and of his own unworthiness took possession of his soul, as to overwhelm him. From that day he dated his entrance into a new life.

I am told that, a few months ago, a lady, visiting the Presiden-tial mansion, was invited to a seat in the family carriage. In the course of the ride, the conversation turned on the subject of religion. The President was deeply interested, and begged the visitor to describe, as clearly as possible, what was that peculiar state of mind in which one might know himself to be a Christian. She repeated to him the simple story of the cross; and explained, that when a poor sinner, conscious that he could not save himself, *looked to Jesus*, and saw in his death a *full atonement* for the sinner's sins, and *believed* that Christ's death was accepted as a *substitute* for the sinner's death, he felt himself to have been delivered from Divine wrath, and to be "at peace with God through our Lord Jesus Christ." The President replied, in a tone of satisfaction, *"That is just the way I feel."*

Who can read his second Inaugural, and fail to see the evidences of a Christian spirit? What State paper, in all our official literature, ever revealed such sense of Divine justice, and such sublime faith in God? It reads as if the writer had been wandering over the earthly boundary, and drank of the spirit of that better land of which so soon he was to be a resident.

And now I come to meet a question which will disturb every Christian mind. The President was shot in the theatre. We would have had it otherwise. Pulpits will speak of it. The press will comment on it. The people in the streets will talk about it. Let us look at it with a calm judgment.

It cannot be said that the President went to the theatre because he loved to be there. He was not, in the common acceptance of the term, a theatre-goer. It is known that he went with great reluctance. He was in no state of mind to enjoy a scene like that. But the newspapers had announced that the President and General Grant would be there on that evening. The people thronged the house to do honor to the great men who had saved the country. General Grant, who had no time to waste in amusements, left Washington in the evening train, to superintend the removal of his family to Philadelphia. The President knew that the people would be disappointed, if they saw neither of the faces that they delighted to honor. Weary as he was, he decided to go. He went, not to see a comedy, but *to gratify the people*. If he had a weakness, it was that he might contribute to the joy of the people. For the people he had spent four toilsome years in lofty self-abnegation. For the people he gave up his life on the night of that fatal Friday.

There is another consideration. In all the countries of Christendom, the rulers are expected to visit the theatre as an *act of state*.

We may deplore the custom, but it is, nevertheless, universal. It is an observance that stretches back through long generations. There is a supposed necessity for it. It is only there that the Executive can receive the formal acclaims of all classes of citizens. There they feel free to give him the tribute of popular plaudits. They cannot so recognize him at church, nor in public receptions, nor in casual appearances abroad. The President's box, like the reception room, is an arrangement of state policy. It is an established point of contact between the chief magistrate and the people. From a religious standpoint, we cannot approve of it. But we must not confound the act of the President, prompted by high considerations of state, with the visit of a private citizen, moved thereunto by the low desire of a mere selfish gratification.

With what profound awe we contemplate this mystery of permissive providence! We close our mouths before the mandate of the Almighty – "Be still, and know that I am God." We cannot understand it. We can only receive it. God employs his instrument according to his own sovereign purpose. His principle of selection confounds all our philosophy. He creates – he destroys. If Moses was the best man to form a great people for a higher nationality, Joshua was a better one to lead them into the promised land. God chose Abraham Lincoln because no other could do his work so well. What if his work were done, and other hands were needed to perfect that he so successfully begun? We have seen too plainly the goodness and wisdom of God in our national affairs, to doubt that he will sanctify to us this awful calamity. We have learnt to acknowledge God in triumph and in defeat, as never before in our history. And God is bringing us closer to himself in this severest of all his dealings. He gave us the best of Presidents. He has taken away our prop, that we might all the more trustfully lean on him. That he will cause "the wrath of man to praise him," who can question? "He hath not dealt so with any nation" as with ours. In this unparalleled affliction he will not desert us. Let us look for the good hand of our God in this calamitous visitation. The tender heart that has been laid low by violence, may have shrunk from the stern duties of the coming time. He was so free from bitter vindictiveness, so prone to lenient dealing even with his enemies, that even the just infliction of punishment on the worst of traitors, might have been too hard a task for a nature so generous and charitable. The good he has done will embalm his name to the latest generation. Thank God that he ever blessed us with Abraham Lincoln!

And who is this new instrument of God, into whose hands thus suddenly and fearfully has been cast the leadership of the nation? No man would have chosen him for President, but God has thrust him on a prostrate, bewildered people. The scene of the inauguration day filled us with shame, and now affects us with apprehension. But, has God mistaken his instrument, or been foiled in his purpose? Already we hear voices that dispel the dark foreboding. General Burnside, Senator Foster, Representative Odell, speak words in the popular ear that lift up the new President from the shadow that enveloped him. We will rally around the new man whom God has given to us. If we prayed for President Lincoln, let us pray all the more for President Johnson. We know there is a providence in all this, and we cannot doubt that God will interpret it to us in his own good time.

Two qualities loom before us in the character of our new chief. First, he is *patriotic*. In the dark hour when the faithful were few, he loved his country too much to love his section. In the very dawning of the insurrection, he stood firm in his place, and denounced the arch traitors who were plotting their country's ruin. He has been tried in the hottest fires of persecution, and betrays no alloy in the gold of his patriotism. We may trust him as possessing the full measure of devotion which the warmest patriot could demand.

Secondly, he is *radical*. We live in times when child's play is criminal. Andrew Johnson has "understanding of the times." He has measured the atrociousness of rebellion. He has sounded the wickedness of slavery. He will make no compromises with traitors. He will not plane down treason into a mere difference of opinion. He is a bold man to meet a bold evil. President Johnson has no glove on his hand. President Johnson has no velvet in his mouth. Treason, to him, is the worst of crimes, and the traitor will struggle against justice in vain.

See the effect on the people of this dastard blow! We are melted down into *unity*. Who speaks a word against Lincoln now? Who stands aloof from the government now? Who dares sympathize with traitors now? We have rubbed out our party lines, and fly together as if nothing had divided us. In a common fraternity of suffering, we weep as with one sorrow, and burn as with one indignation. The government may do anything now against treason, and the people will approve the righteous deed.

We have lost all sentiment of *clemency*. Satan overleaped himself when he lifted the deadly weapon. If we indulged mercy to rebels before, now we have none. There is one deep, loud cry for *justice*! The *animus* of the rebellion has betrayed itself. The bullet that entered our loved President's brain, lodged in the heart of the people. It rankles there. It needed the assassin's foul deed to nerve us to the punishment of traitors. I speak not the name of this heaven-abandoned wretch. I call him THE ASSASSIN. He has lifted us to a new view of this colossal conspiracy. We see the unmitigated turpitude of the huge crime. It is the same spirit that buried our soldiers at Bull Run with faces downward, and made trinkets of their bones – that starved our unhappy prisoners in the pens of Andersonville – that butchered our men in cold blood at Fort Pillow – that devoted the peaceful inhabitants of Lawrence to indiscriminate massacre – that froze our veterans to death on Belle Island – that crowded our officers in the damp dungeons of Richmond, till you could gather the mold from their beards by the handful! And we call on President Johnson to close his hard, hammer hand, and bring it down with its heaviest blows, till he shall crush in the brazen front of this infernal rebellion, and hurl its foul carcass from the land it has polluted!

This land is not large enough to hold the leaders of the rebellion. The flag they have sought to dishonor should not be allowed to cover them. They have forfeited, a thousand times over, the mercy of the government they assailed. And this last and vilest culmination of their crimes puts them beyond the possibility of pardon. Let us make this soil red-hot to the foot of every traitor. Let the warm breath of our holy indignation sweep from our cities every rebel sympathizer. Let us vow, in God's house to-day, that treason shall be destroyed, trunk and branch, root and rootlet, till not one hand be left to give the sword such a vintage of blood again. Then will our land be a land of peace and freedom. Then will our nation be the joy of the whole earth!

Part II:

Southern Sermons

SLAVERY

Even as Northern preachers began their major attacks upon slavery in the 1830s, so Southern pulpits began their strong defense of the institution in the same period of time. The powerful and even defiant proslavery stance of Southern preachers in the 1830s is rather remarkable when it is remembered that most of the Southern evangelical clergy – basically Baptists, Methodists, and Presbyterians, who by the early nineteenth century comprised an overwhelming religious majority in the South[1] – were opposed to slavery in the eighteenth century. In 1784 the Methodists had passed a series of strict rules for the purpose of eliminating slavery from their churches. In 1790 the Virginia General Committee (Baptist) declared slavery to be "a violent deprivation of the rights of nature, and inconsistent with a republican government," and recommended "every legal measure to extirpate the horrid evil from the land." Many Virginia Baptists, however, did not receive the Committee's declaration favorably.[2]

About the turn of the century, as slavery became more firmly entrenched in the South, the Southern pulpits adopted a stance of silence on the issue. Retreating from their earlier antislavery positions, Southern clergy began to affirm that slavery was a civil matter and not a religious concern. This stance, sometimes called "the spirituality of the church," was most likely introduced by Presbyterians in the South, and was soon adopted by most Southern religious bodies. Donald G. Mathews has written that Southern evangelicals developed a kind of litany:

> Slaveholding is a civil institution;
> and we [churches and clergy] will not interfere.
> The character of civil institutions is governed by politics;
> and we will not interfere.
> Politics are beyond the scope of the church;
> and we will not interfere.[3]

James Henley Thornwell, the eminent voice of Southern Presbyterianism, in an 1861 address before the General Assembly of the Presbyterian Church in the Confederate States of America, declared that the church had neither the right nor the competence to deal with the subject of slavery:

> We have no right, as a Church, to enjoin it as a duty, or to condemn it as a sin. . . . The social, civil, political problems connected with this great subject transcend our sphere, as God has not entrusted to his Church the organization of society, the construction of Government, nor the allotment of individuals to their various stations.[4]

Thornwell's position on the necessity of pulpit silence in regard to slavery, along with that of other Southern clergy who proclaimed a similar necessity, was burdened with a major inconsistency. The preachers had not been silent on slavery since the 1830s; quite the contrary, the pulpit had been a primary instrument in the defense of slavery as an institution ordained of God. Thornwell himself had delivered a strong proslavery sermon in 1850 which will be examined at the end of this chapter. The silence imposed was upon those who opposed slavery or espoused emancipation. Loveland has summarized what had happened in the South during the early years of the nineteenth century: "The churches' retreat from antislavery would not have been so important a factor in shaping the southern evangelical view had some ministers in the South continued to voice antislavery opinions. But in the early nineteenth century, preachers who opposed slavery either left the South or fell silent."[5]

An example of Southern unwillingness to even hear a different point of view would be the reaction to Richard Fuller's address before the American Colonization Society on January 21, 1851. Fuller was a noted and popular Baptist minister from South Carolina, who not long before the address had moved to Baltimore. In the speech Fuller was critical of both abolitionism and Southern extremism. He suggested that the South was overly sensitive on the subject of slavery and should allow open debate on the issue. He urged the North to make concessions, and for the South to do the same. The South must realize, exclaimed Fuller, that slavery "fosters indolence and luxury. . . . Slavery is not a good thing, and a thing to be perpetuated." He offered colonization as a "middle ground." Congress should grant money for the purchase of slaves from masters and then pay the passage of these former slaves to Liberia. The previously popular and influential Fuller stirred up great hostility and resentment toward himself throughout the South because of this "middle ground" speech. In spite of efforts to explain and tone down his address, Fuller never regained his previous stature.[6]

What happened in the 1830s to bring about such an uncompromising, and sometimes angry, defense of slavery? For one thing, in August of 1831 a visionary black preacher, Nat Turner, led a slave uprising that resulted in the slaughter of about sixty white Virginians, mostly women and children. It was not lost upon the Southern populace that earlier in the year Garrison had published the first edition of the *Liberator,* which demanded immediate emancipation of the slaves. That Garrison's demands and the Nat Turner revolt were related the South had no doubts. Northern abolitionism was perceived as a dangerous threat to the Southern way of life and its peculiar institution. Ahlstrom has noted that Garrison "did far more than any other man to heighten Southern opposition to emancipation."[7] Frightened and angry, the Southern whites tightened their control over the black population and vigorously defended the practice of slavery. The sermons of the white preachers reflected this emotionally laden Southern response.

Throughout the 1830s, 1840s, 1850s, and Civil War years, the preachers developed several themes in their defense of slavery and the Southern way of life. Different preachers would, of course, choose to put their emphasis upon different points, but the following themes were dominant in Southern preaching during the mid-nineteenth century.

The first, a theme that was the foundation of all other themes for the preachers, was the "discovery" that slavery was a God-ordained, biblically sanctioned institution. Theodore Clapp, in an 1838 sermon at the First Congregational Church in New Orleans, spoke of the transformation in his own life on the subject of slavery, a transformation experienced by many Southern clergymen. He related that after many years of uncertainty, and even involvement in emancipation schemes, he was at last "fully convinced of the rectitude of slavery." According to Clapp, the most significant factor for this revolutionary change was his study of the Scriptures.[8]

In 1837 Samuel Dunwoody, a Methodist preacher from South Carolina, claimed that God, in the Bible, made provision for perpetual slavery. The Negro race was condemned to an existence in slavery. Dunwoody further insisted that Christians were to be obedient to civil authorities, which, for him, meant obedience to the laws and policies which allowed for and protected the existence of slavery. A slaveholder who acted according to the law, said Dunwoody, could not be condemned as a sinner. Therefore, asserted the preacher, the pulpit should be silent on the subject of slavery.[9] Once again, the contradiction!

On November 29, 1860, Benjamin Morgan Palmer, at the prestigious First Presbyterian Church of New Orleans, where he served as pastor, continued the theme. The South had been given a trust by God, he said, "to conserve and to perpetuate the institution of slavery as now existing." The preserving of this trust was a "duty to ourselves, to our slaves, to the world, and to Almighty God." Because of this God-given responsibility, Palmer challenged: "Let the people in all the Southern States . . . reclaim the powers they have delegated. . . . Let them, further, take all the necessary steps looking to separate and independent existence, and initiate measures for framing a new and homogeneous Confederacy."[10] It is important to note that Palmer's belief in slavery as a God-ordained trust led him to advocate secession before it happened. His proposal preceded political action.

During the war years I. T. Tichenor, a Baptist from Alabama, summarized in a sermon the basic biblical texts in support of slavery:

> That slavery is sanctioned by the Bible seems scarcely to admit of a doubt. Founded upon the divine decree that "Canaan should be a servant of servants unto his brethren," existing in the days of the patriarchs, twice spoken of in the ten commandments, with laws written in the New Testament for its regulation, it stands as an institution of God.[11]

A subtheme of the concept that slavery was a God-ordained, biblically sanctioned institution was that those who opposed slavery were anti-God and anti-Bible. Thus, the North in general, and the abolitionists in particular, were castigated as heretics and infidels. Tichenor denounced the North because it demanded "an anti-slavery Constitution, an anti-slavery Bible, and an anti-slavery God."[12] In 1844 W. T. Hamilton delivered a sermon in which abolitionists were denounced as antislavery radicals who should be denied communion with other Christians.[13] Loveland has summarized: "Given the southern evangelicals' insistence that the Bible sanctioned slavery, it is not surprising that they more and more tended to view the sectional controversy as a conflict between those who acknowledged the authority of the Bible and those who repudiated it – in other words, between Christians and infidels."[14]

Yet another theme that was imperative for the justification of slavery was the doctrine of racial inequality. The doctrine held that those of the black race were inferior to those of the white race. The Southern preachers once again turned to their well-used Bibles to support the inequality theme. Through strained exegesis the belief in black inferiority was supported through the biblical stories of the curse of Ham and/or the punishment of Cain.[15]

Doctrines of natural rights and the concept that all men are created equal were anathema to many Southern preachers. In late 1844 and early 1845 the Rev. Richard Fuller, a Southern Baptist minister referred to earlier in this chapter, and the Rev. Francis Wayland, a Northern Baptist clergyman, wrote a series of letters to each other on the subject of slavery. Fuller defended the institution; Wayland opposed it. In one of his letters Fuller, a moderate man by many standards, challenged the idea of natural rights as an argument against slavery. "Government is restraint," he asserted; "the very idea of government includes an abridgement of that personal freedom which a savage has in the forest." Fuller then asked: "Is it, then, necessarily a crime for a government to discriminate between those whom it controls, in the distribution of civil privileges and political liberty? It surely would be prepostrous to affirm this." Fuller continued: "Every government . . . has a right . . . to establish those regulations which shall best promote the good of the whole population."[16]

Other clergy were even more emphatic than Fuller. One said that it was a fallacious concept which held that "all men, simply from the fact of being men, have a natural right to an equal amount of property, or an equal share of personal liberty." People were placed in different circumstances and social relations "under the providence of God." Therefore, "some are rulers, some subjects; some are rich, some poor; some are fathers, some children; some are bond, some free. And if a man is justly and providentially a ruler, he has the rights of a father; and if a slave, only the rights of a slave."[17] It was an order that God had ordained.

Mathews makes the point that many Southern evangelical preachers, in their desire to establish the doctrine of human inequality, insulted and demeaned a majority of their own constituency with the same . . . insensitivity which they usually reserved for talking about black people. In tract upon tract, male writers emphasized the subordination of women as built into the very nature of human society by God himself, citing scripture to that effect and rewarding the submissiveness of women with elaborate praise to her grace, "passive fortitude," and "enduring love."[18]

Mathews then cites the declaration of Frederick Ross, a Presbyterian minister from Huntsville, Alabama, who bound together the subservient positions of slaves and women. "Do you say," asked Ross, "the slave is held to involuntary service? So is the wife. Her relation to her husband, in the immense majority of cases, is made for her, and not by her." He reminded the wives that they, like the slaves, were "under service," and "bound to obey their husbands." Ross continued: "Do you say the slave is sold and bought? So is the wife the world over."[19] Ross, along with many other Southern clergy, spoke and wrote about the inequality of women to justify the position of the inequality of blacks.

There were so many ways in which those of the black race were different from those of the white race. There were anatomical and physiological differences. It was generally held that blacks were less intelligent and more emotional than whites. They were also more sensual and superstitious, less disciplined and less orderly. One had only to look at human behavior in Africa, the original habitat of blacks, to become aware of how different in culture, values, and social mores the blacks were from whites. Africans conducted human sacrifices, ate one another, and "worshipped the devil, practiced witchcraft, and sorcery, disregarded the marriage rites, murdered, swore false, practiced all kinds of dissimulation."[20]

For some Southern preachers blacks were not innately inferior but culturally flawed. Coming from the "dark continent," what more could be expected of them? Whether inferiority had its roots in genetics or culture, blacks could only benefit by their exposure, even as slaves, to the higher and better civilization of the white world. It was a balm for one's conscience to believe that slavery worked for the good of blacks as well as their white masters. In May of 1861 the Southern Baptists declared that the slaves had been "elevated . . . far above the condition of their race in the motherland."[21] E. T. Winkler sermonized that the slaves had been "civilized and christianized out of the depths of barbarism."[22] A Baptist association in Georgia affirmed: "God has placed them [the slaves] here for their good and his glory."[23]

Because a significant number of "inferior" and "degraded" blacks dwelt in the midst of a "highly civilized" white society, there was a need for a well-defined and firmly established social structure to maintain an orderly society.[24] The 1831 Nat Turner revolt in Virginia was all the evidence most Southerners needed for the necessity of maintaining a tight social control within the slave states. The Southern preachers fanned the fires of fear in the South of what would happen if the blacks were loosed from white control. Further slave revolts meant more bloodshed and death, widespread chaos, the complete breakdown of social order, and the rule of anarchy.

The preachers feared rule by the mob, a society where equality was preached and practiced, a culture where social distinctions which imposed order and regulation had collapsed. Some pointed with horror to the French Revolution of the previous century as an example of what happens when the masses gain control and power. James H. Thornwell, in an 1850 sermon, spoke of these issues: "The parties in this conflict are not merely abolitionists and slaveholders – they are atheists, socialists, communists, red republicans, jacobins, on the one side, and the friends of order and regulated freedom on the other. In one word, the world is a battleground – Christianity and Atheism the combatants; and the progress of humanity at stake."[25]

Mathews points out that Southern evangelicals, who justified slavery as a means of establishing order in society, were influenced by Federalist ideas from the eighteenth century. The Federalists, according to Mathews, "supplied southerners with two important intellectual tools for putting together a slaveholding ethic. The first was a body of thought which made room for the principle of social inequality and hierarchy in Republican ideology; the second was a conspiratorial theory of history. Both ideas grew out of Federalist responses to the French Revolution." Mathews continued:

> The dangers of liberty, fraternity, and equality were obviously not perceived by many Americans, and Federalists ... thought they ought to warn their fellow countrymen. Accordingly they argued that Republican institutions were safe only so long as the mob – the mass of people – were controlled by institutions which taught submission to authority, self-restraint, and resignation to social inequality. French Jacobins had mischievously preached the doctrine of equality to a people who could not appreciate the necessity for self-restraint and social disci-

pline, and the result of their wicked irresponsibility was violence and tyranny.[26]

The first sermon at the end of this chapter represents yet another theme emphasized by Southern preachers in those decades before the Civil War — the need of evangelicals to give religious instruction to slaves which would lead to their conversion and a better acceptance of their station in life. The leader and most noted representative of this movement — often referred to as the Mission to Slaves — was the Presbyterian cleric Charles Colcock Jones. Jones, noted as the "Apostle to the Blacks," practiced his mission in Liberty County, Georgia, and through preaching and writing urged that a similar Mission be conducted throughout the South. The sermon included in this volume was delivered in 1831, and in it Jones described his Mission and the rationale for it, sought to answer possible objections to it, and stated those things he expected the Mission to accomplish. Jones in his earlier years had been strongly opposed to slavery, denouncing it as "a violation of all the laws of God and man at once."[27] Over time, however, the Mission became a substitute for emancipation.

Donald Mathews has noted that the objectives of the Mission were threefold.[28] There was, first of all, the "mission to society." Through proper instruction of the slaves the South would become a safer and more orderly society. To those who contended that religious instruction of the slaves might lead to hostility and insurrection, Jones argued in his sermon that quite the opposite would be the effect. "Every intelligent man ought to know," he said, "that there is no more effectual method to present what is suggested by the objector, than to instruct our Servants in the principles of Christianity, to be present ourselves in all their assemblies for religious purposes, and to know who are their teachers." Jones was, as were most Southerners, highly suspicious of black preachers: "We have colored ministers and exhorters, but their numbers are wholly inadequate . . . and while their ministrations are infrequent and conducted in great weakness, there are some of them whose moral character is justly suspected and who may be considered blind leaders of the blind." If white teachers would properly instruct the slaves, Jones's sermon emphasized, "there will be greater subordination and a decrease of crime amongst the Negroes." The Northern abolitionists were quick to condemn this argument as a plot to strengthen the slave system in the South.

The second emphasis was a "mission to masters." The slaves were culturally inferior Africans, but their mistreatment as slaves had exacerbated and perpetuated their inferiority. Only a change in the attitudes and behavior of white masters could bring about a change in blacks. Jones argued that "having reduced them [the slaves] to ignorance, and by our neglect of duty confirmed them in vice, we now quarrel with their stupidity and obduracy."[29] Mathews has summarized the "mission to masters."

> To bridge the chasm between blacks and whites, Evangelical theorists argued, masters first had to take an interest in slaves as persons—a reasonable expectation, really, because the effective control of any work force avoided physical coercion and relied instead upon a sense of mutual support and trust. Masters had to begin the necessary transformation by taking into consideration the slaves' feelings, personal pride, and individual integrity. More specifically, they were told to take an interest in the family life and personal cares of their slaves, and see to it that when discipline was required it was unquestionably fair, a measure designed to reassure everyone concerned that they could count on orderly, rational, predictable government.[30]

In this sermon Jones emphasized that most whites were unaware of the responsibilities that they had to the slaves. "We doubt not," he said, "that there are many of our fellow citizens . . . who have never given themselves the trouble to inquire into the number and nature of those duties which they owe to their Servants, and are in reason and conscience, bound to perform." At another time Jones elaborated even further on those duties:

> In short, if you fail to impress your people with the belief that you are really their friend, and desire their best good for this world as well as for the next, and that you honestly intend to promote it, as far as lies in your power, they cannot, they will not value your instructions. They will view your efforts as hollow-hearted, purely selfish, intended for effect. You desire them to be Christians that you may have less trouble in their management, your work more honestly done, and your pecuniary interest more prospered. "Thou, therefore, which teachest another, teachest thou not thyself?" "First cast the beam out of thine own eye."[31]

A third emphasis was a "mission to slaves." Blacks needed the Gospel, which could only be known fully to them through white religious instruction. Jones sermonized that masters were bound to give their slaves the Gospel "by humanity ... by consistency ... by the spirit of religion, love ... and by the express commandment of God." When the Gospel is faithfully presented to the slaves, not only will spiritual benefits accrue to blacks for time and eternity, but temporal benefits will come to the masters. Jones's sermon states that as a result of biblical instruction, "It will be noticed that obedience is inculcated as a Christian duty, binding on the Servants, and thus the authority of Masters is supported by considerations drawn from eternity.... Will the authority of the Masters be weakened by instructions of this sort? No, it will be strengthened.... For the duty of obedience will never be felt and performed to the extent that we desire it, unless we can bottom it on religious principle." Jones wrote and published a catechism to be used among the blacks. A sample passage went:

Q. Tell me some of God's goodness to you.
A. He gives us father and mother, meat and drink, and clothes to wear; and when we are sick he makes us well.
Q. Is it not great goodness in God to make us live in a Gospel land and to give us his holy word?
A. Yes.[32]

The mission eventually failed. Most masters were not willing to consider the concept that they might have duties and responsibilities to their slaves. Blacks, on the other hand, were not as passive as Jones imagined. Most would not listen to a Gospel that was interpreted for white advantage, or a religion that encouraged black subservience to white masters. The Mission was a major factor in causing the slaves to look more than ever before to ministers of their own race.[33]

The second sermon at the end of this chapter is by James H. Thornwell. Sometimes referred to as the "Calhoun of the Church," Thornwell went north for his theological education. Uncomfortable with the liberal climate of Andover Seminary and the Harvard Divinity School, he returned to his native South Carolina in 1834 without completing his formal theological training. His career included several pastorates, a professorship of metaphysics at South Carolina College, a four-year presidency of the same institution, and a professorship of theology at the Presbyterian Theological Seminary at Columbia. His fame and influence was extended in 1847 when he founded the *Southern Presbyterian Review,* which became a popular and powerful vehicle for the dissemination of his views. He was a leading influence in the organization of the Presbyterian Church in the Confederate States of America. Thornwell died prematurely in 1862 of consumption which had been aggravated by overwork and the excitement of war.

Thornwell did not support the idea of secession until 1860.[34] He then supported secession and later the war, with great vigor until his death. Six weeks before his death, at the time McClellan was beginning what would prove to be a failed threat upon Richmond, Thornwell issued a pamphlet which attempted to awaken the Confederacy as to the crisis it faced. He asserted that Southerners must sacrifice private interests and factionalism if victory was to be accomplished. Should the South lose the war, he warned, her homes would be pillaged, her cities destroyed, her men hanged, and her women would become "the prey of brutal lust." The noble and glorious Southern way of life would pass from this earth.[35]

In 1850 Thornwell delivered the sermon "The Rights and the Duties of Masters," which has become a classic defense of the institution of slavery. The discourse was prepared for and delivered at the dedication of a church which had been erected for the religious instruction of black people. Throughout the sermon Thornwell sought to answer the various charges being made by Northern abolitionists that slavery was immoral and contrary to the spirit of the Gospel. He argued that slavery was not inconsistent with personal rights and moral obligations. Drawing a distinction between a man and his labor, Thornwell contended that though a master owned another's labor, he did not own the laborer. The preacher further contended that a master had the right to discipline his slaves even as society had a right to discipline its erring members. Thornwell viewed slavery as a temporary institution in a fallen world. In the meantime, masters had an obligation to care for their slaves, who were moral human beings, and to preach the Gospel to their slaves in order to prepare them for heaven, where distinctions would cease.

NOTES

1. C. C. Goen has written: "Eighty-two percent of all churches in the eleven states that formed the Confederacy were either Methodist or Baptist." *Broken Churches, Broken Nation* (Macon: Mercer University Press, 1985), 134.

2. Anne C. Loveland, *Southern Evangelicals and the Social Order 1800–1860* (Baton Rouge: Louisiana State University Press, 1980), 191.

3. Donald G. Mathews, *Religion in the Old South* (Chicago: University of Chicago Press, 1977), 157.

4. Quoted in Goen, *Broken Churches*, 165. Goen's book contains a brief but helpful description of the doctrine of "the spirituality of the church" (164–69).

5. Loveland, *Southern Evangelicals and the Social Order*, 192.

6. *Address Before the American Colonization Society* (Baltimore: Office of the Trust Union, 1851).

7. Sydney E. Ahlstrom, *A Religious History of the American People* (New Haven: Yale University Press, 1972), 652.

8. *Slavery* (New Orleans: John Gibson, 1838).

9. *A Sermon upon the Subject of Slavery* (Columbia: S. Weir, 1837).

10. "Slavery a Divine Trust: Duty of the South to Preserve and Perpetuate It," *Fast Day Sermons* (New York: Rudd & Carleton, 1861), 57–80.

11. *Fast Day Sermon* (Montgomery: Montgomery Advertiser Book and Job Printing Office, 1863).

12. *Fast Day Sermon.*

13. *Duties of Masters and Slaves Respectively; or, Domestic Slavery as Sanctioned by the Bible* (Mobile: F. H. Brooks, 1844).

14. Loveland, *Southern Evangelicals and the Social Order*, 261.

15. Donald Mathews has summarized this "imaginative" biblical interpretation: "If one were really imaginative, he could find the origins of black people in the unnatural coupling of the accursed and exiled Cain with a female from among 'pre-Adamites,' who had been created before humanity. For the more traditional bibliophile there was a sufficient explanation in the curse of the drunken Noah upon the descendants of his son, Ham (Africans), because of an invasion of the patriarch's privacy. And a few expositors argued – just to complete the circle no doubt – that Ham had actually married into the race of Cain, thus making blacks twice cursed. That anyone was converted by such explanations is doubtful, for they were merely a way of lending legitimacy to views already shaped by personal experience, psychic need, and social interaction." *Religion in the Old South*, 171.

16. Richard Fuller and Francis Wayland, *Domestic Slavery Considered as a Scriptural Institution* (New York: Lewis Colby, 1845), 147–48.

17. Loveland, *Southern Evangelicals and the Social Order*, 201–02.

18. Mathews, *Religion in the Old South*, 169–70.

19. *Religion in the Old South*, 170. Frederick A. Ross, *Slavery Ordained of God* (Philadelphia: J. B. Lippincott & Company, 1859), 55–58, 124–25.

20. Josiah Priest, *Bible Defense of Slavery: and Origin, Fortunes and History of the Negro Race* (Glasgow, KY: W. S. Brown, M.D., 1852), 228–29. Charles Colcock Jones, the Presbyterian cleric from Liberty County, Georgia, who worked so diligently to establish a sense of community between blacks and whites in the South, confessed that "the degraded moral character of the Negroes" would make community a difficult task to accomplish. "From childhood we have been accustomed to their slovenly, and too frequently, their scanty dress; to their broken English, ignorance, vulgarity, and vice.... Whatever is idle, dissolate, criminal, and worthless attaches to them." Jones did say, however, that white masters must bear some of the responsibility for such undesirable black character-

istics. *Religious Instruction of the Negroes in the United States* (Savannah: Thomas Purse, 1842), 103–04.

21. *Proceedings of the Southern Baptist Convention,* May 10–13, 1861 (Richmond: MacFarlane and Fergusson, 1861), 35.

22. *Duties of the Christian Soldier* (Charleston: A. J. Burke, 1861).

23. *Minutes of the Forty-fifth Anniversary of the Cahaba Baptist Association,* Oct. 18–20, 1862 (Marion: George C. Rogers, Printers, 1862), 11.

24. Prior to the Civil War the eleven Confederate states had a population of approximately nine million; about three and a half million of that number were slaves.

25. *The Rights and the Duties of Masters* (Charleston: Steam Power Press of Walker and James, 1850).

26. Mathews, *Religion in the Old South,* 165. Larry Tise carries the argument even further. He challenges the concept that Southerners adopted their proslavery stance as a response to the abolitionist movement. Rather, the proslavery doctrine grew out of what Tise calls Proslavery Republicanism. His argument is that New England Republicans or Federalists, concerned about the damaging effects of the French Revolution, and desiring to establish order and tradition in early America, supported slavery. When Southerners defended slavery, they heavily borrowed ideas from Federalist writings, writings which were national, not sectional, in character. In a composite biography of 275 proslavery clergymen in the South, Tise demonstrates that the great majority of these clergymen were from the North, were educated in the North, and developed their ideas in the North. Tise's well-researched and very readable book, however, from this writer's perspective raises more questions than it answers. His thesis is fresh, but debatable. *Proslavery: A History of the Defense of Slavery in America, 1701–1840* (Athens: University of Georgia Press, 1987).

27. Quoted in Donald G. Mathews, "Charles Colcock Jones and the Southern Evangelical Crusade to Form a Biracial Community," *The Journal of Southern History* 41 (Aug. 1975): 301.

28. Mathews, *Religion in the Old South,* 140–46.

29. Quoted in Mathews, "Charles Colcock Jones," 307–08.

30. Mathews, *Religion in the Old South,* 142. Jones gave very specific instructions as to the manner of preaching that would be most effective among the slave population. See Jones, *Religious Instruction of the Negroes in the United States,* 250–62.

31. Jones, *Religious Instruction of the Negroes in the United States,* 187.

32. Charles Colcock Jones, *A Catechism of Scripture, Doctrine, and Practice, for Families and Sabbath Schools, Designed Also for the Oral Instruction of Colored Persons* (Savannah: Thomas Purse, 1837); 4.

33. See chapter 9 below.

34. For the evolution of Thornwell's thoughts on secession, see the following chapter, "Sectionalism and Secession."

35. James W. Silver, *Confederate Morale and Church Propaganda* (New York: Norton, 1957), 83–4.

The Religious Instruction of the Negroes

Charles Colcock Jones

1831

Note: *The following Address has been delivered, within a few weeks, before two Societies formed for the Religious Instruction of the Negroes—one in McIntosh, and the other in Liberty County—and by both Societies it was requested for publication. It is my earnest desire that it may awaken the attention of the public to a subject, long neglected, but of vital importance to us, as citizens of the South, whether we consider it in a civil or in a moral point of view. The Address appears as it was delivered, and refers exclusively to Plantation Negroes.*

And he said unto them, *Go ye into the world and preach the Gospel to every creature.*
—Mark XVI, 15—

Men and Brethren: The Lord Jesus Christ was standing on the Mount of Olives surrounded by his deciples. Beneath them lay Jerusalem with its walls, and palaces, and towers, and holy temple, lighted up by the risen sun; and around, as far as the eye could reach, the cities of Palestine, peering above the foilage of the forests, or standing exposed on the plains; the hills and vallies covered with fields of grain, and vineyards and habitations of men. The work which his Father had given to him to do was now finished. He was about to ascend to the right hand of God. The bright cloud which was to receive him out of their sight, was fast floating along in the clear blue sky, to overshadow the place where he stood. And what now should be his *last* commands to his disciples? He seemed with them from the Mount, to survey the world. He had taught them that He was the Redeemer of the world. He had taught them that the field in which this truth should be sown was the world. Then directing their eyes abroad on the scene before them, and spreading forth his hands over it, he cries out: *Go ye into all the world and preach the Gospel*

(Princeton, NJ: D'Hart & Connolly, 1832).

to every creature. To procure the power and privilege of giving this command, Christ died and rose again.

The disciples were the representatives of his church on earth. The command is to his church, and is of perpetual obligation. It is obligatory not only upon ministers of the church, to whom the office of preaching the Gospel is specially committed; but also upon all members of the church, to whom God has given the ability to support the preaching of the Gospel, or talents that qualify them to become teachers of the unlearned. The command implies that all men in the world, no matter of what nation or complexion or condition, are the moral and accountable creatures of God. That they are *lost,* and need the Gospel of Salvation. Whenever, therefore, any people come within the range of our influence, we, who are acting under this command, have two questions, and but two to settle. *Do they need the Gospel? and, Has God put it in our power to give them the Gospel?* The Negroes of our country come fairly within the range of our influence. We believe that they are men – the creatures of God, and like ourselves are moving onward to the retributions of eternity; and as philanthropists and Christians, we are bound to propose to ourselves and to answer these questions in regard to them.

I. *Do they need the Gospel?*

We can return but one answer to this question, and it is an affirmative one. The description which the Apostle Paul, in his Epistle to the Romans, gives of the Heathen world, will apply, with very little abatement, to our Negroes. They lie, steal, blaspheme; are slothful, envious, malicious, inventors of evil things, deceivers, covenant breakers, implacable, unmerciful. They are greatly wanting in natural affection, improvident, without understanding and grossly immoral. Chastity is an exceeding rare virtue. Polygamy is common, and there is little sacredness attached to the marriage contract. It is entered into for the most part without established forms, and is dissolved at the will of the parties. Nor is there any sacredness attached to the Sabbath. It is a day of idleness and sleep, of sinful amusements, of visiting, or of labor. They are generally temperate through necessity; when ardent spirit can be obtained, they will freely drink it. Numbers of them do not go to church, and cannot tell us who Jesus Christ is, nor have they heard so much as the Ten Commandments read and explained. Of the professors of religion among them, there are many of questionable piety who occasion the different churches great trouble in discipline, for they are extremely ignorant, and frequently are quilty of the grossest vices. We cannot go more fully into the moral condition of these people at present. Indeed, it is unnecessary. Generally speaking, they appear to us to be without Hope and without God in the world. A nation of Heathen in our very midst. And if we will believe the testimony of our own eyes and ears, and the testimony of those who know these people most intimately, we must conclude that they need the Gospel, and need it as much as any people in the world do.

II. *Has God put it into our power to give them the Gospel?*

We think that he has. The civil law does not forbid us to give them the Gospel *orally*. We can therefore employ or permit men to visit our plantations for the purpose of instructing them, or we can undertake to instruct them ourselves. And having our plantations, the time and persons of our servants wholly under our control, we can arrange the manner and frequency of our instructions, as we please, and the period of these instructions with as much punctuality, and with as little interruption, as we can arrange the morning and evening devotions of our own fire-side. Our very children might become, to some extent, teachers, by reading to them plain portions of the Bible, or plain Tracts and things of such sort. And who can condemn us for doing what we conceive to be duty? Or who can hinder us? We infringe no law, neither do we violate any man's property or liberty. These two questions, then, being answered in the affirmative, it follows that we are in duty bound to give our Negroes the Gospel.

We are bound to give the Gospel — *by Humanity.* Were we to see a sheep fallen into a ditch, we would lift it out. Were our ox famishing in the stall, we would loose it and lead it away to watering. Much more, then, should we lift up our servants from the pit of moral pollution and death, into which they have fallen. Much more should we strive to loose them from the bonds of sin and Satan, and lead away their famishing souls to the water of life. How much better is a man than a sheep or an ox? When their bodies are diseased we physic and nurse them. And how can we neglect their diseased soul? Are not their souls more precious than their bodies?

We are bound to give them the Gospel — *by Consistency.* We are actually contributing of our substance — or giving our prayers and best wishes to the various benevolent operations of the present day. We pray that Christ's Kingdom may come, and that his Gospel may be preached to every nation and people under the whole heaven. In

consistency with this prayer we have assisted in sending missionaries to the Heathen, thousands of miles from us, and to destitute
settlements in our country. We have assisted in printing Bibles and
Tracts, and in sending them into every family in our land and in
foreign-lands. We have assisted in preaching the Gospel in our public
prisons – in the harbors of our sea-port cities, to those who do business on the great waters. We have assisted in gathering the children
of all parents into Sabbath Schools; and we have assisted in staying
the swellings of the fiery waves of intemperance. But what have we
done for our poor Negroes? With shame must we confess that we
have done *nothing!* An enemy, nay, a friend, might well say to us,
how can you contribute to all these benevolent works and pray for
their success? How can you pray for Christ's Kingdom to come; how
can you pray that God would enable you to do something to hasten
its coming, while you are neglecting a people perishing for lack of
vision around your very doors? And what answer could we return in
justification of our conduct? None. We could do no more than honestly confess our inconsistency.

We cannot cry out against the Papists for withholding the Scriptures from the common people, and keeping them in ignorance of the
way of life, for we withhold the Bible from our Servants, and keep
them in ignorance of it, while we *will* not use the means to have it
read and explained to them. We have been shocked at the death of
forty thousand men annually, by intemperance, and our community
has been thrown into commotion by it. But it is probable that as
many die annually among the Negroes in slave-holding States, whose
death is equally as hopeless as that of the drunkard, and yet we have
not thought of this, neither have we felt it. We have been horror-
struck at the cruelties of the Heathen, who cast their aged and in-
firm, and their tender infants into the rivers to be devoured by crock-
odiles. But we have manifested no emotions of horror at abandoning
the souls of our Servants to the adversary, the roaring lion that
walketh about, seeking whom he may devour. Our inconsistency in
withholding the Gospel from our Servants, both as Philanthropists
and Christians, is most glaring, nor can we deny it.

We are bound to give them the Gospel – *by the spirit of the Religion which we possess.* Religion is comprehended in one word – Love.
Love to God and love to man. This love, as manifested to man, consists in a tender regard for his interests and an earnest desire for his
happiness, not so much, however, in reference to this world as that

to come. Hence it is that the Christian feels such an interest in the conversion and salvation of men, that he is willing to make any sacrifice to obtain this object. Indeed, the very design of God in converting men is to promote his glory, by using them as instruments in the conversion of others. It is therefore, an indication of radical defect of Christian character; or most lamentable, may we not say criminal, ignorance of duty, when the Christian is insensible to the condition of those who are perishing around him, and makes no effort for their salvation. The desire of the Christian to give men the Gospel, should be in proportion to the difficulty to be surmounted, and the need in which they stand of it.

The great, the golden rule of conduct, which Christ prescribes to his followers, is this: *"All things whatsoever ye would men would do unto you, do ye even so to them."* Admitting, then, that we were in the condition of the Negro, and he in our condition, able to read and appreciate the Gospel; experimentally acquired with it; a partaker of its privileges and of its eternal hopes; would we not think it his duty to make known to us the Gospel, which is every thing to perishing sinners, and which alone could yield us happiness in our humble lot? We surely should. And what would we think of him if he denied it to us? *Could* we believe that he possessed the spirit of his religion? *Could* we believe that he sincerely believed and felt all the amazing and soul stirring truths which it contains; No – we could not. Shall we not, then, by passing over the spiritual wants of our Servants, be deficient in the very spirit of our religion? We feel that we shall; and we tremble to think that should we continue to neglect them, our neglect might not only shut their souls out of heaven, but our own.

And once more – we are bound to give them the Gospel – *by the express command of God.* We are commanded by Christ to go into all the world and preach the Gospel to every creature, as we have seen. But more particularly is it said to us, as owners of slaves, "Masters give unto your Servants that which is just and equal, knowing that ye also have a master in heaven." Col. iv. 1. – i.e. Treat your Servants with justice and in an equitable manner, for you have a Master in heaven to whom you are accountable for your treatment of them. Now, we cannot come up to the spirit and letter of these commands, unless we give them the Gospel.

Yes, our Servants are men – They need the Gospel. God has put it into our power to give them the Gospel; and we are bound to do it, by *Humanity – by Consistency – by the Spirit of the Religion we profess –* and by *the Express command of God.* This obligation has been resting upon us for years. May we not say that its age gives it weight? Yea, an awful weight! We have heretofore neglected our duty. If we continue to neglect it, we shall be as heretofore, *without excuse.*

We cannot excuse ourselves, by saying – *that the Negroes have the Gospel already.* Their opportunities of hearing the Gospel are limited. For although, generally speaking, all are permitted to go to church on Sabbath, yet *only a part* of the plantations can go on each Sabbath, as it is not permitted, nor can we say that it is desirable, that all should leave the plantations at a time. And even of this minority, (and an exceeding small minority it is, when we reckon children and youth,) *only a part* attended church. So that the majority do not hear the Gospel for weeks and months together. And, as it is among the whites, so it is among them, many never go to church at all.

But whenever the Negroes hear the preaching of the Gospel, they hear it at a very great disadvantage. The sermons are almost wholly delivered to their masters, and are not only, for the greater part, inapplicable to them, but entirely above their comprehension, both as to language and thought. The Gospel is preached to them in an unknown tongue. Occasionally they are particularly addressed, while worshipping with their masters; and perhaps as often, a regular discourse is delievered at their place of meeting. We have colored Ministers and exhorters, but their numbers are wholly inadequate to the supply of the Negroes; and while their ministrations are unfrequent, and conducted in great weakness, there are some of them whose moral character is justly suspected, and who may be considered blind leaders of the blind.

Nor have the Negroes, at any other time than the Sabbath, any system of stated religious instruction, if we except a few plantations on which they are gathered together and instructed in the evenings. So that on the whole, considering the fewness of the numbers that attend church, the disadvantage under which they hear the Gospel, and the little attention which is paid to their private instructions on the plantations, we must say to our condemnation, that our Servants do not enjoy the privileges of the Gospel. Hence their ignorance of the nature of true religion, and of its fundamental doctrines.

Nor can we excuse ourselves by saying – *that they are incapable of receiving Religious Instruction.* It is customary amongst us to entertain very low opinions of the intellectual capacity of the Negroes. Whether this be right or wrong, we leave every man to judge for himself, and to judge likewise whether their mental weakness is to be attributed to the circumstances of their condition, or to any difference as made by the Author of their existence between them and other men. But to suppose them too ignorant to comprehend the plainer and more essential doctrines of Christianity, is certainly to disregard the testimony of God's word, as well as the testimony of facts.

It is said that "God is no respecter of persons; but, in every nation, he that feareth Him and worketh righteousness is accepted with Him." And again, "He hath made of one blood all nations of men that dwell on all the face of the earth" (Acts, 10: 34–35, 17: 25–26). What then can be plainer than that all men have one common origin, and that all are capable of exercising proper affections towards God; and this necessarily implies a *capability* of understanding the Divine Law, no matter under what dispensation of law they live, whether natural or revealed. If it be allowed that the Negroes are men, then these things are true in regard to them, and thus by the word of God does it appear that they are capable of understanding the Gospel. And this is further evident from fact: Are there not colored communicants in our churches who understand, and in their lives adorn, the doctrine of Jesus Christ? We must believe that their general ignorance on Divine subjects is wholly owing to their want of proper instruction, and not at all to any natural defect of mental constitution.

Nor can we excuse ourselves – *because the Gospel meets with so little success amongst them.* The great wonder with us should be, not that the Gospel meets with *so little success,* but that it meets with any success at all; for we have seen that it is not preached to them in its fullness and connexion – nor is it preached to them generally, nor intelligibly. And we have also seen that the Negroes are extremely ignorant and vicious; and, like other men, they naturally hate the light. It should, therefore, be very far from a matter of discouragement to us, that the Gospel, as they have heretofore been accustomed to receive it, has met with so little success. On the contrary, it should be a matter of *encouragement.* For if it has met with *any success at all,* under a feeble and inadequate dispensation of it, what success may we not hope for under a more energetic and adequate dispensation of it?

The world and the glory of it, are outweighed in value by the soul. If, therefore, only *one* soul is saved from amongst them, the Gospel meets with great success; and were it now revealed to us, that the most extensive system of instruction we could devise, requiring a vast amount of labor and protracted through ages, would result in the salvation of the soul of only *one poor African,* we should feel ourselves warranted in cheerfully entering upon the work, for our reward would exceed our toil and care above the computation of any finite mind. But further, if the Gospel meet with no success at all, it would be no reason why we should not undertake the religious instruction of the Negroes; for if we certainly determine that it is our *duty* to give them instruction, we should do it. The *success* of that instruction *belongs to God.* This is the view which every Christian should take of the subject. God has evidently been speaking to us in favor of our Servants. He has called many of them into his kingdom, and made them rich in faith, as we do know. We have not, as yet, listened to his voice. It is time that we should. He tells us that he is willing to bless the preaching of the Gospel to their salvation. Shall we neglect them? Shall we despise God's voice?

Nor can we render as an excuse for not giving religious instruction to our servants – *that there are before us, peculiar and great difficulties hard to be overcome.* For in every enterprise of benevolence, there are difficulties; and if we wait, in our efforts to do good, until all difficulties are removed, we shall never commence. Times have suddenly and strangely altered in this world, if Christians can do good without encountering much that will try the purity and the firmness of their purposes. Against new enterprises, there are always men in readiness to magnify difficulties and to multiply objections. But when we enter upon them, and have a mind to the work, and the work be of God, difficulties and objections gradually vanish away. One thing is certain: – whatever difficulties now exist with regard to the religious instruction of our Servants, will continue to exist; for there are no causes now in operation adequate to their removal, nor is there the slightest possibility that there will be any. It is, therefore, the dictate of wisdom to commence our work at once. And again, if we are called of God to this work, we must, in the best way we can, attempt it, leaving it to *Him* to remove all obstacles to our progress in it. And it will be a proof of the ardor of our feelings and of our sincerity in the work, if we can cheerfully and manfully grapple with difficulty.

No, we have no excuse for our neglect of our Servants. Before God we must plead guilty, both we and our fathers, and render thanks unto God that his mercy and forbearance have preserved us from merited punishment. From the first introduction of these people into our country, they have been neglected. They have lived and died without the consolations of religion. They have worn out their lives to furnish us with the necessaries and luxuries of life. They have supported us in ease and fulness; and yet after they have thus communicated to us of temporal things, we have ungratefully failed to make them partakers of our spiritual things. Are they debtors to us? or are we debtors to them? Let the conscience of every man answer.

The religious instruction of the Negroes properly devolves on us, their legal owners; for they are wholly at our disposal. None are better acquainted with our laws, our local prejudices, the condition and character of the Negroes, than we; and consequently none are better able to devise and carry into effect unexceptionable systems of instruction.

Now, there are a number of our fellow-citizens, who feel deeply for the spiritual welfare of their Servants, but have been greatly at a loss to know *what* to do. No system of instruction has been proposed for their adoption, and they have felt a delicacy in coming before the public with anything of their own. But it is time to adopt some plan of instruction. Our duty is plain, our Servants must have the Gospel. On this point there can be but one opinion.

But what shall our plan of instruction be?

Before we proceed to answer this question, we should take into consideration the character of the people and the sort of instruction which they need. They are an ignorant and wicked people, from the oldest to the youngest. Hence, instruction should be committed to them *all*, and communicated *intelligibly*. And that it may be impressed upon their memories, and good order promoted amongst them, it should be communicated *frequently and at stated intervals of time*.

We would wish then to communicate religious instruction to *all* our servants, *intelligibly, frequently*, and *statedly*.

What plan is there then that will secure all these necessary ends?

1. *Shall we employ Missionaries to devote their whole time to the Negroes?* While we allow that the employment of Missionaries for this purpose would be attended with very great advantages, and where it can be done, it ought to be done; yet, there are objections to this plan, as falling short of the attainment of the ends which we have in view.

The first is, we could not procure Missionaries. It must be remembered that we want *Southern Men.* Can our churches furnish them? Where are they? Again, if we could procure Missionaries, the question of their support must be decided. Will our churches, or will communities pledge themselves for the necessary funds?

And again, suppose the Missionaries and funds for their support obtained, they would, in a majority of cases, be set over extensive territories, and would be compelled to visit the plantations in rotation, so that several weeks would intervene before these visits could be repeated. Their labor would necessarily be stinted. And remembering that the Negroes for the most part must be instructed at night, we may ask, where are the men of such iron constitution as would live in such service in the low country? The difficulty on the score of health would not exist in the up-country.

2. *Shall we establish stations contiguous to a number of plantations, and give instruction on the Sabbath?* We admit that this is an excellent plan as far as it goes. But it does not meet the wants of the Negroes. There is a radical defect in it. Only a part of every plantation is allowed to be away at any one time, and admitting that this part attended at the stations for instruction on the Sabbath, *a very small part* only of the whole population would enjoy the privileges of the Gospel. But of those who are permitted to leave the plantations on the Sabbath, all would not attend at the stations for instruction, and thus this very small part would be made much smaller.

3. The most efficient plan – the plan which seems to secure all the important ends which we desire, in conveying the Gospel to the Negroes, is that which your Society has adopted, and which is followed by the society in Liberty and by the citizens of Bryan county. It is a plan that embraces the two already mentioned and much more in addition: and for the information of those who are not acquainted with it, let us briefly state it. The plan is this. The Planters form themselves into a *voluntary* association, and take the religious instruction of the colored population into their own hands. And in this way: – As many of the association as feel themselves called to the work, shall become teachers. An Executive Committee is to regulate the operations of the Society, to establish regular stations, both for instruction during the week and on the Sabbath, and to appoint teachers who shall punctually attend to their respective charges, and communicate instruction altogether *orally,* and in as systematic and intelligible a manner as possible, embracing all the principles of the

Christian religion as understood by orthodox Protestants, and carefully avoiding all points of doctrine that separate different religious denominations.

The teachers are not to be sent to any plantation without the cordial consent of the owner. Nor shall they attend at any time than that specified by him. His wishes and arrangements are to be consulted and complied with. They are to confine themselves to the *religious instruction* of the Negroes *wholly;* nor are they to intermeddle with the concerns of the plantation in any manner, nor repeat abroad what their ears hear, or their eyes see on them. They are also to make Reports of their labors to the Executive Committee, which Committee shall make a general report to the Society at some specified time. In addition to the instructions of the teachers, where it is practicable, a Missionary may be employed to take a general supervision of the whole, occupy Sabbath stations, preach also during the week on plantations, and assist in framing courses of instruction, etc.

The only difficulty in the execution of this plan, is the procurement of a sufficient number of efficient teachers. In certain sections of our country, no teachers can be found; the white population is so sparse and so few of them, if any are pious. In these sections, recourse must be had to one or the other of the two plans first mentioned.

Such is the plan which you have adopted. It has thus far answered your expectations. – But we will not contend for its perfection; we will hold ourselves in readiness to receive light from any quarter; it may have its faults. Indeed there have been several *objections* urged against this plan, which as they may lodge in the minds of some to whom the plan is new, it may not be improper to consider.

1. *The plan may succeed in a small neighborhood, but not in a large one.* The success of the plan in any neighborhood depends upon the number of efficient teachers; only secure a sufficient number of teachers, and the neighborhood may be increased to any size. And admitting that there are not a sufficient number of teachers in a neighborhood, yet much good may be done by a few. If we can cultivate only a part of our field, let us do it. It is better to cultivate a part, than let the whole run to waste. Let us not despise the day of small things. Let us trust in God, who may at some future time enable us to cultivate the whole.

2. *This plan of instruction will be the means of introducing amongst us men and principles, hostile to our present system of things, and*

will lead us into trouble. But in what way? Is not the plan our own. Do we not carry it into effect ourselves? Are we not interested persons? Will we commission men to go on our plantations to sow discontent and revolt! Are not the Executive Committee charged with the oversight of the teachers? Have they not power to check or depose from office those who give improper instruction? Our society professes to have nothing to do with the civil instruction of the Negroes, nor do we desire it. We are concerned with them only as moral and accountable beings. Such a thing as stated in the objection cannot take place, unless we ourselves bring it to pass. It is presumed no one will suspect us of it. Every intelligent man ought to know that there is no more effectual method to prevent what is suggested by the objector, than to instruct our Servants in the principles of Christianity, to be present ourselves in all their assemblies for religious purposes, and to know who are their teachers. Our plan carries our security in it.

3. *This plan interferes with the Planter's arrangement, and will probably expose him to the slanders of the Teachers.* The plan cannot interfere with the Planter's arrangements. If he pleases to permit teachers to come on his place, they will come at whatever time he shall appoint, and continue the meetings no longer than may be agreeable to him. The Planter is to please himself. He is not to conform to the arrangements of the Society, but the Society is to conform to his; for the Society very well knows that it has no more right to interfere in his plantation arrangements, than they have to interfere in those of his family. That the Planter will suffer from the slanderous reports of the teachers, we hope may never be the fact. When the teacher comes on a plantation, he comes as it were into a private family. It would almost be unpardonable in a man to come with professions of friendship to do us the kindness and service of religiously instructing our Servants, and then discovering something which he may deem improper in our treatment of our Servants or in their conduct towards us, to go away and make it a matter of public notoriety. He betrays the confidence reposed in him. He is unfaithful to his trust. We hope the Society may never hold in its bosom such a man. We hope it may never shake the hand of fellowship with him. In order to avoid every thing of this nature, it should be the duty of the Executive Committee to appoint as teachers men of judgment and discretion, and to inculcate in their private conference with them, the Christian duty of abstaining from any comment whatever, upon

what they see or hear while engaged in the discharge of their important duties.

4. *This plan will take up much of the Teacher's time, and subject him to great inconvenience.* What great and good work is there that requires no sacrifice of time and convenience? And is the sacrifice of time and convenience in the present work so great as to deter us from it? Let us see if it is.

As to time, the teacher will devote perhaps, at most, but one evening to the instruction of the Negroes, and surely he can so arrange his business as not to suffer other engagements to interfere with this. And now what is it for us to devote one evening in the week to our Servants when their whole time is devoted to us? Especially too, when we seek to promote the salvation of their immortal souls? It is a shame for any man to talk of the sacrifice of time.

As to inconvenience, the teacher will not ride at the extent, more than a few miles. He may sometimes have his zeal and resolution tested by a dark or rainy evening. But what is the inconvenience of a short ride, and sometimes on a stormy night, for the benefit of those who are employed in labor for us, through all the changes of weather during the year: and who have *no other time* in the week to attend religious meetings? It is a shame for any man to talk of the sacrifice of convenience.

The trouble of preparation for his meetings should be something to the teacher. He is engaged in most important and momentous labors; they reach into eternity, and he should discharge them to the best of his abilities. He should bring forth out of his treasures things new and old, so as always to interest and instruct his charge. But considering how many excellent helps we now have in interpreting and illustrating Scripture, he may make his trouble comparatively light. And what is the trouble of preparation to a man who feels the value of the soul – to a man engaged in the work of converting men unto God? The trouble is not then thought of. Do then, teachers who are interested in their work, complain of the trouble of preparation? No. They know by experience that the Scripture is true which saith, *He that watereth, shall himself be watered.* They are watered in having their skirts clear of the blood of souls; in obtaining a more intimate acquaintance with the word of God; and in enjoying the happiness consequent upon sincere labors in the cause of Christ. We feel that if we can see our Servants attentive to our instructions, improving in morality – above all, heartily embracing religion, we shall feel amply compensated for any sacrifice of time and convenience to which we shall be subjected. And by the blessing of God, may we not hope for this?

5. *This plan of instructing the Negroes will do no good; it will only make them worse hypocrites and worse men. It has been tried before.* We confess that we are unable to feel the force of this objection. Our object will be to teach as God shall enable us, *the Gospel* to the Negroes. Will any man say that the *tendency* of the Gospel is to make men worse than they are? If any man says this, we earnestly hope that he will put himself to the trouble of examining the Gospel itself, and its legitimate effects upon mankind. We think that he will be convinced of his error. Wherever *the Gospel* is statedly and faithfully preached, the result is favorable to the piety and morality of the people. We can see no reason whatever, why it should produce an effect on our Negroes, contrary to that which it is designed by infinite wisdom and benevolence to produce, and which it actually produces on all other men, and on some whose condition is worse than that of our Negroes. And from what people did *we*, with all our piety and morality, and knowledge, spring? From a people once as degraded as Negroes. And what has lifted us so far above our progenitors? *The Gospel,* and nothing else. Is there not then a redeeming power in the Gospel for the Africans? We firmly believe that there is. Without this belief, we would not make an effort to give it to them. The unintelligible or corrupt preaching of the Gospel may make men worse, but never the preaching of the pure Gospel.

We are quite sure that no plan of instruction like the present, has ever been in operation in this country. The efforts heretofore made, have been quite partial and for the most part irregular. And it would not be proper for us, considering God's general course in providence and in grace, to expect much decided good from such efforts. And even admitting that the Negroes have hardened themselves, and grown worse under former advantages, this should not discourage us from attempting something more in their behalf. It should operate as an additional and a very powerful reason why we should attempt something more in their behalf. But may we not go further? Admitting we were assured before hand, that our labors would be contemned, and result only in great indifference to religion and in increased hardness of heart, even this assurance ought not to deter us from duty. God, sometimes in the accomplishment of his purposes, and of his great mercy, commands advantages to be multiplied to those who will certainly abuse them. The Jews, in the days of Christ, were a remarkable instance of this. (Matt. 23: 33, 39.)

But it may be questioned if this objection is supported by a solitary fact. On the contrary, we believe, that in the judgment of sober, unprejudiced men, whenever the Negroes have enjoyed for any reasonable time the privileges of the Gospel, they will, in point of order and morality, be found in advance of those who have not enjoyed them.

These are some of the objections which have been urged against our plan of conveying religious instruction to our Servants, and after duly considering them, we do not think that they are of sufficient weight to deter us from our purpose. It is a matter of astonishment, that there should be any objection at all; for the duty of giving religious instruction to our Negroes, and the benefit flowing from it, should be obvious to all. The *benefits*, we conceive to be incalculably great, and some of them are the following:

1. *There will be a better understanding of the mutual relations of Master and Servant.* We doubt not that there are many of our fellow citizens, and we would implicate ourselves in the charge, who have never given themselves the trouble to inquire into the number and nature of those duties which they owe to their Servants, and are in reason and in conscience, bound to perform. Nor do we think that our Servants generally, understand their duties towards us, and from what motives they should be performed. In many instances, they learn them after failure to perform them, through punishment, which might have been saved by a little timely instruction. And although the relative duties of Master and Servant are so important, and are so often insisted upon and defined in the Scriptures, we do not recollect ever to have heard a sermon from the pulpit concerning them.

2. *There will be greater subordination, and a decrease of crime amongst the Negroes.* It is well known that Slavery existed in the Roman Empire during the life of Christ and his Apostles, and that many Slaves became converts during their preaching. It appears that they did not interfere at all with the civil condition of the Slaves, nor pass any opinion concerning it, but preached to them the plain Gospel which is limited to every class and condition of men, and inculcated the duty of obedience in a very high degree. The following passages will suffice as a specimen: "Servants be obedient to your masters according to the flesh, not with eye-service as men pleasers, but as the servants of Christ, doing the will of God from the heart."

"Servants obey in all things your Masters according to the flesh, and whatsoever ye do, do it heartily as to the Lord, and not unto men." "Let as many Servants as are under the yoke count their Masters worthy of all honor, &c." And the Apostle Paul commands Ministers to "Exhort Servants to be obedient unto their own Masters and to please them well in all things, &c." (Eph. 6: 5, 6; Col. 3: 22; 1 Tim. 6: 1; Titus 2: 9,) and other passages of like import which any one may see for himself by consulting the New Testament; particularly the Epistle to Philemon, where it appears that the Apostle Paul sends back Onesimus, a runaway slave to his Master.

It will be noticed that obedience is inculcated as a *Christian duty,* binding on the Servants, and thus the authority of Masters is supported by considerations drawn from eternity. Now it would be a prime object with the Teachers to tread in the footsteps of the Apostles. Will the authority of the Masters be weakened by instructions of this sort? No, it will be strengthened. And we believe that their authority can be strengthened and supported *in this way only;* for the duty of obedience will never be felt and performed to the extent that we desire it, *unless we can bottom it on religious principle.*

Our Patrol Laws are not efficiently executed now, and this proposed plan of operation will, to some extent, supply their place. For the simple presence of a white man at stated times amongst the Negroes, will tend greatly to the promotion of good order.

It has been said, that religious instruction tends to create insubordination, and that religious meetings of the Negroes are nurseries for every sort of irregularity, and we have been pointed for an example to the affair in Charleston of 1822. But the example adduced, refutes the very point it was intended to prove. Those meetings which were held in Charleston for the purpose of exciting the colored population, *were not religious meetings.* They were meetings held under color of religion; but religion, properly speaking, had nothing to do with them; nor had the Negroes composing them any connexion with any white church or congregation.

Supposing that it was religion itself that excited those people? (which we deny with all our might,) men are religious beings. They will meet for religious purposes again. And in what way shall we prevent the recurrence of the same consequences? Only by being present in their meetings ourselves. If our plan of sending a white instructor into every assembly of Negroes for religious purposes, had been in operation in Charleston in 1822, there would never have existed any difficulty. As we said before, our plan seems to carry our security in it.

To shew the influence of true religion upon the Negroes, the case of somewhat an extensive insurrection in one of the West India Islands may be cited, wherein all the Negroes attached to the Moravian Missionary Churches, *to a man, supported the authority of their Masters against the insurgents.* Now, these Moravian Missionaries, as we understand, will have nothing whatever to do with the civil condition of the Slaves, but confine themselves entirely to the work of preaching the Gospel of Christ Jesus and him crucified. In the Danish West Indies, their congregations number 10,000 Negroes who profess faith in Christ; and in the British West Indies 15,000. Again – have we not heard individual planters say, that some of their best Servants are those who profess religion and appear to have the root of the matter in them? Without doubt, *crime* will be diminished. For Teachers, in order to induct a sense of guilt, must charge upon the Negroes those particular sins to which they are so much addicted, and to expose their enormity and consequent punishment in the world to come. Many of them are guilty of notorious sins and know not that they are sins at all. And they will be led to respect each other more; to pay greater regard to mutual rights; the strong will not so much oppress the weak; family relations will be less liable to rupture; in short, all the social virtues will be more honored and respected. Short as has been the existence of your Society, you can testify to the influence of your instructions in restraining crime on some plantations. The same may be said of the instructions on some plantations in Bryan county. Indeed the improvement of the Negroes in morality seems to keep pace with the religious privileges they enjoy.

The plan of instruction pursued by your Society will afford new facilities, and better opportunities of bringing them under the influence of Temperance Societies. It is a matter of astonishment that Masters who are members of Temperance Societies, or advocates of Temperance, take no steps to prevent the sale of ardent spirit to their slaves, especially too when they have it amply in their power. In this matter they seem to lose sight of their own *interest,* to say nothing of their *duty* to their Negroes.

And again, the religious instruction of the Negroes will deliver them from being made dupes and instruments of sin, by those to whom God in his mercy has given greater light, and who ought to know, and do better. The guilt of those must be tremendous who take advantage of their standing, and knowledge, and power, to entice and compel to sin, their poor degraded fellow creatures.

Happy then shall we be, if we can increase the spirit of obedience in our Servants, and cherish it by considerations drawn from eternity. Happy shall we be if we can raise the standard of their moral character, and place them in some good measure above the influence of evil seducers, and deliver their Masters from the pecuniary loss and the pain of severe discipline, consequent upon their negligence and crime.

3. *Much unpleasant discipline will be saved to the Churches.* The offences of colored communicants against Christian character and church order, are very numerous and frequently very heinous; the discipline is wearisome, difficult and unpleasant. Excommunications are of continual occurrence, and are usually in short time followed by applications for readmission. There never will be a better state of things until the Negroes are better instructed in religion.

4. *The Church and Society at large will be benefitted.* The way to strengthen and increase holiness in the soul, is to abound in works of holiness. It is by giving our talents to the exchangers that we gain other talents. By taking in hand the religious instruction of the Negroes, a sufficient field is thrown open for the most vigorous exercise of the piety and zeal, and talents of the church. And allowing that her labor proves of no avail to the Negroes, yet for the sake of the benefit to herself, she should persevere in them.

Society at large will also be benefitted. Benefitted in a *pecuniary point of view.* For a faithful Servant is more profitable than an unfaithful one. He will do more and better work, be less troublesome, and less liable to disease.

And benefitted in a *moral point of view.* We are so accustomed to sin, in the Negroes, which in them appears as a matter of course, that our sensibilities become blunted; we cease to abhor it, and then fall into sin ourselves. We also associate every thing that is mean and degrading with the Negroes, and almost necessarily so, from their mean and degraded characters. The consequence is, they do not seem worthy of our regard, they lose all our respect, and it is no marvel if our conduct towards them is dictated by our opinion of them. Planters will generally confess that the management of them is not only attended with trouble and vexation, but with provocations to sin. And the demoralizing influence which they exert over children and youth, when they are permitted to associate much with them, is well known to us all. In fine, the influence of the Negroes on the morals of our white population is exceedingly pernicious. It is like a millstone hanged about the neck of society. But when we shall see them assuming a higher standard of morals, the current of their opinion turning against vice, their appearance and deportment becoming more respectful, then shall we be favorably affected ourselves. Both classes of society will rise together, and *in this way only can they ever rise,* so great is the influence of the one over the other.

5. *The Souls of our Servants will be saved.* The great object for which we would communicate religious instruction to them is that their souls may be saved. To this all other objects should be subordinate. We believe that God will bless our instructions according to our desire. Strengthened by our faith, let us be willing to sow in tears, for we shall reap in joy. Let us be willing to go forth weeping and bearing precious seed, for we shall come again with rejoicing, bringing sheaves with us. If the rest of Heaven is sweet to any human being, it is sweet to the poor African. If the cheering hopes of a blessed immortality are necessary to any human being, to animate and sustain him in his pilgrimage below, they are necessary to the poor African. The glory of God may be advanced as much in the salvation of his soul, as in the salvation of the soul of any other man whatever.

6. *We shall relieve ourselves of great responsibility.* God, in his mysterious providence has cast this people down under our feet. We rule over them. Why he has subjected them to this bondage, we know not. But one thing we do know: – They are his accountable creatures, and the manner of our treatment of them as such, cannot be a matter of indifference to us, if we have any regard whatever to his approbation or disapprobation. In the exercise of that supreme power over them, vested in us by the laws of our country, we can forbid any man's coming on our plantations for the purpose of religiously instructing them; we can forbid all meetings for religious purposes on our plantations; we can refuse to instruct them ourselves; we can forbid them the privileges of God's sanctuary on the Sabbath; we can literally bar the door of entrance into Heaven against them; nor is there any power in our government that can compel us to swerve a hair from such treatment of them. The moral destinies of these people are submitted to our disposal, and our responsibilities we

may neglect, we may despise. But we cannot be delivered from them. They press upon us with the weight of a mountain, and we can meet them only by giving them the Gospel according to the measure of Christ, *"Freely ye have received, freely give."*

Some have thought that God has permitted the Africans to be brought to this country, that *His truth* might be made known to them. If He has, then may we exclaim: "How unsearchable are His judgments, and His ways past finding out!" He has not only caused the wrath, but the cupidity of man to praise Him. It is certain that the salvation of one soul will more than outweigh all the pain and woe of their capture and transportation, and subsequent residence amongst us. How slow have we been to second the designs of God! How astonishing is it that we have remained so long ignorant of our duty! May we not hope that at these times of ignorance God has winked; but now commands all men every where to repent? May we not hope that our repentance in this region has already begun? You, men and brethren, have reason to bless God that he has put it into your hearts to form the first Society for the Religious Instruction of the Negroes, ever formed, so far as we know, in the Southern States. From the altar which you have raised, fire may be borne to light up altars throughout our country, on which all the sons of Africa may offer sacrifices to God. *A public sentiment* on this subject has now begun its existence. It must live. It must be cherished. It must become as universal as that on Temperance, or on any other work of philanthropy and Christian benevolence. We hope that the attention of our countrymen will be turned to the moral and religious condition of the Negroes; and that after a lapse of time, it will be unusual to find a plantation deprived of the means of grace.

The work itself is great – It is difficult. There is much in it to dampen ardour and induce discouragement. To preach the Gospel to any people however improved and however favorably situated, is discouraging; but to preach it to the most ignorant and degraded, laboring under every disadvantage, is discouraging in the extreme.

But it is the work of God. He can cause mountains to become plains, and rough places to become smooth. In Him must be our trust. In Him there is a sufficiency of power, and wisdom, and grace. And there is a glory in the work which the Apostle to the Gentiles, were he alive, would covet. In imitation of his Master, he was foward to remember the poor. He strove to preach the Gospel, not where Christ was named, lest he should build upon another man's foundation. We tread an untrodden field of enterprise, and the subjects of our regard are the poorest of the poor.

Finally, Men and Brethren – The cry of our perishing servants comes up to us from the sultry plains, as they bend at their toil. It comes up to us from their humble cottages, when they return at evening to rest their weary limbs. It comes up to us from the midst of their ignorance, and superstition and adultery, and lewdness. Shall we disregard it? The cry is passing up to God and *He* will hear it. In a little while our opportunity of doing good to our servants will be done forever. In a little while we shall have done with the artificial distinctions of this world. We shall sleep in the ground, side by side, with them, and return to dust as soon as they. In a little while we shall meet them before Christ the Judge, the Great Master of all, with whom there is no respecter of persons. He will say to us – "These were your servants on earth. They labored for you ten, fifteen, twenty, thirty years. They wore out their lives to supply you with the food, and raiment, and conveniences, and luxuries, of your mortal life. You had them wholly at your disposal. You had my Gospel in your hands. I made you the almoners of my grace to them. Did you remember their never-dying souls? – While they communicated to you of temporal things, did you communicate to them of spiritual things? Did you urge and entreat them to come to me, who alone could give the weary and heavy laden rest? Did you allow them time to seek my face? Or did you neglect their eternal interests? Did you treat them like the beasts that perish? Were they merely the instruments of your profit or of your pleasure? Did you forget that they were your fellow creatures? Did you forget the price that I paid for their redemption? Did you leave them to perish eternally?"

Every owner of slaves has an account to render to God for his treatment of them. O, how fearful will be his account, who, knowingly and wilfully, will permit them to go down from his fields, and from his very dwelling into the bottomless pit, without making a solitary effort to save them? "He that ears to hear, let him hear!"

The Rights and the Duties of Masters

James H. Thornwell

May 26, 1850

Masters, give unto your Servants that which is just and equal; knowing that ye also have a master in Heaven.
—Colossians IV, 1—

God has not permitted such a remarkable phenomenon as the unanimity of the civilized world, in its execration of slavery, to take place without design. This great battle with the Abolitionists, has not been fought in vain. The muster of such immense forces – the fury and bitterness of the conflict – the disparity in resources of the parties in the war – the conspicuousness – the unexampled conspicuousness of the event, have all been ordered for wise and beneficient results; and when the smoke shall have rolled away, it will be seen that a real progress has been made in the practical solution of the problems which produced the collision. . . .

Truth must triumph. God will vindicate the appointments of His Providence – and if our institutions are indeed consistent with righteousness and truth, we can calmly afford to bide our time – we can watch the storm which is beating furiously against us, without terror or dismay – we can receive the assault of the civilized world – trusting in Him who has all the elements at His command, and can save as easily by one as a thousand. . . . It is not the narrow question of abolitionism or of slavery – not simply whether we shall emancipate our negroes or not; the real question is the relations of man to society – of States to the individual, and of the individual to States; a question as broad as the interests of the human race.

These are the mighty questions which are shaking thrones to their centres – upheaving the masses like an earthquake, and rocking the solid pillars of this Union. The parties in this conflict are not merely abolitionists and slaveholders – they are atheists, socialists, communists, red republicans, jacobins, on the one side, and friends of order and regulated freedom on the other. In one word, the

(Charleston: Steam Power Press of Walker and James, 1850).

world is the battle ground – Christianity and Atheism the combatants; and the progress of humanity the stake. One party seems to
regard Society, with all its complicated interests, its divisions and
subdivisions, as the machinery of man – which, as it has been in-
vented and arranged by his ingenuity and skill, may be taken to pieces,
re-constructed, altered or repaired, as experience shall indicate de-
fects or confusion in the original plan. The other party beholds in
it the ordinance of God; and contemplates "this little scene of human
life," as placed in the middle of a scheme, whose beginnings must
be traced to the unfathomable depths of the past, and whose development and completion must be sought in the still more unfathomable
depths of the future – a scheme, as Butler expresses it, "not fixed, but
progressive – every way incomprehensible" – in which, consequently,
irregularity is the confession of our ignorance – disorder the proof of
our blindness, and with which it is as awful temerity to tamper as
to sport with the name of God. . . .

The part accordingly, which is assigned to us in the tumult of
the age, is the maintenance of the principles upon which the security
of social order, and the development of humanity depends, in their
application to the distinctive institutions which have provoked upon
us the malediction of the world. The Apostle briefly sums up all that
is incumbent, at the present crisis, upon the slaveholders of the South,
in the words of the text – Masters, give unto your servants that which
is just and equal, knowing that ye also have a Master in Heaven. It
would be an useless waste of time to spend many words in proving,
that the servants contemplated by the Apostle were slaves. Finding
it impossible to deny that slavery, as an existing element of society,
is actually sanctioned by Christ and His Apostles, those who would
preserve some show of consistency in their veneration of the Scriptures, and their condemnation of us, resolve the conduct of the founders of Christianity into motives of prudence and considerations of
policy. While they admit that the letter of the Scriptures is distinctly
and unambiguously in our favour, they maintain that their spirit is
against us, and that our Saviour was content to leave the destruction of whatsoever was morally wrong in the social fabric, to the
slow progress of changes in individual opinions, wrought by the silent influence of religion, rather than endanger the stability of governments by sudden and disastrous revolutions. . . .

But it may be worth while to expose the confusion of ideas, from
which this distinction, betwixt the letter and the spirit of the Gos-

pel, has arisen, and which has been a source of serious perplexity, both to the defenders and the enemies of slavery. . . . If it can be shown that slavery contravenes the spirit of the Gospel – that as a social relation it is essentially unfavourable to the cultivation and growth of the graces of the Spirit – that it is unfriendly to the development of piety and to communion with God – or that it retards the onward progress of man – that it hinders the march of society to its destined goal, and contradicts that supremacy of justice, which is the soul of the State, and the life-blood of freedom – if these propositions can be satisfactorily sustained, then it is self-condemned – religion and philanthropy alike require us to labour for its destruction, and every good man amongst us would feel bound to contribute to its removal; and even the voice of patriotism would demand that we should wipe from our country the foul reproach of standing in the way of the destined improvement of mankind.

The confusion upon this subject has arisen from a two-fold misapprehension – in relation to the nature of the slavery tolerated in the letter of the Scriptures, and the other in relation to the spirit of Christianity itself.

It is common to describe slavery as the property of man in man – as the destruction of all human and personal rights, the absorption of the humanity of one individual into the will and power of another. "The very idea of a slave," says Dr. Channing, "is that he belongs to another, that he is bound to live and labour for another, to be another's instrument, and to make another's will his habitual law, however adverse to his own." "We have thus," says he in another place, "established the reality and sacredness of human rights, and that slavery is an infraction of these, is too plain to need any laboured proof. Slavery violates not one but all, and violates them not incidentally, but necessarily, systematically, from its very nature." In other words, in every system of slavery, from the operation of its inherent and essential principles, the slave ceases to be a person – a man – and becomes a mere instrument or thing. Dr. Channing does not charge this result upon the relation as it obtains under particular codes, or at particular times, or in particular places. He says, distinctly and emphatically, that it violates all human rights, not *incidentally*, but *necessarily, systematically* from *its very nature*. It belongs to the very essence of slavery to divest its victims of humanity.

"Slavery," says Professor Whewell, "is contrary to the fundamental principles of morality. It neglects the great primary distinction of Persons and Things—converting a person into a thing, an object merely passive, without any recognized attributes of human nature. A slave is, in the eye of the State which stamps him with that character, not acknowledged as a man. His pleasures and pains, his wishes and desires, his needs and springs of action, his thoughts and feelings, are of no value whatever in the eye of the community. He is reduced to the level of the brutes. . . ."

If this be a just description of slavery, the wonder is, not that the civilized world is now indignant at its outrages and wrongs, but that it has been so slow in detecting its enormities, that mankind, for so many centuries, acquiesced in a system which contradicted every impulse of nature, every whisper of conscience, every dictate of religion—a system as monstrously unnatural as a general effort to walk upon the head or think with the feet. I have, however, no hesitation in saying, that whatever may be the technical language of the law, in relation to certain aspects in which slavery is contemplated, the ideas of personal rights and personal responsibility pervade the whole system. It is a relation of man to man—a form of civil society, for which persons are the only elements, and not a relation of man to things. Under the Roman code, in which more offensive language than that employed by ourselves was used in reference to the subject, the Apostles did not regard the personality of the slave, as lost or swallowed up in the propriety of the master. They treat him as a man—possessed of certain rights, which it was injustice to disregard, and make it the office of Christianity to protect these rights by the solemn sanctions of religion—to enforce upon masters the necessity, the moral obligation, of rendering to their bondmen that which is just and equal. Paul treats the services of slaves as duties—not like the toil of the ox or the ass—a labor extracted by the stringency of discipline—but a moral debt, in the payment of which they were rendering a homage to God. "Servants," says he, "be obedient to them that are your masters, according to the flesh, with fear and trembling in singleness of your heart, as unto Christ; not with eye-service, as men-pleasers, but as the servants of Christ, doing the will of God from the heart; with good will doing service, as to the Lord, and not to men; knowing that whatever good thing any man doeth, the same shall he receive of the Lord, whether he be bond or free." I need not say to those who are acquainted with the very elements of moral philosophy, that obedience, except as a figured term, can never be applied to any but rational, intelligent, responsible agents.

It is a voluntary homage to law–implies moral obligation, and a sense of duty, and can only, in the way of analogy, be affirmed of the instinctive submission of brutes, or the mechanical employment of instruments and things.

The apostle not merely recognizes the moral agency of slaves, in the phraseology which he uses, but treats them as possessed of conscience, reason and will–by the motives which he presses. He says to them in effect that their services to their masters are duties which they owe to God–that a moral character attaches to their works, and that they are the subjects of praise or blame according to the principles upon which their obedience is rendered. . . .

The state of things so graphically described and eloquently deplored by the great father of Unitarian Christianity in America, is a palpable impossibility. The constitution of the human mind is in flagrant contradiction to the absorption of the conscience, will, and understanding of one man into the personality of another–it is a thing which cannot be conceived–and if it ever could take place, the termination of all responsibility on the part of the slave would render it ridiculous to labour for his spiritual improvement, or attribute to him any other immortality, than that which Indian fables ascribe to the dog as the faithful companion of his master. And yet upon this absurdity, that slavery divests its victims of humanity–that it degrades them from the rank of responsible and voluntary agents to the condition of tools or brutes–the whole philosophical argument against the morality of the system, as an existing institution–is founded. . . . We grant most cheerfully, and we make an admission in no way inconsistent with Southern slavery, or the slavery sanctioned in the Bible, that though "the human soul may be lost, it cannot either be sold or be made a gift of to another–that conscience may be bound or may be slaughtered, but cannot be transferred to another's keeping–that moral responsibility, instead of being shifted entirely from one to another, or instead of being shared between two, each taking a half or a portion, is doubled, whenever it is attempted to be transferred, or to be deposited, or to be pawned."

The property of man in man–a fiction to which even the imagination cannot give consistency–is the miserable cant of those who would storm by prejudice what they cannot demolish by argument. We do not even pretend that the organs of the body can be said strictly to belong to another. The limbs and members of my servant are not mine, but his–they are not tools and instruments which I can sport with a pleasure, but the sacred possession of a human being, which cannot be invaded without the authority of law, and for the use of which he can never be divested of his responsibility to God.

If, then, slavery is not inconsistent with the existence of personal rights and of moral obligation, it may be asked in what does its peculiarity consist? What is it that makes a man a slave? We answer, the obligation to labour for another, determined by the Providence of God, independently of the provisions of a contract. The right which the master has is a right, not to the *man*, but to his *labour;* the duty which the slave owes is the service which, in conformity with this right, the master exacts. The essential difference betwixt free and slave-labour is, that one is rendered in consequence of a contract; the other is rendered in the consequence of a command. The labourers in each case are equally moral, equally responsible, equally men. But they work upon different principles. . . .

The Providence of God marks out for the slave the precise services, in the lawful commands of the master, which it is the Divine will that he should render; the painful necessities of his case are often as stringent upon the free labourer, and determine, with as stern a mandate, what contracts he shall make. Neither can he be said to select his employments. God allots to each his position – places one immediately under command – and leaves the other not unfrequently a petitioner for a master.

Whatever control the master has over the person of the slave, is subsidiary to this right to his labour; what he sells is not the man, but the property in his services – true he chastises the man, but the punishments inflicted for disobedience are no more inconsistent with personal responsibilities than the punishments inflicted by the law for breaches of contract. On the contrary, punishment in contradistinction from suffering, always implies responsibility, and a right which cannot be enforced, is a right, which society, as an organized community, has not yet acknowledged. The chastisements of slaves are accordingly no more entitled to awaken the indignation of loyal and faithful citizens – however pretended philanthropists may describe the horrors of the scourge and the lash – than the penalties of disgrace, imprisonment, or death, which all nations have inflicted upon crimes against the State. All that is necessary in any case, is that the punishment should be *just.* . . . It is not part of the essence of slavery, however, that the rights of the slave should be left to the caprice or to the interest of the master; and in the Southern States, provisions are actually made – whether adequate or inadequate it is useless here to discuss – to protect him from want, cruelty, and unlawful domination. Provisions are made which recognize the doctrine of the Apostle, that he is a subject of rights, and that justice must be rendered to his claims. . . .

This view of the subject exposes the confusion, which obtains in most popular treatises of morals, of slavery with involuntary servitude. The service, in so far as it consists in the motions of the limbs or organs of the body, must be voluntary, or it could not exist at all. If by voluntary be meant, however, that which results from hearty consent, and is accordingly rendered with cheerfulness, it is precisely the service which the law of God enjoins. Servants are exhorted to obey from considerations of duty; to make conscience of their tasks, with good will doing service, as to the Lord, and not to men. Whether, in point of fact, their service, in this sense, shall be voluntary, will depend upon their moral character. But the same may be said of free labour. There are other motives beside the lash that may drive men to toil, when they are far from toiling with cheerfulness or good will. . . .

There is a moral bondage, the most galling and degrading species of servitude, in which he may be held, as with chains of brass, who scorns to call any man master on earth. Those who have most patiently studied the ends of government and the theory of political society, who are best prepared to solve the problems connected with the nature and extent of the individual restraints, which the security of public order demands – those who have most profoundly investigated the whole question of civil and political liberty, may yet be slaves. They may submit to the sway of a fiercer and more cruel tyrant than any despot who ever wielded a sceptre on earth. "Jesus answered them, Verily, verily I say unto you, whosoever committeth sin is the servant or slave of sin." There is a freedom which is the end and glory of man; the only freedom which the pen of inspiration has commended, and which, from its very nature, is independent of the degrees of kings, or the mandates of States. It is *the* freedom which God approves; which Jesus bought by his blood, and the Holy Spirit effectually seals by His grace; the liberty wherewith Christ has made us free. It consists essentially in the dominion of rectitude, in the emancipation of the will from the power of sin, the release of the affections from the attractions of earth, the exemption of the understanding from the deceits of prejudice and error. It is a freedom which the *truth* of God brings with it – a freedom enjoyed by the martyr at the stake, a slave in his chains, a prisoner in his dungeon, as well as the king upon the throne. Independent of time or place, or the accidents of fortune, it is the breath of the soul as regenerated and redeemed; and can no more be torn from us than the atmosphere of Heaven can be restrained. If the Son shall make you free, you shall be free indeed. . . . This freedom makes man truly a man; and it is precisely the assertion of this freedom – this dominion of rectitude – this supremacy of right, which the Apostle enjoins upon slaves – when he exhorts them to obey their masters in singleness of heart as unto Christ – to despise eye-service, but to do their work as in the eye of God. To obey under the influence of these motives, is to be slaves no longer. This is a *free* service – a service which God accepts as the loyal homage of the soul – and which proclaims them to be the Lord's freed-men, while they honour their masters on earth. Such slavery might be their glory – might fit them for thrones in the kingdom of God. So far was the Apostle, therefore, from regarding involuntary servitude as the characteristic of slavery, that he condemns such servitude as a sin. He treats it as something that is abject, mean, despicable; but insists on the other hand, that slavery dignifies and ennobles the servant, who obeys from the heart.

But while it may be admitted that slavery is not absolutely inconsistent with moral responsibility, nor the freedom of a moral agent, it may be asked whether the slave is not stripped of some of the rights which belong to him essentially as a man; and in this view, whether the relation is not incompatible with the spirit of the Gospel, which asserts and promotes the dignity and perfection of our race. In other words, whether there is not a limitation upon the moral freedom of the slave – whether his situation does not preclude him from discharging his *whole* duty as a man; and, therefore, whether the relation is not ultimately destructive of the full complement of human rights.

This question, it seems to me, comprises the whole moral difficulty of slavery; and it is at this point of the discussion, that the friends and enemies of the system are equally tempted to run into extravagance and excess; the one party denying the inestimable value of freedom; the other exaggerating the nature and extent of human rights, and both overlooking the real scope and purpose of the Gospel, in its relation to the present interests of man.

That the design of Christianity is to secure the perfection of the race, is obvious from all its arrangements; and that when this end shall have been consummated, slavery must cease to exist, is equally clear. This is only asserting that there will be no bondage in heaven. Among beings of the same nature, each relatively perfect, there can be no other inequalities than those which spring from superior endowments – the outward advantages of all must be of the same kind, though they may vary in degrees proportioned to the capacities of the individuals to enjoy them. If Adam had never sinned and brought death into the world, with all our woe, the bondage of man to man would never have been instituted; and when the effects of transgression shall have been purged from the earth, and the new heavens and the new earth, wherein dwelleth righteousness, given to the saints, all bondage shall be abolished. In this sense, slavery is inconsistent with the spirit of the Gospel, that it contemplates a state of things – an existing economy, which it is the design of the Gospel to remove. Slavery is a part of the curse which sin has introduced into the world, and stands in the same general relations to Christianity as poverty, sickness, disease or death. In other words, it is a relation which can only be conceived as taking place among fallen beings – tainted with a curse. It springs not from the nature of man as man, nor from the nature of society as such, but from the nature of man as sinful, and the nature of society as disordered.

Upon an earth radiant with the smile of heaven, or in the Paradise of God, we can no more picture the figure of a slave than we can picture the figures of the halt, the maimed, the lame and the blind; we can no more fancy the existence of masters and tasks than we can dream of hospitals and beggars. These are the badges of a fallen world. That it is inconsistent with a perfect state – that it is not absolutely a good – a blessing – the most strenuous defender of slavery ought not to permit himself to deny; and the devout believer in Revelation would be made to close his eyes to the fact, that the form in which it is first threatened, in the Bible, is as a punishment for crime. . . . When we consider the diversities in moral position, which sin has been the means of entailing upon the race, we may be justified in affirming, that, relatively to some persons and to some times, slavery may be a good, or to speak more accurately, a condition, though founded in a curse, from which the Providence of God extracts a blessing. We are not to judge of the institutions of the present, by the standard of the future life – we are not to confound the absolute and relative. For aught that we know slavery may stand in somewhat the same relation to political society, in a world like ours, in which mortality stands to the human body; and it may be as vain to think of extirpating it, as to think of giving man immortality upon earth. It may be, and perhaps is, in some of its forms, essential to an imperfect society; and it may be, and perhaps is, the purpose of God that it should be found among men, as long as the slime of the serpent is over the earth. Admit, then, that slavery is inconsistent with the spirit of the Gospel, as that spirit is to find its full development in a state of glory—yet the conclusion by no means follows, that it is inconsistent with the spirit of the Gospel, as that spirit operates among rebels and sinners, in a degraded world, and under a dispensation of grace. The real question is: whether it is incompatible with the spiritual prosperity of individuals, or the general progress and education of society. It is clearly the office of the Gospel to train men, by virtue of the discipline of temptation, hardship and evil, for a state of perfection and glory. Nothing is inconsistent with it which does not present obstacles to the practice of duty, which its own grace is inadequate to surmount. Whoever, therefore, would maintain that slavery is incompatible with the present relations of the Gospel to man, must maintain that it precludes him, by its very nature, from the discharge of some of the duties which the Gospel enjoins. It is nothing to the purpose to speak of it generally and vaguely as an evil—it must be shown to be an evil of that specifick kind which necessitates the commission of sin, and the neglect of duty. Neither is it sufficient to say that it presents strong temptations to sin, in the violent motives which a master may press upon a slave, to execute unlawful commands. This can be affirmed of numberless other situations, in which none will contend that it is unlawful to be found. The question is—not whether it is the state most favourable to the offices of piety and virture—but whether it is essentially incompatible with their exercise. This is the true issue.

The fundamental mistake of those who affirm slavery to be essentially sinful, is that the duties of all men are specifically the same. . . . The argument, fully and legitimately carried out, would condemn every arrangement of society, which did not secure to all its members an absolute equality of position; it is the very spirit of socialism and communism.

The doctrine of the Bible, on the other hand, is that the specifick duties—the things actually required to be done, are as various as the circumstances in which men are placed. . . . The circumstances in which men are placed in this sublunary state are exceedingly diversified, but there is probably no external condition in which the actual discipline to which men are subjected may not terminate in the temper of universal holiness. Some are tried in one way, some in another – some are required to do one set of things, some another – but the spirit of true obedience is universally the same – and the result of an effectual probation is, in every case, a moral sympathy with the moral perfections of God. The lesson is the same, however different the textbooks from which it has been taught.

Now, unless slavery is incompatible with the habitudes of holiness – unless it is inconsistent with the spirit of philanthropy or the spirit of piety – unless it furnishes no opportunities for obedience of the law, it is not inconsistent with the pursuit or attainment of the highest excellence. It is no abridgement of moral freedom; the slave may come from the probation of *his* circumstances as fully stamped with the image of God, as those who have enjoyed an easier lot – he may be as completely in unison with the spirit of universal rectitude, as if he had been trained on flowery beds of ease. Let him discharge his *whole* duty in the actual circumstances of his case, and he is entitled to the praise of a perfect and an upright man. The question with God is – not *what* he has done – but *how;* – man looketh at the outward circumstances, but God looketh at the heart. . . . The slave is to show his reverence for God – the freedom of his inward man – by a cheerful obedience to the lawful commands of his master; – the master, his regard for one who is his master in heaven, by rendering to the slave that which is just and equal. The character of both is determined, in the sight of God, by the spirit which pervades their single acts, however the acts may differ in themselves.

If slavery is not essentially incompatible with the discharge of the essential duties, as a spiritual service, it is not destructive of the essential rights of humanity. All political organizations, our enemies themselves being judges, are subservient to the interest of the individual. . . .

All this the grace of God, through the instrumentality of the gospel, may accomplish in the person of one who is bound to labor under the direction and authority of another. The servant of men may be the freeman of the Lord. If his situation is compatible, as it confessedly is, with the achievement of the great end of his existence – if in the school of bondage he may be trained for the glorification and enjoyment of God, he is not divested of any of the rights which belong to him essentially as *man*. He may develop his moral and religious nature – the source and measure of all his rights – and must, consequently, retain every characteristick of essential humanity. . . .

There are rights which belong to men in other situations, to which he is by no means entitled; the rights of the citizen, for example, and the free member of the commonwealth. They are not his, for the simple reason that they are not essential, but contingent; they do not spring from humanity simply considered, for then they would belong to women and children – but from humanity in such and such relations.

As to the influence of slavery upon the advancement of society, there can be no doubt, if the government of God be moral, that the true progress of communities and States, as well as the highest interests of individuals, depend upon the fidelity with which the duties are discharged, in every condition of life. It is the great law of providential education, that to every one that hath shall be given and he shall have abundance; but from him that hath not shall be taken away even that which he hath. In this way the reign of universal justice is promoted, and wherever that obtains, the development of the individual, which is the great end of all social and political institutions, must infallibly take place. The prosperity of the State at the same time is secured, and secured, too, without the necessity of sudden changes or violent revolutions. . . .

Besides the arguments drawn from considerations of justice and the essential rights of humanity, the incompatibility of slavery with the spirit and temper of the Gospel, is not unfrequently attempted to be made out, from the injunction of the Saviour to love our neighbor as ourselves, and to do unto others as we would have them to do unto us. The principle, however, upon which the precept of universal benevolence is interpreted in this case, makes it the sanction of the grossest wickedness. If we are to regulate our conduct to others by the arbitrary expectations which, in their circumstances, our passions and selfishness might prompt us to indulge, there ceases to be any other standard of morality than caprice. The humour of every man becomes law. The judge could not condemn the criminal, nor the executioner behead him – the rich man could not claim his possessions nor the poor learn patience from their sufferings. If I am bound to emancipate my slave because if the tables were turned and our situations reversed, I should covet this boon from him, I should be found, upon the same principle, to promote my indigent neighbors around me, to an absolute equality with myself. That neither the Jews, in whose law the precept was first formally announced, nor the Apostles, to whom it was more fully expounded by the Saviour, ever applied it in the sense of the Abolitionists, is a strong presumption against their mode of interpretation. The truth is, it is nothing but the inculcation of *justice* from motives of love. Our Saviour directs us to do unto others what in their situations, it would be right and reasonable in us to expect from them. We are to put ourselves in their situations, that we may duly weigh the circumstances of their case, and so be prepared to apply to it the principles of universal justice. . . .

The instances which are usually urged to prove that slavery is inconsistent with the rights of man, unfortunately for the argument, are not peculiar to slavery. They are incidents to poverty, wherever it prevails in a distressing form; and a wise system of legislation could much more easily detach them from the system of slavery than from the deep indigence which is sure to crush the laborer where a crowded population obtains. They are, at best, only abuses in the one case which might be corrected, while in the other, they seem to be inseparable elements.

Enough has been said to show that slavery is not repugnant to the spirit of the Gospel, in its present relations to our race. It is one of the conditions in which God is conducting the moral probation of man – a condition not incompatible with the highest moral freedom, the true glory of the race, and therefore, not unfit for the moral and spiritual discipline which Christianity has instituted. It is one of the schools in which immortal spirits are trained for their final destiny. If it is attended with severer hardships, these hardships are compensated by fewer duties, and the very violence of its temptations gives dignity and luster to its virtues. The slave may be fitted, in his humble and if you please, degraded lot, for shining as a star in the firmament of heaven. In his narrow sphere, he may be cherishing and cultivating a spirit which shall render him meet for the society of angels and the everlasting enjoyment of God. The Christian beholds in him, not a tool, not a chattel, not a brute or thing – but an immortal spirit, assigned to a particular position in this world of wretchedness and sin, in which he is required to work out the destiny which attaches to him, in common with his fellows, as a man. . . .

The important question among us is, that which relates to the discharge of our own duties as masters – what are the things which are just and equal that we are required to render to our slaves.

But before attending to this inquiry, it may be well to notice the popular argument against slavery, drawn from the fact, that as it must have begun in the perpetration of grievous wrong, no lapse of time can make it subsequently right. Prescription can never sanctify injustice. The answer turns upon the distinction between the wrong itself and the effects of the wrong. The criminal act, whatever it may have been, by which a man was reduced to the condition of bondage, can never cease to be otherwise than criminal, but the relations to which that act gave rise, may, themselves, be consistent with the will of God and the foundation of new and important duties. The relations of a man to his natural offspring, though wickedly formed, give rise to duties which would be ill-discharged by the destruction of the child. No doubt the principle upon which slavery has been most largely en-grafted into society as an integral element of its complex constitu-tion – the principle, that captivity in war gives a right to the life of a prisoner, for which his bondage is accepted in exchange, is not consis-tent with the truth of the case. But it was recognized as true for ages and generations – it was a step in the moral development of nations, and has laid the foundation of institutions and usages, which cannot now be disturbed with impunity, and in regard to which, our conduct must be regulated by the fact of their existence, and not by speculation upon the morality of their origin. Our world exhibits, every where, the traces of sin – and if we tolerate nothing but what we may expect to find in a state of perfection and holiness, we must leave this scene of sublunary distraction. The education of States is a slow process. Their standards of rectitude slowly approximate the standard of God, and in their ages of infancy, ignorance and blindness, they establish many in-stitutions upon false maxims, which cannot subsequently be extir-pated without abandoning the whole of the real progress they have made, and reconstituting society afresh. . . .

In treating slavery as an existing institution, a fact involving most important moral relations, one of the prime duties of the State is to protect, by temporal legislation, the real rights of the slave. The moral sense of the country acknowledges them – the religion of the country to a large extent, ensures their observance, but until they are defined by law and enforced by penalties there is no adequate pro-tection of them. They are in the category of imperfect and not of perfect rights. The effect of legal protection would be to counteract whatever tendencies slavery may be supposed to possess to produce servility and abjectness of mind. It would inspire a sense of personal responsibility – a certain degree of manliness and dignity of charac-ter, which would be, at once, a security to the master and an immense blessing to the slave. The meanness, cunning, hypocrisy, lying and theft, which accompany a sense of degradation, would give place to the opposite virtues, and there would be no foundation in our social relations for that slavery which Cicero defines — *obedientia fracti animi et abjecti, et arbitrio carentis suo.*

In the different systems of slavery, taken collectively, all the essential rights of humanity have been recognized by law — showing that there is nothing in the relation itself, inconsistent with this legal protection. The right to acquire knowledge — which is practically admitted by us, though legally denied, was fully recognized by the Romans, whose slaves were often the teachers of their children, and the scholars of the commonwealth. The right of the family was formally protected among the Spaniards; and the right to personal safety is largely protected by ourselves. But, without stopping to inquire in which way temporal legislation may, most effectually, protect the rights of the slave, we hesitate not to affirm that one of the highest and most solemn obligations which rests upon the masters of the South, is to give to their servants, to the utmost extent of their ability, free access to the instructions and institution of the Gospel. The injustice of denying to them food and raiment, and shelter, against which the law effectually guards, is nothing to the injustice of defrauding them of that bread which cometh down from Heaven. Their labor is ours. From infancy to age, they attend on us — they greet our introduction into the world with smiles of joy, and lament our departure with a heartfelt sorrow; and every motive of humanity and religion exacts from us, that we should remunerate their services by putting within their reach, the means of securing a blessed immortality. The meanest slave has, in him, a soul of priceless value. "No earthly or celestial language can exaggerate its worth. . . ." That soul has sinned — it is under the curse of the Almighty, and nothing can save it from an intolerable hell but the redemption that is in Christ Jesus. They must hear this joyful sound or perish. For how shall they believe in Him of whom they have not heard, and how shall they hear without a preacher, and how shall they preach except they be sent? Our design in giving them the Gospel, is not to civilize them — not to change their social condition — not to exalt them into citizens or freemen — it is to save them. The Church contemplates them only as sinners, and she is straitened to declare unto them the unsearchable riches of Christ. . . . Christian knowledge inculcates contentment with our lot; and in bringing before us the tremendous realities of eternity, renders us comparatively indifferent to the inconveniences and hardships of time. It subdues those passions and prejudices, from which all real danger to the social economy springs. "Some have objected," says a splendid writer,* "to the instruction of the lower classes, from an apprehension that it would lift them above their sphere, make them dissatisfied with their station in life, and by impairing the habits of subordination, endanger the tranquility of the State; an objection devoid surely of all force and validity. It is not easy to conceive in what manner instructing men in their duties can prompt them to neglect those duties, or how that enlargement of reason which enables them to comprehend the true grounds of authority, and the obligation to obedience, should indispose them to obey."

Our highest security in these States, lies in the confidence and affection of our servants, and nothing will more effectually propitiate their regards than consistent efforts, upon our part, to promote their everlasting good. They will feel that those are not tyrants who are striving to bring them unto God; and they will be slow to cast off a system which has become associated in their minds with their dearest hopes and most precious consolations. Brutal ignorance is indeed to be dreaded – the only security against it, is physical force – it is the parent of ferocity, of rashness, and of desperate enterprises. But Christian knowledge softens and subdues. Christ Jesus in binding his subjects to God, binds them more closely to each other in the ties of confidence, fidelity, and love. We would say, then, to you and to all our brethren of the South, go on in your present undertaking; and though our common enemies may continue to revile, you will be consolidating the elements of your social fabrick, so firmly and compactly, that it shall defy the storms of fanaticism, while the spectacle you will exhibit of union, sympathy and confidence, among the different orders of the community, will be a standing refutation of all their accusations against us. Go on in this noble enterprise, until every slave in our borders shall know of Jesus and the resurrection; and the blessing of God will attend you – and turn back the tide of indignation which the public opinion of the world is endeavouring to roll upon you. Go on in this career, and afford another illustration of what all experience has demonstrated, that Christianity is the cheap defence of every institution which contributes to the progress of man.

*Robert Hall. *Advantages of Knowledge to the Lower Classes.* Works. Vol. I, p. 202.

SECTIONALISM AND SECESSION

James W. Silver, in his brief but powerful book *Confederate Mo-rale and Church Propaganda,* was emphatic in making the point that Southern religion, motivated and energized by the preachers, led the South into secession and the Civil War. His thesis: "The Church was the most powerful organization influencing the lives of men and women in the South in the days before and during the Confederacy. Clergymen led the way to secession." Silver charged: "As no other group, Southern clergymen were responsible for a state of mind which made secession possible, and as no other group they sustained the people in their long, costly, and futile War for Southern In-dependence."[1]

Even as many Northern preachers looked upon the South as an inferior culture, so the Southern clergy looked upon the North as inferior and debased. The North was a den of iniquity where law and order had broken down. Vice, crime, and mob rule were everywhere rampant. Basic to this cultural breakdown in the North was a decline in true and orthodox religion. A Southern religious journal had declared: "our societies [Southern] enjoy profound tranquility so far as doctrinal speculations or pseudo reform of organic principles of government are concerned. We are not troubled—as they are in New England, with Mormonism, Millerism, Comeouterism, Universalism, or with an American edition of German Rationalism. The Southern States are not the soil on which such absurdities flourish."[2]

One of the primary ways that Southern religion "made secession possible" was through example. When the Presbyterian, Methodist, and Baptist denominations divided more than fifteen years before secession and war, a strong national cohesiveness was broken and an example was set for future political division. John C. Calhoun recognized the significance of the religious schisms. In March of 1850 a speech Calhoun had written was delivered before the United

States Senate. Too feeble and weak to deliver the speech himself, Calhoun had it delivered by another. The speech began by recognizing the importance of religious cords in binding the nation together. "The cords that bind the States together," wrote Calhoun, "are not only many, but various in character. . . . The strongest of those of spiritual and ecclesiastical nature, consisted in the unity of the great religious denominations, all of which originally embraced the whole union." Taking note that the religious cords had snapped – he singled out the Methodists and Baptists as points of focus – Calhoun warned of what would happen if the turmoil continued. "If the agitation goes on," he cautioned, "the same force, acting with increased intensity, as has been shown, will finally snap every cord, when nothing will be left to hold the States together except force."[3]

The first denominational rupture took place in 1837, when the Presbyterian Church in the U.S.A. divided between the Old School (those with great reservations about revivalism) and the New School (those enthusiastic about revivalistic activities). Though the break was not strictly a North–South division, most Southerners tended to side with the Old School. A powerful reason for this was that Southerners saw an alarming amount of abolitionist activity in the New School. When the Presbyterian General Assembly assured Southerners that discussion of slavery would cease, Southerners voted with the Old School to purge the New School synods from their midst. The presbyteries in the South that at first sided with the New School came over to the Old School in 1857, no longer able to endure the influence of abolitionism, and the North–South division of the Presbyterian denomination was complete.

The Methodists formally expressed their disapproval of slavery in 1784 when the denomination was formally organized in America. However, no national rules were ever enforced, and slavery became a local option. Abolitionists in the North began forcing the issue. In 1843 there was a large defection of antislavery Methodists who organized the Wesleyan Methodist Church. The next year the General Conference voted that a Southern bishop, James O. Andrew, could no longer hold his office because he owned slaves. The Southerners withdrew from the denomination and the following year established the Methodist Episcopal Church, South, as a proslavery denomination.

The national Baptists, who were loosely organized around societies and boards for missionary purposes, divided in 1845, one year after the Methodist schism. In that year Alabama Baptists asked the Foreign Mission Board if it would appoint a slaveholder for missionary service. After struggling to find a way around the dilemma, the Board responded negatively. Baptists from the South withdrew and formed the Southern Baptist Convention, a Baptist denomination more tightly organized than anything Baptists had ever experienced in their history.

Not only did the churches and their preachers promote secession by example, but they, perhaps more than any other group in the South, called for political schism. James W. Silver has noted several examples of preachers calling for their states to secede from the Union: "Thomas W. Caskey, minister of the Christian Church in Jackson, set out with the Attorney General to 'talk the people out of the Union.' Bishop Francis H. Rutledge promised to pay into the Florida treasury, five hundred dollars when the state seceded." After Lincoln's election, denominations joined individuals in calling for political division: "North Carolina Presbyterians, professing to speak for four-fifths of the Southern clergy and church members, called on all the slave states to make common cause. . . . The Alabama, Mississippi, and South Carolina Baptists officially considered it the duty of their states to secede immediately."[4]

Most Southern preachers had to be "converted" to pro-secession convictions. An example is James H. Thornwell. In 1850 Thornwell passionately opposed the idea of secession. Writing to a friend, he declared: "The prospect of disunion is one which I cannot contemplate without absolute horror. . . . I have hardly been able to sleep in consequence of my deep conviction with which I am oppressed of the evils that threaten us."[5] Early the following year he wrote an article in the *Review* which was severely critical of South Carolina's bent toward disunion. "Single-handed secession," he declared, "however it might be justified in a crisis in which the Federal Government had become openly pledged to the extinction of slavery, under the present circumstances of our country is recommended by not a single consideration that we are able to discover, of wisdom, patriotism or honour."[6]

Ten years later Thornwell changed his mind. On November 21, 1860, two weeks after Lincoln's election, in a sermon at the First Presbyterian Church of Columbia, he called for secession, and reminded that "even though our cause be just, and our course approved of Heaven, our path to victory may be through a baptism of blood. Liberty has its martyrs and confessors, as well as religion."[7] In late December of the same year, a few days after South Carolina had become the first state to pass an ordinance of secession, Thornwell wrote in a letter: "I believe that we have done right. I do not see any course that was left to us. I am heart and hand with the State in her move."[8] He then wrote an article in which he tried "to influence public opinion in states which have not seceded," and declared, "a free people can never consent to their own degradation." He held out the hope that the division could take place and two nations could be formed "without a jostle or a jar."[9] Anne C. Loveland has commented that Thornwell's transformation on secession was "representative of the majority of southern evangelicals. Although opposed to disunion in the 1850s, they supported secession in 1860–1861."[10]

The preachers attempted to spell out their reasons for secession. After the election of Lincoln in November of 1860, R. K. Porter spoke of the need for Southern duty and a defense against the aggressive, lustful North, which had departed from the truth of God.[11] In the same month Benjamin Morgan Palmer, after defending slavery as a trust and duty given to the Southern people from God, challenged the Southern states to secede from the Union.[12] The following month Lucius Cuthbert, Jr., developed a sermon on the theme "The Scriptural Grounds for Secession from the Union."[13] Soon after his native South Carolina had seceded from the Union, Benjamin Palmer called it an act of sublime moral heroism. Relying on nothing "save the righteousness of her cause and the power of God, she took upon her shield and spear as desperate and as sacred a conflict as ever made a state immortal. . . . The Genius of history has already wreathed the garland with which her brow shall be decked."[14]

On May 26, 1861, J. Jones, at the Presbyterian Church of Rome, Georgia, delivered a sermon to the Rome Light Guards and Miller Rifles, in which he reminded his audience why the South had seceded: (1) the hostility of the North; (2) hostility that was thoroughly organized; (3) the Northern opposition to slavery had damaged the South; (4) the North intended to abolish slavery in the South; (5) the Constitution had been violated; (6) secession was a right with a long history; and (7) slavery was an institution derived from the Word of God.[15]

Phillip Slaughter, a Confederate chaplain, preached a sermon in a camp near Centerville, Virginia, wherein he proclaimed an often-stated reason for secession.

Our duty as Christians is equally clear upon general principles. . . .
While the Scriptures recognize government as a divine institution . . .
they tell us in the same breath that *legitimate* rulers are the "ministers
of God" for good. . . . Hence, when governments become a "terror to
the good," and "a praise to the evil," they cease to be legitimate . . . and
it becomes the right of the people to abolish them, and to institute in
their place such new governments as shall seem most likely to effect
their safety and happiness.[16]

The sermon at the end of this chapter is from the mind and heart
of Benjamin Morgan Palmer. It states the Southern rationale for
secession about as well as that idea can be represented. Palmer, pastor of the prestigious First Presbyterian Church of New Orleans, was
an ardent and vociferous proponent of secession. No preacher in the
South equaled Palmer in his denunciations of the North, his defense
of slavery and the Southern way of life, and his advocacy of separation from the Union. Silver has written: "Benjamin Palmer ranged
up and down the country during the whole of the war, assuming the
appearance of a prophet of the Lord. A general in Mississippi declared Palmer to be worth a thousand soldiers to the cause."[17]

Palmer held Presbyterian pastorates in Savannah, Georgia, and
Columbia, South Carolina, before becoming the minister of the First
Presbyterian Church in New Orleans in 1854, a position he held until
his death in 1902. Though he had been an advocate of slavery for
many years, it was "the election of Lincoln to the presidency [that]
brought Palmer openly into the secessionist camp."[18] Twice upon the
approach of Union troops Palmer had to flee, knowing that his out-
spokenness had made him a marked man. In the spring of 1862 he
fled from New Orleans before forces led by Commodore David G. Far-
ragut, and less than three years later he fled from Columbia, South
Carolina, as Sherman's army drew near.

Throughout the war he challenged and cajoled his fellow Southerners to greater and more sacrificial efforts in order to beat back
Northern threats. Even when defeat seemed inevitable, Palmer refused to give up. On December 10, 1863, before the General Assembly
of South Carolina, he attempted to instill a renewed hope, courage,
and effort into the South. He was not abandoning the Confederate
cause, and challenged others not to despair.[19] But Palmer did, eventually, despair. Mary Chestnut, after the fall of Atlanta, wrote in her
diary about hearing a Palmer who had little left to offer.

> This man is so eloquent, it was hard to listen and not give way. Despair was his word, and martyrdom. He offered us nothing more in this world than the martyr's crown. . . . He spoke of our agony, and then came the cry, "Help us, O God! Vain is the help of man." And so we came away shaken to the depths.[20]

The war's end found Palmer in deep despair. He acknowledged that he was "very sad." "Just now the earth is very dark," he said, "and I thank God that I have faith, when I cannot have knowledge."[21]

Soon after the war concluded, Palmer resumed his pastoral responsibilities at the First Presbyterian Church of New Orleans. An editorial note in the *New Orleans Times* on July 17, 1865, commented upon Palmer's return. The journalist wrote that Palmer "had lost none of those powers which gave such a charm to his pulpit oratory. He seemed, however, to be more chastened and subdued than he was before."[22]

Palmer's "chastened and subdued" spirit was only momentary. As he had been an important and dynamic leader in the prewar years, so he became instrumental in forming the civil religion that characterized the postwar South. Despair gave way to faith in a future vindication. Palmer asked: "Can a cause be lost which has passed through such a baptism as ours? Principles never die, and if they seem to perish it is only to experience a resurrection in the future."[23]

Palmer said and did much to help fulfill his prophecy of a future resurrection. When reconstruction measures required previously all-white schools to admit black students, Palmer's church led the way in establishing parochial schools for white pupils only. In 1872 he delivered an address in which he set forth his strongly held belief in segregation, a belief that would be pervasive in the civil religion of the South for many years to come. "It is indispensable," claimed Palmer,

> that the purity of race shall be preserved on either side. . . . There is no escape from the corresponding testimony, biblical and historical, that the human family, originally one, has been divided into certain large groups, for the purpose of being kept historically distinct. And all attempts, in every age of the world, and from whatever motives, whether of ambitious dominion or of an infidel humanitarianism, to force these together, are identical in aim and parallel in guilt with the usurpation and insurrection of the first Nimrod.[24]

In 1869 Palmer wrote a series of seventeen articles in which he protested against any attempts to reunite the Northern General Assembly to the Southern Presbyterian Church. Palmer argued that the Southern church must keep itself separate from its Northern counterpart because that body

> has involved itself in criminal errors touching the kingly office of Christ; ignoring, persistently, His spiritual kingdom, the Church – betraying her spirituality and independence, and perverting the power of the keys to uphold the State, and introducing terms of ecclesiastical communion, unwarranted by Holy Scripture, and contradictory to the commands of Christ.[25]

Palmer raised most of the prewar issues in his protest and then added others, defending and promoting a position that would prevail among Southern Presbyterians until the mid-twentieth century.

In an address on June 27, 1872, at Washington and Lee University, Palmer warned the South about the encroaching evils of industrialism and materialism coming from the North. He was afraid that "the fine sense of honor which formed the beautiful enamel of Southern character may be rubbed away, to be followed by a swift decay of virtue."[26] He concluded by challenging the college youth to keep their value system firmly anchored in the past, and he set before them the heroes of the American Revolution and the Confederacy to serve as their examples.

In the lengthy but eloquent sermon "National Responsibility Before God," Palmer raised almost all of the issues that were important to the Confederate states. It was delivered on June 13, 1861, only two months after the Union surrender of Fort Sumter. Palmer reaffirmed the reasons for secession. After justifying the institution of slavery through Noah's curse on Ham, a curse which condemned Ham's descendants (blacks) to "the doom of perpetual servitude," Palmer spoke at length about five national sins which made the South's separation from the Union imperative and inevitable. He complained that the "Founding Fathers" had failed to recognize God in the Constitution. Charging that the nation's leaders were "tinctured with the free-thinking and infidel spirit ... which brought forth ... the horrors of the French Revolution," Palmer looked to the Confederacy as a means to correct such heretical trends. He was appalled at the lack of reverence for authority and law, and denounced those who appealed to "the pretensions of 'higher law,' which has involved half the nation in the guilt of perjury."

Because of these offenses, "God has let loose upon us this political storm" that "the moral atmosphere will be purged." Palmer saw the present conflict as an event paralleling the American Revolution. He reaffirmed the Jeffersonian doctrine that when a government abuses its power, the people have a right to form a new and good government. After castigating the North, Palmer exclaimed: "The last hope of self-government upon this Continent lies in these eleven Confederated States." From the earliest days of American history, "two nations were in the American womb," and the separation of North and South had been "decreed of God." Palmer's sermon, which is an example of superb prose, summarizes most of the Southern justifications for secession.

NOTES

1. James W. Silver, *Confederate Morale and Church Propaganda* (New York: Norton, 1957), 93, 101.
2. Quoted in Anne C. Loveland, *Southern Evangelicals and the Social Order 1800–1860* (Baton Rouge: Louisiana State University Press, 1980), 259–60.
3. Quoted in C. C. Goen, *Broken Churches, Broken Nation* (Macon: Mercer University Press, 1985), 104–05.
4. Silver, *Confederate Morale and Church Propaganda*, 17, 18–19.
5. Benjamin Morgan Palmer, *The Life and Letters of James Henley Thornwell* (Richmond: Whittet & Shepperson, 1875), 477–78.
6. "Critical Notices," *Southern Presbyterian Review* 4 (Jan. 1861): 452.
7. "Our National Sins," *Fast Day Sermons* (New York: Rudd & Carleton, 1861), 56.
8. Palmer, *Life and Letters of Thornwell*, 486.
9. Silver, *Confederate Morale and Church Propaganda*, 16–17.
10. Loveland, *Southern Evangelicals and the Social Order*, 258.
11. *Christian Duty in the Present Crisis* (Savannah: John M. Cooper, 1860).
12. "Slavery a Divine Trust: Duty of the South to Preserve and Perpetuate It," *Fast Day Sermons*, 57–80.
13. (Charleston: Welch, Harris & Co., 1861).
14. *A Vindication of Secession and the South* (Columbia: n.p., 1861).
15. *The Southern Soldier's Duty* (Rome, GA: D. H. Mason, 1861).
16. *Coercion and Conciliation* (Richmond: Macfarlane & Fergusson, n.d.).
17. Silver, *Confederate Morale and Church Propaganda*, 78.
18. Margaret B. DesChamps, "Benjamin Morgan Palmer, Orator-Preacher of the Confederacy," *Southern Speech Journal* 19 (Sept. 1953): 16. This article is a brief but excellent account of Palmer's activities during the war.

19. *A Discourse Before the General Assembly of South Carolina* (Columbia: Charles P. Pelham, State Printer, 1864).
20. *A Diary from Dixie* (1908; Cambridge: Harvard University Press, 1980), 434–35.
21. Quoted in Charles Reagan Wilson, *Baptized in Blood: The Religion of the Lost Cause 1865–1920* (Athens: University of Georgia Press, 1980), 66.
22. Thomas Cary Johnson, *The Life and Letters of Benjamin Morgan Palmer* (Richmond: Presbyterian Committee of Publication, 1906), 74.
23. Wilson, *Baptized in Blood,* 74.
24. Johnson, *Life and Letters of Palmer,* 355.
25. Johnson, *Life and Letters of Palmer,* 328.
26. Johnson, *Life and Letters of Palmer,* 357.

National Responsibility Before God

Benjamin Morgan Palmer

June 13, 1861

> If thy people go out to war against their enemies by the way that thou shalt send them, and they pray unto thee toward this city which thou hast chosen, and the house which I have built for thy name; then hear thou from the heavens their prayer and their supplication, and maintain their cause.
>
> *—2d Chronicles VI, 34–35—*

This day is one of surpassing solemnity. In the gravest period of our history, amidst the perils which attend the dismemberment of a great nation and the reconstruction of a new government, we are confronted with another more instant and appalling. Our late Confederates, denying us the right of self-government, have appealed to the sword and threaten to extinguish this right in our blood. Eleven tribes sought to go forth in peace from the house of political bondage: but the heart of our modern Pharaoh is hardened, that he will not let Israel go. In their distress, with the untried sea before and the chariots of Egypt behind, ten millions of people stretch forth their hands before Jehovah's throne, imploring him to "stir up his

(New Orleans: Price-Current Steam Book and Job Printing Office, 1861).

strength before Ephraim and Benjamin and Manasseh, and come
and save them." It was a memorable day when the Hebrew tribes,
having crossed the Jordan, stood, the one-half of them upon Mount
Ebal and the other half upon Mount Gerizim, and pronounced the
solemn Amen to the curses and blessings of the divine law as proclaimed by the Levites. Not less grand and awful is this scene today,
when an infant nation strikes its covenant with the God of Heaven.
This vast assembly is not simply a convention of individuals engaged in acts of personal worship. It is not even the Church holding
communion through priestly rites. But, as an integral part of this
young nation and in obedience to the call of our civil head, we are
met to recognize the God of nations. Confessing the sins of our fathers
with our own, and imploring the divine guidance through all our fortunes, the people of these Confederate States proclaim this day,
"the Lord our God will we serve, and his voice will we obey." It is this
sacramental feature of our worship which lends to it such dreadful
solemnity. At the moment when we are crystalizing into a nation, at
the very opening of our separate career, we bend the knee together
before God – appealing to his justice in the adjudication of our cause,
and submitting our destiny to his supreme arbitration. The bonds
of this covenant, which we seal this day to the Lord, are entered upon
the register in which the Recording Angel writes up the deeds of time,
before the Eternal throne.

The question then arises at the threshold of our proceedings,
what principles underlie and support this act of public and national
homage? Our external actions are a mockery, except as they are concrete expressions of some secret and vital truth. As the body is but
the organ of the soul, and each gesture but a symbol of the power
which reigns within – so in all intelligent action some dominant idea
resides, the soul by which it is quickened and informed. The worship
now offered in this sanctuary will be found to turn upon the great
truth, that the nation is in a clear sense a sort of *person* before God –
girded with responsibilities which draw it within his comprehensive
government. We must renounce the shallow nominalism which would
make such a word as "nation" a dead abstraction, signifying only the
aggregation of individuals. It is an incorporated society, and possesses a unity of life resembling the individuality of a single being.
It can deliberate and concur in common conclusions which are carried out in a joint action, analogous to the powers of thought and
will in a single mind. It stands in definite moral relations, out of

which spring such duties and obligations that we can properly speak of the law of nations in which they are expounded, and by which the intercourse with every similar society is regulated. In these respects a nation becomes a *person* capable of executing a trust, and conscious both of rights and obligations. Each has its own precisely defined character, fulfils its appointed mission, is developed through a providential training, and is held to a strict providential reckoning. The importance of this principle is sufficiently apparent. It not only gives significance to these religious solemnities; but it suggests the duty of this new-born nation to consider the part assigned it in the great drama of History, and its dependence upon the blessing of Him who "ruleth in the kingdom of men and giveth it to whomsoever he will." I shall, therefore, be justified in pausing for a moment upon its illustration.

If we ascend the stream of history to its source, we find in Noah's prophetic utterances to his three sons, the fortunes of mankind presented in perfect outline. The benediction upon Shem marked his descendants out for a destiny predominantly religious; and through all time, in ancient days and in modern, both in a true direction and in a false, and as seen in the two representative nations of the Shemitic stock, history attests the fulfillment of this mission. Through the entire interval between Abraham and Christ, the Hebrews were appointed to testify for the unity of God against the idolatry of mankind; and all Hebrew history turns upon the execution of this trust as its pivot. Since the Christian era, the Arabians, belonging to the same group, moving in a false direction, but yielding a blind obedience to what may be termed their Shemitish instinct, gave birth to the Mahometan imposture, a religion without a mystery and without sacrifice, which, transforming a religious enthusiasm into martial fanaticism, has tingled the whole current of their history. Still further to mark the destiny of this group, the only members of it, which have left no permanent trace upon the history of mankind, were those upon the banks of the Euphrates, who were seduced by a fertile agriculture and a flourishing commerce from their religious trust, and lapsed into the idolatry and worldliness of the other races.

In like manner, enlargement was promised to Japhet; and through all the past, the hardy and aggressive families of this stock have spread over the larger portion of the earth's surface, fulfilling their mission as the organ of human civilization. In ancient and in modern times – through the Greeks and Romans once, through the English,

French and Germans now – the world has been indebted to Japhet for its intellectual culture, for the discoveries of science, for the inventions of art, for the solution of all the great problems of State policy and public law. It would not be difficult to show how this general work of civilizing the world has been providentially subdivided between the families of this great stock – that as of old Greece was supremely devoted to intellectual culture, and Rome to political philosophy, so in later times the same partition of duties has practically been made between the great nations of Europe. Still further to show the controlling power of God over nations, wild and nomadic tribes have been held in reserve, bursting, at appointed times, the bounds of their enclosure and recruiting the wasted energies of a decaying civilization.

Upon Ham was pronounced the doom of perpetual servitude – proclaimed with double emphasis, as it is twice repeated that he shall be the servant of Japhet and the servant of Shem. Accordingly, history records not a single example of any member of this group lifting itself, by any process of self-development, above the savage condition. From first to last, their mental and moral characteristics, together with the guidance of Providence, have marked them for servitude; while their comparative advance in civilization and their participation in the blessings of salvation, have even been suspended upon this decreed connexion with Japhet and with Shem.

These facts are beyond impeachment; and nothing can be more instructive than to see the outspreading landscape of all history embraced thus within the camera of Noah's brief prophecy. In the largest classification of the human race, we see the hand of God upon nations – not only "appointing the bounds of their habitations," but impressing upon each the type of character that fits it for its mission. If from this wide generalization we turn attention to particular States, we have the same evidence of their separateness and individuality. Thus, from the earliest moment that Egypt was cradled amidst the bulrushes of her own sacred Nile, she exhibits a character throughout and intensely Egyptian; a character as clearly distinct from the Hebrew and the Persian, as these in their turn differ from the Roman and the Greek. And the spaces which all these respectively fill upon the chart of universal history are as exclusively their own, as the places which they occupy upon the surface of the globe. It is noteworthy in this connection that as nations have their assigned missions, so they are preserved in being till their work is done; after which they sink into decrepitude, or are expunged from the roll of the living. Thus Greece was perpetuated until she had carried the arts of sculpture and painting, of poetry, eloquence and song, to a perfection which has never been surpassed; and when she could do no more in philosophy and science, she was trodden in the dust beneath the iron-heeled legions of Rome. When Rome, too, had built up an empire as wide as the world, and could do no more by her systems of jurisprudence and schemes of state-craft, she slid into a military despotism – and the world having no need of experiments in that direction, her mighty fabric gave way under the pressure of barbarian hordes, the present congress of European nations springing ultimately from the political chaos which was thereby induced. So it has been through all the past; so it will continue to be through all the future; and the grand conclusion is but the lesson which is impressed upon us to-day. This lesson is, that nations are in a weighty sense *persons* before God, with individual characters mysteriously impressed upon the parent stock, and fully developed through a providential training; that they work out their historic missions which are unequivocally assigned by a higher power; that girt about with grave responsibilities, they are held to account for their fidelity to their trusts; and that their solemn duty is to recognize in every stage of their career that Being by whose guidance and blessing they are conducted to their destinies. In the acknowledgement of this truth we to-day bow the knee before the God of Heaven, whom we have chosen to serve as the God of this nation forever.

Parallel with this truth of the nation's personal responsibility, is another which determines the form of our worship by humiliation and fasting as well as by prayer. I refer to the continuity of a nation's life through a long succession of individuals that die. While the elements which compose the nation are continually passing away, the nation remains entire without disintegration. As the body of a living man is continually wasting and as continually repaired, through the ceaseless flux of its particles; so in the state "one generation goeth and another generation cometh," but the nation preserves its identity through the whole succession. In consequence of this it is that, in God's government over them, the sins of a nation are often punished in generations long posterior to that which is immediately guilty. The measure of criminality being at last filled up by these, the accumulated chastisement descends. This principle our Lord declared to the Jews of his day: that they "filled up the measure of their fathers;" that "upon them would come all the righteous blood shed upon the earth, from the blood of righteous Abel unto the blood of Zacharias, the son of Barachias, whom they slew between the temple and the altar; verily I say unto you, all these things shall come upon this generation." It is in virtue of this principle that we undertake to confess the sins of our fathers as well as our own; which, upon any other ground, would be a mockery and a sham. As nations in their corporate form cannot be subject to the retributions of the final judgment, the divine government must be enforced along by temporal sanctions; and the probation which nations enjoy passes along the current of national life through succeeding generations, bringing at last the avenging punishment upon one generation out of many which are equally implicated. If this should seem severe, it should be remembered that it is unavoidable under a state of discipline and probation; and it has the practical comfort, that repenting posterity may often, by humility and faith, turn aside the descending judgment, and secure still the favor and protection of Heaven, forfeited by their fathers.

Under this exposition of principles which underlie our worship, let us, my brethren, like Daniel of old, "confess our sins and the sins of our people, and present our supplication before the Lord our God, in this his holy mountain." There is obviously a distinction between the sins committed really by individuals, but which from their universality we may in a sense bewail as national, and those sins which are referrable to the nation itself in its organized and corporate form. For example, intemperance is painfully prevalent among all classes of our people; yet it is not properly chargeable upon the nation as an organic whole, except so far as the government by its unwise or insufficient legislation may be responsible for the same. So again, "because of swearing the land mourneth," that profane use of God's holy name which dishonors the lips of multitudes; and which one of England's classic writers describes as "the superfluity of naughtiness," "a sort of peppercorn rent" which men gratuitously pay to the Devil. Yet in a strict sense it is the sin of individuals who presumptuously say "our lips are our own, who is Lord over us!" In like manner, Sabbath-breaking is affirmed in Scripture to be one of those offences which peculiarly draw down upon a people the righteous resentment of God. Yet the nation is not held answerable for it, except as rulers in their official acts, or the law by its postal and other arrangements, may wantonly tread it in the dust. However proper it might be to comment upon these forms of transgression and to bewail them upon this day of public fasting, as the common sins of our people, I prefer for special reasons to restrict your attention to that class of sins which are properly national, as being committed by the people in their public association and in their corporate existence.

1. *We bewail then, in the first place, the fatal error of our Fathers in not making a clear national recognition of God at the outset of the nation's career.* The record of the divine dealings with America was, from the beginning, singularly a religious record. It was certainly remarkable that this Western Continent should have been locked up between two oceans from the knowledge of mankind, through fifteen centuries of the Christian era: and quite as remarkable that its discovery should be ordered at a time when an asylum was required for the victims of religious persecution in the old world. It is certainly true that religious zeal operated as a constraining motive with those who first took possession of these shores. In all the proclamations and grants of Spain and Portugal, the planting of the cross upon these heathen and savage coasts was urged as the leading motive for conquest and colonization – and the Continent was formally taken possession of by the first discoverers as distinctly in the name of Almighty God, as by the authority of their Christian Majesties, Ferdinand and Isabella. It is familiar even to our children that the hardships of the first settlement in these United States, were cheerfully endured through the faith and patience of those who simply sought "amidst the depths of the desert gloom" "freedom to worship God." Yet will it be credited, when this most religious people, after the lapse of a century and a half, undertook to establish an independent government, there was a total ignoring of the divine claims and of all allegiance to the divine supremacy? It is true that in the eloquent paper which recited their grievances before the world, and proclaimed the Colonies independent of the British throne, the signers of the Declaration appealed to the Divine Omniscience "for the rectitude of their intentions," and pledged their faith to each other "with a firm reliance on the protection of divine Providence." It is therefore the more remarkable that, eleven years after, in that great instrument by which the several States were linked together in a common nationality, and which was at once the public charter and the paramount law of the land, not a word is found from which one could possibly infer that such a being as God ever existed. The omission was a fearful one; and it is not surprising that He who proclaims his jealousy of his own glory, should let fall the blow which has shattered

that nation. Probable reasons may be suggested for its explanation. It certainly was not due to the irreligiousness of the masses, for they were predominantly Christian. But the public leaders of the time were largely tinctured with the free-thinking and infidel spirit which swept like a pestilence over Europe in the seventeenth and eighteenth centuries, and which brought forth at last its bitter fruit in the horrors of the French Revolution. It may have been due likewise to the jealousy entertained of any union between Church and State, at a time when the novel, grand and successful experiment was first tried of an entire separation between the two. But to whatever causes we refer it, the certain fact is that the American nation stood up before the world a helpless orphan, and entered upon its career without a God. Through almost a century of unparalleled prosperity, this error has been but partially retrieved: as the religious spirit of the people has silently compelled the appointment by executive authority, of days of public thanksgiving and prayer – yet to this day, in the great national act of incorporation there is no bond which connects the old American nation with the Providence and Government of Jehovah.

Thanks be unto God, my brethren, for the grace given our own Confederacy, in receding from this perilous atheism! When my eye first rested upon the Constitution adopted by the Confederate Congress, and I read in the first lines of our organic and fundamental law a clear, solemn, official recognition of Almighty God, my heart swelled with unutterable emotions of gratitude and joy. It was the return of the prodigal to the bosom of his father, of the poor exile who has long pined in some distant and bleak Siberia after the associations of his childhood's home. At length, the nation has a God: Alleluia! "the Lord reigneth let the earth rejoice." And now in the beautiful proclamation of our President our whole people through eleven States are called to ratify the covenant, and to set up the memorial stone thereof. It is indeed no ordinary State Paper, filled with cold and starched commonplaces, which by their icy formality so often freeze up the very piety they seem to invoke. But a religious unction pervades every clause and line; and the child of God can recognize the dialect which his ear loves to hear. It summons us to "recognize our dependence upon God," to "humble ourselves under the dispensations of divine providence," to "acknowledge his goodness" and "supplicate his merciful protection." Under the conviction that "none but a righteous cause can gain the divine favor," it "implores the Lord of Hosts to guide and direct our policy in the paths of right, duty, justice and mercy; to unite our hearts and our efforts for the defence of our dearest rights; to strengthen our weakness, crown our arms with success, and enable us to secure a speedy, just and honorable peace," "to inspire us with a proper spirit and temper of heart and mind to bear our evils, to bless us with his favor and protection, and to bestow his gracious benediction upon our government and country." This is truly a Christian patriot's prayer. It breathes no malignant revenge; but it calls the nation to nestle beneath the wings of Almighty power and love. Upon this central truth – that "God is and that He is the rewarder of them that diligently seek him" – all of us can stand. Hebrew or Christian, Protestant or Catholic – all can subscribe this ultimate truth: and here we all meet to-day to say that He is our trust in whom nations as well as men "live and move and have their being." This day is therefore one of infinite solemnity: it is our nation's first Sabbath, when it meets to confess its God. If it shall hold fast to this testimony, it will have an immortal career: and had I a voice loud as seven thunders, I would proclaim from the Potomac to the Rio Grande, that a nation drives against the rocks which denies its responsibility before the God of Heaven. I speak this not as if it were my trade: but as a man, and in full view of all that constitutes true manhood, under the pressure and dictation of the highest philosophy, I affirm that to know and fear God is the perfection of wisdom. He is most a man, who brings up all parts of his nature with an equal culture; and to cleave sacrilegiously between these parts and to throw away those religious longings which can be satisfied only in God, is to forego our highest prerogative and to approximate the level of senseless apes chattering upon the trees of the forest. My God keep this nation under the power of those religious convictions, which to-day moves the hearts of our people as they were never moved before.

2. *We have sinned against God in the idolatry of our History, and in the boastful spirit it has naturally begotten.* It is a melancholy proof of human frailty, that our noblest virtues so easily degenerate into the meanest vices. A generous heart cannot but rejoice in an honorable ancestry; and love of country is a filial virtue, which must feel complacency in a public history illustrated by magnanimity and truth. A just self-reliance too is only the off-shoot of true manliness; characteristic of all, whether nations or men, by whom any thing historic is ever achieved. Were these high virtues always sanctified by a religious sense of dependence upon God, they would

never be corrupted into the weaknesses either of vanity or arrogance. But woe to the nation that with pride of heart lifts itself against God! The terrible infliction upon Nebuchadnezzar of old, is a lesson for all time. The poor monarch, driven among the beasts of the field and drivelling in his insanity, proclaims through his affecting experience that all "those who walk in pride God is able to abase." Never was such a debt of gratitude for providential blessings contracted by any people, as that due to God from the American nation. He gave them a broad land and full of springs – He emptied out its former inhabitants who melted away as the Canaanites before Israel – and His gracious providence was a wall of fire around their armies through a long and painful war. Yet we have seen how speedily they forgot the God of their salvation, and made an idol of themselves. Looking out from their palaces and towers, they have cried, saying, "is not this great Babylon that we have built for the house of the kingdom, by the might of our power and for the honor of our majesty?" They have lifted up their golden image upon the plain of Dura, and "at the sound of the cornet, flute, harp, sackbut and psaltery, they have fallen down and worshipped it." With insufferable arrogance they have taunted other nations with their adherence to institutions and usages, which are the growth of time, and cannot perish in an hour. Assuming that Constitutional freedom can only be enjoyed under Republican forms, as propagandists of their own political faith, they have sometimes rudely challenged every other creed as heretical and monstrous. It is too often forgotten that forms of government are not the arbitrary products of legislation, but are an outgrowth from the nation's life – as it were, secreted from within and crystalizing around it as an external shell. Hence the burning resentment created by a crusade against usages which are endeared by habit and consecrated by time. Certainly from this charge of officious intermeddling, a portion of the American people have not been free, springing, even where it is most innocent, from the egotism and self-conceit which says, "we are the people, and wisdom will die with us." But it was reserved to our own day to carry this haughtiness to its climax, in denying the right even of political existence to those who will not pronounce the Shibboleth of Federalism. The empty menaces, too, which have been poured into our ears, and into the ears of all Europe, would be disgusting from their arrogance if they were not contemptible from their impotence. But in the public laughter which they have drawn down from all the world, we cannot fail to see the righteous retribution of God upon this national idolatry of self. Let us — so far as in the past we may have been implicated in this transgression — deeply repent of it. Let us, in the opening of our national career, lay deep the foundations of public virtue in a sense of dependence upon God. Let us, to the end of our history, aim to preserve that modesty of carriage which distinguishes the nobleman from the parvenu, and which always remembers that a nation is great only through the divine favor.

3. Another form of national sin has been *a too great devotion to Party, coupled with the flagrant abuse of the Elective Franchise.* We may indulge no Utopian dreams of exemption from the collisions of party; nor would complete political repose, if long continued, be an advantage. Under a free government where men are permitted to think, they must be expected to differ. Discussion, too, gives light; for truth, like fire, comes out from the contact of flint and steel. Parties which spring from honest and different views of public policy, are seldom sectional. Embracing the whole country they are perfectly consistent with genuine patriotism; and may even form bonds of union between those who might else be separated by local interests. The simple existence of parties, therefore, is not an evil; or if it be, like the antagonism between the forces of nature, it is conducive to a higher good. This presupposes, however, that the arena of conflict is the hall of legislation, and the weapons of warfare are those of honorable debate. But when it comes to this, that party usurps the place of country — when caucus becomes king, and by boot and thumbscrew all individuality of opinion is crushed out of men — when public platforms become the oracles of inspiration, higher than the constitution and the law — when tricksters and under-whippers, who drill the rank and file of party, take the place of statesmen who expound and defend great and lofty principles — when, above all, supple cunning carries out, by base and crooked measures, the decrees of secret cabals: then may be seen the handwriting upon the wall, and the glory has departed. Alas! my brethren, am I not reciting the sad and bitter tale of the past? What but this fell spirit of party has riven to its base a government which, a little while ago, we thought as enduring as the everlasting hills? The great statesmen passed away whose hearts could embrace a continent, and we came to men who, whatever their genius, fall under the cutting rebuke of Goldsmith — to men

> "Who, born for the universe, narrowed their mind,
> And to party gave up what was meant for mankind."

We have lived to see fulfilled in the reign of sectionalism the remarkable prophecy of Mr. Jefferson, uttered forty years ago with such startling emphasis: "I had ceased," writes he, "to pay any attention to public affairs, content to be a passenger in our bark to the shore from which I am not distant. But this momentous question (the Missouri controversy) *like a fire bell in the night,* awakened and filled me with terror. *I considered it at once as the knell of the Union.* It is hushed for a moment; but this is a reprieve only, not a final sentence. *A geographical line coinciding with a marked principle, moral and political, once conceived and held up to the angry passions of men, will never be obliterated.*" A turbulent and wicked faction, working through a generation and laying its obscene touch upon everything holy in Church and State, at length sprung like the old man of the sea astride of the nation's neck. The work of ruin was accomplished; and now the deep, awful chasm of eternal separation yawns between North and South. May God in his mercy forgive the authors of this mischief, for it never can be repaired!

But what shall be said of the *abuse of the ballot,* the very symbol and instrument of the people's power? What, of the timidity, or indifference, or disgust of some who abstain from their privilege, and suffer every true interest of the country to pass by default into the hands of base and designing men? What, of the profaneness of others, like Esau, who for a mess of pottage sell their American birthright? What, of the political brokerage which trades in this dreadful immorality, and sets up the offices of government virtually at public outcry to the highest bidders? What, of the trained ruffianism which hustles with violence from the polls all honest men who can be browbeaten? "Oh! the offense is rank, and smells to Heaven!" Can my poor voice contribute aught this day towards arousing the public conscience to the enormity of measures, by which all national morality is secretly sapped, and the foundations of public liberty are surely undermined? Let us be deeply humbled before God for sins like these; and let us fervently pray they may belong only to the record of the past. For the love of God and Country, let us strive to bring back the purer days of the republic: when honest merit waited, like Cincinnatus at his plow, to be called forth for service, and before noisy candidates cried their wares at the hustings like fishwomen in the market – when a ribald press did not thrust its obtrusive gaze into the sanctities of private life, and the road to office did not lead through the pillory of public abuse and scandal – and when the votes of the people only expressed their virtuous and unbiased will. If not – then in the loss of our national virtue we shall become as incapable of serving God and history, as the poor nation which we have just seen stranded upon these abuses and wrecked forever. May these things be only of the past! May the brand of Cain be on the forehead of him who first attempts, in our new government, to corrupt the ballot! May he go forth a fugitive from men, until his dishonor shall hide itself in a nameless grave!

4. *As a nation, we have sinned in a grievous want of reverence for the authority and majesty of law.* You remember that fine passage in Hooker which embalms, in words of amber, the whole philosophy of obedience: "of law there can be no less acknowledged than that her seat is in the bosom of God, her voice the harmony of the world; all things in heaven and earth do her homage: the very least as feeling her care, and the greatest as not exempted from her power; both angels and men and creatures of what condition soever, with uniform consent, admiring her as the mother of their peace and joy." Like the attraction of gravitation in physics, law binds together all the spheres of human duty and holds them fast to the throne of God. In all the concentric circles of society, obedience is man's first obligation. Not one is so much a master, but he owes fealty to a power higher than his own. The spirit of insubordination is therefore the highest treason, for it breaks the tie which binds the universe of moral beings together: as though in nature apostate orbs should fly from their centres, and wildly clash in the regions of space.

But if disregard of law be in this general view a crime of such magnitude, it assumes a new malignity when committed by a people living under such a government as ours. Its distinctive folly and wickedness are seen in the fact that it involves the abdication of our supremacy. In a republic, the sovereign is the people; and the laws they obey are the expressions of their own will. To trample upon these is, therefore, to trail their own sovereignty in the mire, to abdicate their own power, to extinguish the national life by shameful felo de se. When a monarch like Charles V lays aside the insignia of his royal state and retires to a convent, we can understand the weariness of care and disgust of the world, which induced the step. But no censure mingles with our compassion, because the state survived.

His abdication simply transferred the symbol and substance of power to the hands of another, and there was no break in the continuity of the nation's life. But where the people are the ruler no less than the ruled, abdication is a felony; for it can only take place through self-murder. Insubordination to authority is with us therefore the commencement of political destruction—at once the most flagrant and the most senseless of crimes. There is the greater necessity for grinding this truth into the minds of our people, inasmuch as through the simplicity of our republican institutions the ensigns of power are not flaunted before the eye. Under a monarchy, the king and his court become the symbol of authority, the living representative of the law in its majesty. It is an unquestionable advantage of that form of government, that law should be presented in this embodied and concrete form before the masses; who are insensibly taught reverence by the very pomp and ceremony, which many decry without considering this incidental benefit which accrues. But with us, the administration of law is necessarily stripped of this outward splendor: the people should, therefore, be taught the dignity of obedience, as springing from the self-respect which is due to their own sovereignty. Need I pause to show the disasters which, in a popular government, must flow from irreverence of the law? Alas! the present history of our own distracted land furnishes a commentary for the text. It is a sad tale—a tale, sad as that which renewed the grief of Æneas before the Tyrian queen.* It is this arrogant competition of individual opinion finding its climax in the pretensions of "a higher law," which has involved half the nation in the guilt of perjury, and broken the bond of the holiest covenant ever sworn between man and man. It is this same recklessness of obligation, which has lifted up the sword to butcher those who will not bend nor yield to a merciless proscription. It is the same spirit mounting to phrenzy, which has seized upon wise and venerable ministers of the church; who have turned away from the gospel of God, in order to hound on this war of exterminating and bitter revenge. And it is the same demon of misrule which, in three short months, has swept away every guard of private as well as public liberty; and erected, under the shadow of the tomb of Washing-

---

*"Infandum, Regina, jubes renovare dolorem,
Trojanes ut opes et lamentabile regnum
Eruerint Danai. . . . Quis talia fando
Temperct a lachrymis? —"Æneid, Lib. 2

ton, a despotism as irresponsible and cruel as any which has ever crushed the hearts and hopes of mankind.

In this particular manifestation of lawlessness, the South has rather been "sinned against than sinning." But then we have the *lex talionis;* the spirit, whose unrelenting cry is "an eye for an eye – a tooth for a tooth." This right of retaliation finds recognition with us; not softened, as with the ancient Hebrews, by cites of refuge, whither the man-slayer may betake himself. By a too general consent individuals assume the prerogative of the magistrate, in redressing their own wrongs. It may be true, that certain outrages cannot be restrained by the inadequate defences of public law; and when the safety of society may require instant retribution at the hands of the sufferer, who is substantively transformed into the magistrate. But these cases are exceptional and extreme; and if not provided for by special enactment, they are at least sustained by a virtuous sentiment based upon the instinct of self-preservation, characterizing the State as well as the person. Yet, in a civilized and Christian land, when the broad shield of law is supposed to cover all the interests and rights of men, it is flagrant wickedness to live as though society was resolved into its primordial elements: amid all the paths of business or pleasure, to have the treacherous hand trembling upon the concealed weapon, which is ready, in the sudden brawl, to leap forth upon its unsuspecting victim. This spirit must be exorcised from the land, else it will work the destruction of government. Let us choose wise legislators, who shall frame a code sufficient for the public protection. Let us clothe our Judges with the purest ermine, that they may make the temple of justice awful and holy as the sanctuary of God. Let us create a robust and healthy public sentiment, which shall everywhere support the law by an influence as diffused and silent as the pressure of the atmosphere. Let us train our youth to habits of obedience, teaching boys to remain boys, else they will be beaten with rods. Thus may reverence for law pervade all classes; and the daily conduct of our citizens come up as the swelling chorus of that song, which Hooker beautifully describes as "the harmony of the world." We have sinned in this against our race and against God: let our repentance to-day be the deep bass, which shall give the keynote of that song.

5. *As a people, we have been distinguished by a grovelling devotion to merely material interests.* A nation loses its tone when it becomes intensely utilitarian, when noble deeds are weighed in the

scales of merchandise, and expediency stands behind its counter to measure off virtue by the ell, and weigh honor by the pound avoirdupois. The American devotion to material interests is by no means inexplicable. A great and practical race like our own, thrown upon a new Continent, and turning its Saxon energy upon the development of hidden treasures, elsewhere unparalleled, finds its covetousness reacted upon by its own prosperity. The age too is an age of physical science, which, exploring the secrets of nature, and subordinating her powers to the uses of man, renders it utilitarian by system. Besides all this, the stimulus of our Republican institutions develops the activity of our people into almost superhuman energy, and sharpens their wit to the highest shrewdness. With the total obliteration of caste, we start together from the same level of democratic equality. Yet, with the avenues to power and distinction open to all aspirants, is it strange that a general competition should exist amongst our people in the accumulation of wealth, which is at once the most obvious and the most easily attained instrument of power? Thus, the greed of gain has rusted into the hearts of our people – the most sordid of all passions, and the most fruitful source of individual and national corruption. The prevalence of this spirit has exposed us to the bitter sarcasm that, as a nation, we have set up the Golden Calf in the midst of the camp as the God of our idolatry. Every interest of the land has suffered from the corroding influence of this sordid utilitarianism. It has infected our schools of learning, cutting down the standard of intellectual discipline until sound scholarship is fast becoming a thing obsolete as the mythology of Greece. It has contaminated our Courts of Justice, until jury trial has, in a measure, become a shield for crime, and immunity from punishment is regulated by a graduated tariff. It has seated itself in halls of legislation, and discounts at the tables of the money-changers the rights and claims which a just legislation should protect. The spirit of speculation sweeps over the land with its expansion of credit and its inflated prosperity, until, as periodically as the equinox, we look for financial disaster, which dashes to the ground colossal fortunes as easily as the hurricane lays prostrate the giants of the forest.

It is all wrong, my hearers: offensive to God, and ruinous to ourselves. And I do not wonder that, to save us from total demoralization, God has let loose upon us this political storm, in order to bring up from the depth of the nation's heart its dormant virtue. We are learning by the sacrifices of the times, in the same school with our heroic forefathers, that liberty is better than gold, and honor more precious than fortune. The accumulated treasures of past industry and thrift are now cheerfully laid upon the altar of your country's safety. Fathers are consecrating their sons to that Country's service, with an oath more solemn than that which bound Hannibal to eternal enmity with Rome: and tender mothers buckle the shield around them, as did the Spartan mothers of old, saying with equal heroism, "come back with it a conqueror, or be borne back upon it a martyr." I thank God for the storm. It has come in time to redeem us from ruin. Though the heavens be overcast, and lurid lightnings gleam from the bosom of each dark cloud, the moral atmosphere will be purged – and from our heroism shall spring sons and daughters capable of immortal destinies. Let me sound it out as with the trumpet of the Resurrection day: the men in all ages who have made history, have been men of faith – men who could hide a great principle deep in their heart, work it out as a potential and substantive myth and abide the verdict of posterity. All the Poets, all the Statesmen, all the Warriors of the past, were men of faith. Believing in the grand and the true, they could put their heel upon the present; and lifting up the curtain which hides the far off future from other men, they drew up that future by a magnetic attraction to themselves, and lived abreast of it. Any man can do the things that can be done; but they who do the things that can't be done – they are the immortals. It is a heroic day in which to live! Let the pulse of a high and generous patriotism beat in our breasts: that the history we work out may be the school-book from which our children's children shall learn to be true, and brave, and pure, as it becomes the children of the great to be.

I had designed, in connexion with our national responsibilities, to speak of *the obligations we owe to our slave population*. But the subject is excluded by its own largeness from discussion now. It will bear postponement. When this unnatural war shall be concluded, and we shall be free from the impertinent interference with our domestic affairs by which we have been so long annoyed, there will be opportunity to say all that the moralist and Christian should utter, and what it will be fitting the legislator and the master should hear. We can afford to bide the time.

In conclusion, permit me to say that the present is by far the most important and glorious struggle through which the nation has ever passed. The parallel which has been drawn between it and the contest of the Revolution, has not been seen in its full significance by many even of those who have suggested it; certainly not by those who have derided it in terms of measureless contempt. The principles involved in this conflict are broader and deeper than those which underlay that of the Revolution, rendering it of far greater significance to us and to our posterity and to mankind at large. Our Fathers fought for no abstract rights as men, but for chartered rights as Englishmen. They claimed that the fundamental principle of English liberty was invaded, when the Colonies were taxed without representation. They were abundantly able to pay the duty which was stamped upon the Royal paper, and the tax levied upon the tea which they threw into the harbor of Boston: but they were not able to submit to any infraction of their Constitutional rights. For this they resisted unto blood: and had the British Ministry been wise, the day had been long postponed before the Crown had lost its brightest jewel, and England found a rival in those very Colonies which once owed her fealty and love. But *our* Revolution rests upon the broader principle laid as the corner stone of the American Constitution: "that governments derive their just powers from the consent of the governed; and that whenever any form of government becomes destructive of the ends for which it was formed, it is the right of the People to alter, or to abolish it, and to institute a new government, organizing its powers in such form as to them shall seem most likely to effect their safety and happiness." The true issue of to-day is not precisely what it was in November last, nor in January last, nor yet in March, when was exhibited the spectacle of the inauguration at Washington. The issue which now unites our whole population as the heart of one man, is *whether ten millions of people have not the inherent right to institute such a govenment, "as to them shall seem mostly likely to secure their safety and happiness."* This right is denied to us; and its denial lays the foundation of a despotism under which we cannot consent to live, for it was distinctly repudiated in the Declaration of 1776. We should be unworthy of our Fathers, if we flinched from maintaining to the last extremity the one, great, cardinal principle of American constitutional freedom. I could perhaps manage to live, if Providence had so ordained, under the despotism of the Czar, for it is not wholly irresponsible: the order of the Nobles would be interposed between me and the absolute will of the Autocrat. I could perhaps submit even to the Turk: for he is held in check by fear of his own Janizaries. But I will not – so help me God! – I never will submit to the despotism of the mob. It is not the occupant of the White House who is the tyrant of to-day; but the starving millions behind the throne. Hence the wild outburst of revenge and hate, which now astonishes the world. It is the wail of concentrated agony and despair of the unpaid labor which asks for bread, and capital gives it a stone; and which hopes through our extermination and the deportation or massacre of our slaves, to find room for itself upon the broad Savannas of the South. May a merciful God help them of the North! They have sowed the wind, they must reap the whirlwind. They cannot retrieve the past, they must drive on and meet the future: perhaps to experience the fate of Acteon, and be eaten up by their own hounds.

The last hope of self-government upon this Continent lies in these eleven Confederated States. We have retained the one, primary truth upon which the whole fabric of public liberty was reared by our fathers, and from which the North has openly apostatized. We have too in the institution of Slavery a great central fact, living and embodied, lifting itself up from the bed of history as the mountain cliff from the bed of the deep, blue sea; and in defending it against the assaults of a "rose-water philanthropy," we may place ourselves against all the past and feel the support of God's immovable Providence. Dare we then – dare any of us, man, woman or child – falter upon the path of such a destiny? Dare we quench in eternal night the hope which for a hundred years has been shedding its light upon the world, that man be self-governed and free? I do not doubt the bravery of our people – I do not distrust their willingness to make all possible sacrifices to maintain their right. But I do fear the absence of sufficient trust in the power and grace of Almighty God. Whatever may be the strength of our self-reliance, let it be built up through a sacred confidence in God as our shield and buckler. Whatever hopes we may cherish from the diplomatic influences which are destined to bear upon this quarrel, let us remember the jealousy of Him who forbade Israel to "go down into Egypt for horses." Let us trust in God, and with an humble self-reliance take care of ourselves; prepared to recognize that gracious Providence which will work our deliverance.

The division of the American people into two distinct nations has not taken me by surprise. It was clearly enough foreshadowed by the parliamentary conflicts through which we have passed; and it has its root deep down in the different nationalities, of which our eclectic population is composed. The analogies of history should have led us to anticipate it. Through all time, nations have been formed first by agglutination, and then by separation. In their original weakness, the most heterogeneous elements are combined and held together by the pressure of necessity: but in their maturity, those concealed differences spring up, which have their root often in the type of character impressed upon the parent stock; and which no lapse of time can obliterate, and no political chemistry can make permanently to coalesce. We have vainly read the history of our Fathers, if we failed to see that from the beginning two nations were in the American womb; and through the whole period of gestation the supplanter has had his hand upon his brother's heel. The separation of North and South was as surely decreed of God, and has as certainly been accomplished by the outworking of great moral causes, as was the separation of the Colonies from their English mother; as the genesis of the modern nations of Europe, out of the destruction of ancient Rome. In effecting this separation, the most glorious opportunity has been missed of demonstrating the power of our Republican principles, the progress of American civilization, and the effective control of the Gospel over human passions. In past ages, the sword has been the universal arbiter, and every issue has been submitted to the ordeal of battle. How fondly many of us hoped and pleaded for the rejection of this brutal argument; and for such an adjustment of our difficulties, as both the civilization and the religions of the age demanded! But our overtures of peace were first fraudulently entertained, and then insultingly rejected. I accept that rejection. I will go to my God, and will tell him how we have desired peace. I will tell him how we have sought to realize the scripture idea of "beating the sword into the plowshare:" and then I will remit those who have rejected our treaties of amity and commerce, to his retributive judgment. But in this act, let us bow in low humility before His throne; confessing our sins with prayer and fasting, and trusting in His promise to reward them that diligently seek Him. Oh! my country! "there is none like unto the God of Jeshurun, who rideth upon the heaven in thy help, and in his excellency on the sky. The eternal God is thy refuge, and underneath are the everlasting arms: and He shall thrust out the enemy from before thee, and shall say, destroy them. Israel then shall dwell in safety alone: the fountain of Jacob shall be upon a land of corn and wine; also his heavens shall drop dew. Happy art thou, O Israel; who is like unto thee, O People saved by the Lord, the shield of thy help, and who is the sword of thy excellency! and thine enemies shall be found liars unto thee, and thou shalt tread upon their high places."

WAR

As was noted in the introduction of this volume, a dominant belief in the mid-nineteenth century was that God was actively involved in and guided the affairs of individuals, nations, and history. War was not excluded from God's providence. God led nations into war. God provided victory and God caused defeat. The Southern clergy proclaimed in unmistakable terms that God had called the South to war and God would bring triumph.

In varying degrees the Northern clergy had looked upon the war as a righteous cause, a holy conflict that deserved the commitment of all Christian citizens. The Northern preachers, however, paled in significance to their Southern counterparts in seeing and declaring the war a holy struggle. For Benjamin Palmer the war was the holiest battle of history. It was a struggle to the death for freedom, family, home, civilization, and religion.[1] In a sermon on July 7, 1861, Alexander Gregg, the Episcopal Bishop of Texas, echoed most preachers in the Confederacy when he tied patriotism and religion into an inseparable knot. He declared that in all of history there had never been a higher or more noble duty than the one to which the South was now called.[2] In 1863 Dr. Joseph Stiles gave a vigorous expression of this faith.

> Oh, how far you live from the light! Why, let the North march out her millions of men on the left, and array upon the right all the veteran troops of England, France, Russia and Austria; and bring up the very gates of hell in all their strength to compose the center of her grand invading army. What then? Why, everything in God and from God assures us that these Confederate States would hear a voice from heaven: "The battle is not yours, but mine. Stand ye still and see the salvation of the Lord." If they dared to advance one step, a righteous and angry God would fire off upon the aliens terrible thunder that angel ears never heard . . . and fling down upon them cataracts of angry power that hell herself never felt, and . . . shake the very earth from under their feet.[3]

If a war is to be deemed just and fought with enthusiasm, the enemy must be perceived as a wicked and unscrupulous villain. The preachers in the South spared no words or emotions in portraying Northerners, even Northern preachers, as the very incarnation of evil. Meeting one month after the firing on Fort Sumter, the Southern Baptist Convention denounced the evil of the North. The minutes of their meeting speak of "the fanatical spirit of the North" which is "deluging the country in fratricidal blood." Even Northern churches and ministers were "breathing out slaughter and clamoring for sanguinary hostilities," something the Southern Baptists would have thought impossible "among the disciples of the Prince of Peace." The Convention then went on to pass ten resolutions in support of the Confederacy, and a pledge was made to do whatever was necessary to preserve the institutions and manhood of the South.[4]

Confederate sermons and publications were filled with accusations about the wicked North. An 1861 sermon by Edwin T. Winkler referred to the Yankees as "a hostile people . . . perverted into a tyranny."[5] George Foster Pierce, a Methodist bishop, in the spring of 1863 delivered a sermon in which he drew a sharp contrast between the wicked North and the God-fearing South. "We are fighting," he proclaimed, "against robbery and lust and rapine; against ruthless invasion, a treacherous despotism, the blight of its own land, and the scorn of the world. . . . The triumph of our arms is the triumph of right and truth and justice. The defeat of our enemies is the defeat of wrong, malice and outrage."[6]

As the war progressed, Union soldiers were depicted as barbarians ready to devour an innocent South. In 1863 Sylvanus Landrum declared: "Nothing on earth can surpass the beastly brutality and wickedness which the enemy has shown us. Still we have refused to imitate their example.'"[7] Even as some Northern ministers resorted to atrocity stories, some Southern ministers did the same. The stories multiplied in the final stages of the war. James Silver has written: "The triple-edged combination of horrors at the North, atrocities of Northerners in the South, and the threat of overwhelming barbarism if the Confederacy failed, moved into high gear in the last two years of the war. Stories of desecrated churches, desolated homes, and outraged women became common."[8]

In contrast to the wicked and heretical North stood the righteous South. Southerners were God's chosen and special people. The Rev. J. William Jones, a Baptist evangelist who labored to promote revivalism in the camps of General Lee's Army of Northern Virginia, spoke of the "God of Israel, God of the centuries, God of our forefathers, God of Jefferson Davis and Sidney Johnston and Robert E. Lee and Stonewall Jackson, and God of the Southern Confederacy."[9] The Confederacy was the latest successor to the ancient Hebrews in having a unique place in the providence of God.

The preachers continually emphasized the rightness of the Confederate cause. On November 15, 1861, at the Christian Church of Augusta, J. S. Lamar stated the typically declared rightness of the South: "In the contest between North and South, we are absolutely in the right. . . . Dissolution . . . far from being wrong, was the correction of a wrong."[10]

Again and again the preachers reminded their hearers of the purposes for which the South was fighting. In the summer of 1861 Episcopal Bishop Stephen Elliott, in Christ Church of Savannah, enumerated those principles for which the Confederacy was fighting:

> We are engaged in one of the grandest struggles which ever nerved the hearts or strengthened the hands of a heroic race. We are fighting for great principles, for sacred objects . . . to prevent ourselves from being transferred from American republicanism to French democracy . . . to rescue the fair name of our social life . . . from dishonor . . . to protect and preserve a race who form a part of our household, and stand with us next to our children . . . to drive away the infidel and rationalistic principles which are sweeping the land and substituting a gospel of the stars and stripes for the gospel of Jesus Christ.[11]

In 1863 I. R. Finley delivered a sermon at Lloyd's Church in Sussex County, Virginia, in which he enumerated the various characteristics of the divine rule on earth: (1) a spirit of gratitude and rejoicing, (2) a trust and hope in God, and (3) reverence for and obedience to God. Finley then asked where one might look for the rule of God. Responding to his own question, he said: "Will anyone be insane enough to look for it in the land of anarchy and tyranny – the North? Assuredly not. Where, then, is it to be found, but in this noble sisterhood of States – the Southern Confederacy?"[12]

Because the Confederates were in the right, because they were God's special and chosen people, the preachers continually proclaimed assurances of victory. About two months before the war began, Charles Cotesworth Pinckney delivered an optimistic sermon at Grace Church in Charleston. Anticipating trouble, Pinckney declared: "With that all pervading blessing to crown our work; with our acknowledged advantages, agriculture, commercial, social and religious, with a united people, walking in the fear of the Lord, and the faith of the Gospel, we may expect to retain the favor of heaven."[13] Early in the summer of 1861 Alfred MaGill Randolf, Episcopal Bishop of Southern Virginia, suggested that the ungodly Union might succeed for a time, but God was only raising it to a conspicuous position "in order to render more widely instructive the mockery of its triumph and the story of its fall."[14]

Later in the summer, after the Confederate victory at Manassas, John T. Wightman, in a sermon at the Methodist Church in Yorkville, South Carolina, introduced yet another reason for certain Confederate victory. "Cotton is King," declared Wightman, and the South, therefore, was the economic balance of the world. Furthermore, "the cotton trade keeps the Bible and the press under the control of Protestantism." After a strong biblical defense of slavery Wightman testified that the victories at Manassas and Fort Sumter, in the face of greater numbers and power, were proof that God favored and would bring final victory to the Confederate cause.[15]

Most Confederate preachers had no trouble reconciling war and religion. Edwin T. Winkler, in a sermon delivered only a few weeks prior to the war, declared: "I know that some have contended that war is not lawful according to Christian principles; but you have now to learn that it was God's guidance which led the Israelites to the conquest of Canaan." Winkler went on to give other biblical examples of war and soldiering which he declared were ordained and approved by God. He also told his listeners that Jesus' teachings about turning the other cheek did not apply to "the privilege of self-defense or the argument for a righteous war."[16]

James Silver reminds his readers that there were a few, a very few, Southern preachers and religious institutions who were critical of using religion to support and sanction war. The Baptist Association of Columbus, Georgia, for instance, was concerned about those who were "exercised more by the war spirit than by the spirit of the Gospel."[17] Such expressions, however, were very much the exception. Like their Northern counterparts, many Southern preachers extolled the virtue that warfare could bring about. Thomas V. Moore, on November 15, 1861, in a sermon at Richmond before the congregations of the First and Second Presbyterian Churches, affirmed that God used war as a means of disciplining nations. A prolonged peace tended "to emasculate and corrupt a people," while war breaks down "mammon worship and effeminacy."[18]

A primary role of clergymen in the South during the years of the war was the building and sustaining of Southern morale. Silver has written: "As its greatest social institution, the church in the South constituted the major resource of the Confederacy in the building and maintenance of civilian morale."[19] Because the cause of the Confederacy was just, Southern preachers urged their listeners to make any necessary sacrifice in order to ensure the triumph of good over evil. Early in 1864 Thomas Dunaway issued the challenge: "We must be willing, moreover, to contribute of our substance liberally and cheerfully – to sacrifice private rights and interests for the public good."[20]

So, too, strong denunciations were heaped upon those who sowed doubt, destroyed confidence, or were in any way disloyal to the Confederacy. The Baptists in Elon, Virginia, recorded their thoughts about those who failed to carry out their responsibilities: "The man who is not willing to work for the freedom which God has given us, is a traitor to his country, a hypocrit in the church and unfit to die."[21] Many sermons thundered words of judgment upon any who would question the objectives and the leaders of the Confederacy. Thomas Dunaway's 1864 sermon was representative.

> Whoever deals in inflamatory speeches, or heavy complaints, is not the friend but the enemy of his country. Whoever seeks to bring our rulers, civil or military, into disrepute, and thus lessen the confidence of the people in the government of their choice, or in any manner sows the seed of discontent, is working against the peace and welfare of the country.

The Southern clergy spoke with a nearly unanimous voice in support of the war. There were a few like James Lyon of the First Presbyterian Church in Columbus, Mississippi, who "opposed secession, criticized Davis, condemned the war as the work of demagogues, and favored Reconstruction," and somehow held the esteem of his parishioners throughout the war.[22] Lyon was a rare exception. Even as the North sometimes enforced loyalty, so the South had its ways of establishing homogeneity. Richard Beringer has written that most Southern clergymen who expressed pro-Union or anti-Confederate sentiments were dismissed from their pulpits and even expelled from church membership.[23] In some instances far more stringent measures were used to produce conformity among the Southern clergy. Several dissident Southern ministers were imprisoned and a few were killed.[24]

Many Southern clergymen sought to inspire their countrymen by example as well as by words. They enlisted in the armed services as soldiers, officers, and chaplains. One source has estimated that "half of the Southern clergy was in the service by the spring of 1862."[25] In 1864 a Baptist association in Mississippi complained that many churches were without pastors because so many ministers were serving in the Confederate army either as soldiers or in a religious capacity.[26]

Nine times during the life of the Confederacy, Jefferson Davis called for a day of national fasting, either in thanksgiving or humiliation, or both. These days were instrumental in reaching the largest number of people with a message Southern leaders wanted them to hear. Other such fast days were called for by Congress, state legislatures, and denominational bodies. The ministers were scrupulous in observing such special days. Fast days served as a means of unifying the Confederate States and people, and helped them to come to grips with the sacrifices that had to be made if their cause was to prevail.

As did Northern ministers, Southern clergy also saw the Civil War in millennialistic terms. In May of 1861 the Baptist Special Committee on the State of the Country emphasized that the administration of Jefferson Davis was "contributing to the transcendent Kingdom of our Lord Jesus Christ."[27] In 1863 Presbyterian Joseph Stiles joined together the South's mission and the coming millennium. God would bring in the millennium by plucking "some one nation out of the ranks of the world to take ground for God and man under the ranks of the gospel." Stiles was certain that chosen nation would be the Confederacy.[28]

The millennium, most Southern preachers assured, would have a place for slavery. Three months prior to the war Joseph R. Wilson, in a sermon delivered at the First Presbyterian Church of Augusta, projected a millennialistic view of the future in which a prominent feature would be "the institution of domestic slavery, freed from its stupid servility on the one side and its excess of neglect and severity on the other," acclaimed by all as a blessing to masters and slaves.[29] A Presbyterian minister from Georgia prophesied that twenty years after a Confederate victory "abolitionist individual-rights ideas would vanish from the world, and slavery, stronger than ever in the South, would flourish also in many Northern states and foreign countries."[30]

Robert M. Calhoon has summarized: "Proslavery millennialists proclaimed without a trace of irony that slavery's infinite capacity for improvement and moral enhancement made it an ideal activity within which to observe the onset of the millennium."[31]

With the assurances that their cause was God's cause, that the Confederacy was a successsor to ancient Israel in the role of God's chosen people, Southern preachers could confidently hold out hope when all seemed hopeless. God may chastise and discipline his special people, but he would not allow them to ultimately fail. Throughout the war, therefore, the South fought with unusual ardor because they were anxious to prove that God was on their side. Beringer has written: "Religion can inspire like no other force, and in America as in other cultures, war and religion might walk hand in hand, despite the teachings of Christ."[32] It was the ministers who inspired and motivated the South to keep on fighting, to continue the shedding of blood, to perpetuate the carnage, when others were tempted to give up. Thus, in the spring of 1863 Drury Lacy, in a sermon delivered at the General Military Hospital in Wilson, North Carolina, held out not only hope but assurances. After blaming recent military defeats upon Southern sins, he confidently asserted: "What, then, if Lincoln does muster in the field his 3,000,000 of men? Like those before them, they will be driven as chaff before the wind."[33] In December of the same year, five months after Vicksburg and Gettysburg, S. H. Higgens declared: "Of this, we have no doubt whatever. In spite of all reverses, we shall yet prevail — we shall overcome at the last — our enemy will be driven backward — but, God will have the glory."[34] In 1864 the venerable Bishop of Georgia, Stephen Elliott, was still exuding hope. All that was needed was for the people to come "boldly up to the throne of Grace, firmly believing that our prayers . . . will return to us laden with blessings from . . . the God of the Armies of Israel."[35]

The sermon which concludes this chapter was delivered in May of 1862 by the Rev. J. W. Tucker to his Presbyterian congregation in Fayetteville, North Carolina. It touches upon many themes that have been alluded to in this chapter. Tucker's basic premise was that "everything is of providence and under the control of God." That included the present conflict. God, in his wisdom, had ordained the war in spite of human efforts to prevent it. There was no doubt as to whose side God favored. "God is with us. . . . He is on our side. . . . Our cause is just." The suffering caused by the war resulted in purification. There was no reason to doubt ultimate victory, and complete confidence must be placed in civil and military leaders. A sharp contrast was drawn between the North and South. "It is a conflict of truth with error – of the Bible with Northern infidelity – of pure Christianity with Northern fanaticism – of liberty with despotism – of right with might."

NOTES

1. Margaret B. DesChamps, "Benjamin Morgan Palmer, Orator-Preacher of the Confederacy," *Southern Speech Journal* 19 (Sept. 1953): 18.
2. *The Duties Growing Out of It, and the Benefits to Be Expected from the Present War* (Austin: Office of the State Gazette, 1861).
3. *National Rectitude the Only True Basis of National Prosperity* (Petersburg, VA: Evangelical Tract Society, 1863).
4. *Proceedings of the Southern Baptist Convention*, May 10–13, 1861 (Richmond: MacFarlane and Fergusson, 1861), 62, 64.
5. *Duties of the Christian Soldier* (Charleston: A. J. Burke, 1861).
6. *Sermon* (Milledgeville, GA: Groughton, Nisbet, and Barnes, 1863).
7. *The Battle Is God's* (Savannah: E. J. Purse, Printers, 1863).
8. James W. Silver, *Confederate Morale and Church Propaganda* (New York: Norton, 1957), 87.
9. Quoted in Charles Reagan Wilson, *Baptized in Blood: The Religion of the Lost Cause 1865–1920* (Athens: University of Georgia Press, 1980), 33.
10. *A Discourse* (Augusta, GA: Office of the Constitutionalist, 1861).
11. *God's Presence with the Confederate States* (Savannah: W. Thorne Williams, 1861).
12. *The Lord Reigneth* (Richmond: Soldiers' Tract Association, M. E. Church, South, Chas. H. Wynne, Printer, 1863).
13. *Nebuchadnezzar's Fault and Fall* (Charleston: A. J. Burke, 1861).
14. *Address on the Day of Fasting and Prayer* (Fredericksburg: Recorder Job Office, 1861).
15. *The Glory of God, The Defense of the South* (Charleston: Steam-Power Press of Evans & Cogswell, 1861).
16. *Duties of the Christian Soldier*, 6–7.
17. Silver, *Confederate Morale and Church Propaganda*, 33–34.
18. *God Our Refuge and Strength in This War* (Richmond: W. Hargrave White, 1861).
19. Silver, *Confederate Morale and Church Propaganda*, 101.
20. *A Sermon* (Richmond: Enquirer Book & Job Press, 1864).
21. Quoted in Silver, *Confederate Morale and Church Propaganda*, 75.
22. Silver, *Confederate Morale and Church Propaganda*, 19–20.
23. Richard E. Beringer et al., *Why the South Lost the Civil War* (Athens: University of Georgia Press, 1986), 97.
24. For other examples of dissidents among the Southern clergy, see Silver, *Confederate Morale and Church Propaganda*, 19–24.
25. *Confederate Morale and Church Propaganda*, 77–78. Silver tells the story of a

chaplain who became a commander in the heat of battle. "There were ... many stories of fighting Confederate chaplains. One concerned a Virginian who had taken command in battle, after the officers had been killed. He ordered his men to hold their fire until the enemy closed in, and then, his face aglow with excitement, he blurted out: 'May God have mercy on their souls; give 'em hell, boys! give 'em hell!'"

26. *Minutes of the Twenty-fifth Anniversary of the Chickasaw Baptist Association,* Sept. 16-18, 1864 (Meredian, MS: Clarion Book and Job Office, 1865), 2.
27. *Proceedings of the Southern Baptist Convention,* May 10-13, 1861, 63.
28. *National Rectitude the Only True Basis of National Prosperity.*
29. *Mutual Relations of Masters and Slaves as Taught in the Bible* (Augusta: Steam Power Press of Chronicle and Sentinel, 1861).
30. Quoted in Jack P. Maddex, Jr., "Proslavery Millennialism: Social Eschatology in Antebellum Southern Calvinism," *American Quarterly* 31 (Spring 1979): 58.
31. Robert M. Calhoon, *Evangelicals and Conservatives in the Early South, 1740-1861* (Columbia: University of South Carolina Press, 1988), 188.
32. Beringer, *Why the South Lost the Civil War,* 100.
33. *Address* (Fayetteville, NC: Edward J. Hale & Sons, 1863).
34. *The Mountain Moved; or, David upon the Cause and Curse of Public Calamity* (Milledgeville, GA: Boughton, Nisbet, Barnes and Moore, State Printers, 1863).
35. *Gideon's Water-Lappers* (Macon: Burke, Boykin & Co., 1864).

God's Providence in War

J. W. Tucker

May 16, 1862

I form the light, and create darkness: I make peace, and create evil: I the Lord do all these things.
— *Isaiah XLV, 7* —

We have met together in obedience to the proclamation of our beloved President, to supplicate the blessing of God upon our arms. Our Chief Magistrate in making this call to prayer, and this congregation in cheerfully responding to it, alike recognize the hand of God in the origin and progress of this conflict. As a christian people, we

(Fayetteville: Presbyterian Office, 1962).

look not to fortune nor to accidents for help in this hour of our country's peril, but to the God of battles and of nations. The reason is apparent: If the teaching of the Bible, and the revelation of the christian religion be true, there is no such thing as fortune; there can be no accidents. An accident is an effect without a cause; fortune is an act or a series of acts, without an agent. But it is an axiom in Philosophy, and a first principle in all religion, that there can be no effect without a cause; no acts without responsible agents as their authors. What is generally regarded as accident and fortune, are those effects, the causes for which are unknown, and for those acts, the agents producing which are unseen. But are we to conclude that because we are ignorant of the cause producing a certain class of effects, that therefore, they have no cause? or that as the agent in a certain series of actions is unknown to us, that they must of necessity be acts without an agent? We certainly cannot pretend that we know all the causes, and are acquainted with all the agents operating in God's vast empire. There can be then no such thing as fortune or accidents – everything is of providence and under the control of God. Every power in nature and man works for God. Every thing that is comes to pass by the permission or the decree of God. All acts are provided for in God's plan and over-ruled by his providence, for the advancement of his glory and the well being of his people. It will not do to say that God cannot prevent men from acting as they do without destroying their moral agency, and that therefore, sin is in the world, not by the permission, but in defiance of all the perfections of God.

We pray to God to prevent the wickedness of men, every day, without destroying their moral agency. Every prayer we address to God asking him to succour our friends in temptation; to bring them to repentance; to give our enemies better hearts and change their purposes of wickedness towards us, is a request for him to do the very thing that it is here assumed he cannot do.

He certainly controls some men in perfect harmony with their moral liberty. Every good man is an illustration of this. He lives and acts under constant divine influences and attains his highest freedom under this divine control. If God may, and does thus control some men without infringing upon their moral agency, why may he not thus control all men? As every thing is either decreed or permitted by God, he certainly has a purpose in all he permits or decrees. No intelligent or rational being would act or permit others to act without a purpose. It is a mark of intelligence not to act without a motive or reason for acting. Whenever God, who is the supreme, the infinite intelligence, acts, in decreeing that others shall act, or in permitting them to act, he has a purpose for doing so.

This being true, it is evident that God has a plan and a purpose in reference to all nations, revolutions and wars. All these things are brought about in accordance with the divine plan, and in fulfillment of the divine purpose, which was drafted in the mind of God before the world was called into being. He has a providence in all national revolutions. He directs, controls, governs and regulates them. They are made to subserve his purposes, to advance his glory, and to promote his cause.

1st. This is clearly taught in the Bible – "Is there evil in the city and the Lord hath not done it. I form the light and create the darkness: I make peace and create evil: I the Lord do all these things." "All things work together for good to them that love God: to them who are the called according to his purpose."

2d. Men have universally believed this. The heathen nations who have no revelation, and are therefore, guided along by the light of nature and their own moral and spiritual intuitions, recognise God's providence in all social convulsions and national revolutions. They consult their oracles in reference to wars; they ask God to give them victory on the day of battle, and turn away from them the ruin of defeat. In the house of victory they return unto him thanksgiving, and offer sacrifices in token of gratitude. Christian nations act under the influence of the same conviction, in appointing days of national humiliation, fasting and prayer for the blessing of God upon their arms. Is this universal faith without a foundation in truth? Does the race act under the influence of a falsehood? That which is universal is natural; that which is natural is divine – "The voice of nature is the voice of God."

3d. Without this sort of divine control, there could be but little providential protection afforded us. It would afford us but little protection, to save us from the storm and tempest, the flame and the flood, pestilence and famine, and then turn us over without protection to the tender mercies of wicked men and devils. What sense of security could we have under God's providence, if it was confined to the material world, and the whole sphere of its operations was circumscribed to the domain of matter. God's providence is in this war. It must be so if he watches o'er the destiny of men and nations. It was the purpose of no party to bring on this war. All parties tried to prevent it. No one believes, that had all the slave States seceded at once, that there would have been any attempt at subjugation, coercion, or the reconstruction of the Union by force of arms. But the simultaneous secession of the whole South was the plan of the original secessionist. They advocated it as a peace measure; as the only measure that could secure permanent peace, and prevent a bloody war, either in or out of the Union. The war was not desired nor planned by the Union men, either North or South; they deprecated it; it was what they feared – the evil they labored long to prevent; they refused even to consider the question of secession, lest it should result in a bloody war. They pleaded and begged for a compromise, but it was unavailing. The very means they used to prevent it, was the very means that resulted in bringing it about. The manifestation of this strong union feeling confirmed Lincoln in his purpose to put down what he is pleased to term the rebellion by military power. This called forth his proclamation, and this proclamation brought on the war. The Black Republican party North did not desire war; they used all the power of the government to prevent, yet their efforts to prevent it kindled its baleful fires from the banks of the Potomac to the shores of the Rio Grande. In the South we should not criminate each other in regard to the origin, progress and rapid development of this conflict. We all labored, earnestly, honestly, to prevent it, yet that providence which "shapes our ends, rough-hew them as we may," overruled these very means to bring it about for some wise purpose. We are in the midst of it, and we should all try, unitedly and earnestly, to fight through it. American society being what it was, no earthly power could have prevented it. God in his providence did not prevent it, though the whole American people earnestly prayed for him to do so. Though we cannot understand it, we cannot question that it is to answer some wise and benevolent purpose in the progressive development of God's great plan for the elevation of the nations and the salvation of the world. God is with us in this conflict; we think he is on our side in the struggle. We believe this, first, because our cause is just; we have acted and still act purely on the defensive; we have asked nothing but the rights secured to us in the constitution – the privilege of self-government. Having failed to secure this in the Union, we proceeded to come out of it, either in the exercise of the natural right of revolution or the legal right of secession. I care not which you call it: whether natural or legal, it was identically the same sort of State action that took us out of the Union, that was used to place us in it. If it was a legal process when used to place us in the Union, it was equally a legal process when employed to take us out of it. We went in by Sovereign State action; we came out in the same way. Whether in doing this we exercised a natural or a legal right, or both, I care not. It was right if the privilege of self-government is right; and the conflict necessary to the defence of this action, is, as far as we are responsible for it, a religious conflict. It is not of our seeking; we could not avoid it. It has been forced upon us. The fires of fanaticism had been slowly consuming the foundation of our government for years, until at last the nations of the earth were startled in horror by the throes of a political earthquake, that shook into ruins the proudest Temple of Liberty that the sun of heaven ever shone upon. We saw the war cloud as it began to rise slowly but surely; and we used every means in our power to arrest it. Statesmanship, compromise, legislation were all employed, but in vain. It at last covered our political sky with the blackness of darkness, and broke upon us in a fearful storm of fire and blood. Our cause is just, and God will defend the right. Second, God is on our side—is with us in this conflict—because we have had reverses. "Whom the Lord loveth he chasteneth, and scourgeth every son whom he receiveth. If ye are without chastisement, then are ye bastards and not sons." The wise and affectionate father will punish, correct and chastise the children of his love for their good. This principle of the divine administration applies to nations as well as individuals. This must be so because the nation is constituted of individuals. God was evidently with his chosen—the people Israel; but he suffered them to endure the bondage of Egypt. He afterwards brought them out of Egypt with a high hand and an out-stretched arm; but he suffered them to meet with sad reverses in the wilderness. He was evidently with his own chosen nation—the Jews; but they were often defeated in battle by the armies of the surrounding nations.

God has without question been with his church in every age of the world; but he has found it necessary to preserve his people with the salt, and purify them by the fires of persecution. God was with our Revolutionary fathers in their struggle for independence; but he suffered them often to be defeated in their seven years conflict with the mother country; but the eagle bird of Liberty gathered strength while rocked by the storms and tempests of a bloody Revolution. So, God has sent our reverses for our good. They were necessary to humble our pride; to stop our foolish and absurd boasting, and to make us feel the importance of the conflict in which we are engaged. They have tried our patriotism, and have shown to the nations of the earth that it is as pure as the gold which has been tried by the hammer and the fire. Third, our victories indicate the presence of God with our armies in this conflict. Who can read the reports of the battles of Bethel, Bull Run, Manassas Plains, Ball's Bluff, Springfield, Shiloh and Williamsburg, without being convinced that God gave us the victory, and that to him we should render thanksgiving for the glorious triumph of our arms. Every soldier who moved amid the perils and dangers of these bloody conflicts, must feel that the "Lord of host is with us; and the God of Jacob is our refuge." Fourth, another evidence that God is with us is seen in the remarkable preservation of the lives of our troops under circumstances of the greatest apparent danger. The bombardment of Fort Sumter is a miracle and a mystery. The result can only be accounted for by admitting divine protection. Nor was God's protecting providence less evident in the bombardment of the forts of Hatteras, Port Royal, Roanoke Island and Number Ten, than it was in the result at Sumter. In every case there was employed the most formidable armament that the world has ever known, from which there was thrown into our forts a storm of shot and shell, without a parallel in the history of warfare. And yet, ah! mystery and miracle of providence! not fifty of our men were killed in all the engagements. So signally has God manifested his approbation of our cause by the protection of our troops under circumstances of the greatest peril, and most appalling danger, that it should make our whole people grateful to him as the great Giver of all good and the kind Preserver from all evil.

We will close by a few practical remarks:

1st. There is nothing in the present aspect of things, nor in the late reverses to our arms, to cause us to doubt our final success and ultimate victory. The loss of our cities and towns, on the sea-board and large rivers, is the natural result of going into this conflict without a navy; with a people that at present probably has the most formidable navy in the world. We have not had the time nor the material for the construction of a navy; but as ours is an agricultural, and not a manufacturing and commercial society, our strength and national vitality is not in our large cities, on the ocean, but in our rich and fertile fields in the interior. These places are not our whole country; the loss of them is not the loss of our country, nor does it render our cause hopeless. We have got an army of five hundred thousand

men in the field, well equipped, well drilled, well armed and constituted of as good fighting material as any in the world; an army that
has never been whipped by the same number of men on any field:
an army composed of the heroes of Bethel, Manassas, Ball's Bluff,
Springfield, Shiloh and Newbern. Such an army in an open field and
fair fight can never be vanquished. Then why should we fear? Doubt
of success in a just cause with such an army, and the God of nations
and of battles on our side! If, as a people, we deserve to be free,
ultimate failure in such a cause and under such circumstances with
such an ally, is impossible.

2nd. We must have confidence in our government and in our army.
There may have been errors in administration, but neither our President nor his cabinet profess to be infallible; they are but men – with
all the infirmities of men. We should expect them to commit errors.
We should not look for perfection. The fact is the government under
all the circumstances, has been a remarkable success. The severe
criticism in which we sometimes indulge, in regard to the action of
our generals, and the valor of our troops, is irrational, unjust and
ungrateful. We are incompetent to criticise the actions of our generals, for two reasons –

First. We know nothing about the science or the art of war, therefore we should not give a criticism on a subject of which we are to-
tally ignorant. But even if we had military talent, and military training and experience, we, at home, know nothing of the circumstances
and necessities under which they act. To form and express an opinion, disapproving their course, is to show our own ignorance, and to
treat them with great injustice, by condemning them unheard. They
understand it – we do not; they know the facts – we do not; they are
responsible – we are not; they make the sacrifices, and face the dangers – we stay at home; therefore good sense, modesty, justice and
gratitude should make us careful how we censure them. When Johnson evacuated Harper's Ferry, the whole country rang with complaints at the movement; but we now know that it was that movement that gave us the victory at Manassas. When General Albert
Sidney Johnston fell back from Bowling Green and Nashville, the
whole family of croakers were loud in their censure; but it was that
movement that gave us the victory of Shiloh. Now with these facts
before us, we should be careful how we complain of our government,
our generals, and our troops. Judging of the present by the past, we
should infer that the falling back from Yorktown, the evacuation of

Norfolk, and the withdrawing our troops from New Orleans, are movements of as much strategy as those which have been attended with
such fine results. These men, with brave hearts and strong arms,
stand as a wall of fire between the invading foe, and our homes, our
property, and our loved ones; and for this we owe them a debt of eternal gratitude. Shall we repay their sacrifices for us and ours with a
want of confidence?

We should pray to God to give success to our cause, and triumph
to our arms. God will defend the right. We may approach him then
in full assurance of faith; with strong confidence that he will hear
and answer and bless us. Prayer touches the nerve of Omnipotence;
prayer moves the hand that moves the world; prayer is the rod in the
hand of faith, that extracts the fiery curse from the burning bosom of
the dark storm-cloud, and turns from our country and our homes the
thunder-bolts of divine wrath. Prayer will convert darkness into light –
our night into glorious day – our defeat into victory – our disasters
into triumphs – our sorrow into joy – our weakness into strength –
our feebleness into might.

Our cause is sacred. It should ever be so in the eyes of all true
men in the South. How can we doubt it, when we know it has been
consecrated by a holy baptism of fire and blood. It *has* been rendered
glorious by the martyr-like devotion of Johnson, McCulloch, Garnett,
Bartow, Fisher, McKinney, and hundreds of others who have offered
their lives as a sacrifice on the altar of their country's freedom.

Soldiers of the South, be firm, be courageous, be brave; be faithful to your God, your country and yourselves, and you shall be invincible. Never forget that the patriot, like the christian, is immortal
till his work is finished. You are fighting for everything that is near
and dear, and sacred to you as men, as christians and as patriots;
for country, for home, for property, for the honor of mothers, daughters, wives, sisters, and loved ones. Your cause is the cause of God,
of Christ, of humanity. It is a conflict of truth with error – of the
Bible with Northern infidelity – of a pure christianity with Northern
fanaticism – of liberty with despotism – of right with might. In such
a cause victory is not with the greatest numbers, nor the heaviest
artillery, but with the good, the pure, the true, the noble, the brave.
We are proud of you, and grateful to you for the victories of the past.
We look to your valor and prowess, under the blessing of God, for
the triumphs of the future. Then

"Strike till the last armed foe expires,
Strike for your altar and your fires,
Strike for the green graves of your sires;
God and your native land."

Women of the South. We know your patriotism, your bravery, your nobleness of sole. It is not your privilege to fight. You can not move amidst the danger, the perils, the blood and the carnage of the battle-field, beside your fathers, brothers, husbands and lovers. But you can do a work quite as important. You can gird them for the conflict, and with words, looks, glances and smiles, cheer them on to victory and to glory. Every letter you write them from home, should be filled with "thoughts that breath and words that burn," that will catch and kindle from man to man, and heart to heart, until all along our lines shall blaze with a maryr's courage and zeal for country and for home.

You can also, by your fortitude, patience, courage and strength of spirit, shame into silence the fearful, trembling terror-stricken, craven-hearted men in our midst, who are constantly predicting our failure in the glorious struggle in which we are engaged. They absorb all the rays of light, and reflect none – they act as non-conductors in the social chain, that arrest the flow of the currents of patriotism through society – their influence is like the blighting frost upon the flowers. It blasts the hopes of the timid and chills the hearts of the desponding. By destroying confidence in the stability of our government, in the success of our arms, and the ultimate triumph of our cause, they prepare the way, to the extent of their influence, for the ruin of the country by the destruction of our credit and the depreciation of our currency. Wise men, if they cannot be made brave should be taught silence. They should not be suffered to do us harm by their cold comfort, and damn our cause by faint praise.

You can also pray for God's blessing and protection on the loved ones who are absent. Every home should be a sanctuary – every dwelling a Bethel – every spot an altar, from which prayer should be offered for our country, and for our loved ones who are braving the dangers of the battlefield for us, and all we hold dear.

THE LOST CAUSE

After the siege of Vicksburg and the battle of Gettysburg, both culminating in Southern losses on or about July 4, 1863, the pendulum of war swung dramatically in the Union's favor. For objective observers the Confederate Cause had become the Lost Cause. How could the Southern preachers respond? They had confidently proclaimed that the God of War was on their side. The purposes of the Confederacy were God's purposes. How then does a Divine Cause become a Lost Cause? As the preachers sought to answer this troublesome question, they must be admired for their consistency. They were sure that even as God had been a participant in the early stages of the war when so much was going well, so God was still a participant in the latter stages when nothing was going well. Most sermons after the summer of 1863 stressed two points: (1) the South was being punished for her sins, and (2) with due penitence and a renewed commitment the South would even yet become victorious. Thus, the preachers provided a rationale for the continuance of the war when reality would have dictated otherwise.

As Confederate defeats began to mount, so did the accusations of the Confederate clergy that it was the South's sins which were responsible for the calamities. On September 15, 1864, while Sherman's troops were occupying Atlanta, D. M. Gilbert, at the Evangelical Lutheran Church in Savannah, echoed a common Southern religious theme at that time: "It is because of our sins that the Almighty is so severely chastening us."[1]

One sin mentioned by the preachers, perhaps more than any other, was the abuse of slaves throughout the South. The clergy wanted it known that the institution itself was not wrong, but many Southerners had neglected the responsibilities that accompanied the divinely ordained system. As the ministers saw it, slave abuse generally fell into one of two categories. The first kind of abuse was the failure to provide religious training for the slaves. In 1864 some Baptists in Mississippi expressed the thought that because they had been so neglectful in the religious training of slaves, the slaves were now listening to their own "colored preachers" who were doing them more harm than good. "Preachers are rising up among them who are blind—leaders of the blind! They are generally found to be the worst men among them, with few exceptions."[2]

Other Southern ministers and religious institutions were expressing some guilt as to what the South had done to black families. Marriage, too, was an institution ordained by God, and the slavery system had often worked against this divine institution. In 1863 a Georgia association of Baptists passed a resolution urging that the laws of Georgia protect Negro marriages. The Baptists noted that the state laws had failed "to recognize and protect this relationship between slaves," and that present laws were "especially defective, and ought to be amended."[3]

Another sin that was prominently mentioned in Southern sermons during the waning years of the war was greed. There were those in the South who were lining their pockets in the midst of suffering, and the preachers were quick to denounce such profiteers. In mid-August of 1863, about six weeks after the losses at Vicksburg and Gettysburg, the Rev. Sylvanus Landrum declared that the greatest sin of the South was "the lust for gain." He repeated Jefferson Davis's question: "Has not the love of lucre eaten like gangrene into the very heart of the land, converting many among us into worshippers of gain, and rendering them unmindful of their duty to their country, to their fellow men, and to their God?"[4] On that same day LeRoy M. Lee declared that sins were bringing down the Confederacy and warned his congregation to beware of "speculators, forestallers, and extortioners,—if we would escape extermination."[5] Later in 1863 the Baptists of North Carolina, meeting in annual session, complained that the sacrifices in the South "have increased a hundred fold by a spirit of avarice, and a thirst for gain, which like demon spirits, have possessed a large class of our own citizens, of whom we had a right to expect better things."[6] In 1864 Dr. J. L. Burrows thundered: "What intensely selfish greed of wealth. . . . Multitudes are trafficking in their country's distresses, for their own profit."[7]

There were yet other sins for which the Southern preachers thought the South was receiving the judgment of God. Sylvanus Landrum stated that early victories in the war caused Southerners to become too self-reliant, and they then abandoned their dependence upon God.[8] J. L. Burrows spoke of a "reckless chase of amusements . . . Sabbath profanations . . . and groveling drunkenness."[9] Thomas Dunaway enumerated the sins of pride, arrogance, and a trust in troops and cotton.[10] In 1863 Richard Furman, in a letter to the Charleston Baptist Association, wrote: "When we look over our country [the South] and see the greed of gain, the spirit of speculation, the profanity, the ungodliness . . . we fear that still greater bereavements and sufferings await us."[11] The following year Furman wrote another letter to the Charleston Association, reminding the recipients of the biblical passage "Whom the Lord loveth he chasteneth."[12] The implication was that the South was still the object of God's special attention and affection. Because of that, the Almighty expected and exacted a higher standard from Southerners, and they had failed to measure up. Thus the defeats on the field of battle.

If military losses were the direct consequence of Southern sins, then proper repentance would turn the tide of battle once again in the South's favor. The preachers therefore urged the South to repent and fight on — even when ultimate defeat seemed so certain. Early in 1863 W. T. D. Dalzell, in St. Mary's Church of San Antonio, said that he hoped the rash of recent Confederate defeats "may not discourage us. Let it prevent proud boasting. . . Let it remind us that we must still look up to and trust only in God. . . . Let it not lead to any want of faith in His favor."[13] In the spring of 1863 Stephen Elliott delcared that the only hope for the South was to continue the war "which God is working out for our deliverance."[14] The following spring Elliott reminded his congregation that "freedom's battle will never go down in blood and disaster, unless the blows that destroy her come from within."[15] During that same spring Richard H. Wilmer, the Episcopal Bishop of Alabama, traveled throughout his state, seeking to bring encouragement. Though he acknowledged that battlefield reverses were causing many to lose heart, Wilmer contended that such losses were "a part of our discipline . . . a part of our heritage." He compared the present days to the dark days of the American Revolution before victory was achieved. Wilmer assured his listeners that God would bring victory "in His own good time." Meanwhile, "to die for one's country is becoming beautiful."[16]

The preachers issued dire warnings as to what would happen if the North should win. In April of 1864 David Seth Doggett, at the Centenary Church in Richmond, issued frightful predictions of what a Yankee victory would mean. Northern heresies would "surge over the heritage of God. . . . At one fell stroke, religious liberty would be extinguished, and a ruthless tyranny would dictate terms of communion with the polluted crusaders of their altars."[17] In the summer of 1864 Bishop Stephen Elliott delivered the eulogy at the funeral of the bishop-general Leonidus Polk, who had been killed in battle. Elliott took the occasion to denounce Northerners and "the ripening germs of irreligion, of unbelief, of ungodliness, of corruption, of cruelty, of license which have distinguished them." Even at this late date Elliott looked to a glorious future for "a country made independent through his [Polk's] devotion and sacrifice."[18]

The preachers urged their listeners to resist, sometimes at the cost of their lives, the Yankee troops who had invaded their land. On March 27, 1864, the Rev. William Henry Ruffner, speaking at the Presbyterian Church in Lexington, Virginia, urged resistance to the oath of allegiance to the United States and its Constitution that some Union commanders were pressing defeated Southerners to take. "No one," argued Ruffner, "has a right to regard an oath lightly, or question its validity, when taken under any circumstances. . . . There is but one course that is honest in itself, or that will keep the soul clear under the burning eye of God and that is to refuse it – yes, to refuse it, though a thousand bayonets were pointed at his breast."[19]

When the war came to an end, Southern clergymen, at first disheartened, soon found a new role to play. Their task: the promotion of the religion of the Lost Cause. Charles Reagan Wilson, in his book *Baptized in Blood: The Religion of the Lost Cause 1865–1920*, has written of the role that religion played in the South in those years following the war. He begins by stating his basic premise:

> A Southern political nation was not to be, and the people of Dixie came to accept that; but the dream of a cohesive Southern people with a separate cultural identity replaced the original longing. . . . Religion was at the heart of this dream, and the history of the attitude known as the Lost Cause was the study of the use of the past as the basis for a Southern religious–moral identity, an identity as the chosen people.[20]

Not all the clergy nor all the churches in the South perpetuated this postbellum religion, but most of them did. The various denominations continued their debates on various theological differences, but they came together on this single issue: the propagating of the concept that the South was still a holy nation, a special people, more than ever, because they had been "baptized in blood." Because of their commitment to the building of a unique Southern culture, the churches reaped great benefits. Wilson asserts: "The churches' powerful role in the Civil War, and their expansion and dominance after 1865, suggest that if the Confederacy before dying was baptized in blood, Southern religion was likewise symbolically baptized, born again in a fiery sacrament that gave it new spiritual life. The Southern churches thus profited from the holocaust"(8).

The Lost Cause had its own unique theology. There had to be an answer to the haunting question: How can Right be defeated? The preachers had proclaimed that the Confederate cause was God's cause. How could a Divine Cause become a Lost Cause? The churches had an answer. The cause was not wrong. The South lost because of superior Northern military might and because God had visited a special judgment on his chosen people even as he did upon the Israelites of old. J. B. McNeilly, a Presbyterian cleric, recalled the Old Testament accounts of God's chosen people being led into captivity by heathen conquerors, "but that did not prove the heathen to be right in their cause nor that the Israelites were upholding a bad cause"(71). The South's experience of suffering would lead to even greater faith, and there was always the hope of future vindication. "Can a cause be lost when it has passed through such a baptism as ours?" asked Benjamin Morgan Palmer. "Principles never die, and if they seem to perish it is only to experience a resurrection in the future"(74). Warning accompanied theology. Sins must be repented of in order to avoid future judgment. Lost Cause values must be cherished and affirmed. Southern virtue had to be maintained at all costs. "The North was a continual reminder of what Southerners must not become. . . . The hope was that a cultural identity based upon religion and regional tradition could be the answer to Southern fears of decline"(99).

White supremacy was basic to the Southern way of life and "Southern ministers were among the leading defenders of white supremacy"(101). The preachers proclaimed that slavery had been an orderly, God-ordained way of life and any attempts toward racial equality would be a threat to Southern virtue. "Southern denominational assemblies were concerned enough with the issue to justify slavery long after its demise. . . . The Southern Baptist Convention reasserted slavery's religious dimensions in 1892"(103). For most churches, by the 1890s segregation had become the accepted substitute for slavery.

Thus, the clergy in the South were able to turn apparent defeat into a semblance of victory. At least it was a victory for religion, for only religion could provide an answer and philosophy of life that most Southerners could live with in those years after 1865. Only religion could assure the South that their cause and values were still right and that somehow, in some form, the Confederate Cause would live again. Because only religion could provide a satisfactory explanation, a solace, a meaning, and a hope for the defeated South, religion – fundamentally the Protestant churches and their clergy – profited from the carnage of military defeat. As the New South was born and then matured, it grew with a conservative, evangelical religion burning at the center of its cultural being.

The first sermon at the end of this chapter is by the Rev. Stephen Elliott, who before, during, and after the war was the rector of Christ Church in Savannah and the Episcopal Bishop of the Diocese of Georgia. It may be that next to Benjamin Morgan Palmer, Elliott was the most outspoken and tireless defender of the Confederate cause. From 1861 to 1864 his sermons supported slavery, secession, and war; denounced Northerners as heretics, infidels, and evildoers; and urged the South to keep on fighting when all seemed lost. As Palmer fled from invading Yankee forces in New Orleans and Columbia, so Elliot escaped from Savannah just before Sherman's troops arrived in December of 1864. Both men knew that their strong defense of the Confederacy and their equally strong denunciations of the North made them targets for Union retaliation.

On August 21, 1863, Elliott delivered a sermon, "Ezra's Dilemma," in which he addressed the mood of gloom which had settled upon the South. The great defeats at Vicksburg and Gettysburg had taken place the preceding month. He assured his listeners that God was still on their side. God had called them to secession, and slavery was still a divine institution. The North was a wicked adversary, and Providence would not allow them to win. God was biding his time. Reversals were temporary. They served to build character and were a punishment for sins. Elliott enumerated some of those sins for which the South was being punished: failure in duty to slaves, apathy, complaining, and the lust for money. Southerners needed to change their ways and press on to victory. The preacher reminded his audience of the dire consequences that awaited them should the North be victorious.

The second sermon at the end of this chapter is by the Rev. John Paris. Prior to the war Paris was a vigorous proponent for slavery. During the war, as did so many Southern clergymen, he served as a chaplain to Confederate forces. When the war ended, Paris returned to the pastoral ministry, where he became an ardent spokesman on the subject of black inferiority and the need for the segregation of the races. Blacks, according to Paris, simply were not equipped to handle freedom. In their hands freedom became license. These "simple minded people," asserted Paris, once "freed from the restraints that servitude had thrown around them," then "abandoned themselves to a cause of reckless disappation [sic]." Even in their practice of religion the blacks, claimed Paris, showed their inferiority, for they believed "some of the most glaring absurdities"(106, 108).

On February 28, 1864, Chaplain John Paris preached a powerful sermon, which was widely distributed, upon the deaths of twenty-two Confederate soldiers who had been executed by hanging for the crime of desertion. Paris had visited each of the twenty-two North Carolinians in their cells before they went to their deaths. He remarked that these men had been good and honest men, but they had become victims of mischievous home influences. These influences were saying: "We are whipt!" "We might as well give up!" "It is useless to attempt to fight any longer!" These evil voices were urging peace. The soldiers had received the punishment they deserved, but the real culprits were civilians who had spread their "poisonous contagion of treason" to the army. As had Elliott, Paris warned of the terrors that would fall upon the South if the North should triumph. Rather than succumb or submit, Paris urged his listeners "to fight it out to the bitter end."

NOTES

1. *A Discourse* (Savannah: George N. Nichols, 1864).
2. *Minutes of the Twenty-sixth Annual Session of the Choctaw Baptist Association*, Oct. 15 and 17, 1864 (Columbus, MS: J. D. Ryan & Co., Printers, 1865), 5. For a discussion of slave preaching see chapter 9 below.
3. *Minutes of the Bethel Baptist Association*, Oct. 31, 1863 (Macon: Burke, Boykin & Co., 1863), 6.

4. *The Battle Is God's* (Savannah: E. J. Purse, Printers, 1963).

5. *Our Country – Our Dangers – Our Duty* (Richmond: Soldiers' Tract Association, 1863).

6. *Proceedings of the Thirty-fourth Annual Session of the Baptist State Convention of North Carolina*, Oct. 28-31, 1863 (Raleigh: Biblical Recorder Office, 1864), 14.

7. *Nationality Insured* (Augusta, GA: Jas. Nathan Ells, Publisher, Baptist Banner Office, 1864).

8. *The Battle Is God's.*

9. *Nationality Insured.*

10. *A Sermon* (Richmond: Enquirer Book and Job Press, 1864).

11. *Minutes of the One Hundredth and Twelfth Session of the Charleston Baptist Association*, Oct. 31 to Nov. 2, 1863 (Camden: W. K. Rogers Book and Job Printers, 1864), 25.

12. *Minutes of the One Hundredth and Thirteenth Session of the Charleston Baptist Association*, Nov. 5-8, 1864 (Camden: W. K. Rogers Book and Job Printers, 1864), 44.

13. *A Sermon* (San Antonio: Herald Book and Job Press, 1863).

14. *Samson's Riddle* (Macon: Burke, Boykin & Co., Steam Book and Job Printers, 1863).

15. *Gideon's Water-Lappers* (Macon: Burke, Boykin & Co., 1864).

16. *Future Good – The Explanation of Present Reverses* (Charlotte, NC: Protestant Episcopal Church Publishing Association, 1864).

17. *The War and Its Close* (Richmond: Macfarlane and Fergusson, 1864).

18. *An Impressive Summons* (Columbia: n.p., 1864).

19. *The Oath* (Lexington, VA: Gazette Office, 1864).

20. Charles Reagan Wilson, *Baptized in Blood: The Religion of the Lost Cause 1865-1920* (Athens: University of Georgia Press, 1980), 1; future reference to this work noted parenthetically in the text. Wilson's book may be the best single work on the role of religion in the South in those years following the Civil War.

Ezra's Dilemma

Stephen Elliott

August 21, 1863

21. Then I proclaimed a fast there, at the river of Ahava, that we might afflict ourselves before our God, to seek of him a right way for us, and for our little ones, and for all our substance.

22. For I was ashamed to require of the King a band of soldiers and horsemen to help us against the enemy in the way; because we had spoken unto the King, saying, The hand of our God is upon all them for good that seek him; but his power and his wrath is against all them that forsake him.

23. So we fasted and besought our God for this; and he was entreated of us.

— Ezra VIII, 21-23 —

From the beginning of the revolution in which we are yet so sternly engaged, we have boldly assumed the position, that we were fighting under the shield of the Lord of Hosts, of him who "sitteth upon the circle of the earth, and the inhabitants thereof are as grasshoppers." This has been our boast and our consolation. It has supported us under all our sacrifices, and has cheered us through all our days of darkness. The Psalmist never struck his harp to the animating strain – "The Lord of Hosts is with us, the God of Jacob is our refuge" – in more confident faith than we have re-echoed it. Not only has it been chanted in the sanctuaries of Christianity, but our civil rulers have recognized it in their papers of State, and our great Captains have proclaimed it from the head of their armies in victory as well as under defeat. The soldier and the statesman, the man of the sword and the man of the gown, has each borne it upon his escutcheon, and our supreme Legislative assembly has engraven it upon our national seal. All our official documents will go forth in the future, with the sacred inscription "Deo Vindige," and announce to the world our trust and our strength. We have not only nurtured this feeling, which seemed to come upon the Confederacy as an inspiration, within

(Savannah: Power Press of George N. Nichols, 1863).

our own hearts, hugging it there as a part of our religious life – looking to it, in individual faith, as a light shining in a dark place – but we have blazoned it abroad, and are conspicuous this day before the world as a people who have taken the Lord for their God, caring for nothing so much as "for the good will of him that dwelt in the bush." We have said not to one King only, but to all Kings within the reach of our voice – not to earthly Kings merely, but to the King of Kings – "The hand of our God is upon all them for good that seek him; but his power and his wrath is against all them that forsake him." We are bound to this declaration by the most solemn covenants both private and public, and by it must we now stand or fall. We cannot therefore require of any foreign agency – we should be ashamed to do it – "bands of soldiers and horsemen to help us against the enemy in the way." We have deliberately made our choice. We have taken the Lord of Hosts as our Saviour, and to him must we now turn with fasting and with prayer, and "seek of him the right way for us, and for our little ones, and for all our substance."

This is our only resource. We find ourselves in a condition which calls for a wisdom superior to our own, for a power greater than we can control. A day of darkness and of gloominess has unexpectedly settled down upon us, and without being able to perceive any natural causes sufficient to account for it, we are conscious that "our hands hang down and that our knees are feeble," and that we are in peril of our cause. It is a consciousness which has come upon us from on high, and which, I firmly believe, cannot be removed by any earthly means. It must be lifted from our hearts, where it rests like a weight of lead, by the hand of the Lord which placed it there. If we look at our Government, it is as stable as ever, directed by the same clear head and sound judgment which have so well guided our affairs. If we turn to our armies, they are, in proportion to those of our enemy, as numerous and as well appointed as they have ever been, and are commanded, with one immortal exception, by the same skilful Captains, who have so often led them to victory. If we measure our resources, they are greater, in many respects, than they have ever been before. If we examine the field of action, we stand, except in one direction, precisely where we did a year ago. What is it then, which has spread over the Confederate States, so suddenly and without any adequate reason, such a robe of darkness? Two months ago, and our prospects never looked brighter; our hearts were full of hope, and our watchmen thought that they perceived the dawn of a happier day. The cry of "all's well," had just resounded over the land, when, in a moment, all was in eclipse; dark clouds blotted out the promised light; a day of blood and slaughter and captivity rose upon us; the sound of lamentation was heard through the land; our hearts sank within us under the shock and grew as insensible as stone. Nothing like it had occurred even in the worst moments of the past. Twice before had we been defeated and depressed, but we had risen from those disasters chastened yet defiant. From this recent shock we have not rallied as we should have done, had we been stricken by the hands of man alone. We still continue most unaccountably paralysed, as inactive as if we were courting the condition of slaves. It is a visitation from God, to teach us our own weakness; it is the hiding of his countenance from our rulers, from our armies and from our people to make us understand that present victory and final success depend altogether upon his presence and his favour.

We are placed in the like dilemma in which Ezra found himself and his people. We have assumed a very grand but a very solemn position, and we cannot, without utter shame and confusion of face, abandon it, and confess that we have been trusting in vain and unfounded expectations. We are compelled to acknowledge this day, supposing our despondency to have any proper foundation, either that we ourselves have been deceived in supposing that God was on our side, fighting for us against our enemies, or we must declare him to be a Being in whom no reliance can be placed – fickle and faithless – favoring to-day and abandoning to-morrow – puffing up with hope in the beginning, only the more surely to destroy in the end. Let us examine both these positions, and determine whether it is really necessary to lodge ourselves upon either horn of this dilemma; whether God may not be on our side, even while we are suffering defeat and disaster; whether he may not be firm in his purposes and persistent in his good will, even while we are provoking him to anger and forcing him to hide his face from us and from our cause. A review of the grounds upon which we claimed, for so long, the presence of God with us in our conflict, may restore our confidence, and a consideration of the reasons why he is dealing harshly with us, may lead us to repentance and a happier condition.

We believed, when be began this conflict, that the hand of God was with us, because we had the right and the true upon our side under every aspect in which we could view the case between us and our adversaries. We could not think, and we cannot yet think, that

he who rules in righteousness would permit the injured and the oppressed to be overwhelmed by the tyranny of brute force, and con-
signed to degradation and infamy. He might try severely our fortitude – he might chasten heavily our sins – he might keep us long in
the furnace of affliction, but in the end, he would deliver us and
justify our trust in him. "He is the Rock, his work is perfect; for all
his ways are judgment; a God of truth, and without iniquity, just
and right is he."

The question of right in our movement upon general principles
is settled, as between us and those who are trying to subjugate us,
by that charter which was adopted by our forefathers as a declaration of civil rights, and to the observance of whose principles they
pledged their lives, their fortunes and their sacred honour. This charter was not meant only for their times – it was put forth for all the
world, and for all times. It has been held up continually before the
nations by our orators – it has been shaken defiantly in the face of
the old governments of Europe by our statesmen – it has overturned
thrones and broken up dynasties. It belongs to us to-day as fully as
it belonged to our ancestors, and upon it, if we intended to be true
to them and to their principles, we were bound to plant ourselves.
This declaration laid it down as a fundamental principle, "that whenever any form of government becomes destructive of the ends for
which governments were instituted among men, it is the right of the
people to alter or to abolish it, and to institute a new government,
laying its foundation on such principles and organizing its powers
in such form, as to them shall seem most likely to effect their safety
and happiness." Upon this principle, the colonies of Great Britain,
then existing upon this continent, considered themselves justified
in declaring themselves independent of the mother country, and they
declared it with nothing like the show of right which we exhibited
when we followed their example. They were colonies, and assumed
their independence through the right of revolution. We were sovereign
States, and asserted ours by simply resuming our rightful sovereignty.
They flew to arms before any legislative action had given color to
their violence, and thus their proceedings had a smack of rebellion
in them. We dissolved our connection with our sister States, not
after war had already dipped its foot in blood, but through Conventions, constitutionally assembled, chosen freely by the people, whose
ordinances were afterwards ratified by the same people. They rushed
into their conflict with the mother country with quite a half of their

fellow citizens against them. We seceded with an unanimity unparalleled in such a revolution. They fought through the war of independence with many of the very best people of the Colonies against them. We have, up to this time, conducted our conflict with our people firm, determined, and united. If our forefathers were right in their action, then are we right, our enemies themselves being the judges, for they had very much less to complain of than we. The wrongs of the government of Great Britain affected only their civil rights; the wrongs inflicted upon us, threatened our whole social condition. Beginning with the Missouri question we bore, I cannot say patiently, but still we bore, for forty years, wrong upon wrong, and never pronounced for separation at all hazards, until we perceived that every barrier which kept back the angry floods of fanaticism and infidelity had been broken down. All the lessons we had learned from our forefathers not only justified our action, but pointed out to us our duty. Whatever other nations may say of us, the mouth of our present adversaries is stopped upon every principle of justice and truth.

If we pass from the Declaration of Independence, from the general principles upon which our forefathers justified a change of government, to the Constitution which united us, for certain specific and limited purposes, to our sister States, we shall find that we have ever kept the right upon our side. We have never encroached upon the privileges which that Constitution guaranteed to our partners in the Union. We have always been, confessedly, the strict constructionists. We have asked no more than that the Constitution should be observed to its very letter. With a liberality which really amounted to weakness, and which received no return, we yielded point after point, and gave up territory after territory, rather than break up the government under which we had lived at least in safety. We generously stripped ourselves of our rightful heritage, to give our adversaries the means of expansion upon their own principles. Those States which are now persecuting us most implacably, were formed out of territory ceded to the government by the State of Virginia. When by our arms new domain was conquered, the acts which partitioned them into Territories and incorporated them with the United States, were clogged with provisos which excluded us from them as settlers, unless we would consent to sever the ties which bound us to our households. Liberty bills covered the statue books of the Northern States, intended to wrest our property – property most distinctly recognized and guaranteed by the Constitution – from us, if we dared to carry it beyond a certain line. Should we be prudent enough not to carry it, societies were formed, receiving the patronage and encouragement of many of the best people of the North, whose business it was, through secret agents sent among us and living upon our trustful hospitality, to entice our slaves away from their homes, and to receive and protect them until they could be placed beyond the reach of their masters. An armed raid was arranged and carried out against us, which was expected to be accompanied by insurrection and murder and rapine. When its leaders were punished, their memories were held sacred, and their ashes glorified. Against all this we used every constitutional mode of resistance. We appealed to the promises of their forefathers, to the memories of the past, to the better feelings of the present. All was in vain. The conservative portion of the North either could not or would not restrain these aggressions. At last we determined to strike for our homes and for our firesides, but not until a party had been organized and was triumphant, which threatened to overturn our whole domestic and social life. Which party was right in all this? The Northern States in their persistent aggressions, or we in our resistance? Can any man, with any sense of justice, hesitate how to decide? What else could we do? Could we permit every thing that made life valuable to be torn from us, and we the while stand mute and impassive? We did what every high-minded people would have done, transferred the question from the courts of Earth to the courts of Heaven, and committed our cause to him who reigneth in righteousness.

If we go yet a step further, we shall see, that as between us and our adversaries, even admitting all their positions, we still had the right with us. Supposing slavery (for I argue now upon the hypothesis of our adversaries) to have been a wrong to the slave and an evil to the country, I would ask, who did the wrong and who bears the evil? Where did these slaves come from and who brought them here? They came from their native haunts, brought here by the forefathers either of those very men who are fighting this battle with us, or of those who are standing coldly by, seeing us cut each other's throats. These slaves were imposed upon us — imposed upon us, in many cases, against our wills — imposed upon us just so long as it was profitable for those hypocrites to bring them here. And now when they have become interwoven with our whole social life, forming a part of our representation, of our prosperity, of our habits, of our manners, of our affections, all these ties are to be rudely broken asunder, not at

our will or in our own time, but at the will and in the appointed time
of those who forced this evil upon us. Were our people required, upon
any principle of equity, to submit to be the shuttle-cocks of these contemptible gamesters? to be the tools of such mock philanthropy and
such real wickedness? Was this our breeding? Was this the spirit
which Burke foreshadowed as the temper of the slaveholder? Have
they who committed the wrong and took money for it – aye, received
their full bond, flesh and all – the right, whether in the sight of man
or God, to dictate to us, who had paid the bond and rescued the poor
savages from their greedy and bloody grasp and made men and christians of them? And who bears the evil, as they have been pleased
to term it? We bear it, and have borne it, and have endeavored to
turn it into a blessing, and have many of us been martyrs in this
cause. At that day of terrible judgment when the secrets of all hearts
shall be disclosed, many will stand before God, who shall be able to
show that they have sacrificed feelings dearer than life itself for the
benefit of these very slaves, who have spent days of toil and nights
of prayer to understand what was best for their temporal and eternal
state. Many, very many, I know, have been insensible to their duty
and have neglected the great trust committed to their charge, and
for this, punishment has fallen upon us, but many have acquitted
their consciences before God. Let their increase attest their general
comfort! Let their change from the tattooed savage to the well-bred
courteous menial, bear witness to their culture! Let their quiet subordination thro' all this fierce conflict speak trumpet-tongued to the
world of their treatment. Let the numbers who flock to the table of
the Lord attest to the nations the missionary work which is going
on amongst them. Here we are, engaged in one of the bloodiest wars
on record, pressed on every hand, with the enemy at our very doors,
inviting them, alluring them, tempting them, deceiving them, and
yet who wait upon us morning and night? Who keep the keys of our
houses and who nurse and tend upon our children? Who cook the
food we eat and minister to all our necessary wants? These very
slaves! And does the head of any one of us rest less easily upon his
pillow? Does any one tremble as he sees his little ones, dearer to him
than life, nestled in their bosoms and sung to sleep with their lull-
abys? Does any one require a taster of his food, an analyser of his
drink? What does all this mean? How does it harmonize with the
ground assumed by our enemies, that we are inflicting upon these
people a great natural and moral wrong? It means, that upon the score

of humanity, there is no reason for this cruel invasion. It means that we are guiltless of the insulting and calumnious changes which have been laid at our doors. It means that we have been not only masters to these people, but so far as circumstances have permitted us, that we have been friends and instructors. It means that all the blood which has been shed – that all the misery which has been endured – that all the desolation which has been visited upon our land – that all the curse which is laid up in the future, whether for the white race or the black race, is upon our enemies, and that God will require it at their hands.

But beside having reasons like these, depending upon the righteousness of our cause, to believe that God was with us, we had, likewise, another ground of hope arising out of the character and motives of those who were warring against us. We had said in the words which Ezra put into the mouth of his people, not only that "the hand of God is upon all them for good that seek him," but "his power and wrath is against all them that forsake him," and we felt no doubt that the party, which had formed and was directing this crusade against us, had grown up out of elements unchristian and really atheistic. Pretending to a peculiar philanthropy, it was a philanthropy opposed alike to the word and the will of God. Instead of believing in the curse of God upon sin, which curse manifested itself in poverty, in suffering, in slavery, in a thousand forms which made the world as miserable as it is, they determined that human effort could remove them all. Instead of bowing before the word of God, which said "the poor shall never cease out of the land;" instead of submitting to the Divine decree imposed upon Adam and his posterity, "Cursed is the ground for thy sake; in sorrow shalt thou eat of it all the days of thy life;" instead of acquiescing in the triple curse upon the descendants of Ham, "And he said, cursed be Canaan, a servant of servants shall he be unto his brethren. And he said, Blessed be the Lord God of Shem; and Canaan shall be his servant. God shall enlarge Japheth, and he shall dwell in the tents of Shem; and Canaan shall be his servant," they turned their rage against the word of God, and covered it all over with ridicule and with abuse. Catching the echo of the French revolution, they set up liberty, equality, fraternity, as their idols, and virtually dethroned the God of the Bible. They did not work that the evils of social life might fade out quietly under the influence of Christianity, but they defied God, because there were any social evils at all. They were ready, in their fanatical wor-

ship of these terrible delusions – delusions made more terrible than
ever because of the immense developments of physical science and
material prosperity – to blot out all the records of Divine inspiration,
should they be found in opposition to their human conclusions. It
was not Truth which led them on, it was Passion. It was not the path
of pure morality which they were treading; it was the track of a law-
less licentiousness, which led over the ruins and ashes of the altar
and the fireside. At home, its fruits have been fraud, corruption,
unbelief, falsehood, free love. Abroad, wherever their arms have been
victorious, those fruits have been theft, rapine, cruelty, fornication,
desolation. The face of this party was for a time covered with a silver
vail, but the vail has been lifted and lo, the hideous features of the
false Prophet! It carried, for a time, the semblance of wisdom, for
it developed immense material prosperity, but has proved itself to
be "the wisdom which descendeth not from above, but is earthly, sensual, devilish." Can God be with a cause, engendered out of such
materials, led on by such Prophets and Apostles? Will he permit
crime, falsehood, wickedness, unmercifulness, to be triumphant in
the end? Will his power be with those who have forsaken him, and
trampled upon his word and his immutable morality? Impossible; he
is only biding his time while he chastens us for our sins and tries
our faith, and while he ripens them for slaughter and vengeance.

Did any of us ever doubt, in the first years of this conflict, that
God was on our side? Did not the whole land resound with one universal shout of thanksgiving and of praise, as event after event plainly
indicated God's presence with us? Did we not, in solemn festival,
send up our acknowledgement of gratitude, of devotion, of unswerv-
ing faith? Did we not proclaim it from the house tops, that our God
was manifesting himself to us almost as palpably as he had done to
his own chosen people? The remarkable unanimity with which the
seceding States came out of the Union – the harmony with which a
new and permanent Constitution was adopted – the skill with which
vexed questions were avoided, and discordant elements brought into
combination – the recognition of God as our Lord in the face of all
the world, were assumed, on all hands, as tokens of the presence of
his spirit in our Councils and of his good will towards the rising government. And as with our civil affairs so with our military affairs.
The first victory at Manassas, when God smote that proud army
with His fear, and gave us time to gather our resources and discipline our armies for the future – the capture of Norfolk, which sup-

plied us with heavy artillery, while we were preparing to manufacture it for ourselves – the supplies of arms and of ammunition, which
came in from abroad, often at the most propitious moment, to enable
us to sustain the struggle, until we could procure them for ourselves –
the unaccountable delays in the movements of our enemies, when
promptness and decision might have overwhelmed us – the frequent
changes of their Generals at times the most critical for us – the ex-
piration of the term of service of their troops, happening often when
their armies most needed their presence – the marvellous successes
of our little Navy, coming to us just when our hearts were most in
want of comfort and hope – all these and a thousand minuter circumstances which were deeply felt when they occurred, were all taken
to our bosoms and hugged there as precious proofs that God was
with us of a truth. They were to us what the miracles at the Red Sea
and in the wilderness were to the Israelites. Have we forgotten all
these things? Have they faded from our hearts and from our memories because of a few reverses? Are we faithless the moment that
God withdraws himself for a little while from us? O fools and slow
of heart to believe! "God is not a man, that he should lie, neither the
son of man, that he should repent: Hath he said and shall He not
do it? or hath He spoken and shall He not make it good?" And how
could he more plainly have spoken, than by the acts of his Spirit and
of his Providence which we have just recalled to your minds. Even
while he was threatening judgment against the Israelites, his com-
forting words were "For I am the Lord, I change not; therefore ye
sons of Jacob are not consumed."

Why then, you will ask, if God is so clearly on our side, are we
so sorely pressed and made to bleed at every pore? Why do our enemies triumph over us, and spoil our homes and desolate our hearth
stones? Why are our young men smitten and our houses filled with
lamentation? Why does the widow send up her wail before the Lord
and why does the orphan weep because he is fatherless? Why are all
faces filled with anxiety and every brow with care? My hearers, it
requires no research, nor any ingenuity to answer this question. Our
Bibles answer it very directly and very plainly. What you suppose
hard of reconcilement, was asked by the people of Israel thousands
of years ago, and has been asked ever since by the people of God
under whatever dispensation and in whatever condition. Did not
Moses say, when he was recapitulating to the Israelites the wonders
of God in their behalf, "For what nation is there so great, who hath

God so nigh unto them as the Lord your God is in all things that we call upon him for?" And yet this did not hinder but that the Israelites were discomfited in battle, were slain by the sword, were visited with pestilence, were often reduced to very great straits and extremities. Those of whom God is intending to make a nation to do his work upon earth, are precisely those whom he tries most severely. His purpose is to give them not merely victory, but character; not only independence, but righteousness; not peace alone, but the will to do good, after peace shall have been established. His plan, when his hand is upon a people for good, is to discipline as well as to support – to support through discipline, for moral discipline, like military discipline, gives strength and power. His severity goes along with his goodness; he so intermingles them that the one may temper the other and keep down effeminancy and presumption. If you suppose, because God is with you, that you are to run on from victory to victory, without any regard to their moral effect upon you, you will bring upon yourselves much bitter disappointment. The law which God has established for nations as well as for individuals, that any high standard of virtue – virtue which may be relied upon to withstand temptation and to resist corruption – must be gained through the discipline of suffering, is always inflexibly worked out.

When we assume the ground that God has taken us, in spite of our sins, under his especial care and guardianship, we must prepare ourselves to carry on this struggle under the conditions which this sacred relationship involves. We have made our choice before the world, boasting that the Lord is our God – not only boasting of it, but until lately rejoicing in it – and we believe that he has graciously accepted our proffered allegiance. We have said "The hand of the Lord our God is upon all them for good that seek him," and shall we faint and be bewildered, and know not where to turn, the instant we encounter difficulties in the way? Shall we be looking to the right hand and to the left, with trembling limbs and countenances of dismay, when we have boasted to the world that we have such an ally as the Lord of Hosts? Ezra was ashamed, when he had made such an utterance to Artaxerxes, to require of him a band of soldiers and horsemen to help him and his against the enemy in the way. What did he? He proclaimed a fast at the river of Ahava, that he and his might afflict themselves before their God to seek of him a right way for them, and for their little ones, and for all their substance. That was his course; a faithful and a consistent one, and it had its reward, as faithfulness and consistency always will, of entire success. The Lord turned his face once more upon them and showed them that right way which they sought after. "So we fasted," is his simple and beautiful language, "and besought our God for this; and he was entreated of us."

Most surely do we need, my hearers, at this moment, to have the right way pointed out to us – "the right way for us, and for our little ones, and for all our substance." We are sadly out of the way. We have lost sight of the landmarks which directed us so safely upon our first setting out. We seem to have forgotten the resolution with which we entered upon this journey towards the promised land of our national independence – the resolution to suffer anything and to lose everything rather than fail in our purpose. We appear to have abated the enthusiasm which swept everything before it in the outset – which hurried our sons to the field, our wives and daughters to the hospitals, ourselves to any and every work which we could undertake for the advancement of the cause. We have grown apathetic, if not indifferent. We are murmuring and complaining, and some are beginning to ask of our leaders "And wherefore hath the Lord brought us unto this land, to fall by the sword, that our wives and our children should be a prey? were it not better for us to return into Egypt?" What shall we do? How are we once again to regain our lost devotedness and to string ourselves afresh for the duties and the sacrifices which are before us? We must follow the example of Ezra. We must afflict ourselves before our God – we must fast and beseech the Lord to give us true repentance and grace to do the first works.

"In the early history of the Roman Republic, there yawned in the centre of the Forum a deep and dark abyss – an abyss that had opened of its own accord, and had hourly grown wider and wider and threatened to engulph all Rome. The Chief Augur, upon secret consultation with the Senate, uttered these solemn words:

'People of Rome! a heavy doom hangs over our beloved city! The wrath of the Gods has been kindled against you; and in that black abyss you behold its token. See! it gapes with greedy jaws to swallow Rome, and each hour that it remains unclosed, will it become wider and wider, till domestic hearth, sacred altar, Senate house, Capitol, all shall be engulphed.

'Yet may the doom be averted by a fitting oblation. The angry Deities demand a sacrifice – a sacrifice of that, whatsoever it be, which is the most precious of sublunary things. They have not intimated to us what is the sacrifice they demand; that is left to your own judgment and your own faith.

'Choose ye that which ye deem most valuable, and cast it unreluctantly into this gulf. If the sacrifice be acceptable, the chasm will close; if it continues open, seek ye, by a further offering to propitiate the Deities. Is there one, O Romans, who would hesitate a moment to give his best, his most valued, nay all he possesses for his fellow citizens and his country? Shall Rome pass away ere she is out of her infancy, because ye selfishly love aught more than Rome? Or shall she endeavor to fulfil a glorious destiny, purchased by the generous sacrifice of her sons?'

"The augur had scarcely ceased, when he was answered by an unanimous and animated shout – Rome! Rome!! let her be perpetual.

"Down into the abyss were poured showers of glittering coin, the hoarded wealth of the citizens. But the abyss closed not; money was too cheap a sacrifice for such a blessing.

"Next advanced the matrons of Rome in regular order, each bearing the caskets in which were contained her most valued ornaments and her most precious jewels. And as they passed, they sang a solemn chant and cast into the abyss their sparkling gems. One flash of light and they were gone. But the abyss closed not; Gems were too cheap a sacrifice for such a blessing.

"There was a dead silence, and a troubled eye was fixed upon that greedy abyss, that had received so much and yet demanded more.

"Suddenly a shout arose upon the outskirts of the crowd. The tramp of a steed was heard; the throng gave way and a noble warrior dashed towards the abyss, reined up his steed and with a motion of his spear commanded silence.

"'Romans,' said Curtius, 'ye have offered sacrifice of your possessions, of your treasures, of your affections, but who has offered the sacrifice of self? Trust me, Romans, it is the sacrifice of self that is the most precious.'

"With these words, rider and steed plunged into the unfathomable abyss. There was a moment of dreadful feeling – a moment that seemed an age. Slowly the abyss closed; the self sacrifice was received, and Rome was delivered."

Has not this legend of ancient Rome, thus graphically described by an English writer, a deep and rich moral for us at this critical moment! We have freely cast into the black abyss of this war our wealth, our treasures, our children, but have we sacrificed self? Have we de-

termined to give up everything, if need be, for the cause of our country; to lay down upon its altar our private and personal griefs; to
overcome our prejudices, to forget our enmities, to put under foot
our jealousies? Have we resolved to bear all things from man or God,
neglect, humiliation, suffering, rather than be a hindrance in the way
of success? It is far easier to cast into this gulf such things as property, money, treasures, gems, and even sons, than it is to strip ourselves of vanity, of self-conceit, of pride of opinion, of ambition, of
evil habits, of those things which make up our identity. Self! Self!!
in how many subtle, deceitful guises does it dress itself! under how
many high sounding names does it mask itself? How terrible it is
to think that the like features of a noble nature, the deep earnestness, the heroic self-denial, the labor night and day, the intense con-
centration, can arise from impulses so opposite, and that patriotism,
one of the noblest, and selfishness, one of the meanest motives, have
but the same machinery to work with. And yet so it is. The impulse
which would make a man a hero, a martyr, a being to live in his country's heart forever, is as wide apart from that which makes him a
selfish creature, living within himself and for himself, with no aspira-
tions higher than his own interests or his own wants, as is inspiration from heaven and cunning from earth, and yet the instruments
of their work are strikingly alike, so strikingly as to make not only
others, but ourselves, unable to distinguish them. It is very often by
their fruits only – the one reaping in the end honour, admiration, the
world's immortality; the other, the ashes of all their expectations –
that we can finally separate the wheat from the chaff, the pure gold
from the worthless dross.

In turning ourselves, therefore to God in fasting and prayer, let
us truly humble ourselves and beseech Him to show us our own
hearts and to convict us especially of those sins which are offensive
to him and which have placed us in the wrong way. There should be
great searchings of heart to-day. From the President of the Confederate States, who now occupies, for a time, the most responsible position in the world, to the humblest person who is involved in their
destiny, each one of us should examine himself and find out, if possible,
wherein he has offended God and turned away his face from us. Let
us not be looking at and criticising others; let each one look at himself. We shall find sins enough in ourselves to mourn over, without
laying all the blame upon our neighbour's doings. Let the spirit of
the Publican – "God, be merciful to me a sinner" be with us rather

than that of the Pharisee which is now so common; "I thank thee, O God, that I am not as other men are, extortioners, unjust, adulterers, or even as this Publican." My pride of opinion, if I be one in authority, may be doing as much harm to the cause, both with man and God, as another man's covetousness. My vanity and self-conceit may work as much mischief, if I be in a position to make them felt, as your love of ease or your indifference to the cause. It is the aggregate of sinfulness that is working our ruin, that is eating out the heart and spirit of the cause, eating it out naturally and consequentially, for one sin leads inevitably to another. The confidence which grew out of continued victory led to presumption and presumption led to security and the feeling of security begat within the community the desire of wealth, which circumstances seemed to place within every man's grasp. And this making haste to be rich took rapid possession of the minds and hearts of the whole people. Commencing with those who were legitimately engaged in commerce and trade, it soon extended to the farming interests of the country and from them was communicated to the soldier in the camp and the officer in the garrison. Every man became anxious to take part in this game which was to enrich himself, without seeing that it would, most certainly, ruin his country. Men were seen skulking in every way to avoid service in the army, not from cowardice, not from any doubt about the value of the conflict or the certainty of its success, but that they might be at liberty to mingle in this mad hunt after money. Feeble substitutes were put in the place of able bodied men; hundreds sought exemption upon pleas which they would never have dreamed to offer except under the influence of this all-pervading madness, and the soldier, who had retained his early enthusiasm and was ready to sacrifice every thing for the cause, grew dissatisfied when he perceived that he was to bear and to suffer, while others, as able-bodied as himself and as deeply interested in the struggle, remained at home to speculate and grow rich upon his endurance and his sufferings. Just as victory was foreshadowed at the beginning in the earnestness of every heart, in the devotion of every spirit, in the one concentrated idea of victory and independence, so was defeat just as plainly foreshadowed in the distraction of the public mind, in the struggle which rapidly grew up between the administration and the people, in the complaining and the murmuring against the inefficiency of the armies, which was but the natural result of the demoralization of the country. And man could not arrest it. He might force the body, but he could not give the spirit. He might carry the man to the camp, but he could not impart the dash which distinguishes him whose heart is in the work. What we should now ask of God is, that he would revive within us those qualities of mind and of heart – so near akin to the graces of the spirit – which qualify us for carrying on our conflict successfully, earnestness, singleness of purpose, honesty, integrity. The whole people need to be aroused and the government should take the lead, under God, in doing it. The chord of sympathy which vibrated so harmoniously in the past, must be touched anew. This is not a warfare which can be coldly left to the Government and the army; it is the cause, emphatically, of the whole nation – of every man, woman and child in the Confederacy. In vain are conscriptions and impressments; in vain are proclamations and fastings, unless after we shall have fasted and prayed, we use means to rekindle the sacred fire of patriotism which burned so vividly in the outburst of this revolution. Where is the orator? Where is the statesman? Where are the voices which, like a trumpet's blast, led on the soldier to the field of glory – of glory, because the field of duty? They are all mute; some silent in death, some wrapped in inglorious ease. Is this the time for him who has the divine gift of eloquence to keep it pent within his own burning bosom? Is this an hour when any man, who can sway his fellow men, who can enkindle his hope with lips touched with a live coal from off the altar, or excite his fears with the dark shadows of coming events, should leave his country and his country's hopes to drift to ruin without one effort to arrest the misery? Where are the people themselves? Where is that influence of the multitude which is so terrible for evil, so powerful for good? Where is the low sweet voice of woman which has mingled so harmoniously thro' all this tumult with the clangor of the trumpet and the clash of arms? Why is it unheard? Has grief frozen it within her bosom or has terror hushed it into silence? Awake to the reality of things and arouse yourselves, children of the sun, or God's hand will not be with you. "Wherefore criest thou unto me," said the Lord to Moses, when he and his people were hedged up among the mountains, with the fierce Egyptians in their rear, and the deep waters of the red sea before them, "speak unto the children of Israel that they go forward."

Forward, my hearers, forward, with our shield locked and our trust in God, is our only movement now. It is too late even to go backward. We might have gone backward a year ago, when our armies were victoriously thundering at the gates of Washington and were keeping at successfal bay the Hessians of the West, had we been content to bear humiliation for ourselves and degradation for our children. But even that is no longer left us. It is now victory or unconditional submission; submission not to the conservative and christian people of the North, but to a party of infidel fanatics, with an army of needy and greedy soldiers at their backs. Who shall be able to restrain them in their hour of victory? When that moment approaches, when the danger shall seem to be over and the spoils are ready to be divided, every outlaw will rush to fill their ranks, every adventurer will hasten to swell their legions, and they will swoop down upon the South as the hosts of Attila did upon the fertile fields of Italy. And shall you find in defeat that mercy which you did not find in victory? You may slumber now, but you will awake to a fearful reality. You may lie upon your beds of ease and dream that when it is all over, you will be welcomed back to all the privileges and immunities of greasy citizens, but how terrible will be your disappointment! You will have an ignoble home, overrun by hordes of insolent slaves and rapacious soldiers. You will wear the badge of a conquered race, Pariahs among your fellow creatures, yourselves degraded, your delicate wives and gentle children thrust down to menial service, insulted perhaps dishonored. Think you that these victorious hordes, made up in large part of the sweepings of Europe, will leave you any thing? As well might the lamb expect mercy from the wolf. Power, which is checked and fettered by a doubtful contest, is very different from power victorious, triumphant and irresponsible. The friends whom you have known and loved at the North; who have sympathized with you in your trials and to whom you might have looked for comfort and protection, will have enough to do then to take care of themselves. The surges that sweep over us, will carry them away in its refluent tide. Oh! for the tongue of a Prophet to paint for you what is before you, unless you repent and turn to the Lord and realize that "His hand is upon all them for good that seek him." The language of Scripture is alone adequate to describe it – "The earth mourneth and languisheth; Lebanon is ashamed and hewn down: Sharon is like a wilderness. They that did feed delicately are desolate in the streets: they that were brought up in scarlet embrace dung-hills. They ravished the women in Zion and the maids in the cities of Judah. They took the young men to grind, and the children fell under the wood. The joy of our heart is ceased; our dance is turned into mourning. The crown is fallen from our head: wo unto us that we have sinned."

Let us turn then this day to the Lord our God with all our heart
and soul and mind, believing that His hand is upon all them for good
that seek him, trusting that He will shew us the right way for us
and for our little ones, and for all our substance. Let our prayer be
that which Milton offered against the enemies of his country – "Let
them all take counsel together and let it come to nought; let them
decree and do thou cancel it; let them gather themselves and be scat-
tered; let them embattle themselves and be broken; let them embattle
and be broken, for thou art with us."

Funeral Discourse

John Paris

February 28, 1864

Note: *On the morning of the first of February, Brig. Gen. R. F.
Hoke forced the passage of Batchelor's Creek, nine miles west from
Newbern; the enemy abandoned his works and retreated upon the
town. A hot and vigorous pursuit was made, which resulted in the
capture of a large number of prisoners, and the surrender to our forces
of many others, who were cut off from escape by the celerity of the
pursuit, and our troops seizing and holding every avenue leading into
the town, near the enemy's batteries.*

*Among the prisoners taken, were about fifty native North Caro-
linians, dressed out in Yankee uniform, with muskets upon their
shoulders. Twenty-two of these men were recognized as men who
had deserted from our ranks, and gone over to the enemy. Fifteen of
them belonged to Nethercutt's Battalion. They were arraigned before a court martial, proved guilty of the charges, and condemned
to suffer death by hanging.*

*It became my duty to visit these men in prison before their ex-
ecution, in a religious capacity. From them, I learned that bad and
mischievous influences had been used with every one to induce him to*

(Greensborough, NC: A. W. Ingold & Co., Book & Job Printers, 1864).

desert his flag, and such influences had led to their ruin. From citizens
who had known them for many years, I learned that some of them
had heretofore borne good names, as honest, harmless, unoffending
citizens. After their execution I thought it proper, for the benefit of
the living that I should deliver a discourse before our brigade, upon
the death of these men, that the eyes of the living might be opened,
to view the horrid and ruinous crime and sin of desertion, which had
become so prevalent. A gentleman from Forsyth county, who was pres-
ent at the delivery of the discourse solicited a copy for publication,
which has been granted. For the style and arrangement, as it was
preached as well as written in the camp, no apology is offered. Hav-
ing no pecuniary interest in its publication, it is respectfully submit-
ted to all who go for the unqualified independence of the Southern
Confederacy.

—Hoke's Brigade, April 1st, 1864

> *3. Then Judas which had betrayed him, when he saw that he*
> *was condemned, repented himself, and brought again the thirty*
> *pieces of silver to the chief priests and elders.*
> *4. Saying, I have sinned in that I have betrayed the innocent*
> *blood. And they said, what is that to us? See thou to that.*
> *5. And he cast down the pieces of silver in the temple, and*
> *departed, and went and hanged himself.*
> *—Matthew XXVII, 3-5—*

You are aware, my friends, that I have given public notice that
upon this occasion I would preach a funeral discourse upon the death
of the twenty-two unfortunate, yet wicked and deluded men, whom
you have witnessed hanged upon the gallows within a few days. I do
so, not to eulogize or benefit the dead. But I do so, solely, for the
benefit of the living: and in doing so, I shall preach in my own way,
and according to my own manner, or rule. What I shall say will either
be true or false. I therefore request that you watch me closely; weigh
my arguments in the balance of truth; measure them by the light
of candid reason, and compare them by the Standard of Eternal Truth,
the book of God; what is wrong, reject, and what is true, accept, for
the sake of the truth, as responsible beings.

Of all deserters and traitors, Judas Iscariot, who figures in our
text, is undoubtedly the most infamous, whose names have found a
place in history, either sacred or profane. No name has ever been
more execrated by mankind: and all this has been justly done. But

there was a time and a period when this man wore a different character, and had a better name. A time when he went forth with the eleven Apostles at the command of the Master to preach the gospel, heal the sick and cast out devils. And he, too, returned with this same chosen band, when the grand, and general report was made of what they had done and what they had taught.

But a change came over this man. He was the treasurer of the Apostolic board; an office that warranted the confidence and trust of his compeers. "He bare the bag and kept what was put therein." Possibly this was the grand and successful temptation presented him by the evil One. He contracted an undue love for money, and Holy Writ informs us "the love of money is the root of all evil;" so must it ever be when valued above a good name, truth or honor. Now comes his base and unprincipled desertion of his blessed Master. He goes to the chief priests. His object is selfish, base and sordid, – to get money. He enters into a contract with them, to lead their armed guards to the place to which the Saviour had retired, that they might arrest him. Thirty pieces of silver is the price agreed upon, – about twenty-two dollars and fifty cents of our money. A poor price, indeed, for any man to accept for his reputation, his life, his soul, his all. When Judas saw that the Saviour was condemned, it is stated in the text that "he repented himself, and brought again the thirty pieces of silver to the chief priests and elders, saying, I have sinned in that I have betrayed the innocent blood." "And he cast down the thirty pieces of silver in the temple, and departed and went and hanged himself." The way of transgressors is truly hard. As sure as there is a God in heaven, justice and judgment will overtake the wicked; though he may flourish as a green bay tree for awhile, yet the eye of God is upon him and retribution must and will overtake him.

Let us now consider what this man gained by his wicked transaction. First, twenty-two dollars and fifty cents. Secondly, a remorse of conscience too intolerable to be borne. An immortality of infamy without a parallel in the family of man. What did he lose? His reputation. His money. His apostleship. His peace of conscience, his life, his soul, his all.

Well may it be said that this man is the most execrable of all whose names stand on the black list of deserters and traitors that the world has furnished from the beginning until now. – Turning to the history of our own country, I find written high on the scroll of infamy the name of Benedict Arnold, who at one time stood high in the confidence of the great and good Washington. What was his crime? Desertion and treason. He too hoped to better his condition by selling his principles for money, to the enemies of his country, betraying his Washington into the hands of his foes, and committing the heaven-insulting crime of perjury before God and man. Verily, he obtained his reward; an immortality of infamy; the scorn and contempt of the good and the loyal of all ages and all countries.

Thus, gentlemen, I have brought before you two grand prototypes of desertion, whose names tower high over all on the scroll of infamy. And I now lay down the proposition, that every man who has taken up arms in defence of his country, and basely deserts or abandons that service, belongs in principle and practice to the family of Judas and Arnold. But what was the status of those twenty-two deserters whose sad end and just fate you witnessed across the river in the old field? Like you they came as volunteers to fight for the independence of their own country. Like you they received the bounty money offered by their country. Like you they took upon themselves the most solemn obligations of this oath: "I, A.B. do solemnly swear that I will bear true allegiance to the Confederate States of America, and that I will serve them honestly and faithfully against all their enemies or opposers whatsoever, and observe and obey the orders of the Confederate States, and the orders of the officers appointed over me, according to the rules and articles for the government of the Confederate States, so help me God."

With all the responsibilities of this solemn oath upon their souls, and all the ties that bind men to the land that gave them birth, ignoring every principle that pertains to the patriot, disowning that natural, as well as lawful allegiance that every man owes to the government of the State which throws around him the ægis of its protection, they went boldly, Judas and Arnold-like, made an agreement with the enemies of their country, took an oath of fidelity and allegiance to them, and agreed with them for money to take up arms and assist in the unholy and hellish work of the subjugation of the country which was their own, their native land! These men have only met the punishment meted out by all civilized nations for such crimes. To this, all good men, all true men, and all loyal men who love their country, will say, Amen!

But who were those twenty-two men whom you hanged upon the gallows? They were your fellow-beings. They were citizens of our own

Carolina. They once marched under the same beautiful flag that waves over our heads; but in an evil hour, they yielded to mischievous influence, and from motives or feelings base and sordid, unmanly and vile, resolved to abandon every principle of patriotism, and sacrifice every impulse of honor; this sealed their ruin and enstamped their lasting disgrace. The question now arises, what are the influences and the circumstances that lead men into the high and damning crimes of perjury and treason? It will be hard to frame an answer that will fit every case. But as I speak for the benefit of those whom I stand before to-day, I will say I have made the answer to this question a matter of serious inquiry for more than eighteen months. The duties of my office as Chaplain have brought me much in contact with this class of men. I have visited twenty-four of them under sentence of death in their cells of confinement, and with death staring them in the face, and only a few short hours between them and the bar of God. I have warned them to tell the whole truth, confess everything wrong before God and man, and yet I have not been able to obtain the full, fair and frank confession of everything relating to their guilt from even one of them, that I thought circumstances demanded, although I had baptized ten of them in the name of the Holy Trinity. In confessing their crimes, they would begin at Newbern, where they joined the enemy, saying nothing about perjury and desertion. Every man of the twenty-two, whose execution you witnessed, confessed that bad or mischievous influences had been used with him to influence him to desert. All but two, willingly gave me the names of their seducers. But none of these deluded and ruined men seemed to think he ought to suffer the penalty of death, because he had been persuaded to commit these high crimes by other men.

But gentlemen, I now come to give you my answer to the question just asked. From all that I have learned in the prison, in the guard house, in the camp, and in the country *I am fully satisfied, that the great amount of desertions from our army are produced by, and are the fruits of a bad, mischievous, restless, and dissatisfied, not to say disloyal influence that is at work in the country at home.* If in this bloody war our country should be overrun, this same mischievous home influence will no doubt be the prime agent in producing such a calamity. Discontentment has, and does exist in various parts of the State. We hear of these malcontents holding public meetings, not for the purpose of supporting the Government in the prosecutions of the war, and maintenance of our independence, but for the purpose of finding fault with the Government. Some of these meetings have been dignified with the name of "peace-meetings;" some have been ostensibly called for other purposes, but they have invariably been composed of men who talk more about their "rights," than about their duty and loyalty to their country. These malcontents profess to be greatly afflicted in mind about the state of public affairs. In their doleful croakings they are apt to give vent to their melancholy lamentations in such words as these: "The country is ruined!" "We are whipt!" "We might as well give up!" "It is useless to attempt to fight any longer!" "This is the rich man's war and the poor man's fight;" &c. Some newspapers have caught the mania and lent their influence to this work of mischief; whilst the pulpit, to the scandal of its character for faith and holiness, has belched forth in some places doctrines and counsels through the ministrations of unworthy occupants, sufficient to cause Christianity to blush under all the circumstances. I would here remark, standing in the relation which I do before you, that the pulpit and the press, when true and loyal to the Government which affords them protection, are mighty engines for good; but when they see that Government engaged in a bloody struggle for existence, and show themselves opposed to its efforts to maintain its authority by all constitutional and legal means, such a press, and such pulpits should receive no support for an hour from a people that would be free. The seal of condemnation should consign them to oblivion.

Such sentiments as we have just alluded to, are sent in letters to our young men in the army, by writers professing to be friends; often with an urgent and pressing invitation to come home; and some have even added that execrable and detestable falsehood, the quintescence of treason, "the State is going to secede." Letters coming into our camps on the Rappahannock and Rapidan sustain this position. What are the effects produced upon our young men in the ranks? With the illiterate, they are baleful indeed. The incautious youth takes it for granted that the country is ruined and that the Government is his enemy. The poisonous contagion of treason from home gets hold in his mind and steals into his feelings. This appeal from home has overcome him. The young man of promise and of hope once, now becomes a deserter. Is guilty by one false step of the awful crimes of perjury and desertion. The solemn obligations of his oath are disregarded; he takes to the woods, traverses weary roads by night for days, until he reaches the community in which he claims his home; but for what? To engage in any of the honorable vocations of life? No, gentlemen. But to lie hidden from the face of all good true and loyal men. But for what purpose? To keep from serving his country as a man and a citizen. To consume the provisions kept in the country for the support of the women and children, families of soldiers who are serving their country, indeed; and lastly, to get his living in part, at least, by stealing and robbing. And here allow me to say, I am not sufficiently skilled in language to command words to express the deep and unutterable detestation I have of the character of a deserter. If my brother were to be guilty of such a high crime, I should certainly make an effort to have his name changed to something else, that I, and my children after me, might not feel the deep and lasting disgrace which his conduct had enstamped upon it.

I hold, gentlemen, that there are few crimes in the sight of either God or man, that are more wicked and detestable than desertion. The first step in it is perjury. Who would ever behove such an one in a court of justice again? The second, is treason. He has abandoned the flag of his country; thus much he has aided the common enemy. These are startling crimes, indeed, but the third is equally so. He enstamps disgrace upon the name of his family and children.

From amidst the smoke and flames of Sinai God has declared that He "is a jealous God, visiting the inequities of the fathers upon the children unto the third and fourth generations of them that hate me." The infamy that the act of disloyalty on the part of a father places his children in after him, is a disability they cannot escape: it was his act, not theirs; and to them it has become God's visitation according to the text quoted above. The character of infamy acquired by the tories of the revolution of 1776, is to this day imputed to their descendants in a genealogical sense. Disloyalty is a crime that mankind never forget and but seldom forgive; the grave cannot cover it.

Many cry out in this the day of our discontent, and say, "we want peace." This is true, we all want peace, the land mourns of account of the absence of peace, and we all pray for peace. You have often heard me pray for peace, but I think you will bear me witness to-day that you have never heard me pray for peace without independence. God forbid that we should have a peace that brought no independence.

But how are we to obtain peace? There are but two modes known by which to obtain this most desirable boon. First: to lay down our arms, cease to fight, and submit to the terms of our enemy, the tyrant at Washington. Fortunately for us, we already know what those terms are. They stand recorded in his law books, and in his published orders and edicts, – and constitute with our enemies, the *law of the land*, as far as we are concerned.

1. The lands of our citizens are to be sold for the purpose of paying the enormous public debt of the Yankees. This part of the programme has already been put into operation at points held by the enemy, as in Fairfax county, Va., and Beaufort, S.C. In the latter place, the lands have been laid off into thirty acre lots, and bought mostly by negroes.

2. The negroes, everywhere, to be declared free, and placed upon a state of equality with the whites.

3. Every man who has taken any part in the war, denied the right of voting at the polls.

4. Our Governors and Judges appointed by the Federal Government at Washington, and sent to rule over us at his pleasure.

5. Even the men selected to administer to us in holy things at the altars of our God, must be men approved and appointed by his military authorities; as it is now done in Norfolk and Portsmouth, where I am acquainted.

In addition to this, gentlemen, we of course will have to endure the deep and untold mortification of having bands of negro soldiers stationed in almost every neighborhood, to enforce these laws and regulations.

These things would be some of the "*blessings*," we would obtain by such a peace. Tell me to-day, sons of Carolina, would not such a peace bring ten-fold more horrors and distress to our country than this war has yet produced? Can any people on the face of this earth, fit to be freemen, ever accept a peace that will place them in such a condition? Never! never! never!

The great and good Stonewall Jackson, a few weeks before his death was talking with a friend about the probable issue of the war; the conversation turned upon the possibility of the Confederate States being brought again under the rule and authority of the United States; when our illustrious chief remarked, that if he could have his choice in view of such a contingency, he would prefer the grave as his refuge. What patriot would not? What soldier would not? What freeman would not? This was the noble sentiment of a man whom we all believed to be fit to live, or fit to die.

The other mode by which to obtain peace, is to fight it out to the bitter end, as our forefathers did in the revolution of 1776, and reduce our enemies, by our manly "defence," to the necessity of acknowledging our independence, and "letting us alone." – We are involved in this bloody war, and the question before us is, not how did we get into it, but how shall we get out of it?

Many tell us the war cloud looks dark and impenetrable to moral vision. This is all true. But are we not men? Have we not buckled on the armor, putting our truth in the Lord of hosts, as the arbiter of our destiny as a nation? Shall we then lay down our arms before we are overthrown? God forbid! Sons of Carolina, let your battle-cry be, Onward! Onward! until victory shall crown the beautiful banner that floats over us to-day with such a peace as freemen only love, and brave men only can accept. We are engaged in a mighty work, the establishment of an empire, which we trust by the blessing of God will become the freest, the best and the greatest on the face of the earth. Every man must act his part in this great work. Let us then look to the manner in which we perform the part which duty assigns, that there may be no regrets or heart-burnings hereafter. For just as sure as this cruel war began, it will have an end, and that end is nearer now than when it began. And when the sweet and lovely days of delightful peace return to cheer us, and friend meets with friend, and talk over the trials, the perils and sufferings we have endured in freedom's cause; with what emotions of pleasure shall we speak of the soldier ever true and faithful who stood by us, faithful alike both in the sunshine and storm of war. But what will then be said of the miserable skulker? May God give him a better heart that he may become a better man and a better soldier.

From the position which I occupy, I have been enabled to notice deserters and skulkers closely, and I have made it my business to inquire into their history, and I am happy to say for the credit of Christianity, that among the multitude I have known guilty of desertion, only three of that number professed to be members of any Church, and they had been no credit to the religion they professed, as it lived only upon their lips and was a stranger in their hearts.

The true Christian is always a true patriot. Patriotism and Christianity walk hand in hand. When perils and dangers gather around the country that protects him, he then belongs to no party but his country's party; his loyalty must stand unquestioned and unquestionable. As one that fears God, he knows that, if a man is not for his country, he is against it. Hence, there is no neutral ground or position for him to occupy; but to stand by his country as its fast, unwavering friend, that its triumph may be his triumph, and its destiny his destiny. There is no toryism in a Christian's heart. The two principles cannot dwell together.

War is the scourge of nations. God is no doubt chastising us for our good. When the ends of His providence are accomplished, He will no doubt remove the rod. But the ways of His providence are generally dark to mortal vision. Yet He is able to bring light out of darkness. We are only drinking now from a cup, from which every nation upon the face of the earth have drank before us. We have walked the bloody road of revolution for three years; and still we face the foe. Our fathers trod it for seven, and in the end were successful.

The pious Dr. Watts tells us in one of his beautiful hymns, that,

> "God moves in a mysterious way,
> His wonders to perform;
> He plants his footsteps in the sea,
> And rides upon the storm."

His ways with the nations of the earth are deeply mysterious to mortal vision, and whilst they are the exhibitions of His majesty and power, we should regard them likewise as the evidences of His goodness and mercy towards fallen man. As He deals with individuals, so does He deal with nations. He lifteth up one and putteth down another; but all this is done for the good of the whole. Righteousness exalteth a nation, but sin is a reproach to any people, is the doctrine laid down in Holy Writ. Proud Egypt, the cradle of the arts and sciences, has sadly fallen from her ancient glory and splendor. Ezekiel, speaking as the oracle of God, and accusing her of her sins, declared "she shall become the basest of the kingdoms," and the words of the Seer have become verified to the letter. For transgression, the chosen people of God, the Israelists, were compelled to wander forty years in the Arabian desert, thus suffering the chastisement of the disfavor of offended Deity. And when they were permitted to cross over Jordan into the land of promise, they were required to do a strange and wondrous work; namely, to destroy the nations of this goodly land and possess it for their own inheritance. The sins of these nations had cried unto heaven, and Israel became the instrument in the hand of God by which the judgments of offended Justice was meted out to the guilty nations. Jerusalem, the lovely, queenly Jerusalem, whose beautiful temple was the glory of the whole earth, in which the presence of the Eternal Shekinah was visible annually to mortal eye, and where Solomon in all his glory once reigned – sinned with an high hand against God; she knew not the day of her visitation, the cup of her iniquity was full; the judgment of offended heaven overtook her; her glory departed; the besom of destruction swept over her, and she is now trodden down by the gentiles – a crumbling monument of her departed greatness.

Babylon, once the proud mistress of the East, whose spacious walls, hanging gardens, and lofty temples stood as the wonders of the world, and Daniel, the prophet, robed in the vestments of royal honors, once spake and wrote by heaven's prompting of things to come – has fallen; her greatness is lost; her walls have perished; her palaces have crumbled; her temples are entombed, and the wandering Arab now nightly pitches his tent over the spot where Belshazzar held his impious feast. Where is Nineveh? The mighty Nineveh? And Tadmor, and Persepolis, and hundred-gated Thebes? They belong only to the past; the silence of death has spread its sepulchral pall over them, and the relics of fallen greatness alone remain to mark the spot where they lie entombed. Sparta has departed from the map of nations, and Athens is but the tomb of the Athens that was. These have all sinned, and "there is a God that judgeth in the earth."

Four years ago, these Confederate States formed an integral part of the U. States. Perhaps no nation of people ever sinned against more rights and abused more privileges than the United States. The Northern pulpits hatched and fostered the spirit that produced this cruel and bloody war; but cruel and bloody as it is, I believe in God, to-day, that great good will come to us of the South as a people, if we will only depart from our sins and lean upon the Almighty Arm. If He be for us, who can stand successfully against us? He gave to our fathers a Washington, a man who feared God, to guide them through the revolution of 1776. He has give to us a Lee, a man of like faith and of like hopes, to be our leader in these dark days of trial, and we all love to follow where he leads.

He lent to us a Jackson, that bright and shining light of Christianity, whose ardent piety and strong faith always presented the same beauties, in the halls of science, at the altars of God, around the camp-fires, or on the battle-field. Oh, what a model of a Christian soldier! Well do I remember how his presence cheered us as he rode along our line on the morning of the first battle of Fredericksburg, after the artillery began to roar heavily. His very appearance seemed to be the presage of victory. He seemed like one sent by God. But God has seen proper in His providence to take him away, and whatsoever He doeth is right. Let us then bow to the hand that afflicts in such dispensations as this, take courage, and press onward.

Let us then humble ourselves before God as a people, confess our sins, and implore His protecting power to guide us through this mighty struggle to a successful issue. He has certainly done great things for us as a people, whereof we should be glad.

I think you will bear me witness that I have never been hopeful of an early peace in my intercourse among you. But to-day I fancy that I can discover a little cloud, in the political heavens as large as a man's hand at least, that seems to protend peace. Take courage, then, companions in arms. All things around us to-day bid us be of good courage. History fails to tell us of ten millions of freemen being enslaved, who had determined to be free. A braver or more patriotic army than we have, never followed their chief to victory. Their endurance challenges the admiration of the world. When I have seen our brave men in winter's cold and summer's heat, marching from battle-field to battle-field, bare-footed as they were born, and without a murmur, I could not doubt our final success. *Such men as these were never born to be slaves*. Again, when I have turned my eye homeward from the camp, and witnessed the labors of our fair country women, in preparing clothing to meet the wants of the suffering in the field, and witnessed their untiring devotion to the relief of the sick and wounded in the hospitals, I knew that the history of no country, and of no age afforded anything like a parallel, and my faith assured me we never were born to be the slaves of Yankees. Then let your trust to-day be strong in the God of nations.

Surely, then, no man can be found in all our land who owes allegiance to his country, that is so lost to himself, and to all that is noble and patriotic, as to say, "I am for the Union as it was." Such an one could only merit the good man's scorn, and desire the tory's infamy for himself, and disgrace for his children.

Gentlemen, I have followed your fortunes for twenty months, leaving wife and children far behind me. I have rejoiced in your prosperity, and mourned over your adversity. Marches, battles, sufferings are before us still. By the help of God I am with you, and hope still to be with you to share in your triumphs, your sufferings and your joys. If these be the days to try men's souls, for my country's sake I am willing to be tried, by bearing my humble part in this mighty struggle.

For, standing before you to-day, you must permit me to say in the language of a noble patriot, "I am for my country right, yea, for my country wrong." My loyalty to her is unqualified, and without any conditions. Her cause is always my cause. If her cause be right, she shall have my free support; if it be wrong, she shall have my unqualified support. Therefore, when I shall sleep in the dust, you must not say to my children, "your father was a conservative, (or any other name,) when his country was engaged in a bloody struggle for existence." Then you would do me wrong, and do them wrong also. I belong only to my country's party. But it may be said, that I can afford to use strong language when I am not required to take position in the front ranks on the battle-field. The duties of my office require me, as you are aware, to take position in the rear, to assist with the wounded, – but yet at Fredericksburg, Williamsport, Mine Run, and Batchelor's Creek, I was under the fire of both artillery and musketry, and I will here add that if ever my country calls upon me to fall into ranks in her defence with a musket on my shoulder, my answer shall be, "here am I."

Then, to-day, in the light of this beautiful Sabbath sun, let us take courage, and with renewed trust in God, resolve to do our whole duty as patriots and soldiers, and leave the event to the Arbiter of nations. *Amen!*

Part III

Black Sermons, South and North

BLACK PREACHERS

There has been no mention in this book of black preaching and sermons during the sectional crisis in America. The omission was by design, for black preaching simply was not a primary factor in the conflict between the North and South. Both sections were dominated and controlled by the white population. Black preachers and their sermons did play some role, however, and a work on the pulpit and the sectional crisis would be remiss if this role went unrecognized.

When the Great Awakening swept the colonies, blacks, both slave and free, were among those touched by the wave of religious excitement. It was a time when many in the black community were converted to Christianity and especially to the Baptist and Methodist denominations.

By the eve of the Civil War, Christianity was prevalent throughout the slave community in the South. The white society devised two basic means of meeting the worship needs of the Christianized slaves. Black converts were invited to worship with the whites in mixed, though segregated, congregations. It was not unusual for the slaves, who sat in the galleries or back pews, to outnumber the whites in both attendance at and membership in a particular church. About the 1820s some white masters allowed the slaves to have their own separate services under the supervision of white ministers.

For many in the black society, both of the above alternatives soon proved to be unacceptable. Leon Litwack has written: "Nearly every white preacher faced a problem of credibility when he addressed the slaves. Not only did they perceive him as an instrument of the white master, capable of twisting the word of God to make it serve the white man's ends, but what he told them . . . had little relevance for their own lives and hopes."[1] It was difficult, if not impossible, for the slaves to reconcile Christian instruction and the masters' complete control over their lives. Though the slaves tended to condemn most white people, the white ministers in particular were singled out as special targets of condemnation. Above everyone else in the white society blacks saw the preachers as the biggest hypocrites. From the slaves' point of view, the white preachers misinterpreted the Bible to promote white interests, used the Bible as a means of promoting docility and acceptance of station among the slaves, and many of the preachers were themselves slaveholders, some cruel slaveholders. Susan Boggs, an ex-slave from Virginia, remembered that "the man who baptized me had a colored woman tied up in yard to whip when he got home. . . . We had to sit and hear him preach and her mother was in church hearing him preach."[2]

The slaves could not accept the ethical concepts as delivered by the white ministers. When those ministers told the slaves, "Do not steal," the blacks turned deaf ears, for they themselves were stolen property. Josephine Howard illustrated the moral contradiction of white ethical pronouncements: "Dey allus done tell us it am wrong to lie and steal, but why did de white folks steal my mammy and her mammy? Dey lives clost to some water, somewheres over in Africy, and de man come in a little boat to de sho' and tell dem he got presents on de big boat . . . and my mammy and her mammy gits took out to dat big boat and dey locks dem in a black hole what mammy say so black you can't see nothin'. Dat de sinfulles' stealin' dey is."[3] Thus, writes Albert Raboteau, "lying and deceit, normally considered moral vices, were virtues to slaves in their dealings with whites."[4]

Because the white ministers had such little credibility among the slaves, black preachers, many of whom themselves were slaves, arose to meet the spiritual needs of the black Christian community.[5] Sometimes these preachers were ordained by the Baptist or Methodist denominations after proving themselves worthy of such recognition. In other denominations – Presbyterian, Lutheran, Disciples, Episcopalians, Moravians – slave preachers were almost nonexistent.[6] Many slave preachers were merely called and ordained "by the Spirit." A former slave preacher told of his calling from God.

Yer see I am a preacher. De Lord call me once when I was workin'. . . . He call me and told me, in imagination, you know, that he wanted me to preach. I told him I didn't know enough – that I was ig'nant, and the folks would laugh at me. But he drew me on and I prayed. I prayed out in the woods, and every time I tried to get up from my knees He would draw me down again. An' at last a great light came down sudden to me, a light as big as the moon, an' struck me hard on the head and on each shoulder and on the bress, here and here and here. . . . And den same time warm was in around my heart, and I felt that the Book was there. An' my tongue was untied, and I preached ever since and is not afraid. I can't read de Book, but I has it here, I has de text, and de meanin', and I speaks as well as I can, and de congregation takes what the Lord gives me.[7]

These preachers became very influential among the slaves, who recognized the preachers as a source of authority and inspiration. They presided over slave weddings, funerals, and baptisms. They preached, often with eloquence, at religious meetings. The words and behavior of these black ministers were closely monitored by the white masters who greatly mistrusted people of such enormous influence. There was the danger, these masters felt, that slaves could be inspired to revolt and rise up against their masters in the name of God. They could not forget the Nat Turner revolt.[8] Thus, the slave preacher found himself trying to find ways and words to meet the needs of his congregation and at the same time not stir up the suspicions of white observers. He became skilled in the art of obfuscation and double meanings. Anderson Edwards told of the dilemma in which the slave preacher found himself:

When I starts preachin' I couldn't read or write and had to preach what massa told me and he say tell them niggers iffen they obeys the massa they goes to Heaven but I knowed there's something better for them, but daren't tell them 'cept on the sly. That I done lots. I tell 'em iffen they keeps prayin' the Lord will set 'em free.[9]

A black preacher who had been a slave addressed a congregation of freedmen soon after the Union had secured victory. He remembered what it was like during the war when the outcome was still uncertain. "I listened to your prayers," he said,

but I did not hear a single prayer offered for the President of the United States or for the success of the American Army. (Amen! O, yes, I prayed all last night, etc.) But I knew what you meant. You were not quite sure that you were free, therefore a little afraid to say boldly what you felt. I know how it is. I remember how we used to have to employ our dark symbols and obscure figures to cover up our real meaning. The profoundest philosopher could not understand us. (Amen! Hallelujah! That's so.)[10]

Freedom and equality were subjects the white masters most often prohibited the slave preachers from discussing. Preachers who

ignored the prohibition found themselves in trouble. Raboteau has
recorded a few such occasions.

> Sarah Ford told how "one day Uncle Lew preachin' and he say, 'De
> Lawd make everyone to come in unity and on de level, both white and
> black.' When Massa Charles hears 'bout it, he don't like it none, and
> de next mornin' old Uncle Jake git Uncle Lew and put him out in de-
> field with de rest." Henry Clay Bruce retold the story of an old preacher
> named Uncle Tom Ewing, "who was praying on one occasion, after the
> close of his sermon, in the church near Jacob Vennable's place.... The
> old fellow got warmed up, and used the words 'Free indeed, free from
> work, free from white folks, free from everything.' After the meeting
> closed, Jacob Vennable, who sat in front of the pulpit, took Tom to
> task and threatened to have his license revoked if he ever used such
> language in public." Bruce concluded: "I heard Uncle Tom preach and
> pray many times after the above described occurrence, but never heard
> him use the words quoted above." Uncle Lew and Uncle Tom got off
> light; Rev. R. S. Sorrick, a slave preacher in Washington County, Mary-
> land, was placed in prison in 1841 for three months and eight days "for
> preaching the gospel to my colored brethren."[11]

When William Russell, a war correspondent for the *London Times*,
toured the South in 1861, he discovered whites who were indeed
suspicious and fearful of black preachers. They "do the niggars no
good," he was told; "they talk about things that are going on elsewhere and get their minds unsettled." Russell also learned that there
were Southern whites who had great reservations about exposing
their slaves to the Christian religion at all. On one occasion, when
Russell was conversing with a slave lad of about ten years of age on
religious matters, the conversation was abruptly interrupted and
halted by the overseer. Pulling Russell aside, the overseer commented
to him: "We don't think it right to put those things into their heads
so young, it only disturbs their minds, and leads them astray."[12]

Because the presence of white masters at their religious meetings was both inhibiting and intimidating, the slaves began to meet
in secret and secluded places – the woods, thickets, swamps, the bottoms, an out-of-the-way old cabin, and gullies – late at night. They
devised ingenious ways of stifling voices that were lifted in prayers,
songs, or preaching. It was a dangerous thing to participate in these
secret meetings, for severe punishment was inflicted upon those who
did. One ex-slave recalled that his brother-in-law, a slave preacher,
"was flogged, and his back pickled" for preaching at a secret meeting

out in the woods. Even the listeners were flogged and "forced to tell who else was there." The same ex-slave claimed that there were slaves who were whipped "if they are found singing or praying at home." It seems that the slaves were so desirous of practicing religion in their own way, and hearing the Gospel from their own preachers, that they risked floggings and other forms of punishment from their earthly masters in order to worship their "Divine Master" in a manner that had meaning for them.[13]

The slaves had their ways of announcing a secret religious meeting. Wash Wilson, a former slave, recalled: "When de neggars go round singin' 'Steal Away to Jesus,' dat mean dere gwine be a 'ligious meetin' dat night. Dat de sig'fication of a meetin'. De masters . . . didn't like dem 'ligious meetin's, so us natcherly slips off at night, down in de bottoms or somewhere. Sometimes us sing and pray all night."[14]

Though slave preachers were usually unlettered, they were often eloquent. George Hepworth, a war correspondent, wrote of hearing a slave preacher behind the Union lines:

> He was simply a genius, – gifted far beyond most men, and needing only education to enable him to take position among those who make rather than follow public opinion. . . . I remember, too, some of his phrases: they were very beautiful, and were epic in grandeur. He spoke of "the rugged wood of the cross," whereto the Saviour was nailed; and after describing that scene with as much power as I have ever known an orator to exhibit, he reached the climax, when he pictured the earthquake which rent the veil of the temple, with this extremely beautiful expression: "And, my friends, the earth was unable to endure the tremendous sacrilege and trembled." He held his rude audience with most perfect control; subdued them, excited them, and, in fact, did what he pleased with them.[15]

William H. Pipes, a student of old-time black preaching, has described that black preacher and his rhetoric:

> He was illiterate; he reflected the African heritage. Rules of logic and education did not hamper him; his sermons were the product, for the most part, of his imagination. For him, classical standards of rhetoric did not exist; his speeches were imaginative, emotional, and filled with imagery; word pictures became the keys to the mind of the Negro audience. The speaker's information came from life-experiences; therefore, his speeches possessed concreteness drawn from experience, not abstract ideas from books.[16]

The sermons of the slave preacher had much to offer his tired and oppressed listeners. He spoke to them in their words and phrases. He shared with them their experiences. He, too, was a slave, under bondage and without freedom. Though his station in life may have been a bit better than that of the average field hand, he, like them, was severely restricted, was under the watchful eye of the white master, and could be harshly disciplined at any moment.

Because slave religion had many of its origins in the Great Awakening, the preacher continually held out the offer of salvation. Sins could be covered over by the blood of Jesus. Abundant and immediate forgiveness was available to all. God loved the slave. Accompanying the offer of salvation there was the promise of an eternal and wonderful heaven. If this life was drudgery, the next life would be in the plantation mansion. The preachers often talked about the reversal of roles in the life to come. For those with little hope in this life, the thought of eventual bliss must have brightened outlooks and lifted burdens a bit.

But the preachers' messages were not all of the world to come. They offered hope for the here and now. As God had delivered the Hebrew slaves from their Egyptian masters, the same God would bring eventual deliverance to Southern slaves. They must be patient, they must pray; deliverance would come. Of course, such a message had to be disguised if white listeners were at hand, but the congregations knew what their preachers were speaking of, even if the masters did not.

The rhythmic cadences of the preacher, the charge and response that reverberated back and forth between him and his congregation, produced a highly charged emotional atmosphere whereby the black listeners were swept up in ecstasy and thus, for a time, transcended present experiences. Mary Boykin Chestnut, in her famous diary, told of how deeply she was moved by a black religious meeting and how easily she too could have been swept up in the ecstasy of it all, even though "there was literally nothing" in what was said at the meeting.

> Jim Nelson, the driver, . . . was asked to lead in prayer. He became widely excited. . . . He clapped his hands at the end of every sentence, and his voice rose to the pitch of a shrill shriek, yet was strangely clear and musical, occasionally in a plaintive minor key that went to your heart. . . . It was all sound, however, and emotional pathos. There was literally nothing in what he said. The words had no meaning at all. . . .

The Negroes sobbed and shouted and swayed backward and forward . . . responding in shrill tones: "Yes, God!" "Jesus!" "Savior!" "Bless de Lord, amen," etc. It was a little too exciting for me. I would very much have liked to shout, too.[17]

During the war many of the slave preachers kept their congregations informed on the progress of the conflict. The ministers had their ways – somethimes through newspapers that were secretly delivered to them – of discovering the latest news from the battlefield, which was quickly passed on to other slaves. That night a prayer meeting would be called, and in the woods or down in the swamp hopeful blacks would petition the Lord for Union victories. One slave preacher in Georgia, who proclaimed that Yankee victory was inevitable, was covered with tar and set afire by whites who discovered his pronouncements.

It was the slave preacher who kept hope alive in black lives; a hope in a God who loved them and forgave them, a God who would someday bring them to heaven to be with him; a hope of deliverance from contemporary pharaohs; and a hope for Yankee victories.[18]

Black preachers in the North also had their roots in revivalism, but those roots produced a much different product than they did among the slave preachers in the South. Basically, black religion in the North was adaptive and utilitarian as opposed to expressive and nonutilitarian. The Northern blacks were not overly concerned with theological abstractions and philosophical disputes. Theirs was a practical religion. Monroe Fordham has written: "Historically, black religion and black churches in America have functioned primarily to facilitate and enhance the ability of black Americans to act upon their environment and peculiar circumstances, either by adjusting to them (accommodation) or by attempting to change them, to insure their survival as a people."[19]

Other scholars have echoed a similar adaptive theme. Joseph R. Washington, an eminent student of black religion, has written that Northern black religion in the antebellum years was primarily a religion of social protest.[20] Henry Mitchell contends that "because the culture of racism has denied the black man the possibility of realizing his own dignity as a person, all black religion has of necessity been concerned with the affirmation and support of black self-hood."[21]

Northern black preachers, in those years before the war, adopted the basic doctrines of evangelical Protestantism, but gave those doctrines their own unique twists to meet the needs of black people caught in a discriminatory, prejudiced white society. As with all evangelicals the Bible was a source of authority for Northern blacks. Black preachers felt a need to quote from and refer to the Bible in order to legitimatize and authenticate their messages. However, as Mitchell points out, the Bible was interpreted to meet the needs of "black people in a hostile world." Black ministers "labored for God, but they also worked for the political, economic, and social good of God's oppressed black children."[22]

Out of the Charles G. Finney revivals, which were a part of the Second Great Awakening, came the doctrine that man was not so depraved that he could not work for his own and society's perfection. Education, benevolence, and social reform became important by-products of the perfectionist doctrine. Black preachers quickly understood how such emphases could work for the betterment of the black community. Supporting the perfectionist theology was the postmillennial view of the return of Christ; that is, the millennium – the transformed earth, the Kingdom of God – would precede the return of Jesus. Many in mid-nineteenth-century America believed the United States would lead the world in bringing in the millennium. Once again, black preachers were quick to see and adopt this optimistic world view to their own dreams of a better society where all people would be viewed and treated as the children of God. Fordham has summarized those themes which dominated black religion in those years prior to the war. "The major themes," he wrote, "in antebellum northern black religious thought were in large measure the result of the application by blacks of revival doctrines to the environment of circumstances and adaptive needs and concerns of northern black society."[23]

The final discourse in this book is by a black Northern preacher, and it reflects the above themes. It was delivered by the Rev. Theodore S. Wright before the Convention of the New York State Antislavery Society in Utica, on September 20, 1837. The discourse is a response to the Annual Report of the Society, which recognized the progress of the antislavery movement and outlined actions that yet needed to be taken. Theodore Wright was a man who was highly involved in those various movements dedicated to improving life for black people in the United States. Soon after receiving his theological training at Princeton Theological Seminary, Wright assumed the pastorate of the Shiloh Presbyterian Church in New York City, where he served for a number of years. It was there he came in contact with those abolitionists who strongly opposed the colonization movement. As a man of literary attainment and oratorical skill, he was often called upon to express his emancipation views at various antislavery meetings. He became one of the prominent black reformers of his time.

The brief discourse traces the history of the antislavery movement. Wright saw in the Declaration of Independence and the Convention of 1776 a basic antislavery sentiment. He was sure that the nation's founders looked forward to the day when slavery would be abolished. Progress was being made toward this end when it was interrupted by the colonization movement, the "principle of expatriation," a "dark period" for blacks. The discourse is an excellent document for depicting how blacks, especially Northern blacks, felt about colonization. Wright credits the defeat of the colonization movement to Garrison and other early abolitionists, who demanded emancipation as a substitute for colonization. Wright was pleased that abolitionism, which began as a small and despised group, now boasted "hundreds of thousands of members."

Wright's discourse embodies those themes that have been considered. There is reform, progress, and optimism. "We have everything to hope for, and nothing to fear," proclaimed Wright. Reform, which was millennialistic in nature, was led by the hand of God and undergirded by the teachings of the Bible. "God is at the helm," affirmed Wright. "The Bible is your platform – the Holy Spirit will aid you."

But the millennium had not yet come. Prejudice must first be annihilated. Even some abolitionists, though they worked and sacrificed for emancipation, failed to see the black man as a brother. "Prejudice must be killed," warned Wright, "or slavery will never be abolished."

NOTES

1. Leon F. Litwack, *Been in the Storm So Long* (New York: Vintage, 1980), 24.
2. Quoted in Albert J. Raboteau, *Slave Religion: The "Invisible Institution" in the Antebellum South* (New York: Oxford University Press, 1978), 167.
3. George P. Rawick, ed., *The American Slave: A Composite Autobiography*, 19 vols. (Westport, CT: Greenwood, 1972); vol. 4, *Texas*, pt. 2, 163.

288 Black Sermons, South and North

4. Raboteau, *Slave Religion*, 296.
5. Not all of the black preachers in the South were slaves. Several had gained their freedom, remained in the South, and provided an effective ministry to slaves. Some of these preachers had received a limited education and articulated the Gospel message in a rather high quality use of the English language.
6. Raboteau, *Slave Religion*, 207.
7. Frederick Law Olmsted, *The Cotton Kingdom*, 2 vols. (New York: Mason Brothers, 1861), 2:104.
8. The rebellion of Nat Turner—who was himself a preacher, and who used religion as a means of inspiring blacks to revolt—triggered a white backlash in the South against black preachers. Laws were enacted in several states to silence black preachers. Governor John Floyd of Virginia spoke for many, if not most, white Southerners when he proclaimed: "The public good requires the negro preacher to be silenced" (quoted in David Charles Dennard, "Religion in the Quarters: A Study of Slave Preachers in the Antebellum South, 1800–1860" [Ph.D. dissertation, Northwestern University, 1983], 200). Dennard's work is one of the best sources on slave preaching that this writer has encountered. He points out that the black preachers found ingenious ways to get around the restrictions imposed on them after the Turner revolt. He concludes: "All in all, the great majority of slave preachers, both before and after the Turner rebellion, generally practiced their vocation in virtual opposition to all whites in the antebellum South. As such, their presence and continued visibility in the religious life of their people must therefore be attributed essentially to their own deeply held sense of mission, ingenuity, and determination to follow the dictates of their own conscience" (255).
9. Rawick, *The American Slave*, 4, *Texas*, pt. 2, 9.
10. Litwack, *Been in the Storm So Long*, 466.
11. Raboteau, *Slave Religion*, 232–33.
12. William Howard Russell, *My Diary North and South*, ed. Eugene H. Berwanger, (Philadelphia: Temple University Press, 1988), 106, 186.
13. Raboteau, *Slave Religion*, 214–15.
14. Rawick, *The American Slave*, 5, *Texas Narratives*, pt. 4, 198.
15. George H. Hepworth, *The Whip, Hoe and Sword* (1864; Freeport, NY: Books for Libraries Press, 1971), 166–67.
16. William H. Pipes, *Say Amen, Brother! Old-Time Negro Preaching: A Study in American Frustration* (1951; Westport, CT: Negro Universities Press, 1970), 66.
17. Mary Boykin Chestnut, *A Diary from Dixie* (Cambridge: Harvard University Press, 1980), 149.
18. Litwack, *Been in the Storm So Long*, 25.
19. Monroe Fordham, *Major Themes in Northern Black Religious Thought, 1800–1860* (Hicksville, NY: Exposition Press, 1975), 5–6.
20. Joseph R. Washington, Jr., *Black Religion* (Boston: Beacon Press, 1964), 253.
21. Henry M. Mitchell, *Black Preaching* (Philadelphia: Lippincott, 1970), 36.
22. *Black Preaching*, 55.
23. *Major Themes in Northern Black Religious Thought*, 17.

The Progress of the Antislavery Cause

Theodore S. Wright

September 20, 1837

Mr. President: All who have heard the report which has been presented are satisfied it needs no eulogy. It supports itself. But, sir, I would deem it a privilege to throw out a few thoughts upon it — thoughts which arise on beholding this audience. My mind is involuntarily led back a few years to the period prior to the commencement of this great moral effort for the removal of the giant sin of oppression from our land. It is well known to every individual who is at all acquainted with the history of slavery in this land, that the convention of 1776, when the foundations of our government were laid, proclaimed to the world the inalienable rights of man; and they supposed that the great principles of liberty would work the destruction of slavery throughout this land. This remark is sustained by an examination of the document then framed, and by the fact that the term "slavery" is not even named. The opinion that slavery would be abolished — indeed, that it had already recieved a death-blow, was cherished by all the reformers. — This spirit actuated Woolman, Penn, Edwards, Jefferson, and Benezet, and it worked out the entire emancipation of the North. — But it is well known that about 1817 a different drift was given — a new channel was opened for the benevolence which was working so well. The principle of expatriation, like a great sponge, went around in church and state, among men of all classes, and sponged up all the benevolent feelings which were then prevalent, and which promised so much for the emancipation of the enslaved and down-trodden millions of our land. That, sir, we call the dark period. — Oh, sir! if my father who sits beside me were to rise up and tell you how he felt and how men of his age felt, and how I felt (though a boy at that time), sir, it would be seen to have been a dark period. Why, sir, the heavens gathered blackness, and there was nothing cheering in our prospects. A spirit was abroad, which said "this is

Cartin Godwin Woodson, *Negro Orators and Their Orations* (Washington DC: The Associated Publishers, 1925), 86–92.

not your country and home," a spirit which would take us away from our firesides, tear the freeman away from his oppressed brother. – This spirit was tearing the free father away from his children, separating husband and wife, sundering those cords of consanguinity which bind the free with the slave. This scheme was as popular as it possibly could be. The slaveholder and the pro-slavery man, the man of expanded views, the man who loved the poor and oppressed of every hue and of every clime, all united in this feeling and principle of expatriation. But, sir, there were hundreds of thousands of men in the land who never could sympathize in this feeling; I mean those who were to be removed. The people of color were broken-hearted; they knew, sir, there were physical impossibilities to their removal. They knew, sir, that nature, reason, justice and inclination forbade the idea of their removing; and hence in 1817, the people of color in Philadelphia, with James Forten at their head – (and I envy them the honor they had in the work in which they were engaged), in an assembly of three thousand, before high heaven, in the Presence of Almighty God, and in the midst of a persecuting nation, resolved that they never would leave the land. They resolved to cling to their oppressed brethren. They felt that every ennobling spirit forbade their leaving them. They resolved to remain here, come what would, persecution or death. They determined to grapple themselves to their enslaved brethren as with hooks of steel. My father, at Schenectady, under great anxiety, took a journey to Philadelphia to investigate the subject. This was the spirit which prevailed among the people of color, and it extended to every considerable place in the North and as far South as Washington and Baltimore. They lifted up their voice and said, this is my country, here I was born, here I have toiled and suffered, and here will I die. Sir, it was a dark period. Although they were unanimous, and expressed their opinions, they could not gain access to the public mind: for the press would not communicate the facts in the case – it was silent. In the city of New York, after a large meeting, where protests were drawn up against the system of colonization, there was not a single public journal in the city, secular or religious, which would publish the views of the people of color on the subject.

Sir, despair brooded over our minds. It seemed as though everything was against us. We saw philanthropists, for instance, such men as Rev. Dr. Cox, swept away by the waves of expatriation. Other men, such as our President before us, who were engaged in schemes of benevolence in behalf of the people here, abandoning those schemes. It was a general opinion that it would do no good to elevate the people of color here. Our hearts broke. We saw that colonization never could be carried out, for the annual increase of the people of color was 70,000. We used to meet together and talk and weep and what to do we knew not. We saw indications that coercive measures would be resorted to. Immediately after the insurrection in Virginia, under Nat Turner, we saw colonization spreading all over the land; and it was popular to say the people of color must be removed. The press came out against us, and we trembled. Maryland passed laws to force out the colored people. It was deemed proper to make them go, whether they would or not. Then we despaired. Ah, Mr. President, that was a dark and gloomy period. The united views and intentions of the people of color were made known, and the nation awoke as from slumber. The *Freedom's Journal*, edited by Rev. Sam'l E. Cornish, announced the facts in the case, our entire opposition. Sir, it came like a clap of thunder! I recollect at Princeton, where I was then studying, Dr. Miller came out with his letter, disapproving of the editor's views, and all the faculty and the students gave up the paper. Benj. Lundy of Baltimore nobly lifted up his voice. But he did not feel the vileness of colonization. A young man, for making certain expositions touching slavery, was incarcerated in a dungeon, where truth took a lodgment in his heart, where he avowed eternal hatred to slavery, and where before high heaven, in the secrecy of his dungeon, with the chains upon him, he resolved to devote his life to the cause of emancipation. . . . And when the President of the American Antislavery Society stepped forward and paid the fine, we were crying for help – we were remonstrating. We had no other means but to stand up as men and protest. We declared this is our country and our home; here are the graves of our fathers. But none came to the rescue.

At that dark moment we heard a voice – it was the voice of Garrison, speaking in trumpet tones! It was like the voice of an angel of mercy! Hope, hope then cheered our path. The signs of the times began to indicate brighter days. He thundered, and next we hear of a Jocelyn of New Haven, an Arthur Tappan at his side, pleading for the rights of the Colored American. He stood up in New Haven amid commotion and persecution like a rock amid the dashing waves. Ought I not this afternoon to call upon my soul, and may I not ask you to call upon *your souls* to bless the Lord for His unspeakable goodness in bringing about the present state of things? What gratitude is called for on our part, when we contrast the state of things developed in your report with the dark period when we could number the abolitionists, when they were few and far between? Now a thousand societies exist, and there are hundreds of thousands of members. Praise God and persevere in this great work. Should we not be encouraged? We have everything to hope for, and nothing to fear. God is at the helm. The Bible is your platform – the Holy Spirit will aid you. We have everything necessary pledged, because God is with us. Hath he not said – "Break every yoke, undo the heavy burdens, and let the oppressed go free"? – "Remember them that are in bonds, as bound with them"? Why do I see so many who minister at the sacred altar – so many who have everything to lose and nothing to gain, personally, by identifying themselves with this cause? Nothing but the spirit of Almighty God brought these men here.

This cause, noble though persecuted, had a lodgment in the piety of our countrymen, and never can be expatriated. How manifest has been the progress of this cause! Why, sir, three years ago, nothing was more opprobrious than to be called an "abolitionist" or "antislavery man"!

Now you would be considered as uncharitable towards pro-slavery men, whether editors of newspapers, presidents of colleges or theological seminaries, if you advance the idea that they are not abolitionists or antislavery men. Three years ago, when a man professed to be an abolitionist, we knew where he was. He was an individual who recognized the identity of the human family. Now a man may call himself an abolitionist and we know not where to find him. Your tests are taken away. A rush is made into the abolition ranks. Free discussion, petition Anti-Texas, and political favor converts are multiplying. Many throw themselves in, without understanding the breadth and depth of the principles of emancipation. I fear not the annexation of Texas. I fear not all the machinations, calumny and opposition of slaveholders, when contrasted with the annexation of men whose hearts have not been deeply inbued with these high and holy principles. Why, sir, unless men come out and take their stand on the principle of recognizing man as man, I tremble for the ark, and I fear our society will become like the expatriation society; everybody an abolitionist. These points which have lain in the dark must be brought out to view. The identity of the human family, the principle of recognizing all men as brethren – that is the doctrine, that is the point which touches the quick of the community. It is an easy thing to ask about the vileness of slavery at the South, but to call the dark man a brother, heartily to embrace the doctrine advanced in the second article of the constitution, to treat all men according to their moral worth, to treat the man of color in all circumstances as a man and brother – that is the test.

Every man who comes into this society ought to be catechized. It should be ascertained whether he looks upon man as man, all of one blood and one family. A healthful atmosphere must be created, in which the slave may live when rescued from the horrors of slavery. I am sensible I am detaining you, but I feel that this is an important point. I am alarmed sometimes when I look at the constitutions of our societies. I am afraid that brethren sometimes endeavor so to form the constitutions of societies that they will be popular. I have seen constitutions of abolition societies, where nothing was said about the improvement of the man of color! They have overlooked the giant sin of prejudice. They have passed by this foul monster, which is at once the parent and offspring of slavery. Whilst you are thinking about the annexation of Texas – whilst you are discussing the great principles involved in this noble cause, remember this prejudice must be killed or slavery will never be abolished. Abolitionists must annihilate in their own bosoms the cord of caste. We must be consistent – recognize the colored man in every respect as a man and brother. In doing this we shall have to encounter scorn; we shall have to breast the storm. – This society would do well to spend a whole day in thinking about it and praying over it. Every abolitionist would do well to spend a day in fasting and prayer over it and in looking at his own heart. Far be it for me to condemn abolitionists. I rejoice and bless God for this first institution which has combined its energies for the overthrow of this heaven-daring – this soul crushing prejudice.

The successors of Penn, Franklin, and Woolman have shown themselves the friends of the colored race. They have done more in this cause than any other church and they are still doing great things both in Europe and America. I was taught in childhood to remember the man of the broad-brimmed hat and drab-colored coat and venerate him. No class have testified more to the truth on this subject. They lifted up their voices against slavery and the slave-trade. But, ah! with but here and there a noble exception, they go but halfway. – When they come to the grand doctrine, to lay the ax right down at the root of the tree, and destroy the very spirit of slavery – there they are defective. Their doctrine is to set the slave free, and let him take care of himself. Hence, we hear nothing about their being brought into the Friends' Church, or of their being viewed and treated according to their moral worth. Our hearts have recently been gladdened by an address of the Annual Meeting of the Friends' society in the city of New York, in which they insist upon the doctrine of immediate emancipation. But that very good man who signed the document as the organ of that society within the past year, received a man of color, a Presbyterian minister, into his house, gave him his meals alone in the kitchen, and did not introduce him to his family. That shows how man can testify against slavery at the South, and not assail it at the North, where it is tangible. Here is something for abolitionists to do. What can the friends of emancipation effect while the spirit of slavery is so fearfully prevalent. Let every man take his stand, burn out this prejudice, live it down, talk it down, everywhere consider the colored man as a man, in the church, the stage, the steamboat, the public house, in all places, and the death-blow to slavery will be struck.

Bibliography

Bibliography

SERMONS ON SECTIONAL ISSUES
DURING THE MID-NINETEENTH CENTURY

Adams, E. E. *Government and Rebellion*. Philadelphia: Henry B. Ashmead, 1861. On April 28, 1861, at the North Broad Street Presbyterian Church in Philadelphia, Adams asserted that the preservation of government was the cause of God. Thus, rebellion cannot be justified. The Union cause, therefore, was God's cause.

Adams, William. "Prayer for Rulers, or, Duty of Christian Patriots." *Fast Day Sermons*. New York: Rudd & Carleton, 1861. 311–36.
On January 4, 1861, at the Madison Square Presbyterian Church in New York City, the Rev. Mr. Adams preached a sermon seeking conciliation. He asked the North to "cease from all vituperation and angry reproaches." He asked the South to "not force us [the North] to join new issues; nor give resurrection to questions which long ago have been considered as settled by the civilized world. . . . You must not forswear reason, nor put the torch to that edifice which we occupy in common."

Adger, John B. *The Religious Instruction of the Colored Population*. Charleston: T. W. Hayes, 1847.
A proslavery sermon preached in the Second Presbyterian Church of Charleston on May 9, 1847.

Allen, Joseph Henry. *A Reign of Terror*. Bangor, ME: Samuel S. Smith, 1857.
A sermon at the Union Street Church in Bangor protesting the attack upon Sumner on the floor of the United States Senate.

Anderson, Samuel James Pierce. *The Dangers and Duties of the Present Crisis*. St. Louis: Schenck & Co., 1861.
A proslavery sermon at the Union Church in St. Louis on January 4, 1861.

Armstrong, George D. *The Good Hand of Our God upon Us*. Norfolk: J. D. Ghiselin, 1861. On July 21, 1861, at the Presbyterian Church in Norfolk, Armstrong declared God's approval of war based upon his biblical text: "The Lord is a man of war: the Lord is his name" (Exod. 15:3). He referred to the Civil War as the "second war of independence."

————. *Politics and the Pulpit.* Norfolk: J. D. Ghiselin, Jr., 1856.

A proslavery discourse delivered in the Presbyterian Church in Norfolk on November 11, 1856, which asserted the right of ministers to speak out on such subjects.

Atkinson, Joseph Mayo. *God, the Giver of Victory and Peace.* Raleigh: n.p., 1862.

On September 18, 1862, at the Presbyterian Church in Raleigh, Atkinson declared that God had intervened in the war on the side of the Confederacy. If our eyes had been open during a Confederate victory, declared the minister, "we should have seen an angel, terrible as that which smote the host of Sennacherib, hurling back the multitudinous cohorts of our self-confident invaders, filling their ranks with confusion, dismay, and death."

Atkinson, Thomas. *Annual Address to the Convention of the Diocese of North Carolina at Morgantown.* Raleigh: Office of the Church Intelligencer, 1861. On July 10, 1861, the Episcopal Bishop of North Carolina noted the break in the political union of the nation, and asked if there should also be a break in Episcopalian religious ranks. At this point Atkinson seemed uncertain of the answer.

————. *Christian Duty in the Present Time of Trouble.* Wilmington, NC: Fulton & Price, Steam Power Press, 1861.

In the spring of 1861 Atkinson, at St. James Church in Wilmington, declared: "It is God who rides in this storm, and will direct the whirlwind."

————. *On the Causes of Our National Troubles.* Wilmington, NC: Herald Book and Job Office, 1861.

At St. James Church in Wilmington, on January 4, 1861, Atkinson spoke of those sins that were tearing apart the nation: corruption, declining religion, and a declining respect for human authority. "It is only by a general amendment of our ways and doings, by stemming the tide of immorality which is sweeping over the land, that we can avert national judgment."

Atterbury, John G. *God in Civil Government.* New Albany, IN: Geo. R. Beach, 1862.

On November 27, 1862, at the First Presbyterian Church of New Albany, Atterbury spoke of the dangers of too much democracy, of "spurious liberty" and "false independence" which had led to the present conflict. "God has not conceded to man the right to rule himself. So again magistrates, though constituted for the benefit of the people and not their own advantage, are yet not the servants of the people but God's servants. They are above the people, not below them. Though designated for their trust by the people themselves, they yet receive their commission from above."

Atwood, E. S. *The Nation's Loss.* Salem, MA: Salem Gazette, 1865.

Following the death of Lincoln, Atwood, at the South Congregational

Church of Salem, asserted that the South was celebrating the assassination of the president with great glee. Therefore, there was a need for stern judgment upon them.

Bacon, Leonard. *Two Sermons*. New Haven: Thomas H. Pease, 1857.
The pastor of the First Church of Christ (Congregational) in New Haven issued a strong denunciation of slavery. He stated that the law of God must supersede the United States Constitution on the slavery question.

Badger, Henry S. *The Humble Conquer*. Boston: Wm. V. Spencer, 1865.
The Congregational minister from Cambridgeport, Massachusetts, linked the assassination of Lincoln to slavery interests. He called for justice toward the South: "To be just, but not vindictive; to punish, not for revenge, but for future security; to know when mercy is wisdom, and when it is criminal weakness — was never so desirable or so difficult as now."

Barnes, Albert. *The Love of Country*. Philadelphia: C. Sherman and Son, 1861.
On April 28, 1861, at the First Presbyterian Church of Philadelphia, Barnes, one of the best-known spokesmen for the New School Presbyterians, gave a rousing patriotic address. "Of all the civil and political trusts ever committed to any generation of men, that Constitution is the most precious, for it guards higher interests and secures richer blessings in the world than any other."

Barnwell, William Hazzard. *The Divine Government*. Charleston: Edward C. Councell, 1851.
A proslavery sermon delivered on November 21, 1851.

Barrows, E. P., Jr. *The American Slavery Question*. New York: John S. Taylor, 1836.
Two early Northern antislavery sermons delivered at the First Free Presbyterian Church in New York City.

Barrows, William. *Our War and Our Religion and Their Harmony*. Boston: J. M. Whittemore, 1862.
Early in 1862, at the South Congregational Church of Reading, Massachusetts, Barrows described the work of God in the world and the duties of humankind to assist the Deity in militant service.

Barten, O. S. *Fast Day Sermon*. Richmond: Enquirer Book and Job Press, 1861.
This sermon was delivered on June 13, 1861 at St. James Church in Warrenton, Virginia, where Barten was the rector. "The United States Government ... ignores God and makes no reference to an overruling Providence! ... The Government of the Confederate States, thank God! is a Christian Government.... We desire nothing that is not right. The war on our part is not aggressive, but simply defensive, and, once having our independence acknowledged, we desire nothing but to be let alone ... to secure the approbation and blessing of God, whose help we now implore."

Bartholomew, J. G. *The Hour of Peril*. Boston: Abel Tompkins, 1861.

At the Universalist Church in Roxbury, Massachusetts, the minister emphasized that honor and religion were involved in the Civil War. One must take sides. There could be no neutrality.

Bartol, Cyrus A. *The Remission by Blood.* Boston: Walker, Wise, and Company, 1862.

Predicting a long and bloody war in order to adequately atone for sins, the Rev. Cyrus Bartol, in Boston's West Church, advised that the people must "resign [themselves] to whatever agonies Heaven, as terms of pardon, appoints.... Only after a long and painful purification, are we to be released." Bartol went on: "The country bleeds for its sins: it must bleed abundantly; though we trust it will not, like a sacrificial victim on a Hebrew altar, bleed to death."

Bassett, George W. *A Discourse on the Wickedness and Folly of the Present War.* n.p., n.d.

Bassett, who was a militant abolitionist and disaffected New School Presbyterian minister, delivered this address at the Court House in Ottawa, Illinois, on August 11, 1861. He declared that because the war was being waged to preserve the Union, and not to free the slaves, it was a repudiation of the Declaration of Independence and the Constitution. In its attempt to put down Southern independence, the Lincoln administration was adopting the monarchial policies of England which the colonists had repudiated.

Beecher, Charles. *A Sermon on the Nebraska Bill.* New York: Oliver and Brothers, 1854.

A sermon which strongly denounced the Kansas–Nebraska Act.

Beecher, Henry Ward. "Address at the Raising of the Union Flag over Fort Sumter." *Patriotic Addresses.* In this address, preached on April 14, 1865, Beecher summed up what the Civil War had accomplished. "First, that these United States shall be one and indivisible. Second, that States are not absolute sovereigns, and have no right to dismember the republic. Third, that universal liberty is indispensable to republican government, and that slavery shall be utterly and forever abolished."

———. "Against a Compromise of Principle." *Patriotic Addresses.*

On November 11, 1860, less than five months before Fort Sumter was fired upon, Beecher was willing to allow the South her institution of slavery, but pleaded that Northerners not be compelled to be slave catchers under the Fugitive Slave Law. "We do not ask to molest the South in the enjoyment of her institutions. But we will not be made constables to slavery, to run and catch, to serve writs, and return prisoners." Beecher did perceive a vital difference between North and South. "Southern states ... have organized society around a rotten core: slavery; the North ... around a vital heart: liberty."

———. "The Battle Set in Array." *Patriotic Addresses.*

This sermon was preached on April 14, 1861, the weekend that Fort

Sumter was surrendered to Confederate forces. Beecher addressed what he perceived to be a fundamental difference between the North and South. "There has been a spirit of patriotism in the North; but never, within my memory, in the South. I never heard a man from the South speak of himself as an American. Men from the South speak of themselves as Southerners." In 1860 Beecher had been ready to allow the South to secede in peace. When the cannons boomed against Fort Sumter, he changed his position. "For Americans the right of revolution has ceased to exist." Certain situations called for war, as detestable as it might be. "I go with those that go furtherest in describing the wretchedness of war. . . . I hold that it is ten thousand times better to have war than slavery."

———. "Centennial Review." *Patriotic Addresses*.

This address was delivered on November 30, 1876. Earlier in the month was the disputed presidential election between Hayes and Tildon. Beecher reviewed the progress of Reconstruction in the South. Generally, he was pleased. "There have been some outbreaks and outrages . . . but taking the people throughout all the Southern States, they demand and deserve credit for the conduct they have pursued."

———. "Conditions of a Restored Union." *Patriotic Addresses*.

On October 29, 1865, Beecher, in a sermon at Plymouth Church, outlined his plan for Reconstruction. Displaying a magnanimous spirit, he advocated leniency toward the South. "Now that war has ceased from our midst, nothing can better crown its victories than a generous and trustful spirit on the part of the citizens of this nation toward those who have been in error." There was one basic condition to Reconstruction – the abolition of slavery. Nevertheless, Beecher's words portrayed an attitude of white supremacy: "Declaring the colored man's rights to citizenship in this country does not make him your equal socially." He went so far as to advocate property and educational tests as qualifications for black voting.

———. *Freedom and War*. Boston: Ticknor & Fields, 1863.

This is a collection of eighteen Beecher sermons from the year 1859 to 1863. All of the sermons have to do with those issues that were dividing the nation.

———. "Modes and Duties of Emancipation." *Patriotic Addresses*. On November 26, 1861, the first Thanksgiving of the war, Beecher reminded his listeners: "We are fighting, not merely for our liberty, but for those ideas that are the seeds and strengths of liberty throughout the earth." He noted the lack of unity in the North over the slavery question.

———. "National Injustice and Penalty." *Freedom and War*.

On September 28, 1862, six days after the Emancipation Proclamation had been announced, Beecher said: "The American doctrine of slavery is not analogue or derivative of the Hebrew or any mild form of slavery. It is the extremest and worst form of the Roman doctrine of slavery; the harshest that the world has ever seen." In the sermon Beecher protested that the framers of the Constitution had erred in compromising on slavery. "They were afraid that South Carolina – that rottenest of rotten slaves states – would not come in." In an interesting aside Beecher claimed that Southern women, more than Southern men, bore a special blame for slavery. "Southern men have been tame and cool in comparison with the fury of Southern women." He strongly defended Lincoln's use of war powers that were being debated throughout the North.

———. "The Nation's Duty to Slavery." *Patriotic Addresses*.

This sermon was preached on October 30, 1859, while John Brown was in prison awaiting trial for his involvement at Harper's Ferry. It is an ambivalent sermon. On one hand, he was clear as to his hatred for slavery. "It is a great sin . . . it is a national curse; . . . if I could have my way, every man on the globe should be a free man, and at once." He was unclear, however, as to what to do. "I am bound by the great law of love to consider my duties toward the slave, and I am bound by the great law of love to consider my duties toward the white man, who is his master." Though Beecher portrayed some sympathy toward John Brown, he abhorred his methods. He urged the slaves not to revolt, but to wait quietly for their day of deliverance.

———. "Our Blameworthiness." *Patriotic Addresses*.

In this sermon, on January 4, 1860, Beecher declared that the North was not without sin in regard to slavery. "We who dwell in the North are not without responsibility for this sin. . . . You and I are guilty of the spread of slavery unless we have exerted . . . every influence in our power against it. . . . The vengeance and zeal of our hearts toward the South might be somewhat tempered by the reflection that we have been so faithless and wicked."

———. *Patriotic Addresses*. New York: Fords, Howard & Hulbert, 1891.

A collection of thirty-five Beecher sermons, addresses, and articles, from 1850 to 1885, on slavery, the Civil War, and the development of civil liberty in the United States.

———. "Peace Be Still." *Fast Day Sermons*. New York: Rudd & Carleton, 1861.

In this sermon, preached at Plymouth Church on January 4, 1861, Beecher declared that slavery was the greatest national sin, a sin from which many other sins flowed. He acknowledged the North's responsibility for this sin both in the past and present. The North, which Beecher considered "the brain of this nation," had done little, if anything, toward the abolition of slavery. Beecher disputed the idea that slavery could be defended by the Bible. He accused himself of being indolent and passive on the slave question.

———. *Sermons*. 2 vols. New York: Harper & Bros., 1868.

This source contains sermons on a variety of subjects, only some of which are political or social in nature.

———. "The Southern Babylon." *Freedom and War*.

This sermon was delivered on January 4, 1863. It equates the South with ancient Babylon, "the symbol of the injustice and the oppression practised by the commerce of the world." Though Beecher disagreed with the Southern point of view, he admired the Southerners' "heroic spirit. . . . They are on the wrong side; but they put us to shame by their utter enthusiasm for the most accursed cause that ever the sun was permitted to shine on."

———. "The Success of American Democracy." *Patriotic Addresses*.

This sermon was delivered on April 13, 1862, the first anniversary Sunday of the firing on Fort Sumter. In the discourse Beecher makes the point that all society has been corrupted by slavery: "Men brought up under the influence of slavery are contaminated to the very root, and they cannot make good citizens."

Bellows, Henry W. "The Crisis of Our National Disease." *Fast Day Sermons*. New York: Rudd & Carleton, 1861.

This sermon was delivered on January 4, 1861, at All Souls Church in New York City. Taking note of the clouds of war gathering upon the horizon, Bellows declared: "We are not going to war, I trust, to force fifteen States to live under a Government they hate. But we will go to war to save order and civilization, with any faction, conspiracy, rabble, or political party that strives, in illegal and treasonable ways, to break up the Government. We owe it to the intelligence and worth of the South, to believe that they are silenced and tyrannized over by a mob that does not understand nor value their interests and wishes."

Bentley, Edward. *The Lord Our National God*. New York: John A. Gray, 1860.

This sermon was delivered before the congregations of the Methodist Episcopal and Reformed Dutch Churches in the Methodist Church of Ellenville, New York, on November 29, 1860. Bentley urged the North not to compromise with the South, for the "throbbing" of the "national heart" would not cease "till this crowning curse and sin [slavery] is wiped from our national fame."

Bigelow, John F. *The Hand of God in American History*. Burlington, VT: W. H. and C. A. Hoyt, 1861.

The pastor of the Baptist Church in Reesville, New York, delivered this sermon on July 7, 1861. At this time the North was hard pressed to point to any evidence showing God's favor. Bigelow took the long-range approach and attempted to show how God's hand had been evident in national history since colonial days. Therefore, he assured, God "will make their [Confederates'] own wicked rage and demented foolhardiness, if they persevere in the attempts to sunder the Republic, the means of their chastisement, if not their destruction."

Bingham, Joel F. *Great Providences Toward the Loyal Part of This Nation.*
Buffalo: Breed, Butler and Co., 1864.
This sermon, delivered before seven Presbyterian congregations of Buffalo on November 24, 1864, speculated on what America could be like
following the war: "such a home of liberty, such a scene of peaceful order
and contented industry . . . such a land of right and virtue and religion
as would well answer to the figure of millennial glory and the reign of
the Redeemer of men upon earth."
———. *National Disappointment.* Buffalo: Breed, Butler and Co., 1865.
Delivered shortly after the assassination of Lincoln, this sermon rejoiced
in the damages that the Union army had inflicted upon the Confederacy.
The minister memorialized Lincoln by saying that it was fitting "after
having wrought out the painful salvation of the Republic, [he] has been
offered, a bloody sacrifice, upon the altar of human freedom."
Bittinger, J. B. *A Sermon Preached Before the Presbyterian Churches of
Cleveland.* Cleveland: E. Cowles and Co., 1861.
This sermon applauded Lincoln's use of war powers which suspended
certain civil rights. To those who protested such actions, Bittinger replied that "so-called freedom of speech and press" were a mask for "foulness of vituperation" or "unblushing mendacity."
Blackburn, William M. *The Crime Against the Presidency.* Trenton: Mur-
phey and Bechtel, 1865.
This was a sermon delivered at the Fourth Presbyterian Church in Trenton. The sermon blends harsh judgment and eventual mercy toward the
South. "May no degree of calm justice be withheld from them, but may
they not be denied our prayers, nor the saving power of their God. My
prayer is for their arrest, their punishment, and their salvation in death."
Blagden, George Washington. *Remarks, and a Discourse on Slavery.* Bos-
ton: Ticknor, Reed, and Fields, 1854.
The pastor of Old South Church (Congregational) in Boston upheld the virtues of slavery and denounced the horrors of abolitionism.
Blanchard, Jonathan. *Sermon on Slaveholding.* Cincinnati: n.p., 1842.
A sermon before the Synod of Cincinnati (New School Presbyterian) in
1841 on the biblical foundations for abolitionism.
Blitch, J. L. *Thy Kingdom Come.* Augusta, GA: Baptist Banner Press, 1865.
Delivered at the Aberdeen Church, this sermon reminded the hearers
that the kingdom of God was triumphant. "The Christian is continually
fighting against the enemies of Christ and His kingdom. Sometimes he
is badly defeated, and with sorrow bitterly weeps: again, he gains little
ground; then, with exultation, he exclaims, 'through grace, I am the victor, and thus his life is spent. . . . You will come out more than conquerors, through your Lord Jesus Christ."
Boardman, George Dana. *Addresses.* Philadelphia: Sherman & Co., 1865.
This volume contains a sermon in which the pastor of the First Baptist

Church in Philadelphia demands swift and severe punishment upon all Southern leaders following the assassination of Lincoln. He would banish Southern leaders from the borders of the nation, but "speak words of forgiveness and good to the multitudes they have duped."

———. *Loyalty to Law, the Duty of the Christian Patriot*. New York: French and Wheat, 1860.

As the first calls for secession began, Boardman took a mediating stance. He asked for respect for civil authority, toleration of slavery within the slave states, and patient waiting for a change in circumstances.

Boardman, Henry A. *Thanksgiving in War*. Philadelphia: C. Sherman and Son, 1861. A sermon delivered in the Tenth Presbyterian Church of Philadelphia, on November 28, 1861, by a minister who had previously expressed a desire for conciliation with the South. Now he felt betrayed by the Confederacy and could no longer sympathize with those by whom "this rebellion was concocted many years ago. . . . The one cherished object of these men was to destroy the Union." The sermon spoke of those virtues that war could inculcate. "This war promises to arrest in a measure the extravagance and parade, the epicurism and effeminacy into which we were so fast running. It puts our young men upon a training which will nourish their manly virtues. It inculcates, as no moralist could, lessons of economy, of moderation, of patience, of self-control."

———. *What Christianity Demands of Us at the Present Crisis*. Philadelphia: J. B. Lippincott and Co., 1860.

On Thanksgiving Day, November 29, 1860, Boardman asked for reason and forbearance in the present crisis. "The Union is too sacred a trust to be sacrificed except on the most imperative grounds. . . . It is too closely linked with the cause of human liberty, and with the salvation of the world. To destroy it at the bidding of passion; to destroy it until every practical means for preserving it has been tried and exhausted, would be a crime of appalling turpitude against patriotism, against religion, and against humanity."

Booth, Robert Russell. *The Nation's Crisis and the Christian's Duty*. New York: Anson D. F. Randolph, 1861.

In a sermon preached on May 12, 1861, this Presbyterian clergyman proclaimed that the side favored by God would win the conflict. The North must make every effort to win that favor. He used as his text: "If God be for us, who can be against us?"

———. *Personal Forgiveness and Public Justice*. New York: Anson D. F. Randolph, 1865.

The pastor of the Mercer Street Presbyterian Church in Philadelphia combined a theology of justice and mercy in his proposed treatment of a defeated South "We have no right as individuals to be vindictive, but as a nation we must be just. . . . It is the claim of justice that the authors of this tremendous crime of rebellion . . .should be condemned and punished. . . .As solemnly as we are called to punish deliberate transgressors, we are called upon to shelter and protect the ignorant transgressor."

Breckinridge, Robert J. "The Union to Be Preserved." *Fast Day Sermons.* New York: Rudd & Carleton, 1861.
This sermon was delivered on January 4, 1861, at Lexington, Kentucky. With South Carolina already having seceded, and other Southern states ready to do so, Breckinridge denounced secession as a great evil. "Secession is a proceeding which begins by tearing to pieces the whole fabric of government, both social and political. . . . No state in this Union ever had any sovereignty at all, independent of, and except as they were, United States." Regardless of what states in the lower South may do, Breckinridge urged Kentucky "to stand by the Constitution and the Union of the country to the last extremity."

Brooks, Phillips. "Abraham Lincoln." *Addresses.* Philadelphia: Henry Altemus, 1895.
This is an eloquent sermon by the renowned Episcopalian rector which eulogized Lincoln shortly after the president's death. Brooks sharply contrasted a society that defends slavery with a society that opposes the institution. Even the normally gentle Brooks was vehement in his denunciation of Southern cruelty.

Brownlow, William Gannaway. *A Sermon on Slavery; A Vindication of the Methodist Church, South.* Knoxville, TN: Kinsloe & Rice, 1857.
In a sermon delivered on August 9, 1857, at Temperance Hall in Knoxville, Brownlow defended slavery and the proslavery stance of Southern Methodists.

Burrows, John Lansing. *Nationality Insured.* Augusta, GA: Jas. Nathan Ells, Publisher, Baptist Banner Office, 1864.
This sermon, delivered at the First Baptist Church of Augusta on September 11, 1864, spoke of the Confederate sins which were responsible for military defeats: "pride . . . reckless chase of amusements . . . greed of wealth . . . depraved thirst for power and place . . . fearful blasphemies . . . Sabbath profanations . . . drunkenness! Of what crime in the catalog forbidden by God can we not discover samples every day?" The South needed only to repent and military victories would resume.

———. *The New Richmond Theater.* Richmond: Smith, Bailey & Co., 1863.
The pastor of the First Baptist Church in Richmond, on February 8, 1863, denounced the opening of a new theater in Richmond. It was bad enough that such a building should open at any time, but even worse in a time of war. For such sins the South would be punished by God. "The New Richmond Theater is a public assignation house, where any vile man may be introduced to an infamous woman by paying the price of a ticket."

Bushnell, Horace. *The Census and Slavery.* Hartford: Lucius E. Hunt, 1860.
This is a Thanksgiving discourse delivered at the chapel in Clifton Springs,

New York, on November 29, 1860. Bushnell urged a moderating course in the midst of crisis, saying that slavery would fall in the South because it was economically unprofitable.

———. *A Discourse on the Slavery Question.* Hartford: Case Library, 1839.
Bushnell warned against hasty antislavery actions and urged that Southern men be given time to correct the abuses of slavery through gradual legislative actions. This sermon was a response to the work of abolitionists.

———. *The Northern Iron.* Hartford: Hunt & Son, 1854.
This sermon stated that the South was culturally inferior in comparison to the North. The South was proficient in dining, hunting, harangue, and politics. The North had iron which the South lacked.

———. "Popular Government by Divine Right." *Building Eras in Religion.* New York: Charles Scribner's Sons, 1910.
In 1864, the pastor of the North Congregational Church in Hartford, declared that national government is established by divine authority and must, therefore, be obeyed. Bushnell comes very close to the old doctrine of the divine right of kings.

———. *Reverses Needed.* Hartford: L. E. Hunt, 1861.
Shortly after the Northern defeat at the Battle of Bull Run, Bushnell attempted to sustain the morale of his congregation. "The main point for us now is to get ourselves ready for the grand struggle we are in . . . receiving those settled convictions that will stay by us in all the changing moods we are to pass."

Butler, C. M. *Funeral Addresses on the Death of Abraham Lincoln.* Philadelphia: Henry B. Ashmead, 1865.
The pastor of the Church of the Covenant (Presbyterian) in Philadelphia declared that the assassination of Lincoln was just the latest in a long, long list of Southern atrocities. Lincoln was a man marked for slaughter by the South. Therefore, the South should receive harsh judgment.

Butler, Henry E. *God's Way of Leading the Blind.* Burlington, NY: Free Press and Book and Job Printing Office, 1865.
At the First Congregational Church in Keeseville, New York, on April 23, 1865, Butler declared that judgment must come upon the South, but it must be administered with a proper attitude. "But there is danger lest revenge, a passion always bad, should mingle with righteous indignation. America's spirit should be that of Samuel when he hewed the guilty Agag in pieces, sad, serious, determined, God-like."

Butler, J. G. *The Martyr President.* Washington: McGill & Witherow, 1865.
In a sermon delivered shortly after the assassination of Lincoln, at St. Paul's Lutheran Church in Washington, Butler declared that Booth "was but the representation and instrument of the enemies of the Heaven-blessed Government, whose Head they have stricken down."

Butler, William C. *Sermon.* Richmond: Chas. H. Wynne, Printer, 1861.
At St. John's Church (Episcopal) of Richmond, on July 21, 1861, the Sun-

day after the Battle of Manassas, Butler made this appraisal: "It was a fadeless, imperishable triumph of the moral over the physical. It was a voice of thunder from the throne of God, reverberating into the dull, earthy ears of men – Might is not Right, but Right is Might."

Canfield, Sherman. *The American Crisis*. Syracuse: Journal Book and Job Office, 1865.

This sermon, delivered on November 24, 1864, spoke of the importance of going through fire and trial on the way to the millennium. "On its way towards the millennium, the Kingdom of Christ occasions strifes and conflicts by causing a portion of a world lying in wickedness to differ from the rest. The very goodness, frankness, and courage which it produces in its subjects, renders them odious to evil doers."

Cassels, Samuel J. *Servitude and the Duty of Masters to Their Servants*. Norfolk: Press of the Beacon, 1843.

This sermon was delivered in June of 1843 at the Presbyterian Church of Norfolk. Cassels proclaimed that if slavery were "carried out in a scriptural sense, I can scarcely imagine a better state of society than what might thus exist."

Clapp, A. Huntington. *God's Purpose in the War*. Providence: Knowles, Anthony and Company, 1861.

This sermon was delivered in the Beneficent Congregational Church of Providence on May 12, 1861. It predicted a long and bloody conflict that would have major and lasting repercussions. "Other judgments [from God] . . . have made a temporary impression. It will not be so with this [Civil War]."

Clapp, Theodore, *Slavery*. New Orleans: John Gibson, 1838.

At the First Congregational Church in New Orleans, on April 15, 1838, Clapp relates that after years of uncertainty and even involvement in emancipation schemes, "we are [now] fully convinced of the rectitude of slavery."

Clark, Frederick G. *Gold in the Fire: Our National Position*. New York: John H. Duychinck, 1862.

This sermon, delivered at the West Twenty-third Street Presbyterian Church of New York City, on Thanksgiving Day, November 27, 1862, declared that the issuance of the Emancipation Proclamation meant that God was now clearly on the Union side.

Clarke, James Freeman. *Discourse on the Aspects of the War*. Boston: Walker, Wise and Company, 1863.

On April 2, 1863, Clarke told his congregation at the Indiana Place Chapel of Boston that slavery, and the nation's refusal to do anything about it, was the cause of the Civil War.

Cleaveland, Elisha. *The Patriot's Song of Victory*. New Haven: Thomas H. Pease, 1864.

In the Congregational Church of New Haven, on September 11, 1864,

Cleveland declared that God had given victories in response to Northern prayers.

Clough, Simon. *A Candid Appeal to the Citizens of the United States*. New York: A. K. Bertron, 1834.

The Congregational minister at Fall River, Massachusetts, issued an early Northern denunciation of abolitionism as being antibiblical. He suggested that preachers who espouse abolitionist principles should be dismissed by their congregations as false teachers.

Cobbs, Nicholas Hamner. *The Doubting Christian Encouraged*. Uniontown, AL: Daily Herald Book and Job Office, 1864.

The Episcopal Bishop of Alabama declared: "Trials and hardships must be encountered, wearisome journeys, cold and hunger must be his portion, and sometimes he must mingle in the fierce and deadly strife and danger of battle. Let then these weak and desponding believers go onward, notwithstanding all their doubts and fears, 'looking only' to Jesus the author and finisher of their faith."

Confederate Imprints, 1861–1865. A microfilm based on Marjorie Lyle Crandall, *Confederate Imprints: A Check List*, 2 vols. (Boston: The Boston Athenaeum, 1955), and Richard B. Harwell, *More Confederate Imprints*, 2 vols. (Richmond: The Virginia State Library, 1957).

This marvelous collection of Confederate material contains 114 sermons that were preached in the South during the Civil War.

Crosby, Howard. *God's View of Rebellion*. New York: E. French, 1864.

On September 11, 1864, at the Fourth Avenue Presbyterian Church, New York, Crosby urged his congregation not to compromise with those who had rebelled against the nation. "If we compromise with this rebellion we shall bring down [from God] woes most fearful on our country's future." He further affirmed: "We are one people, under one Government; and armed resistance to that Government is rebellion, and rebellion is accursed of God."

Crothers, Samuel. *The Gospel of the Typical Servitude*. Hamilton, OH: Gradner and Gibbon, 1835.

This preacher, who was an Ohio member of the American Antislavery Society, drew a distinction between Hebrew and pagan slavery. Hebrew slavery was a means of paying a debt, and provision was made for eventual emancipation. God's law did not endorse the slavery system of the South, which doomed a person to perpetual bondage.

Cuthbert, Lucius, Jr. *The Scriptural Grounds for Secession from the Union*. Charleston: Welch, Harris & Co., 1861.

This sermon was delivered on December 16, 1860, at Aiken, South Carolina.

Dabney, Robert L. "The Christian's Best Motive for Patriotism." *Fast Day Sermons*. New York: Rudd & Carleton, 1861.

This sermon was preached at College Church in Hampden Sidney, Vir-

ginia, on November 1, 1860. It was an appeal for peace and reconciliation between the North and South. The preacher asked the church of
"thirty-four thousand evangelical ministers, and four millions of Christian adults" to work for those things which made for peace. He warns
his audience not to be taken in by those who cry out for political violence
from a spirit of hate and vengeance. Later on, Dabney would admit to
having second thoughts about this sermon.

Dalzell, W. T. D. *A Sermon.* San Antonio: Herald Book and Job Press, 1863.
This sermon, delivered at St. Mary's Church of San Antonio, sought to
remind its listeners of that for which they could be thankful. Union
troops had not stepped on Texas soil as with other Confederate states.
"Thank God for the high moral virtues which this war has developed in
our state and country." Even with the rash of recent Confederate defeats, Dalzell hoped these "may not discourage us. Let it prevent proud
boasting. . . . Let it remind us that we must still look up to and trust
only in God. . . . Let it not lead to any want of faith in His favor, nor of
thankfulness for the many tokens of that favor in the year past; nor yet
of confidence in the final happy issue."

Darling, Henry. *Chastened, but Not Killed.* Albany, NY: Van Benthuysen's
Printing House, 1864.
On August 4, 1864, at the Fourth Presbyterian Church in Albany, Dar-
ling compared Southern rebellion to Absalom's rebellion against King
David, whereby God had allowed Absalom "a momentary triumph, yet,
in the end, David was certain that it [rebellion] would be destroyed."

De Veaux, T. L. *Fast-Day Sermon.* Wytheville, AL: D. A. St. Clair, Printer, 1861.
"Confession and supplication must precede the attainment of desired
blessings from God." The sermon specifically listed several personal and
national sins for which confession must be made: failure to aid those in
want; failure to study the Scriptures and pray; failure to keep and honor
the Sabbath; failure in the religious education of children; bribery, corruption, greed, drunkenness, and profaning the name of God.

Dexter, Henry Martyn. *What Ought to Be Done with the Freedmen and
with the Rebels?* Boston: Nichols and Noyes, 1865.
Dexter, who later became a noted church historian, delivered this sermon at the Berkeley Street Church in Boston on April 23, 1865. He
spoke of the necessity of dividing rebel lands among the former slaves.
Yet the government must not interfere with questions of social equality.
"If we can trust the grass to grow and the trees to blossom and bear
fruit . . . we can trust the great mass of emancipated negroes to become
thrifty farmers and mechanics, and valuable members of the great industrial body, by natural promptings of opportunity and self-interest,
in the propitious air of freedom."

Dickinson, James Taylor. *A Sermon.* Norwich, CT: Anti-Slavery Society, 1834.
This sermon, preached on July 4, 1834, supported the abolitionist posi-

tion with many references to the Scriptures. Guilt for the sin of slavery was shared by the entire nation which permitted the perpetuation of the institution. Non-slaveholding Christians had a duty to warn slaveholders of God's certain judgment and punishment if slavery persisted. Laws protecting slavery should be nullified by obedience to the higher law of God.

Dickson, A. F. *Plantation Sermons, or Plain and Familiar Discourses for the Instruction of the Unlearned.* Philadelphia: Presbyterian Board of Publication, 1856.
These sermons were intended to be used by masters or mistresses who desired to provide religious instruction for their slaves.

Doggett, David Seth. *A Nation's Ebenezer.* Richmond: Enquirer Book and Job Press, 1862.
On September 18, 1862, at the Broad Street Methodist Church in Richmond, Doggett asserted that God was not an idle spectator in the war. "He will not suffer public justice and integrity to struggle unaided."

———. *The War and Its Close.* Richmond: Macfarlane and Fergusson, 1864.
On April 8, 1864 at the Centenary Church in Richmond, Doggett warned of what would happen if the North should win. Northern heresies would "surge over the heritage of God. . . . At one fell stroke religious liberty would be extinguished, and a ruthless tyranny would dictate terms of communion with the polluted crusaders of their altars."

Doggett, Simeon. *Two Discourses on the Subject of Slavery.* Boston: Minot Pratt, 1835.
A Unitarian minister from Raynham, Massachusetts, delivered a strong and strident defense of slavery.

Dreher, Daniel I. *A Sermon.* Salisbury, NC: Watchman's Office, 1861.
The pastor of St. James' Church in Concord, North Carolina, on June 13, 1861, affirmed the validity of secession. "Nature and nature's God has marked us out for two nations."

Duffield, George. *A Sermon on American Slavery: Its Nature and the Duty of Christians.* Detroit: J. S. and S. A. Bagg, 1840.
This sermon is a warning against hasty antislavery action. It appeals for gradual reform.

Duffield, George, Jr. *The God of Our Fathers.* Philadelphia: T. B. Pugh, 1861.
This widely circulated sermon was delivered at the Coates Street Presbyterian Church in Philadelphia on January 4, 1861. Duffield contended that the nation's crisis was God's punishment for sins. Those sins included ingratitude, intemperance, violation of the Sabbath, infidelity, adultery, murder, unjust wars, and oppression.

———. *The Great Rebellion Thus Far a Failure.* Adrian, MI: S. P. Jermain and Co., 1861.
This sermon, delivered at the Presbyterian Church in Adrian, on November 28, 1861, was critical of extremes in both North and South. "I know

that slavery is the bitter root of all this trouble, and slavery for myself or any other member of the human race, I hate as much as I do its last and bitterest fruit, secession – but between the spirit and sentiments of Calhoun and his followers on the one extreme, and those of Garrison and his followers on the other, I see but little room to choose."

Dunaway, Thomas. *A Sermon*. Richmond: Enquirer Book & Job Press, 1864.
This sermon before the Coan Baptist Church of Richmond in April of 1864 urged Southerners to put forth greater sacrifice. "We must be willing, moreover, to contribute of our substance liberally and cheerfully – to sacrifice private rights and interests for the public good."

Dunwoody, Samuel. *A Sermon upon the Subject of Slavery*. Columbia, SC: S. Weir, 1837.
This Methodist preacher claimed that God, in the Bible, made provision for perpetual slavery. The Negro race was condemned to an existence of slavery. Dunwoody further insisted that Christians were to be obedient to civil authorities, which, for him, meant obedience to the laws and policies which allowed for the existence of slavery.

Dwight, William T. *The Nationality of a People Its Vital Element*. Portland, ME: N. A. Foster, 1861.
In this sermon delivered at the City Hall, on July 4, 1861, Dwight warned that if secession were allowed to succeed, the United States would lapse into the colonial orbit of England or France.

———. *The Pulpit in Its Relations To Politics*. Portland, ME: Francis Blake, 1857.
This Congregational minister from Portland declared that temperance and slavery were fit moral subjects to which sermons should be addressed.

Dwinell, Israel E. *Hope for Our Country*. Salem, MA: Charles W. Swasey, 1862.
This sermon preached on October 19, 1862, at the South Side Church of Salem recognized the importance of the Emancipation Proclamation for the North. Early defeats were due to the North's reluctance to emancipate the slaves. "The cause of the war is clearly slavery; and we tried for a long time . . . to fight the war, and save sin; and God would not suffer it. . . . Now we are openly and directly on the side of God; and now we may hope to have His favor."

Eddy, Daniel C. *The Martyr President*. Boston: Graves & Young, 1865.
In a sermon that was preached soon after the assassination of Lincoln, Eddy charged: "Southern people are a different race." He accused the South of gross atrocities during the war, the assassination of Lincoln being only the latest. He demanded retribution. "The sooner the screws are put on, the better for the nation, and the better for humanity."

———. *Our Country: Its Pride and Its Peril, or Liberty and Union*. Boston: John M. Hewes, 1861.
After a trip to Syria, Eddy delivered this sermon at the Harvard Street Baptist Church in Boston on August 11, 1861. Eddy spoke of the United

States as being representative of all humanity and the necessity of remaining a united and single nation. "We cannot have two or more republics on this soil. God and nature have forbidden it."

———. *Secession, a National Crime.* Philadelphia: American Baptist Publication Society, 1863.

———. *The Union, the Constitution and the Law.* Philadelphia: American Baptist Publication Society, 1863.

This sermon depicts a millennial vision of what the United States would be like following a Northern victory.

Eddy, Richard. *Three Sermons.* Philadelphia: H. G. Leisenring, 1865.

In these sermons from 1865 Eddy, a Universalist pastor in Philadelphia, indicted Jefferson Davis and other Southern leaders for their roles in the Civil War. "Justice shall have its course with those who instigated and led this Rebellion. I speak not of revenge . . . but the justice which comes from judicial trial, the execution of the penalty which the law has provided for treason."

Eddy, Zachery. *A Discourse on the War.* Northampton, MA: Trumbull and Gere, 1861.

Eddy, who had been converted from an apostle of peaceful disunion with the South to a staunch advocate of war, delivered this sermon on April 28, 1861, to the Northampton Volunteers. "If the crusaders, seized by a common enthusiasm, exclaimed, 'IT IS THE WILL OF GOD! IT IS THE WILL OF GOD!' – much more may we make this our rallying cry and inscribe it on our banners."

———. *Secession: Shall It Be Peace or War?* Northampton, MA: Trumbull and Gere, 1861.

This sermon, delivered on April 4, 1861, urged the North to free itself from the burden of union with the South that the North might more fully "develop all the forces of a high, Christian civilization."

Edwards, Henry L. *Discourse Commemorative of our Illustrious Martyr.* Boston: Wright and Potter, 1865.

This sermon, preached in the Congregational Church of South Abingdon, Massachusetts, in June of 1865, sought to blend love and punishment in the treatment of the conquered South. Edwards called for Negro rights. "And let us give, moreover, the long degraded negro his due. Give him the Bible, and the ballot, as well as the bullet. If he has used the one as well as we, he will the other. . . . Qualify the freedman to read, and write, and vote, as soon as possible, and let him make the most of himself that he can."

Eells, W. W. *How and Why We Give Thanks.* Pittsburgh: W. S. Haven, 1864.

This sermon, delivered at the First Presbyterian Church of Pittsburgh, on November 26, 1863, was one of many Northern sermons which declared that the Emancipation Proclamation was the turning point of the war. He [God] interposed . . . and all thoughtful men should know assuredly that true peace in this land should be built upon the foundation of universal emancipation."

Elliott, James H. *The Bloodless Victory*. Charleston: A. E. Miller, 1861.
This sermon was preached in St. Michael's Church (Episcopal) in Charleston on the taking of Fort Sumter by the Confederacy. Elliott declared that the victory was an answer to prayer: "The hand of God seems as plainly in it as in the conquest of the Midianites."

Elliott, Stephen. *Ezra's Dilemma*. Savannah: Power Press of George N. Nichols, 1863.
Elliott blamed recent Confederate defeats upon the sins of the people. "The crown is fallen from our head – woe onto us that we have sinned." The South needed only to repent and all would be well again. He warned of dire consequences should the North win the war.

———. *Gideon's Water-Lappers*. Macon, GA: Burke, Boykin & Co., 1864.
This sermon, preached in Christ Church of Savannah, still held out hope for the Confederacy. All that was needed was for the people to come "boldly up to the throne of Grace, firmly believing that our prayers . . . will return to us laden with blessings from . . . the God of the Armies of Israel."

———. *God's Presence with Our Army at Manassas*. Savannah: W. Thorne Williams, 1861.
This sermon was preached at Christ Church commemorating the Confederate victory at Manassas Junction. The victory was "the crowning token of his [God's] love – the most wonderful of all the manifestations of his divine presence with us. . . . He has smitten our enemies in their most tender and sensitive point, their invincible power, and has taken from us the pride of victory by giving it to us wrapped up in the funeral shroud of the brave and the young."

———. *God's Presence with the Confederate States*. Savannah: W. Thorne Williams, 1861.
On June 13, 1861, in Christ Church, Elliott enumerated the principles for which the Confederacy was fighting. "We are engaged in one of the grandest struggles which ever nerved the hearts or strengthened the hands of a heroic race. We are fighting for great principles, for sacred objects . . . to prevent ourselves from being transferred from American republicanism to French democracy . . . to rescue the fair name of our social life . . . from dishonor . . . to protect and preserve a race who form a part of our household, and stand with us next to our children . . . to drive away the infidel and rationalistic principles which are sweeping the land and substituting a gospel of the stars and stripes for the gospel of Jesus Christ."

———. *How to Renew Our National Strength*. Savannah: Steam Power Press of John M. Cooper & Co., 1861.
On November 15, 1861, at Christ Church, on a day of fasting and prayer

called by President Jefferson Davis, Elliott said that such a fast day, of which there would be many in the history of the Confederacy, was worth more than armaments, as long as "it be kept in spirit and in truth." Realizing that the South was engaged in a war of attrition, Elliott admonished: "We are only at the beginning of a long and bloody conflict, and it is the duty of everyone to consider it so and prepare himself for such a contingency." Elliott defended the strategies of Jefferson Davis and declared that those who questioned and destroyed confidence in the Confederate government were guilty of sin. "We are moving in the light of God's countenance, and the waving of His hand and the flashing of His eye are almost visible to us."

———. *An Impressive Summons*. Columbia: n.p., 1864.
This sermon by the Episcopal Bishop of Georgia is the funeral remarks for the Rev. Leonidus Polk, the bishop-general who was killed in battle in June of 1864. The remarks were published in the fall under the above title. Elliott took the occasion to denounce Northern Christians and "the ripening germs of irreligion, of unbelief, of ungodliness, of corruption, of cruelty, of license which have distinguished them." Even at this late date the bishop looked to a glorious future for "a country made independent through his [Polk's] devotion and self-sacrifice."

———. *New Wine Not to be Put in Old Bottles*. Savannah: Steam Power Press of John M. Cooper & Co., 1862.
This sermon was delivered on February 28, 1862, a time when the war was becoming increasingly burdensome to the South. Elliott reminded his listeners that nations "must win their way to a place in history through the baptism of blood."

———. *Our Cause in Harmony with the Purposes of God in Jesus Christ*. Savannah: Steam Power Press of John M. Cooper & Co., 1862.
In this sermon, delivered on September 18, 1862, at Christ Church in Savannah, Elliott was so certain of Confederate victory that he prophesied: "The summer's sun shall not have passed away, ere we shall find ourselves freed from their power." God would bring judgment upon the North. "God is upon their track and ere this conflict is ended, will bring them to repentance and remorse or else punish them in the way of his wrath." Elliott warned: "Let us not, by any improper exultation, turn away God's wrath from our enemies."

———. *Samson's Riddle*. Macon, GA: Burke, Boykin & Co., Steam Book and Job Printers, 1863.
At the time this sermon was delivered on May 27, 1863, in Christ Church, Savannah, the South was beginning to feel the footprints of the North upon its soil. Elliott declared that the only hope lay in continuing the war "which God is working out for our deliverance."

———. *The Silver Trumpets of the Sanctuary*. Savannah: Steam Power Press of John M. Cooper & Co., 1861.

This sermon was preached in June of 1861 in Christ Church to the Pulaski Guards before they left to join the army in Virginia. "Ye may go to battle without any fear, and strike boldly for your homes and your altars without any guilt. . . . The church will sound the trumpets that shall summon you to battle."

————. *Vain Is the Help of Man.* Macon, GA: Burke, Boykin & Co., 1864. This sermon was delivered on September 15, 1864, in Christ Church, Savannah, shortly after the fall of Atlanta. Elliott exclaimed: "We have nothing left but to follow the example of the Psalmist and crying unto God to 'give us help from trouble,' and to recognize that 'vain is the help of man.'" Elliott denounced Southerners who attempted to live a life of ease in the midst of great suffering and their failure to support the Confederate army. He predicted that if Lincoln was reelected, the South's cause would be aided, for the Confederacy would never surrender while Lincoln was President.

Ewer, F. C. *The National Crisis.* New York: George F. Nesbitt, 1861. This sermon from the rector of St. Anne's Protestant Episcopal Church in New York City shortly after the war began asked the listeners to "let us remember that this is a war of principle, not of vengeance."

Fair, Robert A. *Our Slaves Should Have a Bible.* Due West, SC: Telescope Press, 1854. This sermon was delivered before the Abbeville Bible Society in July of 1854.

Farley, Charles Andrews. *Slavery.* Richmond: James C. Walker, 1835. This Unitarian clergyman, just arrived from Boston, on August 30, 1835, at the Unitarian Church in Richmond, delivered one of the harshest critiques of abolitionism heard in the South during the 1830s.

Fast Day Sermons or the Pulpit on the State of the Country. New York: Rudd & Carleton, 1861. A superb collection of sermons from throughout the nation, representing different points of view, preached from November 1, 1860, through January 4, 1861.

Ferguson, Jesse Babcock. *Address on the History, Authority and Influence of Slavery.* Nashville: John T. S. Fall, 1850. A proslavery sermon preached on November 21, 1850 at the First Presbyterian Church in Nashville.

Finley, I. R. *The Lord Reigneth.* Richmond: Soldiers' Tract Association, M. E. Church, South, Chas. H. Wynne, Printer, 1863. This sermon, at Lloyd's Church in Sussex Country, Virginia, on August 16, 1863, considered the divine rule of God on earth an indisputable fact. If one truly believes this, the following effects will result: (1) a spirit of gratitude and rejoicing; (2) trust and hope in God; (3) reverence for and obedience to God. Where might one look for the rule of God in operation? "Will anyone be insane enough to look for it in that land of anarchy and tyranny – the North? Assuredly not. Where, then, is it to be found, but in this noble sisterhood of States – the Southern Confederacy."

Finney, Charles G. "Doubtful Actions Are Sinful." *Lectures to Professing Christians*. London: Milner and Company, 1837.

Finney never devoted an entire sermon to any social or public issue. In a portion of this sermon the noted evangelist expressed his antislavery views.

Fish, Henry Clay. *The Duty of the Hour: or, Lessons from Our Reverses*. New York: Sheldon and Co., 1862.

Following another Union defeat in the early stages of the war, Fish asked his listeners how long the Union could prosecute the war without taking the proper advantages. The four million slaves in the South, by providing manual labor, allowed the white males to go off to war. "Can we afford to give them this mighty advantage? . . . Tenderness to slavery is tenderness to rebellion." Fish demanded an immediate Union stance for emancipation.

————. *The Valley of Achor a Door of Hope; or, The Grand Issues of the War*. New York: Sheldon and Co., 1863.

On Thanksgiving Day, November 26, 1863, at the First Baptist Church in Newark, Fish told of his confidence for a Union victory. He described his utopian vision of the nation following the war: "I see it. I see it. The war successfully ended; the bondman everywhere a freeman; the degraded white man everywhere educated and ennobled; the diverse elements in the national composition fused and welded inseparably together; local jealousies and animosities at an end; treason and traitors expelled from the country; the heresy of state and secession killed; . . . a school house and church in every district; the people taking the highest type of civilization – intelligent, God-fearing, liberty-loving, self-governed, and bound together in one tender and beautiful brotherhood."

Fisher, George P. *Thoughts Proper to the Present Crisis*. New Haven: Tuttle, Morehouse and Taylor, 1861.

This sermon, delivered in the chapel of Yale College, on January 4, 1861, attacked the compact theory of government: "Society is not a compact to be dissolved at the caprice of the parties which are bound by it."

Foss, Cyrus D. *Songs in the Night*. New York: N. Tibbals and Co., 1861.

In a sermon to Brooklyn Methodists, Foss gave strong support for limiting the freedom of expression. "We talk of the freedom of the press as something sacred. We have exalted it into a demi-god which is profanation to touch or to speak against. . . . Free speech and a free press are essential to the stability of republican institutions, but let neither insolently claim to be in such sense free as beyond check."

Foster, Eden B. *Two Discourses*. Lowell, MA: J. J. Judkins, 1854.

In these sermons Foster, a Congregationalist from Lowell, proposed the secession of the North from the Union as a last resort to check the spread of slavery. Foster also replied to Senator Stephen Douglas, who had delcared that m:nisters were ignorant about political affairs and, therefore, should not comment upon them. The sermons also contain a strong attack upon the Kansas–Nebraska Bill. Inherent in the slavery system, said Foster, were such evils as cruelty, ignorance, immorality, and sin.

Foster, Edwin B. *The Constitution Our Ark in the Storm.* Springfield, MA: Samuel Bowles, 1862.

This sermon, delivered at the First Congregational Church of West Springfield, is filled with atrocity stories about Southern treatment of Yankee soldiers. Some, though apparently not many, Northern sermons resorted to such tactics. A portion of Foster's sermon was as follows. "They dig up decaying remains and tear the scalps from the heads of the departed, as vultures tear the flesh, that they may make drinking cups of the skulls. With strange powers of invention, almost their own ingenuity of mechanism, they manufacture the bones of our dead into rings and castanets and whistles, then hawking them abroad, as an article of merchandise, they coolly pocket the thirty pieces of silver." Foster viewed the war as one of constitutional authority versus the despotism of the few.

Freeman, George Washington. *The Rights and Duties of Slaveholders.* Raleigh: J. Gales & Son, 1836.

This is a sermon on the evils of abolitionism, delivered in Christ Church (Episcopal) of Raleigh on November 27, 1836.

Frotheringham, Octavius B. *The Last Signs.* New York: John A. Gray, 1856.

The issue of "bleeding Kansas" caused this sermon to warn of a spreading slaveocracy. The sermon also charged that the physical attack upon Sumner in Congress demonstrated how brutal and violent the slave system was.

Fuller, Richard. *Address Before the American Colonization Society.* Baltimore: Office of the Trust Union, 1851.

Fuller was a noted Baptist minister who had served for many years in South Carolina and had recently moved to Baltimore. This sermon was delivered in Washington, on January 21, 1851. It was critical of abolitionism and of Southern extremism as well. The South was overly sensitive on the subject of slavery and it was something that needed to be openly discussed throughout the South. After arguing that the North needed to make concessions, he said that the South also did. The South must realize that slavery "fosters indolence and luxury." He then stated: "Slavery is not a good thing, and a thing to be perpetuated." He suggested colonization as a "middle ground" around which the North and South could unite. Congress should grant money for buying slaves from masters and then pay the former slaves' passage to Liberia. Fuller, who had been a very popular minister throughout the South, stirred up great hostility and resentment toward himself in the South because of this speech.

Fulton, Justin R. *Radicalism*. Boston: J. E. Tilton, 1865.
  The pastor of Tremont Temple (Baptist) in Boston made a reply to those in the North who praised the fighting abilities of Robert E. Lee. "We cannot bear to hear such men as Robert E. Lee, Judge Campbell, and others praised. The blood of our starved brothers, in different rebel prisons, cries out against them. . . . It is no honor to be a rebel, and to have bravely fought. Fighting in support of crime is murder."
Furness, William Henry. *A Sermon Occasioned by the Destruction of Pennsylvania Hall*. Philadelphia: J. C. Clarke, 1838.
  This sermon defended the abolitionists' right of free speech and assembly.
Gannett, Ezra S. *Relation of the North to Slavery*. Boston: Crosby, Nichols, 1854.
  After a trip through the South, which the minister of the Federal Street Meeting House in Boston claimed he took with an open mind, he returned convinced that slavery was a grievous wrong, indefensible and unjustifiable.
Gaylord, William A. *The Soldier God's Minister*. Fitchburg, NH: Rollstone Printing Office, 1862.
  This sermon was delivered on October 5, 1862, at the Congregational Church in Fitchburg. During the middle years of the war many Northern ministers changed the emphasis of their sermons as to the meaning of the war. During the early years of the war saving the Union was the primary reason for the conflict. About the middle of 1862 there was an increased emphasis on the abolition of slavery. The salvation of God-ordained government had become subordinate to the emancipation of the slaves. Gaylord's sermon reflected that change.
Gilbert, D. M. *A Discourse*. Savannah: George N. Nichols, 1864.
  On September 15, 1864, in the Evangelical Lutheran Church in Savannah, while Sherman's forces were occupying Atlanta, Gilbert echoed a common Southern religious theme at that time: "It is because of our sins that the Almighty is so sorely chastening us."
Girardeau, John Lafayette. *Conscience and Civil Government*. Charleston: Evans & Cogswell, 1860.
  A proslavery discourse delivered before the Society of Alumni of the College of Charleston on Commencement Day, March 27, 1860.
Gladden, Washington. *Recollections*. Boston: Houghton Mifflin, 1909.
  This noted Congregationalist minister, on the Sunday after Lee surrendered to Grant, delivered a sermon asking for lenient terms toward the South. Gladden said that such a sermon, for the most part, fell on deaf ears.
Goodrich, William H. *A Sermon on the Christian Necessity of War*. Cleveland: Fairbanks, Benedict and Co., 1861.
  Goodness and progress can triumph only when contested on the battlefield. "You will mark it as a fact of general history, that in the estab-

lishment of great rights, and the overthrow of great wrongs, there has always come a point where the issue must be fought out in battle. Rooted wrong and ancient despotism never yield that last point, till they are confronted with force greater than their own. Selfish power, even when deserted by its old advocates, and disowned by the surrounding world, will always make one last stand, and will yield only when conquered and abased."

Goodwin, H. M. "On the Assassination of President Lincoln." The Goodwin Manuscripts: Sermons. No. 393. Hammond Library of Chicago Theological Seminary.

This Congregational minister from Rockford, Illinois, declared that the assassination of Lincoln was a "representative act, deriving its character from sources below and broader than individual wills that planned and executed it. The spirit of the Southern rebellion, the dastardly . . . spirit of slavery is in it, and expressed through it."

Gordon, Adoniram Judson. *The Chosen Fast*. Boston: N. P. Kemp, 1865.

This sermon, delivered at the Baptist Church in Jamaica Plain, on April 13, 1865, as the war neared its end, envisioned an America where perfect freedom was about to obliterate the "wilderness of servitude" and national life would "blossom as a rose."

Green, Beriah. *Four Sermons Preached in the Chapel of Western Reserve College*. Cleveland: Office of the Herald, 1833.

Slavery was a moral, not just a political, issue. An intuitional ethic which is the law of God planted in the heart teaches that slavery is an evil.

Gregg, Alexander. *The Duties Growing Out of it, and the Benefits to be Expected from the Present War*. Austin: Office of the State Gazette, 1861.

On July 7, 1861, the bishop declared the necessity of the present war, and then tied patriotism to religious devotion. Never had there been a higher or more noble duty than the one to which the South was now called.

――――. *Primary Charge to the Clergy of the Protestant Episcopal Church in the Diocese of Texas*. Austin: State Gazette Job Office, 1863.

Delivered at Christ Church in Houston on May 9, 1863, this sermon is a very long and involved discussion about the relationship between church and state and the responsibilities one has to the other.

――――. *A Sermon*. Austin: Texas Almanac Office, 1862.

On July 20, 1862, the Episcopal Bishop of Texas told a congregation at St. David's Church in Austin that the end of the war would soon come. The Confederacy was "a people wonderfully delivered."

――――. *A Sermon*. Austin: Texas Almanac Office, 1863.

Delivered at St. David's Church in Austin, this sermon is a strong denunciation of extortion; "a disposition to go beyond the bounds of a just and lawful gain – to take advantage of times and circumstances by demanding exorbitant prices." This was, more than any other, the sin which was destroying the Confederacy.

Gurley, P. D. *The Voice of the Rod*. Washington: Wm. Ballantyne, 1865.
This sermon, delivered at the New York Avenue Presbyterian Church in Washington on June 1, 1865, was a summary of alleged Southern atrocities. Atrocity stories were not typical of most Northern preachers.

Hall, Nathaniel. *The Limits of Civil Disobedience*. Boston: Wm. Crosby and H. P. Nichols, 1854.
This Congregationalist minister from Dorchester, Massachusetts, stated that obedience to the higher law of God must supersede all human laws. The discourse urged the overthrow of slavery.

————. *The Moral Significance of the Contrasts Between Slavery and Freedom*. Boston: Walker, Wise and Company, 1864.
After a three-week trip through Kentucky and Tennessee, Hall issued a sermon-report on slavery and its effect upon slowing the progress of civilization.

————. *Righteousness and the Pulpit*. Boston: Wm. Crosby and H. P. Nichols, 1855.
A sermon declaring that Christians were called by God to oppose slavery.

Hamilton, W. T. *Duties of Masters and Slaves Respectively; or, Domestic Slavery as Sanctioned by the Bible*. Mobile: F. H. Brooks, 1844.
Hamilton denounced abolitionists as antislavery radicals. They were sinners and should be denied communion with other Christians.

Harris, Samuel. *Our Country's Claim*. Bangor, ME: Wheeler and Lynde, 1861.
This sermon, delivered on July 4, 1861, declared that the most distinctive and important feature of America was the principle of universal justice and individual freedom.

Haven, Gilbert. *A Memorial Discourse on the Character and Career of Abraham Lincoln*. Boston: James Magee, 1865.
This Methodist minister of Boston accused Robert E. Lee of complicity in Lincoln's assassination. "[Booth] was but the dagger's point; Lee [was] its polished handle; slavery the force that drove it home. The yet unharmed general attempted to assassinate a nation. . . . He, too, is a murderer. Let us do justice to the greatest traitors of our land." Haven's plan for reconstruction was to dethrone all rebel leaders and put freed slaves in their place after giving them the right to vote.

————. *National Sermons*. Boston: Lee and Shepherd, 1869.
This is a collection of 25 sermons dealing with national and sectional issues from the Fugitive Slave Law in 1850 to the election of Grant in 1868.

Hendrick, John T. *Union and Slavery*. Clarksville, TN: C. O. Faxon, 1851.
This Thanksgiving sermon, delivered on November 11, 1850, at the Presbyterian Church in Clarksville, declared that the Ten Commandments assumed that slavery would continue "in all time to come." Hendrick also said that the Bible guaranteed the immutability of the current roles of the three races in America.

Higgens, S. H. *The Mountain Moved; or, David upon the Cause and Curse* of Public Calamity. Milledgeville, GA: Boughton, Nisbet, Barnes and Moore, State Printers, 1863.

Higgens declared on December 10, 1863: "Of this, we have no doubt whatever. In spite of all reverses, we shall yet prevail – we shall overcome at the last – our enemy will be driven backward – but, God will have the glory."

Higginson, Thomas Wentworth. *Massachusetts in Mourning*. Boston: James Monroe and Company, 1854.

This Unitarian minister called the Kansas-Nebraska Bill a revolution against liberty and the use of law to enforce tyranny.

Hitchcock, R. D. *Thanksgiving for Victories*. New York, 1864.

On September 11, 1864, Hitchcock attempted to explain why early Northern defeats were now turned to victories. "A bad cause may be successful at the start. . . . The good cause is stunned and staggered by the first onset; but by and by it rallies, warming as it works, and striking harder and harder till the field is won."

Holland, DeWitte, ed. *Sermons in American History*. Nashville: Abingdon Press, 1971.

This book contains two sermons on slavery – one from Theodore Parker and one from James H. Thornwell; and two sermons on the Civil War – one from Henry Allen Tupper and the other from James D. Liggett. Helpful editorial comments accompany the sermons.

Hovey, Horace. *Freedom's Banner*. Coldwater, MI: n.p., 1861.

On April 28, 1861, in a sermon before the Coldwater Light Artillery and the Zouave Cadets, Hovey reminded his listeners as to what the North-South conflict was all about. "Our work as a Model Republic is but half done. We are yet to show the world that we have a cohesion and governmental power; that we are not a mere voluntary association for the promotion of temporary interests – not a mere debating society, but that we are a veritable government, in which the majority rules through agencies established by law; and that armed rebellion can be punished here as well as in a monarchy."

Howe, William Bell White. *Cast Down, but Not Forsaken*. Charleston: Steam Power Presses of Evans & Cogswell, 1861.

This sermon was preached on December 12, 1861, at St. Phillip's Church in Charleston, on the Sunday after the Great Fire. Drawing his text from the book of Job, Howe declared: "We are being tried, not punished. God would prove what our faith is made of: whether it is mere holiday faith, which lasts only when the sun shines, and when all things are prosperous, or whether it is of that robust nature, which will endure a great fight of afflictions. . . . This is the very essence of the trial, to believe that God is with us when, to all appearances, He has deserted us."

Howlett, T. R. *A Discourse*. Washington: Gibson Bros., 1865.

This sermon, preached at the Calvary Baptist Church in Washington, declared that the abettors of the rebellion, North and South, must share in the guilt of Lincoln's assassination. "Not alone upon him who fired the fatal weapon . . . not alone upon the miserable wretches now on trial for their complicity, but upon every . . . abettor of the Rebellion. Ministers who have preached peace and conciliation when they mean aid and comfort to the foe. . . . Upon all these as well as upon Confederate soldiers in arms and the greater conspirators, rests the blood that has been shed during the war."

Humphrey, Herman. *Our Nation*. Pittsfield, MA: Henry Chickering, 1861.
This eminent Congregationalist on January 4, 1861, declared that in spite of the present crisis, the United States would not be deterred from its great divine mission. "Would He have brought us hither and give us so much work in prospect for bringing in the millennium, if He had intended to pluck us up, just as we are entered upon the work?"

Ide, George. *Battle Echos, or, Lessons from the War*. Boston: Gould and Lincoln, 1866.
This Baptist minister declared that payment for slavery must be made in "rivers of blood and oceans of treasure."

Jacobs, Ferdinand. *The Committing of Our Cause to God*. Charleston: A. J. Burke, 1850.
On December 6, 1850, at the Second Presbyterian Church in Charleston, Jacobs affirmed that the Bible presented slavery as a "permanent" relation which "may ever be expected to exist."

———. *A Sermon for the Times*. Marion, AL: n.p., 1861.
On June 13, 1861, after denouncing the spiritual depravity of the North and a Constitution which fails to mention God, Jacobs spoke of the importance and necessity of Southern independence. The struggle would be costly, but through God's providence and human instrumentality it could be won.

Johnston, E. S. *Abraham Lincoln*. Harrisburg, PA: Theo. F. Sheffer, 1865.
The theme of this sermon at the Second English Evangelical Lutheran Church of Harrisburg was that God's vengeance must be executed upon the South and human compassion must not stand in the way of it. "Vengeance belongs to God. To us as a Government he has entrusted the execution of his punishments on the guilty. It is neither wise nor safe for us to arrest the vengeance which does not belong to us, but to God."

Jones, Charles Colcock. *The Religious Instruction of the Negroes*. Princeton, NJ: D'Hart & Connolly, 1832.
A proslavery sermon from a Presbyterian minister who was greatly concerned that slaves should receive a proper religious education.

Jones, J. *The Southern Soldier's Duty*. Rome, GA: D. H. Mason, 1861.
This sermon was delivered in the Presbyterian Church of Rome on May 26, 1861, to the Rome Light Guards and Miller Rifles. Jones reminded his audience as to why the South seceded: (1)hostility of the North, (2) hostil-

ity that was thoroughly organized, (3)Northern opposition to slavery, (4) the North's plan to abolish slavery, (5) the Constitution had been violated, (6) secession was a right with a long history, and (7) slavery is a right derived from the Word of God. "Soldiers, be strong in your cause and realize that honor and interest, patriotism and piety, loved, loving, and dependent ones, your existence, and the prosperity of true religion, and the authority of God's word, all are committed to your keeping."

Junkin, George. *The Integrity of our National Union.* Cincinnati: R. P. Donogh, 1843.

This sermon before the Synod of Cincinnati (Old School Presbyterian) in 1843 was an eight-hour attack on abolitionism.

Kimball, Henry. *The Ship of State Bound for Tarshish.* Boston: Geo. C. Rand and Avery, 1861.

Delivered in the First Congregational Church in Sandwich, Massachusetts, on November 21, 1861, this sermon declared that Union defeats were due to the federal government's failure to take a firm stand against slavery. The ship of state had come upon a storm which would not abate until Jonah (slavery) was thrown overboard. "It is preposterous for us to suppose that we can keep up long before a civilized world, and nourish the very cause of all our disasters. The venom of slavery is in the fang of treason; let us extract the poison, and the teeth of rebellion will be drawn."

Lacy, Drury. *Address.* Fayetteville, NC: Edward J. Hale & Sons, 1863.

This sermon was delivered at the General Military Hospital in Wilson, North Carolina, in March of 1863. After blaming military reversals upon Confederate sins, Lacy assured his audience of eventual Confederate triumph. "What, then, if Lincoln does muster in the field his 3,000,000 of men? Like those before them, they will be driven as chaff before the wind."

Lamar, J. S. *A Discourse.* Augusta, GA: Office of the Constitutionalist, 1861.

On November 15, 1861, at the Christian Church of Augusta, Lamar stated the rightness of the Confederate cause: "In the contest between the North and the South, we are absolutely in the right.... Dissolution,... far from being wrong, was the correction of a wrong. However, if the South was to be victorious in their just cause, they must repent of their sins. Four sins were specified and elaborated upon: pride, covetousness, selfishness, and disobedience.

Landrum, Sylvanus. *The Battle is God's.* Savannah: E. J. Purse, Printers, 1863.

This sermon was preached on August 21, 1863, at the Savannah Baptist Church, a few weeks after the battles of Gettysburg and Vicksburg. The tide of battle had shifted dramatically against the South. Landrum assured his listeners that the battle was still in God's hands. He took special note of the evil emanating from the North. "Nothing on earth can surpass the beastly brutality and wickedness which the enemy has shown us. Still we have refused to imitate their example."

Lanphear, O. T. *Peace by Power*. New Haven: J. H. Benham, 1864.
This sermon, delivered at College Street Church in New Haven on October 9, 1864, urged the reelection of Lincoln as the surest way to realize peace. Lanphear denounced a vote for McClellan, the supposed "peace candidate." "The man who casts his vote, in the election now pending, in favor of a peace not won by the conquests of our armies, does the rebel cause more service, if possible, than he would by joining the rebel army."
Laurie, Thomas. *Three Discourses*. Dedham, MA: John Cox, Jr., 1865.
Delivered at the South Evangelical Church of West Roxbury, Massachusetts, one sermon expressed a fear that Northern victory might be undone by wily politicians. Therefore, "the whole South must be leavened with the Gospel. Its educational and religious institutions must be reconstructed, not by arbitrary dictation, but by loving cooperation."
Lee, LeRoy M. *Our Country – Our Dangers – Our Duty*. Richmond: Soldiers' Tract Association, 1863.
This sermon delivered at the Centenary Church (Methodist) of Lynchburg, Virginia, on August 21, 1863, declared that sins were bringing down the Confederacy. Lee told his congregation to beware of "speculators, forestallers, and extortioners, – if we would escape extermination"; otherwise, "there remaineth nothing but war – fierce, bloody, protracted war." The minister urged his congregation to fight on. "Until they (the North) choose to stop, we are compelled to fight. . . . Compromise would be treason against truth, country and God."
Leeds, S. P. *Thy Kingdom Come: Thy Will Be Done*. Windsor, VT: Bishop and Tracy, 1861.
This sermon, delivered at the Congregational Church at Dartmouth College on September 26, 1861, decried the softness, laxity, and unwarranted leniency that had permeated the country, but rejoiced that the war could bring forth higher virtues. Soft-headed people would be pushed into the background "while men of deeds come to the front."
Liggett, James D. "Our National Reverses." Manuscript, Civil War Collection, Yale University.
This sermon was delivered at the First Congregational Church of Leavenworth, Kansas, in September of 1862, when the war was not going well for the North. The reason for Northern defeats, declared Liggett, was because the eradication of slavery was not the top priority of the Union.
Little, Charles. *Relation of the Citizen to the Government*. New Haven: William H. Stanley, 1864.
On November 24, 1864, at the Congregational Church in Chesire, Connecticut, Little declared that Northern victories were from God.
Longstreet, Augustus Baldwin. *Fast-Day Sermon*. Columbia, SC: Townsend & North, Publishers, 1861.
On June 13, 1861, at the Washington Street Methodist Church in Columbia, Longstreet, after denouncing the wickedness of the North and

its leaders, declared: "I thank God we have separated ourselves from that people. . . . But if, with God's word in our hand, and its verification before our eyes, we do not profit by them – if we do not radically change our conduct and our code, we had as well expect the laws of nature to be reversed, as to expect to escape the judgments which have befallen that people."

Lord, John C. *The Higher Law in Its Application to the Fugitive Slave Bill.* Buffalo: George H. Derby, 1851.
While many preachers in the North were calling for defiance to the Fugitive Slave Law, Lord asked for patience and obedience to law until the courts could decide upon the legality of the law.

Lowry, Robert. "Sermon XVII." *Our Martyr President, Abraham Lincoln: Voices from the Pulpit of New York and Brooklyn.* New York: Tibbals & Whiting, 1865.
This sermon is a call for stern judgment upon the South following the assassination of Lincoln.

McCaine, Alexander. *Slavery Defended from Scripture, Against the Attacks of the Abolitionists* Baltimore: Wm. Woody, 1842.
McCaine was a founder and dominant figure in the splinter Methodist Protestant Church. This defense of slavery was delivered before the General Conference of the Methodist Protestant Church in Baltimore.

Magie, David. *A Discourse Delivered in the Second Presbyterian Church.* New York: Francis Hart and Co., 1863.
This is an atypical Northern sermon, but representative of those who wanted the war to cease in order to allow God to work out the North-South problem.

March, Daniel. *Steadfastness and Preparation in the Day of Adversity.* Philadelphia: C. Sherman and Son, 1862.
This sermon, delivered at the Clinton Street Presbyterian Church in Philadelphia on September 14, 1862, spoke of the work of God in history. "He assigns to nations their periods of trial and conflict, of prosperity and repose. . . . But the active conflict which the powers of darkness are ever waging for the possession of this world, has at last rolled toward that quarter of the field where the Divine Commander has assigned us our station. And we must take our turn in resisting the attack, considering what we do and suffer in this contest is not for ourselves alone, but for the ages and generations of the human family in all the future." March assured that the war would result in "a mountain of holiness for the dissemination of light and purity to all the nations."

Meade, William. *Address on the Day of Fasting and Prayer.* Richmond: Enquirer Book & Job Press, 1861.
The Episcopal Bishop of Virginia delivered this sermon at Christ Church in Millwood on June 13, 1861. Meade was ashamed of the church's part in breaking up the Union and called for peace overtures. Meade even

tually became an enthusiastic Confederate. Such a transformation happened to many ministers in the South.

———. *Sermon*. Richmond: Chas. H. Wynne, Printer, 1861.

This sermon was delivered at the Convention of the Protestant Episcopal Church of Virginia on the day marking Meade's fifty-first year in the ministry and the thirty-second year of his episcopate. "It has pleased God to permit a great calamity to come upon us. . . . I believe that the object sought for will be most perseveringly pursued, whatever sacrifice of life and comfort and treasure may be required. Nor do I entertain any doubt as to the final result though I shudder at the thought of what may intervene before that result is secured." This sermon contains many references to Virginia history.

Michelbacher, Maximilian J. *A Sermon Delivered on the Day of Prayer at the German Hebrew Synagogue, "Bayth Ahabah."* Charleston: Steam Power Press of Evans & Cogswell, 1863.

This sermon, delivered by a rabbi on March 27, 1863, sought to defend Jews from charges of extortion and pledged Jewish support of the Confederacy. "May we not reverently conceive, that the Almighty, in listening to our prayers, has in the High Courts of Heaven, graciously ratified our choice? . . . if this be so, let him beware, who is slow to perform the first duty of the citizen [patriotism]!" The rabbi explained that the dual cause of the Confederacy was independence and self-defense. If these remained the causes then "we [will] retain the blessing of the Great Creator by our humility and righteousness before Him."

Miles, James W. *God in History*. Charleston: Steam Power Press of Evans & Cogswell, 1863.

This sermon was delivered before the graduating class of the College of Charleston on March 29, 1863. Miles contended that the Confederacy was "commissioned by God to contend for and illustrate great principles, intimately connected with the progress of humanity." The South could accept its responsibility and become a glory among the nations, or it could fail and become a warning example.

Minnigerode, Charles. *He That Believeth Shall Not Make Haste*. Richmond: Chas. W. Wynne, Printer, 1865.

This sermon was delivered in St. Paul's Church (Episcopal) in Richmond, early in January of 1865. In the last weeks of the Confederacy this sermon still held out hope. God "chooseth his people in the furnace of affliction. He who believeth . . . cannot become the plaything of every puff of adversity or prosperity. What we need is a stout heart and a firm, settled mind: and oh! may we as a NATION remember, 'he that believeth shall not make haste.'" The minister denounced "coward, faithless, selfish hearts," the "want of faith," the "murmuring against God's providence."

———. *Power*. Richmond: W. H. Clemmitt, Book and Job Printer, 1864.

This sermon, delivered at St. Paul's Church on November 23, 1864, is devoted to the subject of power, as it is found in God and man.

Mitchel, J. C. *Fast Day Sermon*. Mobile: Farrow & Dennett, 1861.

> The pastor of Second Church in Mobile, on June 13, 1861, inquired: "Who can fail to see the hand of God in the whole movement?"

Moore, Thomas V. *God Our Refuge and Strength in This War*. Richmond: W. Hargrave White, 1861.

> This sermon, delivered before the congregations of the First and Second Presbyterian Churches of Richmond on November 15, 1861, declared that God used war as a means of disciplining people and nations. A prolonged peace tends "to emasculate and corrupt a people," while war breaks down "mammon worship and effeminacy."

Nadal, B. H. *The War in the Light of Divine Providence*. New Haven: Tuttle, Morehouse and Taylor, 1863.

> In 1863 this Methodist preacher warned of the consequences should the Southern "rebellion" succeed: "If this rebellion could succeed, the civilized world would experience the beginning of a second deluge, which would leave the broken remnants of human rights clutched in the hands of a few Neros and Napoleons. . . . The world would be subverted . . . and it would be proved that all our notions and hopes in regard to a peaceful and righteous God had been a dream."

New Haven Evening Register. Vol. XXV #89, 1865.

> This newspaper carried the accounts of three sermons that were delivered on a Saturday, on the Green in New Haven, on April 15, 1865. Because of the assassination of Lincoln, all three sermons demanded harsh terms to be imposed upon the South. Dr. Patton received great applause from the gathered crowd as he demanded the most stringest kind of judgment. "Yes, vengeance belongs to God, but he has his human instruments to carry out his vengeance. He will not allow this land to be polluted with the innocent blood unavenged, shed by these rebels. We must wipe it out. . . . The men who have violated their oft repeated oaths of loyalty and hatched and perpetuated this rebellion, I would not trust their oath. . . . If they are not hung, the mildest that we can in justice do them, is to put them on probation for the rest of their lives."

Nichols, Starr H. *Our Sins and Our Repentance*. Mansfield, OH: Prichard, 1861.

> This sermon was delivered in the Congregational Church of Mansfield on September 26, 1861. Nichols stated that a reason for the war was because of the nation's preoccupation with materialism, which had turned the people into headstrong children, "impetuous" and "defiant" of all restraints.

Norwood, William. *God and Our Country*. Richmond: Smith, Bailey and Co., 1863.

> On March 27, 1863, the minister of St. John's Church in Richmond, devoted a large portion of his sermon to a condemnation of speculators and profiteers in the South. Because many Southern businessmen were interested in gaining large profits from the war, widows, orphans, and crippled veterans were without food, clothing and shelter.

Ottman, Sefferenas. *God Always for the Right and Against Wrong*. Pennyan, NY: S. C. Cleveland, n.d.
On January 4, 1861, at the Presbyterian Church of Pulney, New York, Ottman declared that slavery would die whether the Union persisted or not. "In the Union or out of it, slavery must die. God has written upon it its inevitable doom; and universal civilization has pronounced against it."

Paddock, Wilbur. *A Great Man Fallen*. Philadelphia: Sherman & Co., 1865.
At St. Andrew's Episcopal Church in Philadelphia, after the assassination of Lincoln, Paddock declared that Booth was merely a tool of those higher up on the ladder of a slave society.

Paine, Levi. *Political Lessons of the Rebellion*. Farmington, CT: Samuel Cowles, 1862.
On April 18, 1862, Paine declared that people needed to study God's dealings with Israel in order to understand the present crisis. He lamented that, unlike a previous time in American history, "we no longer have a class of men we can call ... statesmen." America had entered an "era of demagogues and traitors and corrupt politicians" who prostitute the nation to "the highest bidder."

Palmer, Benjamin M. *A Discourse Before the General Assembly of South Carolina*. Columbia: Charles P. Pelham, State Printer, 1864.
This sermon, delivered on December 10, 1863, attempted to infuse new life and courage into the South as ultimate defeat seemed to lie on the horizon. "The language of true prayer is never the cry of supine imbecility, nor the wail of craven despondency. It is always the language of hope and expectation. ... I thank God that, in the darkest hour, I have never despaired of the republic."

———. *National Responsibility Before God*. New Orleans: Price-Current Steam Book and Job Printing Office, 1861.
On June 13, 1861, two months after the first shots of the Civil War were fired, Palmer preached on the five national sins that made secession inevitable.

———. "Slavery a Divine Trust: Duty of the South to Preserve and Perpetuate It." *Fast Day Sermons*. New York: Rudd & Carleton, 1861.
This sermon, delivered at the First Presbyterian Church of New Orleans, declared that the South was given a trust by God "to conserve and to perpetuate the institution of slavery as now existing." The preserving of this trust was a "duty to ourselves, to our slaves, to the world, and to Almighty God." Because of this duty, Palmer challenged, "Let the people in all the Southern States ... reclaim the powers they have delegated. ... Let them, further, take all the necessary steps looking to separate and independent existence, and initiate measures for framing a new and homogeneous confederacy." This sermon was delivered on November 29, 1860, shortly after Lincoln's election but before the seces-

sion of South Carolina. Palmer was calling for an "independent existence" prior to its actualization.

———. *A Vindication of Secession and the South.* Columbia: n.p., 1861.
The secession of South Carolina was a sublime example of moral heroism, according to Palmer. Relying on nothing "save the righteousness of her cause and the power of God, she took upon her shield and spear as desperate and as sacred a conflict as ever made a State immortal. . . . The Genius of history has already wreathed the garland with which her brow shall be decked."

Palmer, Ray. *The Opening Future: or, The Results of the Present War.* Albany, NY: J. Munsell, 1863.
This Thanksgiving discourse on November 26, 1863, found the minister grateful that the Civil War had given the United States a real history. "Pilgrims from other lands will come to visit and survey our battlefields, at Fort Donelson and Shiloh, Vicksburg and Port Hudson, Murfreesboro, Antietam and Gettysburg, as we have gone to examine those of Thermopylae and Marathon, of Cannae and Pharsalia, of Bannockburn, Agincourt and Waterloo. So shall we take our place and influence among historic and classic lands."

Paris, John. *Funeral Discourse.* Greensborough, NC: A. W. Ingold & Co., Book and Job Printers, 1864.
This sermon blamed civilian defeatest attitudes for military defections. Hoping to instill renewed faith within his hearers, Paris noted, "The ways of His providence are generally dark to mortal vision."

Parker, Theodore. "The Anti-Slavery Convention." *Centenary Edition,* Vol. 11.
This address at Fanueil Hall on May 31, 1848, found Parker accusing the church of lagging far behind God on the slavery issue. He saw the church as the most conservative of institutions, more concerned with ritual and dogma than with life. He did not hesitate to criticize Northern complicity with slavery. He was especially critical of his own area: "The men who control the politics of Massachusetts, of all New England, do not oppose or dislike slavery." In spite of many obstacles, Parker concluded, the antislavery movement would succeed. "We are certain of success; the spirit of the age is on our side. . . . Do you believe America can keep her slaves? It is idle to think so. . . . Yes, on our side is . . . the religion of Christ; on our side are the hopes of mankind, and the great power of God."

———. "The Boston Kidnapping." *Centenary Edition,* Vol. 11.
On April 12, 1852, before a congregation of 3,000 at the Melodian in Boston, Parker lamented the guilt of the city in sending back to slavery the fugitive Thomas Simms. The sermon is a beautiful demonstration of prose and exhibits an extraordinary grasp of history. Parker exclaimed that Northern money had made the Fugitive Slave Law possible, a law which "in the Yankee . . . has brought out some of the most disgraceful examples

of meanness that ever dishonored mankind." He was particularly disappointed with Boston. "Boston capitalists do not hesitate to own Southern plantations and buy and sell men. . . . Most of the slave-ships in the Atlantic are commanded by New England men. . . . The controlling men of Boston have done much to promote, to extend, and to perpetuate slavery."

———. *Centenary Edition of the Works of Theodore Parker.* 15 vols. Boston: American Unitarian Association, 1907.
Volumes 9 and 11 (especially vol. 11) contain most of Parker's sermons dealing with slavery and other sectional issues.

———. "The Free Soil Movement." *Centenary Edition*, Vol. 11.
In December of 1848 Parker declared that the history of the United States was a history of freedom versus slavery, with slavery being the winner most of the time. Slavery won its first battle in the Constitution. "South Carolina and Georgia were the only slave states thoroughly devoted to slavery at that time. They threatened to withdraw from the Union. . . . If the other States had said, 'You may go, soon as you like . . . ,' it would have been better for us all. However, partly for the sake of keeping peace, and still more for the purpose of making money by certain concessions to the South, the North granted the Southern demands." In the sermon Parker dramatically sketched what he believed were the historical differences between the North and South. "Who . . . has made the nation great, rich, and famous for her ideas and their success all over the world? The answer is . . . the North. . . . Who has filled the presidential chair forty-eight years out of sixty? Nobody but the slaveholders. . . . Who sets at naught the Constitution? The South."

———. "The Function of Conscience." *Centenary Edition*, Vol. 11.
On September 22, 1850, Parker launched a stinging attack on the Fugitive Slave Law of 1850. Throughout the sermon he stressed his determination to disobey the law. Parker associated the human conscience with the moral law of God. This conscience is far more binding upon a person than the Constitution or state laws.

———. "The Mexican War." *Centenary Edition*, Vol. 11.
On February 4, 1849, at Fanueil Hall in Boston, Parker denounced the Mexican War as a conflict to extend slavery. Aware that President Polk has said that it was treason to oppose the war, Parker responded: "Treason is it? . . . If my country is in the wrong, and I know it, and hold my peace, then I am guilty of treason, moral treason."

———. "Reply to Webster." *Centenary Edition*, Vol. 11.
On March 25, 1850, at Fanueil Hall, Parker severely criticized Senator Daniel Webster of Massachusetts for his part in the passage of the Fugitive Slave Law earlier in the month. "I know of no deed in American history, done by a son of New England, to which I can compare this, but the act of Benedict Arnold."

————. "A Sermon of Slavery." *Centenary Edition of the Works of Theodore Parker*, Vol. 11.

This sermon from the famous Boston Unitarian was delivered on January 31, 1841. It was his first antislavery sermon. After denouncing slavery as a grave sin, Parker sought to demolish the arguments as to why the North should not be involved in the slave debate. For those in the North who claimed that slavery was an affair of the South, Parker replied: "If there is a crime in the land known to us, and we do not protest against it to the extent of our ability, we are partners of that crime."

————. "The Slave Power." *Centenary Edition*, Vol. 11.

This discourse was delivered before the New England Anti-Slavery Convention on May 29, 1850. Over the history of the United States, Parker could think of only three instances where freedom had beaten back the forces of slavery: in the prohibiting of slavery in the Northwest Territory, in prohibiting the slave trade in 1808, and in the prohibition of slavery in Oregon. Parker complained that both contemporary political parties supported slavery. He had words of high praise for William Lloyd Garrison, the leader of the abolitionist movement. "There rose up a man who would not compromise, nor be silent, — who would be heard. . . . He found a few others, a very few, and began the anti-slavery movement." Parker predicted that war was the only way to settle the struggle between slavery and freedom. "We cannot have any settled and lasting harmony until one or the other of these ideas is cast out of the council of nations; so there must be war between them before there can be peace."

Patton, A. S. *An Occasional Discourse*. Utica, NY: Curtiss & White, 1865.

At the Tabernacle Baptist Church in Utica, Patton accused the South of secretly approving the assassination of Lincoln. "Tell me not that the leading men of the South disapprove of these acts. Tell me not that they mourn for the death of Lincoln — it is what they wished for, and their barbarous spirit led them to applaud the cowardly Brooks, so in their great secret souls they to-day approve the miscreant murderer Booth."

Peck, George. *Our Country: Its Trial and Triumph*. New York: Carlton and Porter, 1865.

This is a collection of fifteen sermons by a Methodist minister from Scranton, Pennsylvania, on various national themes from 1861 to 1865.

Perkins, A. E. P. *Thanksgiving Sermon*. Boston: T. R. Marvin and Sons, 1865.

At the East Congregational Church of Ware, Massachusetts, Perkins demanded that certain Southern political leaders never hold public office again. "The idea that such men as Breckenridge, Yulee, Benjamin, Hunter, Mason, Toombs, Slidell, and others like them, infamous for perjury and treason, should ever, by any possibility, appear in the halls of Congress, or upon the judicial bench, or should represent us in foreign courts, as they may do if they are restored to their full civil standing, is too great an outrage to every sentiment of decency and patriotism, ever for a moment to be entertained."

Perrin, Lavalette. *The Claims of Caesar.* Hartford: Case, Lockwood, and Co., 1861.

In a sermon at the Center Church of New Britain, Connecticut, on August 18, 1861, Perrin noted that Jesus opposed rebellion against a cruel Roman government, therefore, "how much is this true . . . when rulers are upright and the government is just? . . . Rebellion against it is the highest crime against God and society possible to man."

Pettes, Samuel, Jr. *The Preacher and the Hearer.* Lowell, MA: B. H. Penhallow, 1855.

The minister of the First Congregational Church in Billericia, Massachusetts, discussed whether slavery was an appropriate topic for a sermon. He concluded that it was.

Pharr, Walter W. *Funeral Sermon.* Salisbury, NC: J. J. Bruner, Printer, 1862.

This sermon was delivered on the death of Capt. A. K. Simonton of Statesville, North Carolina. It portrayed the hope of immortality and praised the departed as a man and a soldier.

Phelps, S. D. *National Symptoms.* New Haven: Thomas H. Pease, 1862.

Delivered at the First Baptist Church of New Haven on April 18, 1862, this sermon spoke of the positive traits that soldiering would bring to young men who enlisted for war. Camp life would instill a "hardier and stronger [people], both in physical endurance and in moral vigor." America had been "degenerating and becoming effeminate through luxury and ease." The returning soldiers would provide the nation with "moral and Christian heroes . . . stalwart influences . . . a purer and more stable Republicanism."

Pierce, George Foster. *Sermon.* Milledgeville, GA: Groughton, Nisbet, and Barnes, 1863.

This sermon by a Methodist bishop on March 27, 1863, before the General Assembly of Georgia, attempted to answer those who were skeptical about God's interest in the Confederate cause. Noting Southern victories on the battlefield, Pierce remarked: "The coincidence of these interventions with the prayer of the people have left no room for doubt, and have wrung from profane, even skeptical lips, the confession, God reigneth and God is for us and with us." The sermon drew a startling contrast between the wicked North and the God-fearing South. "We are fighting against robbery and lust and rapine; against ruthless invasion, a treacherous despotism, the blight of its own land, and the scorn of the world. . . . The triumph of our arms is the triumph of right and truth and justice. The defeat of our enemies is the defeat of wrong, malice and outrage." The South needed only to repent of its sins, one being the failure to allow Negroes to read, and all will be well.

————. *The Word of God a Nation's Life.* Augusta, GA: Office of the Constitutionalist, 1862.

This sermon was delivered before the Bible Convention of the Confederate States on March 19, 1862. Pierce noted that the Confederates "have not only dissolved the political ties which connected us to the Northern States, but have broken up our religious societies, our benevolent institutions, and thrown us upon new organizations to meet our responsibilities as a Christian people to the world around us." After outlining the characteristics of a godly society, Pierce urged repentance for Southern sins, especially greed.

Pierce, Henry Niles. "God Our Only Trust." *Sermons*. Mobile: Farrow and Dennett, 1861.

Pierce delivered this sermon on June 13, 1861, to his congregation at St. John's Episcopal Church in Mobile. He commented that the Confederate States only wanted peace but were being forced to fight. "Under these circumstances, we may confidently ask for God's blessing on our cause and look for his protection."

Pinckney, Charles Cotesworth. *Nebuchadnezzar's Fault and Fall*. Charleston: A. J. Burke, 1861.

This sermon was delivered at Grace Church in Charleston on February 17, 1861. Anticipating possible trouble, Pinckney was optimistic: "With that all pervading blessing to crown our work; with our acknowledged advantages, agriculture, commercial, social and religious, with a united people, walking in fear of the Lord, and the faith of the Gospel, we may expect to retain the favor of heaven."

Porter, Abner A. *Our Danger and Our Duty*. Charleston: Letter-Press of E. C. Councell, 1850.

This proslavery sermon was delivered on December 6, 1850, at the Glebe Street Presbyterian Church in Charleston.

Porter, Charles S. *Our Country's Danger and Security*. Utica: R. W. Roberts, 1844.

Concerned about the tearing apart of the American fabric, Porter urged his listeners to reject insurrectionary efforts (the abolitionist movement) which were a greater evil than slavery.

Porter, R. K. *Christian Duty in the Present Crisis*. Savannah: John M. Cooper, 1860.

After the election of Lincoln in November of 1860, Porter spoke of the need for Southern duty and defense against the aggressive, lustful North, which had departed from the truth of God.

Post, Henry. *A Sermon*. Albany, NY: Week, Parsons and Co., 1861.

At the Presbyterian Church in Warrenburgh, New York, on September 16, 1861, Post spoke of what it would mean if the Southern rebellion was a success: "We should sink to the level of the European nations: the hope of the world would turn into a nation too feeble, too inherently jealous, to preserve its high station. . . . The star of the western hemisphere would set amid lurid clouds, no more to rise."

Pratt, Nathaniel Alpheus. *Perils of a Dissolution of the Union.* Atlanta: C. R. Hanleiter & Co., 1856.

This sermon was delivered on November 20, 1856, at the Presbyterian Church of Roswell, Georgia.

Prentiss, George L. *The Free Christian State and the Present Struggle.* New York: W. H. Bidwell, 1861.

This professor at Union Seminary sought to demolish the Jeffersonian argument which would vindicate rebellion and secession, and spoke of the historical and religious necessity of one nation.

Quint, Alonzo. *Annual Election Sermon.* Boston: Wright & Potter, 1866.

Though the war was over, Quint warned that the "conflict of ideas" was not over and that "the doctrine of equal rights has still to be maintained against prejudice, pride, and a mistaken interest."

———. *Southern Chivalry and What the Nation Ought to Do with It.* New Bedford, MA: Mercury Job Press, 1865.

This sermon, delivered at the North Congregational Church in New Bedford on April 16, 1865, was one of the most vitriolic attacks leveled at the South by a Northern preacher. "Carry your perjuries to other shores; England is a good place for you. This land is sick of your presence. You are a stench in the nostrils of honest men. Go, Virginian descendants of transported convicts. Go, you who have lived by oppression and robbery. Never return. Your heritage is gone. Return, and the rope awaits your first step upon our shores. The land of convicted rebels should be taken." Exile, confiscation, and hanging summarized Quint's proposals for the South. Northern missionaries were needed to "Christianize" the South.

Randolf, Alfred MaGill. *Address on the Day of Fasting and Prayer.* Fredericksburg: Recorder Job Office, 1861.

The Episcopal Bishop of Southern Virginia, on June 13, 1861, at St. George's Church in Fredericksburg noted that the ungodly Union government might succeed for a time, but God was only raising it to a conspicuous position "in order to render more widely instructive the mockery of its triumph and the story of its fall."

Rankin, J. E. *The Battle Not Man's, but God's.* Lowell, MA: Stone and Huse, 1863.

Before the United Congregational Churches in Lowell, on August 6, 1863, Rankin emphasized that when the Emancipation Proclamation was issued, God took the war into his own hands and began to administer military defeat to the South.

———. *Moses and Joshua.* Boston: Dakin and Metcalf, 1865.

After the death of Lincoln this sermon, preached at the Winthrop Congregational Church in Charleston, Massachusetts, expressed grave mistrust of Southerners and asked for the law to take its course.

Raphall, M. J. "Bible View of Slavery." *Fast Day Sermons*. New York: Rudd
& Carleton, 1861.
This sermon was delivered at the Jewish Synagogue in New York City on
January 4, 1861. While admitting that he was no friend of slavery, Raphall
stated that there were biblical foundations for it. The slave code of Moses
affirmed slavery, and nowhere does the New Testament contradict or interfere with that code. Slavery was no sin, said Raphall, but there was a difference between Hebrew and heathen slavery. "The Bible view of slavery
derives from its divine source. The slave is a person in whom the dignity
of human nature is to be respected. Whereas, the heathen view of slavery
which prevailed at Rome, and which I am sorry to say, is adopted in the
South, reduces the slave to a thing, and a thing can have no rights." With
this consideration Raphall thought that there could be a meeting place
between the North and South in the slavery debate.

Raymond, H. R. *A Sermon*. Marion, AL: George C. Rogers, Printer, 1863.
This sermon was delivered on February 8, 1863, at the Presbyterian
Church of Marion, commemorating the death of David Y. Huntington,
"who fell on Manassa Plains," August 30, 1862. The discourse, published
by the soldier's parents, noted Huntington's valor and dedication. Raymond declared: "Too much honor can scarcely be accorded to those valor-
ous spirits who, at the call of their country and from patriotic devotion
to her rights and interests, have laid their lives upon the altar. . . . The
obligations of Christianity are superadded to those of patriotism. Every
citizen of this Confederacy should feel bound to do what he can for the
comfort of those whose lives are in daily jeopardy for our defense from
the ruthless invader."

Reed, Edward. *A People Saved by the Lord*. Charleston: Steam-Power Press
of Evans & Cogswell, 1861.
This sermon, early in the war, declared that God was on the side of the
Confederacy. "Unless the Lord has been on our side, they had swallowed us
up quick."

Rees, W. *A Sermon on Divine Providence*. Austin: Texas Almanac Office, 1863.
This sermon, delivered at the Methodist Church of Austin on February 4,
1863, declared: "Because His government is absolute, universal and eternal; therefore, if God be our friend and protector, individually and nationally, no calamity can befall us; but what will ultimate in greater
blessing, and higher good to us."

Renfroe, John J. D. *The Battle Is God's*. Richmond: Macfarlane & Fergusson, 1863.
This sermon, preached on August 21, 1863, before Wilcox's Brigade,
defended and upheld the leadership of Jefferson Davis. Renfroe was
disgusted by the slanderous abuse being "heaped upon the devoted head
of our noble President."

Rice, Daniel. *Harper's Ferry — Its Lessons*. Lafayette: Luse, 1860.
    The federal force used against John Brown at Harper's Ferry in 1859
    was evidence as to how proslavery the national government was.
Robinson, Charles S. *The Martyred President*. New York: J. F. Trowbridge,
    1865.
    This sermon, delivered at the First Presbyterian Church in Brooklyn, on
    April 16, 1865, asked for stern judgment upon the South following Lin-
    coln's death. He made the point that such judgment is not revenge, but
    retribution.
Robinson, James T. *National Anniversary Address*. North Adams, MA:
    W. H. Phillips, 1865.
    With the war at an end, Robinson commented: "The greatest conspiracy
    against the Free Institutions, and progress of mankind, is annihilated. . . .
    The great Republic, tried by fire . . . but terrible and glorious, ascends
    through smoke and flame to unending sway and splendor." Robinson
    was the pastor of the Baptist Church of North Adams.
Ruffner, W. H. *The Oath*. Lexington, VA: Gazette Office, 1864.
    This sermon, delivered on March 27, 1864, at the Presbyterian Church
    of Lexington, gave special attention to the oath of allegiance to the
    United States that many defeated Southerners were being compelled to
    take. "No one has a right to regard an oath lightly, or question its valid-
    ity, when taken under any circumstances. . . . There is but one course
    that is honest in itself, or that will keep the soul clear under the burning
    eye of God and that is to refuse it — yes, to refuse it, though a thousand
    bayonets were pointed at his breast."
Salter, William. *Our National Sins and Impending Calamities*. Burlington,
    IA: Hawk-Eye Book Office, 1861.
    The pastor of the First Congregational Church in Burlington commented
    that the sorrows which had befallen the nation were a judgment of God
    upon national evils: pride, intemperance, licentiousness, slavery exten-
    sion, and crimes against the freedom of speech and of the press.
Schmucker, S. S. *The Christian Pulpit, the Rightful Guardian of Morals, in
    Political No Less than in Private Life*. Gettysburg: H. C. Neinstedt, 1846.
    This sermon declares that the pulpit has a responsibility to shape the
    moral and political directions of society. This included the abolition of
    slavery.
Shannon, James. *On Domestic Slavery, as Examined in the Light of Scrip-
    ture, of Natural Rights of Civil Government, and the Constitutional
    Power of Congress*. St. Louis: Republican Book and Job Office, 1855.
    This proslavery sermon was delivered before the Proslavery Convention
    of the State of Missouri in Lexington, Kentucky, on July 13, 1855.
Sherwood, Adiel. *Suffering Disciples Rejoicing in Persecution*. Atlanta: Frank-
    lin Printing House, Wood, Hanleiter, Rice & Co., 1861.
    This was the introductory discourse before the Georgia Baptist Conven-

tion at Americus in April of 1858. The discourse claimed that religion
never flourished more than when faced with persecution and suffering.
Suffering is a sign of Christian devotion and usefulness. To suffer in and
for the name of Christ, however, is to ultimately reign and rule with Christ.

Simpson, Matthew, and others. *Our Martyr President, Abraham Lincoln:
Voices from the Pulpit of New York and Brooklyn.* New York: Tibbals
& Whiting, 1865.
This is a collection of sermons preached in New York City upon the
assassination of Lincoln. Many of the sermons recommend a harsh recon-
struction of the South as a response to Lincoln's death.

Slaughter, Philip. *Coercion and Conciliation.* Richmond: Macfarlane & Fergusson, n.d.
This sermon was preached in a military camp near Centerville, Virginia,
by the chaplain. "Our duty as Christians is equally clear upon general
principles. . . . While the Scriptures recognize government as a divine institution . . . they tell us in the same breath that *legitimate* rulers are
the 'ministers of God' for good. . . . Hence, when governments become a
'terror to the good,' and 'a praise to the evil,' they cease to be legitimate . . .
and it becomes the right of people to abolish them, and to institute in
their place such new governments as shall seem most likely to effect
their safety and happiness."

Sledd, Robert Newton. *A Sermon.* Petersburg, VA: A. F. Crutchfield and Co.,
1861.
At the Market Street Methodist Church in Petersburg, on September 22,
1861, this sermon was delivered to the Confederate Cadets on their departure for the battlefields. "We fight for our people. The avowed purpose of our enemies is subjugation, the extinction of liberty in our land:
an end which they profess to be resolved to accomplish though it bring
desolution to every home and baptize every foot of southern soil in fire
and blood: a purpose which savors more of the heartlessness of an Alexander or the barbarity of an Attila than of the civilization of the nineteenth century."

Smith, Henry. *God in the War.* Buffalo: Wheeler, Matthews, and Warren, 1863.
The hour for easy repentance was past. "The streams have been turned
to pitch and the dust into brimstone. God is treading the wine press
alone. . . . For the day of vengeance is in his heart."

Smith, Henry B. "Sermon XXI." *Our Martyr President, Abraham Lincoln.
Voices from the Pulpit of New York and Brooklyn.* New York: Tibbals
& Whiting, 1865.
Smith advocated a peace plan that called for elimination of the Southern caste system and the introduction of Northern schools, churches,
and institutions of philanthropy into the South. "Especially must we
use all means to raise up the class of freedmen to the dignity and responsibilities of their new positions, as men and as citizens."

Smith, Henry J. *A Sermon*. Greensboro, VA: James W. Albright, 1862.
  On December 5, 1861, at the Presbyterian Church of Greensboro, Smith
  listed eight matters for which the state of Virginia could give thanks:
  (1) religious advantages, (2) the conservation and steady principles for
  which the state was known, (3) the good and large land which God had
  given to the state, (4) the educational and literary institutions, (5) the
  exemption from sufferings the state had experienced, especially in comparison to several other Confederate states, (6) the unity and harmony
  which existed in the state, (7) the spirit of prayer and humility which
  characterized the state during the separation from the Union, and (8)
  that God had shown his favor in the contest being waged.
Smith, Moses. *God's Honor Man's Ultimate Success*. New Haven: Thomas
  J. Stafford, 1863.
  On September 27, 1863, speaking in Plainville, Connecticut, Smith de-
  clared what the North must do in the South once victory was achieved:
  "The whole South must be supplied with the Bible – the unmitigated
  Bible. . . . The churches and Sabbath schools must bless that land of
  darkness."
Smith, Whitefoord. *God, the Refuge of His People*. Columbia, SC: A. S. John-
  ston, 1850.
  A proslavery sermon delivered before the General Assembly of South
  Carolina on December 6, 1850.
Smyth, Thomas. *The Battle of Fort Sumter: Its Mystery and Miracle: God's
  Mystery and Mercy*. Columbia, SC: Southern Guardian Steam-Power
  Press, 1861.
  In this sermon, delivered at the First Presbyterian Church of Charleston
  on December 5, 1861, Smyth declared that the South has been given
  "the high and holy keeping, above all conservators, of the Bible." The
  sermon made a strong indictment of the Lincoln administration.
Spear, Samuel T. *The Law-Abiding Conscience, and the Higher Law Conscience; with Remarks on the Fugitive Slave Question*. New York: Lambert and Lane, 1850.
  In Brooklyn, Spear, in speaking of the Fugitive Slave Law, asked for lawful measures to correct this unjust legislation. However, man was called
  to obey God's law above the law of man, even if that led him to actions
  for which he must suffer civil consequences.
———. "Sermon XVI." *Our Martyr President, Abraham Lincoln. Voices
  from the Pulpit of New York and Brooklyn*. New York: Tibbals & Whiting, 1865.
  In this sermon following the death of Lincoln, Spear condemned Robert E.
  Lee. "General Lee . . . is a traitor to his country and who richly deserves
  to be hung for his crimes."
———. *The Nation's Blessing in Trial*. Brooklyn: Wm. W. Rose, 1862.
  At the South Presbyterian Church in Brooklyn, Spear declared that the

war would result in the United States being recognized as a great military power, a "first class nation, whose ability to defend its rights will protect it against injury."

———. *Two Sermons for the Times.* New York: Nathan Lane and Co., 1861. A people have no right to revolutionize the political order. To do so would make "government nothing but a rope of sand. . . . If any portion of the people insist upon trying the question of force under the revolutionary right, the Government must insist upon trying the same question under the high, solemn, and majestic attributes of divine sovereignty."

Spencer, Ichabod Smith. *Fugitive Slave Law: The Religious Duty of Obedience to Law.* New York: M. W. Dodd, 1850. This sermon, delivered on November 24, 1850, in the Second Presbyterian Church of Brooklyn, emphasized the Christian responsibility to obey the Fugitive Slave Law. This was a very different stance than the one taken by most Northern ministers.

Sprague, William B. *Glorifying God in the Fires.* Albany, NY: C. Van Benthuysen, 1861. On November 28, 1861, at the Second Presbyterian Church of Albany, Sprague shared an apocalyptic vision of what a Northern victory would mean: "a flood of millennial glory" and "the great Thanksgiving Day of the world."

Spring, Gardiner. *The Danger and Hope of the American People.* New York: John F. Trow, 1843. As sectional differences and tensions increased, this sermon urged a common respect of and loyalty to the U.S. Constitution. Spring declared that this commonality would bind all Americans together.

———. *State Thanksgiving during the Rebellion.* New York: Harper & Bros., 1862. On November 28, 1861, at the New York City Brick Presbyterian Church, Spring told of how Southern actions and attitudes turned him from conciliation to strong opposition. "When the first indications of this conflict made their appearance, all my prepossessions, as is well known, were with the Southern states. . . . But when I hear so few kind words . . . when crafty politicians . . . blind and enslave the minds of people . . . when I learn that secession was preconcerted and determined in years gone by, . . . when I see these things my convictions are strong that we have reached the limit beyond which forbearance may not be extended."

Stearns, William A. *Necessities of the War and the Conditions of Success in It.* Amherst, MA: Henry A. March, 1861. The president of Amherst College spoke of how terrible it would be if the South was successful. "Are we to be broken down for our sins, and our free institutions become a hissing and a by-word over all the earth? . . . Or is there yet a great future before us, and is God leading us across the Red Sea of blood, that he may fit us, by suffering for prosperity?"

Steele, John. *The Substance of an Address*. Washington, OH: Hamilton Robb, 1830.

This sermon was delivered before the Associate Reformed Synod of the West in Steubenville on October 16, 1829. The question before the meeting was communion and slaveholders. Steele argued that slavery was a blameless institution and that there was no conflict between slavery and Christianity.

Stiles, Joseph Clay. *National Rectitude the Only True Basis of National Prosperity: An Appeal to the Confederate States*. Petersburg, VA: Evangelical Tract Society, 1863.

This sermon was a fiery declaration that God would yet bring Confederate victory in spite of recent battlefield reversals. "Oh, how far you live from the light! Why, let the North march out her million men on the left, and array upon the right all the veteran troops of England, France, Russia and Austria; and bring up the very gates of hell in all their strength to compose the center of her grand invading army. What then? Why, everything in God and from God assures us that these Confederate States would hear a voice from heaven: 'The battle is not yours, but mine. Stand ye still and see the salvation of the Lord!'" Stiles denounced extortioners who "churned up an egregious yearning of the bowels after filthy lucre," which greatly hurt the Confederate cause.

Stone, A. L. *The Divineness of Human Government*. Boston: Henry Hoyt, 1861.

Delivered in Boston's Park Street Church, this sermon said that if the Southern rebellion should succeed, all legitimate authority would break down in America, forcing Americans "back from friendships and brotherhoods and all alliances, to the instincts of the forest brute." The sermon urged its listeners to "strike for Law and Union, for country and God's great ordinance of Government."

――――. *Emancipation*. Boston: Henry Hoyt, 1862.

This sermon, delivered at the Park Street Church in Boston on April 3, 1862, declared that the nation needed a renewed interest in the Old Testament, especially that prophetical concept of the Lord as an avenging God.

――――. *The War and the Patriot's Duty*. Boston: Henry Hoyt, 1861.

In a sermon delivered on the Sunday following the fall of Fort Sumter, April 21, 1861, at the Park Street Church in Boston, Stone stated the cause and purpose of the war as he saw it. "It is not an anti-slavery war we wage; not a sectional war; not a war of conquest and subjugation; it is simply and solely a war for the maintenance of the government and the Constitution." He further declared: "If war is a duty, it is a Christian duty, as sacred as prayer, – as solemn as sacraments."

Summers, Thomas Osmond. *Christian Patriotism*. Charleston: C. Canning, 1850.

This proslavery sermon was delivered at the Cumberland Street Methodist Church of Charleston on December 6, 1850. Summers emphasized the importance of obeying the laws of the nation.

Sunderland, Byron. *The Crisis of the Times*. Washington: National Banner Press, 1863.

This sermon, delivered at the First Presbyterian Church in Washington on April 30, 1863, expressed deep pessimism as to when the war would end. This was a prevalent attitude in the North and South at this time. "The day of peace is gone from us; God only knows when, or if ever, it may return to this generation."

Swain, Leonard. *A Nation's Sorrow*. Providence: n.p., 1865.

This sermon by the pastor of the Central Congregational Church in Providence declared that the assassination of Lincoln united the North in demanding harsh reconstruction terms upon the South following the war. He advised stern punishments for the leaders of the Confederacy and mercy for the masses.

Sweetser, Seth. *A Commemorative Discourse on the Death of Abraham Lincoln*. Boston: John Walson & Son, 1865.

This sermon by a Boston Congregationalist demanded a stern justice to be imposed upon the South following Lincoln's assassination.

Thompson, A. C. *Military Success from God*. Boston: T. R. Marvin and Son, 1862.

This minister from Roxbury, Massachusetts, used the following text to explain why God was allowing Northern military defeats in the early part of the Civil War. "If ye forsake him, he will forsake you."

Thompson, Joseph P. "Abraham Lincoln, His Life and Its Lessons." *Our Martyr President, Abraham Lincoln. Voices from the Pulpit of New York and Brooklyn*. New York: Tibbals & Whiting, 1865.

In a sermon delivered at the Broadway Tabernacle Church (Congregational) in New York City, shortly after Lincoln's assassination, Thompson declared that traitors must be hung in a spirit of calm justice. "There can be no doubt that the leading traitors deserve to forfeit their lives for their crime. . . . We must be careful to keep our hands clean of even the imputation of a passionate revenge."

————. *Our National Crimes and Follies*. New York: Thos. Holman, 1861.

This sermon, delivered in New York City, traced the pulpit warnings on slavery over the previous few years and declared that the coming peril had been foretold through preaching.

————. *The Psalter and the Sword*. New York: L. S. Harrison, 1863.

At the Broadway Tabernacle Church in New York, on November 7, 1862, Thompson gave thanks for the Emancipation Proclamation and what it would mean. "The Proclamation of Emancipation has challenged all the powers of darkness to defeat it. . . . We cannot be dismayed. We will still march on with the psalter in our hand; for soon the seventh angel shall pour out his vial into the air, and there shall come a great voice out of the temple of heaven, from the throne, saying, IT IS DONE."

Thompson, M. L. P. *Discourses*. Cincinnati: Gazette Company, 1861.
  These sermons, delivered at the Second Presbyterian Church of Cincinnati on September 26 and November 28 of 1861, declared that the nation was being punished for allowing slavery to exist for such a long
  time. We "left in the heart of our land the very flail with which he is now
  threshing us."
Thornwell, James H. "Our National Sins." *Fast Day Sermons*. New York:
  Rudd & Carleton, 1861.
  On November 21, 1860, this eminent Presbyterian from South Carolina
  accused the Union government of an unconstitutional usurpation of
  power. Lincoln had recently been elected to the presidency, and Thornwell called for secession even though "our path to victory may be through
  a baptism of blood. . . . It does not follow, even if she [the South] should
  be destined to fall, that her course was wrong, or her sufferings in vain."
————. *The Rights and the Duties of Masters*. Charleston: Steam Power
  Press of Walker and James, 1850.
  An early Southern sermon whose main thesis was a defense of slavery.
  The sermon was preached at the dedication of a church erected in Charleston for the benefit and instruction of the slave population.
Tichenor, Isaac Taylor. *Fast Day Sermon*. Montgomery: Montgomery Adver-
  tiser Book and Job Printing Office, 1863.
  In the midst of the Civil War when the tide of battle was beginning to
  turn against the South, Tichenor, pastor of the First Baptist Church in
  Montgomery, assured the General Assembly of the State of Alabama
  that God would even yet vindicate the Confederacy. He defended the institution of slavery but noted that the abuse of slavery was a reason for
  the South's present reversals upon the battlefield.
Tracy, Joseph. *Natural Equality*. Windsor, VT: Chronicle Press, 1833.
  This sermon, delivered before the Vermont Colonization Society on October 17, 1833, was one of the very early attacks on the abolition
  movement.
Trumbull, H. Clay. *Desireableness of Active Service*. Hartford: Case, Lockwood, 1864.
  This sermon declared what a noble and high honor it was to fight and
  even die for one's country.
————. *Good News*. Hartford: Case, Lockwood, 1864.
  This sermon was given in commemoration of the reenlistment of the
  10th Regiment of Connecticut. Trumbull declared: "You have filled well
  your place and performed fully your part, and in nothing have you done
  more to benefit your country than in this noble, new enlistment."
Tucker, Henry H. *God in the War*. Milledgeville, GA: Boughton, Nisbet &
  Barnes, State Printers, 1861.
  Tucker, who was professor of belles lettres at Mercer University, delivered this address before the Georgia Legislature on November 15, 1861.

He emphasized: "God is in the war. He brought it upon us." God often used the wicked for his purposes: "Thus, the guilt of those who wage this diabolical war on the unoffending people of the Confederate States, finds no apology in the providence of God."

Tucker, Joel W. *God Sovereign and Man Free*. Fayetteville, NC: Presbyterian Office, 1862.
Tucker empahsized that every Confederate victory was a sign that Southerners were God's chosen people, and every Confederate defeat was a punishment of sins. Thus, when the battle does not go well for the South: "If the people . . . were to turn with one heart and one mind to the Lord . . . He would drive the invaders from our territories. . . . He can turn them as he turns the rivers of water."

————. *God's Providence in War*. Fayetteville, NC: Presbyterian Office, 1862.
Tucker declared that God ordained the Civil War in spite of human efforts to prevent it.

————. *The Guilt and Punishment of Extortion*. Fayetteville, NC: Presbyterian Office, 1862.
This sermon, delivered on September 7, 1862, denounced the hoarding of consumer goods and profiteering in the South.

Tupper, Henry Allen. *A Thanksgiving Discourse*. Macon, GA: Burke, Boykin & Co., 1862.
On September 18, 1862, at the Baptist Church of Washington, Georgia, Tupper offered thanks that the South had "been delivered from the unnatural and destructive alliance, though it be at the necessary expense of this terrible war." God had led the South into the war and "the mercies of the past should only encourage us to implore further and greater favors." The sermon was a strong attack upon the federal government and declared the necessity of separating from it. "Separation was necessary to salvation, and war to final separation. Hence, the Lord, who would deliver us from the snare, led providentially and imperceptibly into war." The sermon goes on to account for God's favor upon the Confederate armies at the time.

Van Dyke, Henry J. "The Character and Influence of Abolitionism." *Fast Day Sermons*. New York: Rudd & Carleton, 1861.
On December 9, 1860, at the First Presbyterian Church of Brooklyn, Van Dyke delivered a strong denunciation of abolitionism. "This tree of Abolitionism is evil, and only evil—root and branch, flower and leaf, and fruit." Van Dyke built his theme upon four premises. (1) Abolitionism has no foundation in the Scriptures. (2) Its principles have been promulgated chiefly by misrepresentation and abuse. (3) It leads in multiples of cases and by a logical process, to utter infidelity. (4) It is the chief cause of the strife that agitates, and the danger that threatens our country.

————. *The Spirituality and Independence of the Church*. New York: n.p., 1864.

Van Dyke, a Peace Democrat and apologist for slavery, rejected the idea that the Emancipation Proclamation was evidence of the divine indictment of slavery. He also rejected the thought that the war was an apocalyptic struggle to help the United States carry out a divine mission. "I do not believe, but reject as blasphemous, the sentiment so often uttered by Christian ministers, that God cannot do without the United States, that the Church of Christ is in anywise identified with or dependent upon the national existence."

Vedder, C. S. *Offer unto God Thanksgiving*. Charleston: Evans & Cogswell, 1861.
On July 28, 1861, at the Summerville Presbyterian Church in South Carolina, Vedder spoke of early Confederate military victories and exclaimed: "It is God alone who has fought our battles."

Vernor, W. H. *A Sermon*. Lewisburg, TN: Southern Messenger Office, 1861.
This sermon was delivered before the Marshall Guards No. 1 at the Presbyterian Church at Lewisburg on May 5, 1861. It is a strong defense of slavery, which the preacher declared was central to the Confederate cause.

Vincent, Marvin R. *The Lord of War and of Righteousness*. Troy, NY: A. W. Scribner, 1864.
This sermon was delivered on November 24, 1864, at the First Presbyterian Church of Troy. As victory drew near, Vincent reaffirmed that God had caused the war because of the "great national sin" of slavery.

———. *Our National Discipline*. Troy, NY: A. W. Scribner, 1863.
This Thanksgiving sermon was delivered at the First Presbyterian Church of Troy on November 26, 1863. It declared that judgment had come upon the nation because of its unbridled search for profit, which had turned personal liberty into "wild and brutal license which has brought us well nigh to the brink of anarchy."

———. *A Sermon on the Assassination of Abraham Lincoln*. Troy, NY: A. W. Scribner, 1865.
On April 23, 1865, at the First Presbyterian Church in Troy, Vincent called for harsh judgment upon the South following the death of Lincoln. "I call upon the government to put in force against these leading traitors the penalty of the law. And I would their gibbet were so high that every man North and South might see it happen from his housetop, and learn as he looks that treason is not safe for the perpetrator."

Vinton, Alexander H. *Man's Rule and Christ's Reign*. New York: John A. Gray, 1862.
This sermon was delivered on November 27, 1862, at St. Mark's Church in New York City. The preacher blamed early Union defeats upon the North's turning away from God and "profane self-conceit." The rector claimed that "our disasters may be God's method of delay, to bring us more into felt dependence on Him, and so much in harmony with His plans."

————. *The Mistakes of the Rebellion*. New York: George F. Nesbitt, 1863.
This Episcopal rector in New York City delivered a sermon that was a
stinging attack upon Southern character.

Vinton, Francis. "Irreligion, Corruption and Fanaticism Rebuked." *Fast Day
Sermons*. New York: Rudd & Carleton, 1861.
This sermon, delivered in Trinity Church of New York City on January 4,
1861, sought a mediating course in the slavery debate. Vinton declared
that the Bible does uphold slavery, but the South had abused the institution in several ways. He sought to bring about a reconciliation between
North and South by asking both sides to close their ears and hearts to
the voices of extremism and fanaticism. "In the extremes of abolitionism and propagandism, slavery is distorted."

Wadsworth, Charles. *War a Discipline*. San Francisco: H. H. Bancroft and
Company, 1864.
On November 24, 1864, at Calvary Church in San Francisco, Wadsworth
declared that God and God alone brings victory. "We are learning . . .
that our national salvation depends neither upon political sagacity, nor
military strength, but solely on the protection of that great Arm that
ruleth in Zion."

Walker, George Leon. *The Offered National Regeneration*. Portland, ME:
Advertiser Office, 1861.
At the State Street Congregational Church of Portland, on September 21,
1861, with the Civil War in its very early stages, Walker declared that
slavery, "the great sin of human oppression is at length disclosed as the
sin of sins cleaving to the national soul." Walker asked: "What will you
do, O American empire, about this sin of thy soul? Will you submit to
it? Will you be ruined by it? Or will you repent of it and put it away?"

Watson, Alfred A. *Sermon Delivered Before the Annual Council of the Diocese
of North Carolina*. Raleigh: Progress Print, 1863.
Delivered on May 14, 1863, this sermon was a strong defense of the
Confederate cause and the Church's, especially the Episcopal Church's,
relationship to it. The sermon defended slavery and castigated abolitionism. It stated that many churches in the North – again, especially Episcopal churches – were sympathetic to the Confederate cause, though
there were some churches which sided with radical abolitionism.

Webb, Edwin. *Memorial Sermons*. Boston: Geo. C. Rand and Avery, 1865.
This is a collection of three sermons that were delivered toward the end
of the war by the pastor of Shamut Church in Boston. The first sermon's
theme has to do with the Union capture of Richmond; the second re-
views the results of the war; and the third comments upon the assassination of President Lincoln.

Weiss, John. *Northern Strength and Weakness*. Boston: Walker, Wise and
Company, 1863.
A major theme of this sermon, delivered at Watertown, Massachusetts,

on April 30, 1863, was that God was punishing the nation for the sins of slavery and hatred of black people. "The sin of fifty years [slavery] rose up wrathfully, and held its poisoned cup to the trembling lips of the country."

Wentworth, J. B. *A Discourse on the Death of Abraham Lincoln*. Buffalo: Matthews and Warren, 1865.

This sermon, delivered by the pastor of St. Mark's Methodist Episcopal Church in Buffalo, demanded swift and severe punishment upon the South following Lincoln's assassination. Of Robert E. Lee he said: "The greater his talents, the greater his guilt."

West, Nathaniel, Jr. *Establishment in National Righteousness*. New York: John F. Trow, 1861.

Delivered at the Second Presbyterian Church in Brooklyn, this sermon emphasized that when the war was over, God would commission the United States to be "a national Israel and servant of the Lord, fit for the Master's use." Though several groups might contribute to the rebuilding of national life after the war, the leadership would be given by the "bold, energetic Anglo-Saxon race predominating vastly over the rest."

Wheelwright, William H. *A Discourse*. Richmond: Chas. H. Wynne, 1862.

This sermon was delivered to the troops stationed at Gloucester Point, Virginia, on February 28, 1862. It spoke of the sins which had damaged the Confederate cause in recent months. "Self-seeking has cursed our cause for the past six months. . . . Grosser sins have been on the increase, especially in our army – Profanity, Drunkenness, Gaming." He urged his listeners to learn from these past sins, repent, and press on to victory. "Our future well-being may demand that our suffering be great and protracted; that our baptism be of fire and blood; that our cup be of wormwood and gall. Let us not shrink from that baptism, nor put from us the cup; never admit the thought of submission to our foe. All that makes life desirable is at stake: our property, the welfare of our wives, children, and servants; our existence as a free, independent people."

Wightman, John T. *The Glory of God, the Defense of the South*. Charleston: Steam-Power Press of Evans & Cogswell, 1861.

This sermon was delivered on July 28, 1861 – a day set apart for thanksgiving for the victory at Manassas – at the Methodist Church of Yorkville, South Carolina. Affirming that "Cotton is King," Wightman declared that the South was the economic balance of the world. Furthermore, "the cotton trade keeps the Bible and the press under the control of Protestantism." After a strong biblical defense of slavery, the preacher testified that the victories at Manassas and Fort Sumter, in the face of overwhelming numbers and power, proved that God favored and would bring to victory the Confederate cause.

Wilmer, Richard H. *Future Good – The Explanation of Present Reverses*.

Charlotte, NC: Protestant Episcopal Church Publishing Association, 1864.

The Bishop of Alabama preached at several places throughout Alabama during the spring of 1864. His constant theme was the theme of this sermon. Though the present military reverses were causing many to lose heart throughout the South, Wilson contended that they were "a part of our discipline . . . a part of our heritage." He compared the present days to the dark days of the American Revolution, before victory was achieved. God would bring victory to the Confederacy "in His own good time." Meanwhile, "to die for one's country is becoming beautiful."

Wilson, Edmund B. *Reasons For Thanksgiving*. Salem, MA: Observer, 1862.

On April 20, 1862, this Unitarian minister, at the North Church in Salem, spoke of the unity that the attack upon Fort Sumter brought about in the North to prevent secession. "One week before all was uncertainty; there was apathy, doubt, gloom. . . . [Now] we are one people." The North was one people committed to preserving the Union by force of arms.

Wilson, James P. *Our National Fast*. Newark: A Stephen Holbrook, 1861.

This sermon, delivered at the South Park Presbyterian Church of Newark on January 4, 1861, spoke of the danger of too much democracy, whereby legislators vote according to the various whims of the people. The political order should be viewed as a "united family" or a "vast paternity" in which government officials justly demand the citizens' obedience as a father over his family. Democracy does not mean popular rule, but it is a process by which rulers are invested with authority.

Wilson, Joseph Ruggles. *Mutual Relations of Masters and Slaves as Taught in the Bible*. Augusta, GA: Steam Power Press of Chronicle and Sentinel, 1861.

At the First Presbyterian Church of Augusta, on January 1, 1861, Wilson projected a millennialistic view of the future. He looked to a time "when that welcome day shall dawn, whose light will reveal a world covered by righteousness." A prominent feature of this welcome day would be "the institution of domestic slavery, freed from its stupid servility on the one side and its excesses of neglect and severity on the other." It would be a time acclaimed by all as a blessing to both masters and slaves.

Wilson, Joshua A. *Relations and Duties of Servants and Masters*. Cincinnati: Hefley, 1839.

Through this sermon Wilson sought a mediating position. He declared that Christians could not interfere with civil institutions which were legally established. They could, however, change laws by the will of the people expressed constitutionally.

Wilson, Samuel Ramsey. *The Causes and Remedies of Impending National Calamities*. Cincinnati: J. B. Elliott, 1860.

This is a proslavery sermon by the pastor of the First Presbyterian Church in Cincinnati.

Winkler, Edwin Theodore. *Duties of the Christian Soldier.* Charleston: A. J. Burke, 1861.

This sermon, delivered on January 6, 1861, just prior to the Civil War, speaks of those qualities that make for a good soldier.

Winn, T. S. *The Great Victory at Manassas Junction; God, the Arbiter of Battles.* Tuscaloosa, AL: J. F. Warren, at the Observer Office, 1861.

This sermon, preached at the Presbyterian Church in Concord, Alabama, on July 28, 1861, equated the North with the Philistines in the Old Testament and the South with the Hebrews or Jews. The victory at Manassas was compared to David slaying the giant Goliath. As the sermon drew to a close, the preacher reminded his audience: "We meet here as Christians and as patriots . . . not to abuse our enemies, not to exult over their loss, not to boast of our own valor, but to give thanks to Almighty God for the great victory which He, and He alone, has enabled us to achieve. . . . The whole work, from the beginning to the end, was the work of God."

Woodson, Carter Godwin. *Negro Orators and Their Orations.* Washington: Associated Publishers, 1925.

This volume contains a number of pre–Civil War sermons by black ministers from the North who protested against slavery in the South and discrimination in the North.

OTHER WORKS

Adams, Nehemiah. *A South-Side View of Slavery.* Boston: T. R. Marvin, 1855.

Ahlstrom, Sydney E. *A Religious History of the American People.* New Haven: Yale University Press, 1972.

Barnes, Gilbert H. *The Antislavery Impulse 1830–1844.* Introduction by William G. McLoughlin. 1933; New York: Harcourt Brace, 1964.

Barnes, Gilbert H., and Dwight L. Dumond, eds. *Letters of Theodore Dwight Weld, Angelina Grimke Weld, and Sarah Grimke.* 2 vols. New York: Appleton-Century, 1934.

Bartlett, Irving H. *The American Mind in the Mid-Nineteenth Century.* 2nd ed. Arlington Heights, IL: Harlan Davidson, 1982.

Bellah, Robert N. "Civil Religion in America." *Daedalus* 96 (Winter 1967): 1–21.

Beringer, Richard E., Herman Hattaway, Archer Jones, and William N. Stills, Jr. *Why the South Lost the Civil War.* Athens: University of Georgia Press, 1986.

Billington, Monroe L. *The American South: A Brief History.* New York: Scribner's, 1974.

Brigance, William Norwood, ed. *A History and Criticism of American Public Address*. 2 vols. New York: Russell & Russell, 1960.

Brownlow, Paul C. "The Northern Protestant Pulpit and Andrew Johnson." *The Southern Speech Communication Journal* 39 (Spring 1974): 248–59.

Calhoon, Robert M. *Evangelicals and Conservatives in the Early South, 1740–1861*. Columbia: University of South Carolina Press, 1988.

Calhoun, John C. *A Disquisition on Government and Selections from the Discourse*. Ed. Gordon Post. Indianapolis: Bobbs Merrill, 1953.

Cheesebro, Roy A. "The Preaching of Charles G. Finney." Ph.D. dissertation, Yale University, 1948.

Chestnut, Mary Boykin. *A Diary from Dixie*. Foreword by Edmund Wilson; edited by Ben Ames Williams. Cambridge: Harvard University Press, 1980.

Christy, David. *Pulpit Politics: Ecclesiastical Legislation on Slavery and Its Disturbing Influences on American Union*. 1862; New York: Negro Universities Press, 1969.

Cole, Charles C., Jr. "Horace Bushnell and the Slavery Question." *New England Quarterly* 23 (March 1950): 19–30.

———. *The Social Ideas of the Northern Evangelicals, 1826–1860*. 1954; New York: Octagon Books, 1966.

Commager, Henry Steele. *Theodore Parker: Yankee Crusader*. Boston: Beacon Press, 1960.

Craven, Avery O. *Civil War in the Making 1815–1860*. Baton Rouge: Louisiana State University Press, 1959.

Dennard, David Charles. "Religion in the Quarters: A Study of Slave Preachers in the Antebellum South." Ph.D. dissertation, Northwestern University, 1983.

DesChamps, Margaret B. "Benjamin Morgan Palmer, Orator-Preacher of the Confederacy." *Southern Speech Journal* 19 (Sept. 1953): 14–22.

Dunham, Chester Forrester. *The Attitude of the Northern Clergy Toward the South 1860–1865*. Philadelphia: Porcupine Press, 1974.

Emmel, James Robert. "The Persuasive Techniques of Charles Grandison Finney as a Revivalist and Social Reform Speaker, 1820–1860." Ph.D. dissertation, Pennsylvania State University, 1959.

Finney, Charles G. *Lectures on Revivals of Religion*. Ed. William G. McLoughlin. Cambridge: Belknap Press, 1960.

———. *Lectures on Systematic Theology*. 1846–47, rev. 1878; Grand Rapids: Eerdman's, 1964.

Ford, Lacy K. "Republican Ideology in a Slave Society: The Political Economy of John C. Calhoun." *The Journal of Southern History* 54 (Aug. 1988): 405–24.

Fordham, Monroe. *Major Themes in Northern Black Religious Thought, 1800–1860*. Hicksville, NY: Exposition Press, 1975.

Frederickson, George M. *The Inner Civil War: Northern Intellectuals and the Crisis of the Union*. New York: Harper, 1965.

Fuller, Richard, and Francis Wayland. *Domestic Slavery Considered as a Scriptural Institution*. New York: Lewis Colby, 1845.

Goen, C. C. *Broken Churches, Broken Nation*. Macon: Mercer University Press, 1985.

Handy, Robert T. *A History of the Churches in the United States and Canada*. New York: Oxford University Press, 1970.

Hardman, Keith J. *Charles Grandison Finney, 1792–1875, Revivalist and Reformer*. Syracuse: Syracuse University Press, 1987.

Hepworth, George H. *The Whip, Hoe and Sword*. 1864; Freeport, NY: Books for Libraries Press, 1971.

Hibben, Paxton. *Henry Ward Beecher: An American Portrait*. Foreword by Sinclair Lewis. 1942; New York: Beekman, 1974.

Holland, Dewitte, ed. *Preaching in American History*. Nashville: Abingdon Press, 1969.

Hopkins, John Henry. *View of Slavery*. New York: W. I. Pooley, 1864.

Howe, Daniel Walker. "Religion and Politics in the Antebellum North." *Religion and American Politics*. Ed. Mark A. Noll. New York: Oxford University Press, 1990. 121–45.

Hudson, Winthrop S. *Religion in America*. 3rd ed. New York: Scribner's, 1981.

Johnson, Thomas Cary. *The Life and Letters of Benjamin Morgan Palmer*. Richmond: Presbyterian Committee of Publication, 1906.

Jones, Charles Colcock. *A Catechism of Scripture, Doctrine, and Practice, for Families and Sabbath Schools, Designed Also for the Oral Instruction of Colored Persons*. Savannah: Thomas Purse, 1837.

———. *Religious Instruction of the Negroes in the United States*. Savannah: Thomas Purse, 1842.

Linder, Robert D. "Civil Religion." *Dictionary of Christianity in America*. Ed. Daniel Reid. Downers Grove, IL: InterVarsity Press, 1990.

Litwack, Leon F. *Been in the Storm So Long*. New York: Vintage, 1980.

Loveland, Anne C. *Southern Evangelicals and the Social Order 1800–1860*. Baton Rouge: Louisiana State University Press, 1980.

McKivigan, John R. *The War Against Proslavery Religion: Abolitionism and the Northern Churches, 1830–1865*. Ithaca: Cornell University Press, 1984.

McLoughlin, William G. *Modern Revivalism: Charles Grandison Finney to Billy Graham*. New York: Ronald Press, 1959.

———. *The Meaning of Henry Ward Beecher*. New York: Knopf, 1970.

McLoughlin, William G., and Robert Bellah. *Religion in America*. Boston: Beacon Press, 1968.

McPherson, James M. *Battle Cry of Freedom*. New York: Oxford University Press, 1988.

Maddex, Jack P., Jr. "Proslavery Millennialism: Social Eschatology in Antebellum Southern Calvinism." *American Quarterly* 31 (Spring 1979): 46–62.

Mathews, Donald G. "Charles Colcock Jones and the Southern Evangelical

Crusade to Form a Biracial Community." *The Journal of Southern History* 41 (Aug. 1975): 299–320.

———. *Religion in the Old South*. Chicago: University of Chicago Press, 1977.

Minutes of the Bethel Baptist Association, Oct. 31, 1863. Macon: Burke, Boykin & Co., 1863.

Minutes of the Forty-fifth Anniversary of the Cahaba Baptist Association, Oct. 18–20, 1862. Marion, GA: George C. Rogers, Printers, 1862.

Minutes of the One Hundredth and Thirteenth Session of the Charleston Baptist Association, Nov. 5–8, 1864. Camden, SC: W. K. Rogers Book and Job Printers, 1864.

Minutes of the One Hundredth and Twelfth Session of the Charleston Baptist Association, Oct. 31 to Nov. 2, 1863. Camden: W. K. Rogers Book and Job Printers, 1864.

Minutes of the Twenty-fifth Anniversary of the Chickasaw Baptist Association, Sept. 16–18, 1864. Meridian, MS: Clarion Book and Job Office, 1865.

Minutes of the Twenty-sixth Annual Session of the Choctaw Baptist Association, Oct. 15 and 17, 1864. Columbus: J. D. Ryan & Co., Printers, 1865.

Mitchell, Henry M. *Black Preaching*. Philadelphia: Lippincott, 1970.

Moorhead, James H. *American Apocalypse: Yankee Protestants and the Civil War 1860–1869*. New Haven: Yale University Press, 1978.

Nevins, Allen. *Ordeal of the Union*. 2 vols. New York: Scribner's, 1947.

Oliver, Robert T. *History of Public Speaking in America*. Boston: Allyn and Bacon, 1965.

Olmsted, Frederick Law. *The Cotton Kingdom*. 2 vols. New York: Mason Brothers, 1861.

Palmer, Benjamin Morgan. *The Life and Letters of James Henley Thornwell*. Richmond: Whittet & Shepperson, 1875.

Pipes, William H. *Say Amen, Brother! Old-Time Negro Preaching: A Study in American Frustration*. 1951; Westport, CT: Negro Universities Press, 1970.

Potter, David. *The Impending Crisis, 1848–1861*. Completed and edited by Don E. Fehrenbacher. New York: Harper, 1976.

Priest, Josiah. *Bible Defense of Slavery: and Origin, Fortunes and History of the Negro Race*. Glasgow, KY: W. S. Brown, M.D., 1852.

Proceedings of the Southern Baptist Convention, May 10–13, 1861. Richmond: MacFarlane and Fergusson, 1861.

Proceedings of the Thirty-fourth Annual Session of the Baptist State Convention of North Carolina, Oct. 28–31, 1863. Raleigh: Biblical Recorder Office, 1864.

Raboteau, Albert J. *Slave Religion: The "Invisible Institution" in the Antebellum South*. New York: Oxford University Press, 1978.

Rawick, George P., ed. *The American Slave: A Composite Autobiography*. 19 vols. Westport, CT: Greenwood, 1972.

Ross, Frederick A. *Slavery Ordained of God*. Philadelphia: J. B. Lippincott & Company, 1859.

Rozwenc, Edwin C. *Slavery as a Cause of the Civil War.* Boston: Heath, 1949.

Russell, William Howard. *My Diary North and South.* Ed. Eugene H. Berwanger. Philadelphia: Temple University Press, 1988.

Seabury, Samuel. *American Slavery Distinguished from the Slavery of English Theorists and Justified by the Law of Nature.* New York: Mason Brothers, 1861.

Silver, James W. *Confederate Morale and Church Propaganda.* New York: Norton, 1957.

Smith, Timothy. *Revivalism and Social Reform in Mid-Nineteenth Century America.* Nashville: Abingdon Press, 1957.

Stampp, Kenneth M., ed. *The Causes of the Civil War.* Englewood Cliffs, NJ: Prentice-Hall, 1974.

Stanton, Robert Livingston. *The Church and the Rebellion.* 1864; Freeport, NY: Books For Libraries Press, 1971.

Stewart, Charles. "Civil War Preaching." *Preaching in American History.* Ed. Dewitte Holland. Nashville: Abingdon Press, 1969. 235–55.

Sweet, William Warren. *The Methodist Episcopal Church and the Civil War.* Cincinnati: The Methodist Book Concern, 1912.

———. *The Story of Religion in America.* New York: Harper, 1930.

Taylor, Hubert Vance. "Preaching on Slavery 1831–1861." *Preaching in American History.* Ed. Dewitte Holland. Nashville: Abingdon Press, 1969. 168–83.

Thornwell, James Henley. "Critical Notices." *Southern Presbyterian Review* 4 (Jan. 1851): 452.

Tise, Larry. *Proslavery: A History of the Defense of Slavery in America.* Athens: University of Georgia Press, 1987.

Tocqueville, Alexis de. *Democracy in America.* The Henry Reeve text as revised by Francis Bowen; corrected and edited with introduction, editorial notes, and bibliographies by Phillips Bradley. New York: Knopf, 1966.

Washington, Joseph R., Jr. *Black Religion.* Boston: Beacon Press, 1964.

Wiley, Austin. *This History of the Antislave Cause in State and Nation.* Portland, ME: Brown, Thurston and Hoyt, Fogg & Donham, 1880.

Wilson, Charles Reagan. *Baptized in Blood: The Religion of the Lost Cause 1865–1920.* Athens: University of Georgia Press, 1980.

Wilson, Henry. *History of the Rise and Fall of the Slave Power in America.* 3 vols. Boston: James R. Osgood, 1874.

Woodward, C. Vann. *The Burden of Southern History.* Rev. ed. Baton Rouge: Louisiana State University Press, 1968.

Wright, G. Frederick. *Charles Grandison Finney.* Boston: Houghton Mifflin, 1891.

Index